Strengths-Based School Counseling

Promoting Student Development and Achievement

John P. Galassi
and
Patrick Akos

*The University of North Carolina
at Chapel Hill*

LEA LAWRENCE ERLBAUM ASSOCIATES, PUBLISHERS
2007 Mahwah, New Jersey   London

Cover design by Tomai Maridou

Lawrence Erlbaum Associates
Taylor & Francis Group
270 Madison Avenue
New York, NY 10016

Lawrence Erlbaum Associates
Taylor & Francis Group
2 Park Square
Milton Park, Abingdon
Oxon OX14 4RN

© 2007 by Taylor & Francis Group, LLC
Lawrence Erlbaum Associates is an imprint of Taylor & Francis Group, an Informa business

Printed in the United States of America on acid-free paper
10 9 8 7 6 5 4 3 2 1

International Standard Book Number-13: 978-0-8058-6249-2—0-8058-6249-8 (paper)
                                       978-1-4106-1787-3—1-4106-1787-4 (e book)

Visit the Taylor & Francis Web site at
http://www.taylorandfrancis.com

and the LEA Web site at
http://www.erlbaum.com

November 28, 2007

Contents

Preface

Despite calls for a more preventive and developmental mode of functioning, school counseling has tended to be driven primarily by a reactive, and sometimes crisis orientation. Like social workers and school, counseling, and clinical psychologists, school counselors typically function to alleviate deficits, often in a small percentage of the students they serve. Although this orientation has served school counselors well in many instances, it is not empowering; it does not serve all students, and it does not replace those deficits with the type of positive characteristics and abilities that schools are attempting to develop in young people.

The recently developed ASCA National Model for school counseling calls for counselors in the 21st century to change the way they function and represents a significant step forward in the evolution of professional school counseling. The National Model emphasizes outcomes-based, comprehensive school counseling programs that target academic, personal/social, and career development for *all* students.

Strengths-Based School Counseling (SBSC) provides a framework for implementing comprehensive school counseling programs that is both compatible with and enhances the ASCA National Model. SBSC builds upon contemporary theory and research from a variety of areas: (a) developmental psychology, (b) education, (c) positive psychology, (d) resiliency, (e) school counseling, and (f) social work. Research in those fields is beginning to witness a shift away from a deficit-oriented model of human behavior in order to incorporate a more strengths-oriented (positive) perspective. This research has identified the specific student strengths and abilities associated with positive youth development in the academic, personal/social, and career development domains, as well as the environments that have been shown to foster that development for all youth. As such, SBSC is in tune with the main purpose of schooling—the development of culturally and contextually based academic, personal/social, and career-related knowledge, skills, and attitudes that enable students to be successful in life and contribute to the society in which they live.

Six major principles form the foundation of Strengths-Based School Counseling:

1. Promote Evidence-Based Student Strengths
2. Promote Evidenced-Based, Strengths-Enhancing Educational Environments
3. Promote Context-Based Development for All Students

4. Emphasize Promotion over Remediation and Prevention
5. Emphasize Evidence-Based Interventions and Practice
6. Emphasize Promotion-Oriented Developmental Advocacy at the School-Building Level

Thus, the purpose of this book is to offer a contemporary evidenced-based developmental framework that is compatible with the ASCA National Model and applicable to practicing school counselors and those students and faculty involved in school counselor preparation.

Eight chapters comprise this text. Chapter 1 provides an overview of the Strengths-Based School Counseling framework, its six guiding principles, and the conceptual and research foundations on which SBSC is based. In Chapter 1, we situate SBSC with respect to traditional orientations to school counseling and to more contemporary approaches, including the ASCA National Model. Chapters 1 and 7 (Strengths-Based School Counseling in Perspective)—which the reader may find helpful as both a preview and review—present the distinctive features of the SBSC framework.

In Chapter 2 we clarify the often-debated role of the school counselor. The flexible, yet sustainable, SBSC role is to promote the evidence-based student strengths associated with positive youth development for all students and the environments that have been shown to support them. We also demonstrate how the direct (e.g., counseling, assessment) and systems-level (e.g., consultation, advocacy) services/functions flow from the SBSC role, and how these can be more useful than the traditional functions school counselors have performed.

Chapters 3 to 6 focus on promoting development in the three domains—academic, personal/social, and career—identified in the ASCA National Model. Although these developmental domains are mutually influential and are interrelated, we present them as distinct chapters for both clarity and alignment with the ASCA National Model. This focus on outcomes (especially environments) is a departure from traditional school counseling textbooks that focus on functions. To live the SBSC role, developmental outcomes become the primary focus that drives the functions and tasks school counselors perform.

Academic development (Chapters 3 and 4) is afforded two chapters because of the primacy that it has assumed in the contemporary school counselor's role (e.g., the ASCA National Model) and because a large percentage of individuals who enter school counseling lack a background in student learning and academic development. Personal/social and career development are addressed in Chapters 5 and 6. In the case of each developmental domain, we discuss selected evidence-based student strengths that counselor's need to promote and the environments that have been found to promote them. In addition, we provide information about the evidenced-based interventions that have successfully enhanced those student strengths, as well as information about effective environmental modifications. Examples are drawn from a variety of disciplines, including school counseling, school psychology, education, psychology, and social work; also, applications at the elementary, middle/junior-high, and high-school levels are provided.

In Chapter 7, we endeavor to put Strengths-Based School Counseling into perspective. We do this through posing and answering a dozen common questions that readers (school counselors, students, and counselor educators) may have about SBSC.

Chapter 8 is addressed to the counselor educator and those involved in school counselor preparation (e.g., school counselor supervisors). Here we discuss how to incorporate a strengths-based framework into school counselor preparation. We use the 2001 Standards of the Council for Accreditation of Counseling and Related Education Programs (CACREP) as our framework for counselor preparation. In our discussion, we consider preparing strengths-based school counselors both in the context of preparing counselors for other settings (e.g., community counselors, college counselors) as well and preparing them in stand-alone school counselor education programs.

This text has a number of distinctive features:

- A strengths-based, promotion-oriented developmental framework for practice that is compatible with and enhances the ASCA National Model for School Counseling
- A broad empirical basis for the student strengths and strengths-enhancing environments that school counselors need to promote
- Detailed examples of evidenced-based interventions and educational environments that work
- Links to Web sites and other resources for evidence-based approaches to enhancing development for all students in the academic, personal/social, and career domains
- In-depth coverage of principles and interventions the counselor must know in order to increase academic achievement and reduce achievement gaps
- Information about the effects of major educational reform initiatives that relate to local needs that the counselor and other educator address
- Information about the importance of enhancing ethnic identity development for all students

The authors thank Lane Akers of Lawrence Erlbaum Associates (LEA) for supporting our vision of school counseling, and LEA reviewers Drs. Edward Herr and Bruce Wampold for their reviews and insightful comments and suggestions. We also thank the following counselor educators who helped research, review, challenge, and support our ideas: Drs. Kelly Coker, Amy Milsom, Spencer

Niles, and Ken Hughey. In addition, we appreciate the invaluable feedback provided to us throughout the process by a number of school counselors, students, and educators, including Elizabeth Collins, Mary Dillon, Dr. Merna Galassi, Karen Galassi-Ferrer, Sonali Gurjar, Kelli Kirk, Kathy Parramore, Angela Poovey, and Brett Zyromski. Finally, we thank Jane Gorey for helping us to prepare the manuscript.

OVERVIEW

In the 20th century, the school counselor's role and functions underwent a variety of transformations in response to changing student and societal needs (Baker, 2001; Gysbers, 2001; Gysbers & Henderson, 2001; Herr, 2001; Paisley & Borders, 1995). Over the years, that role has focused on vocational guidance (pre-1950s), fostering personal growth (1950s), enhancing individual development (1960s), and, most recently, on implementing comprehensive developmental guidance and counseling programs (1970s–present) (Keys, Bemak, & Lockhart, 1998). In the process, school counseling has evolved (Gysbers & Henderson, 2001). It began as a position consisting of a set of extra duties performed by a teacher and then evolved into an ancillary group of services provided by a specially trained professional, the guidance counselor. It currently involves an effort by a professional school counselor to initiate an organized, comprehensive program that is integral to education and based on a developmental framework (Gysbers & Henderson, 2001).

In Strengths-Based School Counseling (SBSC), we present a framework to guide the practice of school counseling in the 21st century. SBSC is informed by contemporary developmental theory and research from a variety of disciplines. This perspective is both compatible with and operationalizes many of the features of the ASCA National Model for School Counseling Programs (American School Counseling Association [ASCA], 2003). The strengths-based counselor's *primary role* is *to promote and advocate for positive youth development for all students and for the environments that enhance and sustain that development.* In the past, counselors have frequently directed their efforts primarily at the needs of only a segment of students. The needs of poor and minority students; students with limited English skills; students from other cultures; and learning-disabled and other students with exceptional needs have often been underserved or not addressed at all by school counselors. The strengths-based perspective emphasizes the school counselor focusing on positive youth development for all students.

Positive youth development involves nurturing and enhancing a variety of empirically identified student strengths or competencies. We highlight these strengths using the three developmental domains—academic, personal/social, and career—of the ASCA National Model for School Counseling Programs (ASCA, 2003). Research (e.g., Henderson & Milstein, 1996; Osterman, 2000) has demonstrated that the presence of these student developmental strengths is associated with certain types of environmental characteristics (e.g., those in which high expectations for student success are communicated and those in which students' needs for belonging are satisfied). The counselor is a school leader who works with students, teachers, administrators, parents, and other members of the community and promotes these strengths-enhancing environments for all students.

TABLE 1–1.
The Six Guiding Principles of Strengths-Based School Counseling

1. Promote Context-Based Development for All Students
2. Promote Individual Student Strengths
3. Promote Strengths-Enhancing Environments
4. Emphasize Strengths Promotion over Problem Reduction and Problem Prevention
5. Emphasize Evidence-Based Interventions and Practice
6. Emphasize Promotion-Oriented Developmental Advocacy at the School Level

While remediation of deficits and the removal of barriers play a role in this framework, the strengths-based counselor focuses on proactive and preventive approaches to help students build skills and on enhancing the asset-building capacity of the school environment. Thus, the emphasis is on *promoting* student development—academic, personal/social, and career. Strengths-based school counselors employ a variety of direct (e.g., counseling, classroom guidance) and systemic (e.g., consultation, advocacy) level interventions. The purpose of these interventions is to promote the development of student strengths and strengths-enhancing environments. In order to effect these desired outcomes, the counselor chooses evidence-based interventions whenever possible. "High-quality, comprehensive, competence-promotion programs that focus on both children and their socializing environments represent the state of the art in (primary) prevention" (Weissberg, Caplan, & Harwood, 1991, p. 830).

At this point, we will elaborate on six of the guiding principles of strengths-based school counseling. Table 1–1 lists these principles. This section will be followed by a discussion of the relation of the SBSC perspective to current school counseling models and a consideration of some of the conceptual and empirical developments that influence the strengths-based framework.

Promote Context-Based Development for All Students

Focusing on and enhancing student development for all students is by no means new to school counseling. Comprehensive developmental guidance or comprehensive school counseling programs come in a variety of forms and have been a major influence on school counseling for some time (e.g., Dinkmeyer & Caldwell, 1970; Gysbers & Henderson, 1994; 2000; Myrick, 1997; Paisley & Hubbard, 1994; Sink & MacDonald, 1998). Although some preliminary data support their effectiveness (e.g., Borders & Drury, 1992; Lapan, Gysbers, & Petroski, 2001; Whiston & Sexton, 1998), research has demonstrated that (a) these programs are not explicit about the specific developmental theory and research on which they purportedly were built, (b) salient developmental constructs (e.g., developmental tasks) were difficult to find in them, and (c) cultural and ethnic development were rarely addressed (Mac-Donald & Sink, 1999; Sink & MacDonald, 1998).

In addition, existing comprehensive developmental counseling programs tend to be loosely based on older developmental research and *stage theories* of development (e.g., Erikson, 1963, Havighurst, 1972; Kohlberg, 1969; Piaget, 1950) rather than on more contemporary developmental theory and research. Stage theories portray all human development as progressing through a logical, more or less invariant, hierarchical sequence of growth and increasing complexity in which there is a consistent relationship between stage and behavior.

In contrast, the influential and interactive role that context and environment play in human development increasingly has been recognized by contemporary developmental theorists and researchers (e.g., Bronfenbrenner, 1979; Lerner, 1986; Lerner et al., 1998). Environmental and contextual factors can shape, enhance, delay, or even impede student development. As a result, more recent developmental theories and research tend to emphasize contextual rather than stage factors in development (e.g., Gilligan, 1982; Helms, 1994a; Lerner, 1986; Lerner et al., 1998).

Contextual theories emphasize behavioral variability and the role of environmental and social circumstances on development (see Ripley, Erford, Dahir, & Eschbach, 2003 for a discussion of these theories in relation to school counseling programs). Green and Keys (2001), for example, have noted the failure of comprehensive developmental counseling programs to recognize and incorporate the role that culture and contextual factors exert on the development of students, especially for students of color and those in inner city, urban environments. In short, it is questionable whether existing school counseling models of practice are actually based on current developmental theory and research, and whether the premises on which they are based have sufficient explanatory power to drive the interventions needed to serve 21st century education stakeholders (Galassi & Akos, 2004).

In contrast, contemporary developmental theory and research inform and provide considerable support for a strengths-based approach to comprehensive school counseling programs. Research by Bornstein and colleagues (Bornstein, Davidson, Keyes, & Moore, 2003) at the Center for Child Well-Being, for example, focuses on developing strengths from birth throughout childhood and adolescence that nurture a child's ability to thrive in all aspects of life—physically, cognitively, and socioemotionally. Their approach (a) is positive (e.g., strengths-based), (b) is evidence-based, (c) recognizes that different positive characteristics are more or less influential throughout different stages of life (e.g., developmental), (d) acknowledges that child well-being is affected by interactions among parents, children, caregivers, community, and the environment, and (e) is committed to all people having equal access to opportunities and supports for child development.

Wagner (1996) proposed a model of optimal development in adolescence and advocated for counseling psychologists to facilitate this development. The model consisted of six interacting domains: (a) biological, (b) cognitive, (c) emotional, (d) social, (e) moral, and (f) vocational. For each domain, Wagner proposed criteria for optimal development, reviewed the literature on domain-specific development during adolescence, and discussed demographic (e.g., ethnicity, gender) and social (e.g., parents, siblings, peers, community, the environment, and role models) influences on development.

As we have seen, contextual factors play an important role in current perspectives on human development. As such, they need to be acknowledged and incorporated into school counselors' efforts to facilitate positive development for all students.

Promote Individual Student Strengths

Enhancing human development throughout the life span and maximizing student development are important principles of the ethical standards of the American Counseling Association (ACA, 1995) and the American School Counselor Association (ASCA, 1998), respectively; however, the notion of strengths-based counseling has rarely been advanced in general (Arredondo & Lewis, 2001; Harris & Thoresen, 2003; Smith, 2006), or in school counseling specifically. SBSC is characterized by counselors promoting development of student factors or strengths (sometimes referred to as competencies, assets, or other related concepts) such as skills, attitudes, and knowledge that are both modifiable and have been shown to be empirically related to academic success and other indices (e.g., personal/social and career) of positive youth development.

"*Strength* may be defined as that which helps a person to cope with life or that which makes life more fulfilling for oneself and others. Strengths are not fixed personality traits; instead, they develop from a dynamic, contextual process rooted deeply in one's culture" (Smith, 2006, p. 25). A major purpose of schooling is to help students develop the knowledge, skills, and attitudes (i.e., the strengths) that will enable them to live productive and happy lives as citizens in a democratic society. As educational leaders, school counselors are an important part of that strengths-promoting endeavor. Moreover, as we shall discuss later, a strengths-based approach to counseling is applicable to a wide range of concerns presented by students and other educational stakeholders. "Positive approaches are most helpful for working with highly stressed individuals, families and communities—exactly the ones whose behavior often is pathologized" (Arredondo & Lewis, 2001, p. 263). Thus, strengths-based school counseling focuses on helping students build on or further enhance their current strengths and competencies as well as develop additional ones that have been shown to be associated with positive development.

Promote Strengths-Enhancing Environments

As we have discussed, environmental and contextual factors can exert a marked impact on student development. Furthermore, research has demonstrated that certain types of environments are associated with positive youth development. With respect to academic development, for example, Osterman's (2000) review of the literature indicated that the extent to which the school environment satisfies students' need for belonging significantly impacts academic attitudes, beliefs, behaviors, and achievement. Taking a broader environmental perspective on children's academic success, Christenson and Anderson (2002) reviewed the importance of complementary roles for family, school, and community on six factors: (a) standards and expectations set by adults, (b) structure, (c) opportunity to learn, (d) support, (e) climate/relationships, and (f) adult modeling. Thus, student academic success is facilitated when parents and teachers state clear performance expectations, set goals and standards for behavior, discuss expectations with students, and emphasize children's effort when completing tasks. Families and schools also need to provide consistency with respect to instructions for schoolwork, rules for behavior, and age-appropriate monitoring and supervision. Opportunities to learn with support, praise, and explicit feedback, a warm and friendly adult-student relationship, and adults modeling a commitment to learning and hard work are additional environmental factors that are empirically related to student success in school. Contextual and environmental factors are also important influences on student development in the personal/social and career areas. These factors are referred to by a variety of terms including external assets and protective factors, but in SBSC, we will refer to them as strengths-enhancing environments.

Not only do school counselors need to be aware of the impact of these contextual and environmental factors, they also need to promote them actively through collaboration, advocacy, and other system-level interventions that we will discuss in detail later. Strengths-enhancing environments reinforce and help sustain the very student strengths that school counselors are trying to promote through counseling and other direct service interventions.

Emphasize Strengths Promotion over Problem Reduction and Problem Prevention

In SBSC, the focus is on *promoting* positive development rather than on problem prevention and problem remediation, although the two latter functions are certainly important aspects of the school counselor's role. By focusing on promotion, the strengths-based school counseling program addresses the needs of the entire student population. In contrast, a primary focus on remediation and helping students to resolve problems reflects a medical rather than a developmental model of professional functioning for school counselors. It emphasizes pathology, deficit-reduction, and a crisis-oriented perspective that can result in the school counselor targeting services to a relatively small portion of students. In addition, it relegates the school counselor to a reactive mode of functioning.

> Schools—and our society in general—have adopted a rehabilitative, reactive focus for most treatment efforts, and thus significant resources are directed toward resolution of existing problems and maladaptive behaviors (e.g., school detention and suspensions, special education services, Chapter 1 reading programs. (Zins & Wagner, 1997, p. 137)

Not surprisingly, school counseling, with rare exceptions (Paisley & Peace, 1995), has also tended to be preoccupied with treating problems (e.g., individual remediation).

> The strengths-based school counselor certainly does not ignore students who seek help resolving particular problems. As we shall discuss in subsequent chapters, however, the counseling emphasis to problem remediation in SBSC is somewhat different. "Treatment is not just fixing what is broken; it is nurturing what is best within ourselves." (Seligman, 1999, cited in Smith, 2006, p. 13)

Helping students overcome problems once they occur is an important focus of school counseling, but why not emphasize attempts to prevent these problems from ever developing in the first place? Prevention efforts (e.g., dropout prevention, violence prevention, drug abuse prevention) result in the school counselor assuming a more proactive mode of functioning and serving a much larger number of students. While prevention efforts by the school counselor are important, they also suffer from a variety of limitations.

First, success in preventing a problem from occurring does not necessarily mean that we have done much to optimize human functioning. Preventing illiteracy by teaching basic reading skills is an important accomplishment in itself, but it is a long way from instilling intrinsic motivation to read or a commitment to academic excellence. Similarly, Pittman, Irby, Tolman, Yohalem, and Ferber (2001) gave the following example:

> Suppose we introduced an employer to a young person we worked with by saying, "Here's Johnny. He's not a drug user. He's not in a gang. He's not a dropout. He's not a teen father. Please hire him." The employer would probably respond, "That's great. But what does he know, what can he do?" (p. 4)

Thus, prevention is an important but often insufficient goal. "Problem-free does not mean fully prepared" (Pittman & Fleming, 1991, p. 3). Pittman et al. (2001) even step beyond this idea to state that "fully prepared isn't fully engaged," and research on development increasingly emphasizes the importance of participation—"choice and voice"—for adolescents" (p. 6).

In addition, prevention efforts have been only moderately successful in a number of instances. Persistently high levels of risk taking and problem behaviors suggest that new approaches are needed (Moore & Keyes, 2003).

> How can problems like depression or substance abuse or schizophrenia be prevented in young people who are genetically vulnerable or who live in worlds that nurture these problems? How can murderous schoolyard violence be prevented in children who have access to weapons, poor parental supervision, and a mean streak? What we have learned from over 50 years is that the disease model does not move us closer to the prevention of these serious problems. Indeed, the major strides in prevention have largely come from a perspective focused on systematically building competency, not correcting weakness. (Seligman & Peterson, 2003, p. 315)

For example, Pollard and Rosenberg (2003) reported that the Prevent Child Abuse America organization concluded after years of focusing on child abuse prevention that they could be more effective in preventing child abuse by focusing on family and individual strengths and preparing first-time parents to promote positive childhood outcomes. Their intervention consists of home visitors providing new parents with support, education, and referral to services, as well as training and employment opportunities for up to five years after the child is born.

Masten and Reed (2002) asserted that "promoting healthy development and competence is at least as important as preventing problems and will serve the same end. As a society, we will do well to nurture human capital, to invest in the competence of our children" (p. 84). Moreover, there are a number of important reasons for school counselors to emphasize promotion rather than remediation and prevention. As we have already noted, an important purpose of education is to assist students to acquire the knowledge, skills, and attitudes necessary to function as productive adults. Successfully treating and/or preventing problems does not necessarily guarantee that this acquisition will occur. By adopting a strengths-promotion focus, however, the school counselor is aligned with other educators and with the mission of schools to help young people acquire what they need to function as productive adults.

Catalano, Berglund, Ryan, Lonczak, and Hawkins (2002) noted that interest in promoting positive youth development has grown because research has consistently demonstrated that the same individual, family, school, and community factors often predict both positive (e.g., success in school) and negative (e.g., delinquency) outcomes for students. In addition, researchers and practitioners realized that a successful transition to adulthood involved more than just not dropping out of school and avoiding drugs, violence, and early sexual activity. Focusing on the predictors of positive outcomes by promoting social, emotional, behavioral, and cognitive competencies in children was seen as the key to preventing problem behaviors as well as equipping students for adulthood (W. T. Grant Consortium on the School-Based Promotion of Social Competence, 1992). More importantly, however, research is accumulating that many of these strengths-oriented programs are quite effective *both* in promoting positive youth development outcomes and in preventing problematic behaviors (Catalano et al., 2002).

Emphasize Evidence-Based Interventions and Practice

The strengths-oriented school counselor is committed to evidence-based practice. Evidence-based practice involves three important components: (a) promoting evidence-based student strengths and strengths-enhancing environments, (b) employing evidence-based counseling interventions whenever possible, and (c) collecting evidence (e.g., outcome data) about the effects of the interventions that have been employed. We have already introduced the concepts of student strengths and the strengths-enhancing environments that research has shown to be associated with academic success and other indices of positive youth development. Examples of these concepts will be presented in depth in subsequent chapters. We now will briefly consider evidence-based counseling interventions.

In their daily practice, school counselors seek to meet student needs through intervention decisions based on a variety of information sources, including personal hunches, clinical experience, theoretical orientation, and research knowledge. Evidence-based practice is focused on the premise that, of all these sources, research knowledge provides the most reliable single source of guidance (e.g., Sexton, 2001). Thus, evidence-based practice involves the counselor employing best-practice interventions (e.g., those whose effectiveness has been supported by research). At this point in time, research specifically identifying best practices in school counseling is only beginning to accumulate (Baker, Swisher, Nadenichek, & Popowicz, 1984; Borders & Drury, 1992; Gerler, 1985; Eder & Whiston, 2006; McGannon, Carey, & Dimmitt, 2005; Prout & DeMartino, 1986; Sexton, Whiston, Bleuer, & Walz, 1997; St. Clair, 1989; Whiston & Sexton, 1998). The present state of knowledge, however limited, does provide information on general trends that are sufficient to inform intervention decisions (Sexton, 2001). Moreover, the Center for School Counseling Outcome Research at the University of Massachusetts, Amherst regularly updates information about evidence-based school counseling practices through research briefs and research monographs, which are available at http:// www.umass.edu/schoolcounseling/index.htm.

Best-practices and evidence-based interventions are by no means confined to school counseling research. Researchers and practitioners representing a variety of disciplines have developed a number of evidence-based interventions that are relevant to school counseling. A summary of some of these interventions is presented in Table 1–2. In the table, we have organized the resources according to the three developmental areas—academic, personal/social, and career—identified in the American School Counselor Association (ASCA, 2003) National Model for School Counseling Programs. These three areas represent a convenient conceptual organization scheme; however, the three

(*text continues on page 24*)

TABLE 1–2.
Evidence-Based Resources for School Counselors

Source	Website, Citation or Other Location Information	ASCA Domains	Brief Summary of Resource
Some Things DO Make a Difference for Youth: A Compendium of Successful Youth Practice and Programs, American Youth Policy Forum (1997)	http://www.aypf.org/compendium/index.html American Youth Policy Forum 1836 Jefferson Place, NW Washington, DC 20036-2505 Telephone: (202) 755-9731 Fax: (202) 775-9733 Website: http://www.aypf.org	Academic Career Personal/Social	This AYPF Compendium contains evaluations of programs and practices that were found to be successful in propelling youth to rewarding careers and postsecondary education, reducing risky or illegal behaviors, and providing opportunities to youth who had dropped out of school or were leaving the juvenile justice system. Sixty-nine evaluations of 49 programmatic interventions are summarized.
More Things That DO Make a Difference for Youth, American Youth Policy Forum, (1999)	http://www.aypf.org/compendium/index.html American Youth Policy Forum 1836 Jefferson Place, NW Washington, DC 20036-2505 Telephone: (202) 755-9731 Fax: (202) 775-9733 Website: http://www.aypf.org	Academic Career Personal/Social	This AYPF Compendium includes more evaluations of youth programs. It summarizes 64 evaluations of 46 youth programs—career academies, school-to-work, Tech Prep, school reform, juvenile justice and related areas of youth policy.
Summary of Program Characteristics for Some Things and More Things (Matrix),	http://www.aypf.org/RAA/index.htm American Youth Policy Forum 1836 Jefferson Place, NW Washington, DC 20036-2505	Academic Career Personal/Social	A Matrix summarizing the various characteristics of the 85 programs identified in *Some Things DO Make a Difference for Youth: A Compendium of Successful Youth Practice and Programs and More Things That DO Make a*

Resource	Citation / Contact	Focus	Description
American Youth Policy Forum	Telephone: (202) 755-9731 Fax: (202) 775-9733 Website: http://www.aypf.org		*Difference for Youth.* The Matrix describes the focus, the research-based findings, and the key components of each program.
Safe and Sound: An Educational Leader's Guide to Evidence-Based Social and Emotional Learning (SEL) Programs, Collaborative for Academic, Social, and Emotional Learning (CASEL) (March 2003)	http://www.casel.org/1A_Safe_&_Sound.pdf Collaborative for Academic, Social, and Emotional Learning (CASEL) Department of Psychology (M/C 285) University of Illinois at Chicago 1007 West Harrison Street Chicago, IL 60607-7137 Telephone: (312) 413-1008 Fax: (312) 355-4480 Website: http://www.CASEL.org	Academic Personal/Social Career	*Safe and Sound* provides educators with objective, evidence-based information about nationally available programs for the classroom that promote social and emotional learning (SEL). SEL is the process of developing the ability to recognize and manage emotions, develop caring and concern for others, make responsible decisions, establish positive relationships and handle challenging situations effectively. SEL provides schools with a framework for preventing problems and promoting students' well-being and success. Evaluates 80 programs, including 22 "select" programs. Evaluates the strengths and weaknesses of each program based on evidence of effectiveness, availability of professional development, and 5 key social and emotional skills.
Communities That Care: Prevention Strategies: A Research Guide to What Works	Posey, R., Wong, S. C., Catalano, R. F., Hawkins, J.D., Dusenbury, L., & Chappell, P. J., (1996) *Communities That Cares. Prevention Strategies: A Research Guide to What Works,* Seattle, WA: Developmental Research and Programs, Inc.	Academic Personal/Social	*Communities That Care* provides research-based tools to help communities promote the positive development of children and youth and prevent adolescent substance abuse, delinquency, teen pregnancy, school dropout and violence.

(continued)

TABLE 1-2 (*Continued*)

Source	Website, Citation or Other Location Information	ASCA Domains	Brief Summary of Resource
Developmental Research and Programs, Inc. (2000)	Developmental Research and Programs, Inc. 130 Nickerson, Suite 107 Seattle, WA 98109 Phone: (206) 286-1805 Fax: (206) 286-1462		The CTC directory lists over 100 prevention strategies or programs shown to be effective in reducing risk factors and enhancing protective factors. The strategies recommended by CTC are organized into the four areas of family, school, community-based youth programs, and community-focused programs and into six age ranges from prenatal to young adult.
Positive Youth Development in the United States: Research Findings on Evaluations of Positive Youth Development Programs *Journal of Prevention & Treatment* (2002).	Catalano, R., Berglund, M. L., Ryan, J. A. M., Lonczak, H. S., and Hawkins, J. D. (2002). *Positive youth development in the United States: Research findings on evaluations of positive youth development programs.* Prevention & Treatment, 5. http://journals.apa.org/prevention/volume5/pre0050015a.html	Academic Personal/Social Career	The report describes 25 well-evaluated, positive youth development programs in the community, school, and family settings.
Programs that Work and What Works in Youth Development (series)	http://www.iyfnet.org/section.cfm/5 International Youth Foundation 32 South Street, Suite 500 Baltimore MD 21202	Academic Personal/Social Career	IYF identifies programs that are effectively meeting young people's needs in five issue areas—1) *Innovative Learning* to enhance the educational opportunities available to young people both inside and outside of school; 2) *Youth*

| International Youth Foundation (2003) | Telephone: (410) 951-1500
Fax: (410) 347-1188
E-mail: youth@iyfnet.org
Web site: http://www.iyfnet.org | | *Employment* to improve the job and livelihood skills of young people, as well as promote workplace improvements and enhance skills that make their first job experience more positive and productive; 3) *Life Skills* to equip young people with essential skills for living, including self-esteem, effective communications, decision making, critical thinking, teamwork, and leadership skills; 4) *Youth Participation* to promote the role of young people as leaders of positive social change in their communities; and 5) *Health Education and Awareness* to prepare young people to lead healthy lives and make informed decisions concerning key health issues. |
| *Promoting Positive Youth Development as a Support to Academic Achievement,*

National Institute on Out-of-School Time (NIOST) and The Forum for Youth Investment (Sept. 2002) | http://www.afterschoolforall.org/news/LG%20Research/WP_NIOST_final.pdf

The Forum for Youth Investment
7014 Westmoreland Ave.
Takoma Park, MD 20912
Telephone: (301) 270-6250
Facsimile: (301) 270-7144
Website:
http://www.forumforyouthinvestment.org (publications). | Academic
Personal/Social | This report investigates how after-school programs can most effectively promote positive youth development as a support to academic achievement. The paper provides a brief overview of learning theory, explains the features and rationale of the positive youth development approach, and provides local and national examples of programs utilizing positive youth development strategies to support youth development and academic achievement. |

(*continued*)

TABLE 1-2 (*Continued*)

Source	Website, Citation or Other Location Information	ASCA Domains	Brief Summary of Resource
Promoting Healthy Adolescents: Synthesis of Youth Development Program Evaluations *Journal of Research on Adolescence* (1998).	Roth, J. and Brooks-Gunn, J. (1998). *Promoting Healthy Adolescents: Synthesis of Youth Development Program Evaluations. Journal of Research on Adolescence,* 8(4), 423–459.	Academic Personal/Social Career	The article describes 15 well-evaluated, positive youth development programs grouped into three categories: 1) Positive-Behavior Focused Competency/Asset Enhancing Programs; 2) Problem-Behavior Focused Competency/Asset Enhancing Programs; and 3) Resistance Skills-Based Prevention Programs. The article further summarizes the outcome research on these programs.
Raising Academic Achievement: A Study of 20 Successful Programs, American Youth Policy Forum, (2000)	http://www.aypf.org/RAA/index.htm American Youth Policy Forum 1836 Jefferson Place, NW Washington, DC 20036-2505 Telephone: (202) 755-9731 Fax: (202) 775-9733 Website: http://www.aypf.org	Academic	This AYPF publication highlights 20 models of excellence in raising academic achievement. The 20 examples were drawn from the 95 youth initiatives included in AYPF's two previous publications on successful youth programs: *Some Things DO Make a Difference for Youth and Things DO Make a Difference for Youth and MORE Things That DO Make a Difference for Youth.* Evaluations included in the book show evidence of success on multiple measures of academic achievement, such as test scores, high school graduation rates, and college enrollment and retention.

Source	Website/Contact	Focus	Description
Raising Minority Academic Achievement: A Compendium of Education Programs and Practices, American Youth Policy Forum, (2001)	http://www.aypf.org/rmass/pdfs/Book.pdf American Youth Policy Forum 1836 Jefferson Place, NW Washington, DC 20036-2505 Telephone: (202) 755-9731 Fax: (202) 775-9733 Website: http://www.aypf.org	Academic	This AYPF report details a two-year effort to find, summarize, and analyze evaluations of school and youth programs that show gains for minority youth across a broad range of academic achievement indicators. The report provides an accessible resource for policymakers and practitioners interested in promoting the academic success of racial and ethnic minorities from early childhood through advanced post-secondary study. It presents 38 successful programs
Prevention Connection: Promoting Strength, Resilience and Health in Children, Adults, and Families, American Psychological Association (2002)	http://www.oslc.org/spr/apa/home.html	Personal/Social	Provides a searchable data base of summaries of research on the effectiveness of prevention and health promotion efforts with children and adolescents.
Promising Practices Network on Children, Families and Communities (2004)	http://promisingpractices.net/programlist.asp	Academic Personal/Social	The Promising Practices Network (PPN) website highlights programs and practices that credible research indicates are effective in improving outcomes for children, youth, and families. The site contains information on 44 promising and 20 proven programs in a broad prevention spectrum: health and safety, school readiness and success, drug abuse, teen pregnancy, violence, and family initiatives.

(*continued*)

TABLE 1-2 *(Continued)*

Source	Website, Citation or Other Location Information	ASCA Domains	Brief Summary of Resource
Transforming Education for Hispanic Youth: Exemplary Practices, Programs, and Schools By Anne Turnbaugh Lockwood and Walter G. Secada, University of Wisconsin-Madison National Clearinghouse for Bilingual Education (NCBE), Resource Collection Series No. 12 (January 1999).	http://www.ncela.gwu.edu/ncbepubs/resource/hispanicyouth/ and http://www.ncela.gwu.edu/ncbepubs/resource/hispanicyouth/hdp.htm	Academic Personal/Social Career	The document contains six chapters. The first, *The Hispanic Dropout Problem and Recommendations for Its Solution*, provides statistics on the Hispanic dropout rate, and an overview of findings from the Hispanic Dropout Project. Included are the probable reasons for the dropout problem and the best methods of solving it. Chapters Two through Five describe the implementation of effective programs for Hispanic youth in elementary and secondary schools. *Cognitively Guided Instruction (CGI)* in mathematics, *Helping One Student to Succeed (HOSTS)*, and *Success for All* are presented among the successful models. The final chapter incorporates interviews with four members of the Hispanic Dropout Project in a discussion of what leads to Hispanic dropout and how to ensure a better future for the education of Hispanic students.
The Prevention of Mental Disorders in School-Aged Children: Current State of the Field *Journal of Prevention & Treatment* (2001).	Greenberg, M. T., Domitrovich, C., and Bumbarger, B. (2001). *The prevention of mental disorders in school-aged children: Current state of the field.* Prevention & Treatment, 4. http://journals.apa.org/prevention/volume4/pre004000la.html	Academic Personal/Social	This article reviews numerous primary prevention programs that have proven to be effective. The authors identify and describe 34 universal and targeted interventions that have demonstrated positive outcomes.

UCLA School Mental Health Project: Center for Mental Health in Schools	http://smhp.psych.ucla.edu	Personal/Social	This website is a clearinghouse to specialized resources, materials and information related to mental health in schools. The website includes links to *Annotated Lists* of empirically supported/ evidence-based interventions for school-aged children and adolescents. Also included are links that allow the user to download various materials developed by the Center, including materials on Policy Issues & Research Base, Systemic Changes & Enhancing and Sustaining Systems/Programs/ Services, and Developing Comprehensive, Multi-faceted, and Integrated Approaches. In addition, there are links to specific program materials on Classroom Enhancement and Youth Development, Support for Transitions, Crisis Response and Prevention, Home Involvement, Student and Family Assistance, and Community Out-reach (including volunteer participation). There also is a host of resource and training materials on specific Psychosocial and & Mental Health Concerns (e.g., dropout prevention, bullying, anxiety, sexual minorities, teen pregnancy, violence prevention, suicide prevention).
The American Psychological Association, Division of Child Clinical Psychology, Ad Hoc Committee on	APA (1998). The American Psychological Association, Division of Child Clinical Psychology, Ad Hoc Committee on Evidence Based Assessment and Treatment of Childhood Disorders, *Journal of Clinical Child Psychology*, 27, 156–205.	Personal/Social	The APA Committee reviewed outcome studies on the treatment and assessment of childhood disorders. In this special section of the *Journal of Clinical Child Psychology*, the APA published reviews of assessment and treatment interven-tions for anxiety, depression, conduct disorders,

(continued)

TABLE 1-2 (*Continued*)

Source	Website, Citation or Other Location Information	ASCA Domains	Brief Summary of Resource
Evidence-Based Assessment and Treatment of Childhood Disorders			ADHD, and broad-spectrum Autism, as well as a more global view of the field.
The NMHA Directory of Model Programs to Prevent Mental Disorders and to Promote Health	National Mental Health Association 2001 N. Beauregard Street, 12th Floor Alexandria, Virginia 22311 Telephone: (800) 969-6642 Fax: (703) 684-5968	Personal/Social	The NMHA Directory contains summaries of programs that have been selected as model interventions for the prevention of mental disorders and/or the promotion of mental health.
National Mental Health Association (1995)	http://www.nmha.org		
Substance Abuse and Mental Health Services Administration (SAMSA) National Registry of Effective Programs (NREP)	http://modelprograms.samhsa.gov/ template.cfm?page=nrepbutton U.S. Department of Health and Human Services Substance Abuse and Mental Health Services Administration Center for Substance Abuse Prevention Phone: 1.877.773.8546 (toll free)	Academic Personal/Social	Lists three levels of evidence-based programs— promising, effective, and model. A brief description is provided for each as well as prevention classification—universal (targeted to the general population), selective (targeted to a subgroup whose risk is significantly higher than average), and indicated (targeted to targeted to individuals in high-risk environments, identified as having minimal but detectable signs foreshadowing disorder or having biological markers indi-

			cating predisposition. The registry can be searched across a variety of categories such as content (e.g., academic achievement, alcohol), demographics, and setting.
Safe and Drug Free Schools Model Programs	http://www.ed.gov/offices/OESE/SDFS/programs.html	Personal/Social	This site describes various drug and violence prevention programs at the state and national level. The site lists nine exemplary and 33 promising programs.
U.S. Department of Education (2002)	http://www.ed.gov/admins/lead/safety/exemplary01/index.html U.S. Department of Education 400 Maryland Avenue, SW Washington, DC 20202 Telephone: (800) USA-LEARN Fax: (202) 401-0689		
Center for Substance Abuse Prevention Western Regional Center (2001)	http://casat.unr.edu/westcapt/	Personal/Social	This website contains information of best-practices and promising-practices substance abuse prevention programs. It also describes best practices for developing and implementing a substance abuse program. The website also contains a link to download *Achieving Outcomes: A Practitioner's Guide to Effective Prevention*. This Guide presents a process for demonstrating and documenting prevention outcomes
Preventing Drug Use Among Children & Adolescents	http://www.nida-nih.gov/prevention/prevopen.html	Personal/Social	This website contains a research-based guide for parents, educators and community leaders on preventing drug abuse among children and

(continued)

TABLE 1–2 *(Continued)*

Source	Website, Citation or Other Location Information	ASCA Domains	Brief Summary of Resource
National Institute on Drug Abuse (NIDA)			adolescents. The website discusses the principles of prevention and risk factors and protective factors. To help those working in drug abuse prevention, NIDA, in cooperation with the prevention scientists, presented examples of research-based programs that feature a variety of strategies proven to be effective. Each program was developed as part of a research study, which demonstrated that over time youth who participated in the programs had better outcomes than those who did not. The programs are presented within their audience category (universal, selective, indicated, or tiered). *Universal* programs are designed for the general population, such as all students in a school. *Selective* programs target groups at risk or subsets of the general population, such as poor school achievers or children of drug abusers. *Indicated* programs are designed for people already experimenting with drugs.
Drug Strategies (2004)	http://www.drugstrategies.org/pubs.html Drug Strategies 1100 Connecticut Ave., N.W., Ste.800 Washington, D.C. 20036 (202) 289-9070	Personal/Social	Drug Strategies is a nonprofit organization that promotes more effective approaches to the nation's drug problems and supports private and public efforts to reduce the demand for drugs through prevention, education, treatment,

Organization	Contact	Category	Description
			law enforcement and community initiatives. Drug Strategies publishes the following publications: *Treating Teens: A Guide to Adolescent Drug Programs; Revised Making the Grade: A Guide to School Drug Prevention Programs; and Safe Schools, Safe Students: A Guide to Violence Prevention Strategies.*
Exemplary and Promising Safe, Disciplined, and Drug-Free Schools Programs U.S. Department of Education Office of Safe and Drug-Free Schools (2001).	U.S. Department of Education Office of Safe and Drug-Free Schools 1-877-4ED-PUBS	Personal/Social	This program identifies 33 promising and 9 exemplary school and community drug abuse and violence prevention and intervention programs.
The Center for the Study and Prevention of Violence University of Colorado at Boulder (2001).	http://www.colorado.edu/cspv/ Center for the Study and Prevention of Violence Institute of Behavioral Science University of Colorado at Boulder 439 UCB Boulder, CO 80309-0439 Telephone: (303) 492-8465 Fax: (303) 443-3297	Personal/Social	The CSPV Blueprints for Violence Prevention project has reviewed more than 600 programs to date. The project has identified 21 promising programs and 11 model prevention and intervention programs that meet a strict scientific standard of effectiveness and have been shown to reduce adolescent violent crime, aggression, delinquency, and substance abuse.

(continued)

TABLE 1-2 (*Continued*)

Source	Website, Citation or Other Location Information	ASCA Domains	Brief Summary of Resource
Preventing Crime: What Works, What Doesn't, What's Promising. A Report to the United States Congress L. W. Sherman, Denise Gottfredson, et al. (1997). Washington, DC: U.S. Department of Justice.	http://www.ncjrs.org/pdffiles/171676.pdf	Personal/Social	This report reviews programs funded by the Office of Justice Programs for crime, delinquency and substance abuse. The report describes evidence-based crime prevention programs that work, programs that do not work, and programs that are promising. The report focuses on crime prevention programs for families, schools, communities, the workplace, and law enforcement.
Youth Violence: A Report of the Surgeon General U.S. Department of Health and Human Services	http://www.surgeongeneral.gov/library/youthviolence/report.html	Personal/Social	This report details programs to prevent or reduce violent behaviors or associated risk factors among youth. The report identifies 28 programs designated as model or promising with respect to violence impacts or risk factor impacts.

What Works Clearinghouse U.S. Department of Education, Institute of Education Sciences	http://www.whatworks.ed.gov/	Academic Personal/Social	Reviews topics on a wide range or the nation's most pressing issues in education. Current review—Curriculum-base interventions for increasing middle school math. Forthcoming reviews include—interventions for early reading, character education, dropout prevention, English language learning, delinquent, disorderly, and violent behavior, and peer-assisted learning.
Treating and preventing adolescent mental health disorders: What we know and what we don't know. A research agenda for improving the mental health of our youth.	Commission on Positive Youth Development (2005). The positive perspective on youth development. In D. L. Evans, et al., *Treating and preventing adolescent mental health disorders: What we know and what we don't know. A research agenda for improving the mental health of our youth.* (pp. 498–527). New York: Oxford University Press, Inc.	Academic Personal/Social	Brief summaries of 26 literature reviews of model youth development programs that promote well-being and/or reduce problems.

areas are by no means mutually exclusive. Interventions that produce positive changes in one area may or may not produce positive changes in one or both of the other two areas as well. The table also presents the source for the research-based resources, the website, journal, or other location of the resource, and a brief summary of the resource.

One example of the type of information indexed by Table 1–2 is the work of Catalano et al. (2002). They reviewed research on 77 positive youth development programs in the United States. These programs were defined as ones which sought to achieve one or more of the following objectives: (a) promote bonding; (b) foster resilience; (c) promote social, emotional, cognitive, behavioral, and moral competence; (d) foster self-determination; (e) foster spirituality; (f) foster self-efficacy; (g) foster clear and positive identity; (h) foster belief in the future; (i) provide recognition for positive behavior and opportunities for prosocial involvement; and (j) foster prosocial norms (healthy standards for behavior). Twenty-five programs were designated as effective based on empirical evidence presented in the evaluation. Effective programs were shown to result both in positive youth behavior outcomes and the prevention of problem behaviors. The positive changes included (a) significant improvements in interpersonal skills, (b) quality of peer and adult relationships, (c) self-control, (d) problem solving, (e) cognitive competencies, (f) self-efficacy, (g) commitment to schooling, and (h) academic achievement. The significant reductions in problem behaviors involved (a) drug and alcohol use, (b) school misbehavior, (c) aggressive behavior, (d) violence, (e) truancy, (f) high risk sexual behavior, and (g) smoking. A number of the programs served students of color.

Eight of the effective programs took place in one environment, either the schools or the community. The remaining 17 took place in either two (typically, family and school) or three (community, family, and school) environments. School components were used in 22 (88%) of the effective programs, family components in 15 (60%), and community components in 12 (48%). Twenty-four (96%) of the programs used training manuals or other forms of structured curricula, and 20 (80%) intervened for nine months or more. Longer programs (e.g., more than nine months) generally produced better results than shorter programs. Skill building and environmental-organizational change strategies tended to be present in most effective programs.

The most common positive youth development constructs focused on by these programs were competence, self-efficacy, prosocial norms, opportunities for prosocial involvement, recognition for positive behavior, and bonding. In addition to the overall information on positive youth development programs, Catalano et al.'s (2002) review provides a brief description, a summary of the results produced, and a reference for each of the 25 effective programs. Such information can be invaluable to the busy, practicing school counselor who is attempting to build an effective, evidence-based comprehensive counseling program or who, as a school leader, is attempting to help her/his faculty to select an evidence-based program to enhance a particular aspect of student development.

Of course, the fact that a school counselor or other school personnel employ an intervention that research has shown to be effective does not mean that it will necessarily be successful in a particular school or with a given group of participants. How completely the intervention is administered, how consistently it is implemented, as well as the context in which it is implemented, all affect its impact. It is the school counselor's responsibility to collect relevant data (e.g., accountability) in order to assess the impact of a counseling intervention and ultimately of the school counseling program as a whole. Accountability is demonstrated by the extent to which such student indicators as academic achievement, attendance rates, graduation rates, and school safety are positively impacted by counseling interventions. Stone and Dahir (2004) and the Center for School Counseling Outcome Research webpage, http://www.umass.edu/schoolcounseling/leaders.htm, provide useful information about accountability issues and designing applicable measurement instruments for school counselors.

Emphasize Promotion-Oriented Developmental Advocacy at the School Level

The call for school counselors to serve as advocates for students has come from a variety of quarters (The Education Trust, 1999; Eriksen, 1997; Hart & Jacobi, 1992; House & Martin, 1998; Kiselica & Robinson, 2001; Lee, 2001; Lee & Walz, 1998; Lennon, Blackwell, Bridgeforth, & Cole, 1996; Lewis & Bradley, 2000). Critics have charged that school counselors have often functioned as agents of the status quo and gatekeepers for tracking and other practices that have limited educational and career opportunities for poor students, minority students, and other traditionally underserved groups (e.g., limited English proficient students, students with special needs) (Hart & Jacobi, 1992; House & Martin, 1998). In contrast, counselors are being increasingly called upon to assertively advocate for policies and practices that remove these barriers.

Advocacy "is based on the belief that individual and/or collective action must be taken to right injustices or to improve conditions for the benefit of an individual or groups" (House & Martin, 1998, p. 284), and is "the act of speaking up or taking action to make environmental changes on behalf of our clients" (Bradley & Lewis, 2000, p. 3). Client advocacy involves the school counselor working with or on behalf of a client or group of clients to change policies, services, or the environment in order to make conditions more favorable for enhancing the development of that client or client group.

Advocacy may involve removing barriers that block, delay, or even impede development and/or lobbying for policies, conditions, and programs that are likely to promote development. To date, much of the focus on advocacy appears to be directed primarily at removing barriers (e.g., The Transforming School Counseling Initiative) to development (The Education Trust, 1999).

In SBSC, however, the primary focus is on promotion-oriented advocacy—lobbying for practices, policies, and environments that enhance and foster student developmental strengths—rather than merely lobbying against policies that restrict opportunities for development. The difference between the two approaches to advocacy is significant, even though at first glance it may only appear to be subtle. For example, a counselor may advocate against a policy of self-contained classes for learning disabled and other students with special needs. But advocating against that policy is not the same as advocating for inclusion of these students into regular education classes and for providing both the classroom teacher and these students with the necessary instructional and other resources to be academically successful in that environment. With an emphasis on the latter, school counselors push for and contribute to solutions rather than merely expose problems. Similarly, advocating against tracking students is not the same as advocating for effective differentiated instruction so that all students can be academically challenged. Because of the complexity involved with engineering the type of school and community social contexts that nurture positive development, counselors frequently need both to advocate for promotion-oriented change and to collaborate with others to make change happen.

In school counseling, it is useful to distinguish between client advocacy (e.g., working for the interests of one's own clients) and social and political advocacy (Lewis, Cheek, & Hendricks, 2001). In social and political advocacy, counselors are involved in ways to effect change in political, economic, and social systems so that these systems are more responsive to the needs of total communities. Because of the day-to-day responsibilities and demands on school counselors, local promotion-oriented advocacy is likely to be a more central component of twenty-first-century school counseling in the SBSC framework. The counselor will be principally involved within her/his individual school. As such, advocacy efforts will focus primarily on lobbying for system policies and environments that enhance development for all students and secondarily on identifying and removing barriers—rules, regulations, policies, and procedures—that impede academic, career, and personal/social development opportunities for all individuals or particular groups of students. The school counselor's advocacy is concerned with assuring access, equity, and educational justice for all students. While this effort may encompass social and political advocacy, it is more likely that the counselor's day-to-day functioning and advocacy is focused at the building and district level rather than on larger political structures. This focus enables the counselor to build and sustain the types of school, school district, and community change efforts often needed to support successful academic, personal/social, and career development for all students.

Although advocacy efforts can have a much broader impact on student development than more traditional school counseling direct services, advocacy may not be a mode of functioning that comes naturally to school counselors. It involves more risk than many other counseling services. It frequently requires assuming an assertive posture and going against the status quo and against policies that have been established by a principal, a superintendent or other administrator, or by teachers. It may also involve simply lobbying for some positively oriented new practice, but organizations often resist change and those who propose it. School counselors tend to view themselves as team players rather than change agents and are inclined to adhere to administrative policies and procedures rather than to advocate for change even though they may have doubts about whether current policies and procedures are in the best interests of students.

Of course, advocacy does not have to involve open conflict and direct confrontation with administrators or other influential individuals, but even the simple presentation of data and information that contraindicates current practices can generate resistance. Thus, in a number of instances, advocacy can incur potential costs and pitfalls (Kiselica & Robinson, 2001) for the school counselor. These include backlash, undermining support for the counseling program, and possible job loss. As such, the strengths-based school counselor will need to build support for advocacy efforts from others, choose her/his advocacy "battles" wisely, and make effective use of more traditional listening and helping skills in these endeavors in order to minimize possible fallout from the power holders that she/he is attempting to influence. In addition, the school counselor will need to recognize that the potential benefits to student development of promotion-oriented advocacy far exceed its potential risks.

RELATIONSHIP OF STRENGTHS-BASED SCHOOL COUNSELING TO CURRENT SCHOOL COUNSELING MODELS

SBSC is influenced by a number of the current school counseling models. For example, it builds upon and expands the notion of a comprehensive developmental guidance or comprehensive school counseling program (see Galassi & Akos, 2004, for a discussion of these programs). It is also compatible with the concepts included in the American School Counselor Association's National Standards and National Model for school counseling (ASCA, 2003; Bowers & Hatch, 2002; Campbell & Dahir, 1997), but it attempts to operationalize those concepts more fully. We now turn to a brief consideration of some of these models in relation to a strengths-based perspective.

Comprehensive Developmental Guidance Programs

Comprehensive developmental guidance programs (CDGP) are currently the major way of organizing school counseling programs in this country (Gysbers

& Henderson, 2001), and, to date, the Missouri model (Gysbers & Henderson, 1994) has been the most prominent and influential of these programs. The model consists of three elements: (a) content, (b) an organizational framework, and (c) resources (Gysbers & Henderson, 1994, 2000, 2006). The content element involves student competencies grouped by domain (e.g., self-knowledge and interpersonal skills, goals, life-career-planning goals). The conceptual foundation for the model is life career development, which is defined as "self-development over the life span through the integration of roles, settings, and events in a person's life" (Gysbers & Henderson, 1994, p. 62). The second element, organizational framework, activities, and time, comprises three structural components and four program components. A definition of the program, rationale, and set of assumptions provide the structural components. Guidance curriculum (structured groups and classroom presentations), individual student planning (advisement, assessment, placement, and follow-up), responsive services (individual and small group counseling, consultation, and referral), and system support (management activities, research, consultation, community outreach, and public relations) coupled with suggested counselor time distribution by grade levels across these processes constitute the program components. The final element in Gysbers and Henderson's comprehensive guidance program is resources: human (school counselors, teachers, administrators, parents, students, community members, and business and labor personnel), financial, and political (e.g., endorsement of the program by the school board).

SBSC neither replaces nor serves as an alternative to CDGP. Rather, it provides a framework for deciding what should be emphasized in these programs. As is the case for comprehensive school counseling programs generally, the Gysbers and Henderson (1994) model involves the counselor functioning in proactive, preventive, and remedial modes. Although remediation and prevention are also important aspects of the strengths-based counselor's role, promotion and proactive functioning have a more prominent role in a comprehensive developmental guidance program that is strengths-oriented. Moreover, Gysbers and Henderson's model appears to emphasize the importance of particular counseling functions and the recommended percentages of time allocated to each (e.g., guidance curriculum—elementary school 35–45%, middle school 25–35%, high school 15–25%). The strengths-based school counselor, in contrast, is focused on promoting outcomes—evidence-based student strengths and strengths-enhancing environments. As such, the particular modes of functioning (e.g., individual counseling, guidance curriculum, system support) and the percentages of time devoted to each one are more flexible and less prescriptive. In addition, with a focus on environmental enhancement, the strengths-based school counselor is poised to assume a leadership role in the schools and to thrust the school counseling program into an integral position in the education and development of young people.

The Transforming School Counseling Initiative

The Transforming School Counseling Initiative (The Education Trust, 1999) represents an influential effort to reform the graduate-level, pre-service training of school counselors. With its emphasis on the counselor as educational leader and advocate in promoting academic achievement for all students and reducing barriers that impede academic success for poor and minority students, this initiative sought to redirect the emphasis away from the mental health focus that its proponents asserted had dominated school counselor training. Among its major contributions are (a) reinforcing the principle that all students can succeed academically, (b) stressing that school counselors must serve as advocates, leaders, and collaborators with other professionals to reduce the minority achievement gap, (c) emphasizing the importance of school counselors promoting systemic level change, and (d) stressing the necessity of data-based outcomes with respect to increasing academic achievement in school counseling programs.

Among the important differences between SBSC and The Transforming School Counseling Initiative (TSCI) is that development is viewed more holistically and contextually in the strengths-based perspective. While academic achievement and development are important educational goals, these goals need to be considered in context with, rather than apart from, personal/social and career development. As we discussed earlier, research has demonstrated that development in one area impacts development in other areas. As a result, narrowly focused academic interventions may not always be the most effective way to increase academic achievement. At times, the academic achievement of low-performing children may be more effectively enhanced by addressing unresolved social and emotional concerns prior to addressing their learning needs (Shechtman, 2002). For example, in a study of low achieving elementary (grades 2–6) children, Shechtman, Gilat, Fos, and Flasher (1996) randomly assigned students for 20 weeks either to a wait-list group that received 4–6 hours per week of intensive academic assistance for their learning problems, or to a treatment group that received the academic assistance plus 45 minutes per week of interpersonally focused group therapy. Results indicated that 75% of the treatment students improved their grades, whereas wait-list students did not. Treatment students also improved in self-esteem, social status, and self-control; all gains were maintained at follow-up (6–9 months later).

In summary, SBSC is compatible with many of the objectives of the TSCI. At the same time, SBSC differs in emphasis in focusing attention less on reducing barriers to academic success and development and more on increasing avenues that promote that development. Moreover, it adds to the contributions of the TSCI by stressing the importance of holistic development as well as evidence-based interventions regardless of their focus (academic, personal/

social, or career) that facilitate academic development as well as development in the personal/social, and career areas.

ASCA National Standards and National Model for School Counseling

Together, the American School Counseling Association National Standards for School Counseling Programs (Campbell & Dahir, 1997) and National Model (ASCA, 2003) link school counseling closely to the academic mission of schools. In addition, by defining what a school counseling program is, by describing in detail the four elements of the Model (foundation, delivery system, management system, and accountability), and by discussing the role of leadership advocacy, collaboration and teaming, and systemic change, these documents inform counselors, students, parents, and other educators of the contributions that school counselors can make to education.

An extended discussion of the National Standards and the National Model is beyond the scope of this chapter. The point of the discussion is to illustrate how SBSC complements and expands on the developmental framework provided by the National Standards and National Model.

The National Standards were intended to serve as the foundation for developing a national model for school counseling (Bowers, Hatch, & Schwallie-Giddis, 2001). They also attempt to tie school counseling programs to the academic mission and needs of the school and encourage the school counselor to assume a leadership role in education reform. The National Standards assert "the primary goal of the school counseling program is to enhance student achievement and accomplishment" (Campbell & Dahir, 1997, p. 4).

> A comprehensive school counseling program is developmental and systematic in nature, sequential, clearly defined, and accountable. It is jointly founded upon developmental psychology, educational philosophy, and counseling methodology. . . . The school counseling program is integral to the educational enterprise. The program is proactive and preventive in its focus. It assists students in acquiring and using lifelong learning skills. (Campbell & Dahir, 1997, p. 9)

In the form of a set of standards and student competencies in three broad domains of development—academic, career, and personal/social—the National Standards enumerate the attitudes, knowledge, and skills that all students are to acquire as a result of participating in a school counseling program. These standards are further elaborated in the National Model (ASCA, 2003) by over 100 competencies and student indicators, which appear to be loosely tied to developmental theory and research.

In our presentation of SBSC, we adhere to this tri-part (e.g., academic, career, and personal/social) perspective on development partially for reasons of conceptual simplicity and clarity and partially for consistency with the

National Model; however, our previous discussion indicated that development must be viewed more holistically. Thus, the three development domains are by no means mutually exclusive; they are interrelated. Development is a continuous process, and change in one area impacts change in other areas. Moreover, the effects of an intervention applied in one domain are not necessarily limited to effects only in that domain. For example, as we have seen, an intervention that is designed to effect change in personal/social development may trigger improvements in the academic area as well. In addition, an intervention designed to effect change in one developmental domain may not even be as effective in producing change in that domain as an intervention that is usually employed to effect change in another developmental domain. For instance, tutoring (an academic intervention) may be recommended to improve the (academic) performance of high school students who have performed poorly on end of grade or end of course mathematics tests; however, this intervention may be less effective in improving mathematics performance than an internship in a business or other work setting (a career intervention) in which mathematic skills are used on a regular basis and thereby increase students' motivation to acquire these skills and their willingness to exert the necessary time and effort to do so.

In our presentation of SBSC, we incorporate the domains of academic, career, and personal/social development that are stressed in ASCA's National Model. However, our discussion expands on the ASCA Model in a number of ways, including (a) explicitly recognizing that these developmental areas are interrelated and contextually based, (b) identifying and stressing the importance of empirical or evidence-based developmental strengths and evidence-based, strengths-enhancing environments for each of these areas, and (c) whenever possible, identifying and emphasizing the use of evidence-based interventions to facilitate development in these areas.

CONCEPTUAL FOUNDATIONS OF STRENGTHS-BASED SCHOOL COUNSELING

The conceptual foundations of SBSC are rooted primarily in contemporary theories and research in psychology, especially developmental psychology, as well as in best practices and contemporary models for comprehensive school counseling programs. We now turn to an overview of the general psychological conceptual foundations of SBSC. In this chapter, we will briefly consider contributions from developmental contextualism, resiliency, developmental assets, competence, social developmental theory, and positive psychology. In subsequent chapters, we will discuss more specific theories and research that are linked to particular evidence-based student strengths and strengths-enhancing environments.

Developmental-Contextualism

Developmental-contextualism is a meta-theory. As a meta-theory, it provides a framework for examining earlier developmental theories and a guide for practice and research by psychologists who work in schools (Lerner, 1984, 1986, 1995; Lerner et al., 1998; Walsh, Galassi, Murphy, & Park-Taylor, 2002). Developmental-contextualism addresses many of the limitations of earlier developmental theories (see Walsh et al. for a discussion of how this theory can inform the work of counseling psychologists in schools). For example, earlier theories (e.g., Piaget's stages of cognitive development) tended to overemphasize the person side of the person-environment relationship by focusing on the universal aspects of development, the ways in which people are similar to each other. They paid relatively little attention to developmental variability, to the influence of context on the developing person, or to the influence of the person on the developmental context. Earlier theories also tended to: (a) focus primarily on childhood development; (b) examine individual processes of development (e.g., cognitive, physical, moral) in isolation from each other; and (c) be concerned with psychopathology.

Developmental-contextualism asserts a number of key developmental principles. Our discussion addresses four of those principles that have implications for student development and school counseling. First, context exerts a major influence on development. Family, school, neighborhood, community, society, and culture all influence development. Development cannot be fully understood in isolation from these influences. These influences result in variability and plasticity in development. This variability means that there is potential to modify development in new directions throughout the life span rather than the universal fixed stage concept of development proposed by earlier theories. One implication for the school counselor of these multiple developmental influences is that the interventions that we have traditionally used (e.g., those focused solely on the individual student) often need to be coupled with or even supplanted by interventions at the systems level (e.g., school, family, community, etc.)

Second, development is holistic. Development occurs at various levels— biological, psychological, social, and cultural. Events at one level impact development at other levels as these levels reciprocally and continually interact with and influence one another. As a result, the different aspects of a person work together rather than in isolation from the whole. One implication of holistic development is that initiatives to influence one aspect of development (e.g., cognitive and academic achievement) may have limited impact when attempted in isolation from considerations in other areas of development. Thus, attempts to improve academic performance and test scores may have limited impact if biological (e.g., health, nutrition, safety), psychological (e.g., belongingness), and/or cultural (e.g., ethnic identity) developmental issues go unattended. Due to the complexity of human development, effective intervention, prevention, and promotion efforts with students often require coordinated and comprehensive approaches that target multiple feedback loops and a wide range of behavior.

A third point is that earlier developmental theories focused on development from birth to age 18. While that age range encompasses most of the students in pre-K–12 educational settings, it fails to address the developmental issues of parents and family units, which, in turn, have a substantial impact on the development of school-age youth. In contrast, developmental-contextualism endorses a life-span developmental perspective. A life-span perspective tends to be more in tune with a variety of issues that counselors and educators help students address. These issues include transitions, both from one schooling level to another and from school to work, and acquiring the knowledge, skills, and attitudes needed to be successful in life.

Finally, developmental-contextualism incorporates both strengths and deficits. Contemporary developmental theory:

> Views the course of human development as a trajectory that can be modified at any point and can lead to new patterns of risk and resilience as well as corresponding sets of strengths and deficits. Recent research on effective programs for school-children and youth makes clear that a focus on competence enhancement as well as problem reduction is essential for treatment success. (Walsh et al., 2002, p. 693)

Resiliency

Recent advances in theory and research on resiliency have important implications for strengths-based school counseling (e.g., Benard, 1991; Garmezy, Masten, & Tellegen, 1984; Henderson & Milstein, 1996; Rutter, 1985; Werner & Smith, 1992). Resiliency is "the capacity to spring back, rebound, successfully adapt in the face of adversity and develop social, academic, and vocational competence despite exposure to severe stress or simply to the stress inherent in today's world" (Henderson & Milstein, 1996, p. 7). It includes the "capacity to bounce back, to withstand hardship, and to repair yourself" (Wolin & Wolin, 1993, p. 5).

Resiliency has applicability not only to the type of services provided to all students in a comprehensive school counseling program, but is also especially relevant to the at-risk students that counselors serve. Moreover, the developmental research in this area, which has often involved longitudinal studies, has important implications as well. The most well known of these longitudinal research studies is the ongoing, 40-plus year collaboration of Werner and Smith (1992) that followed the development into adulthood of an initial sample of over 600 poor, minority children from Kauai. This and other resiliency research has repeatedly demonstrated that, contrary to popular belief, most people are not permanently overwhelmed by and irreparably damaged by exposure to adverse life circumstances. Typically, 50% or more of children who have unfortunately been reared under conditions of profound adversity (e.g., extreme poverty, child abuse and neglect, homelessness, parent mental illness, family dysfunction, etc.) over a prolonged period of time nevertheless develop into adults who have healthy relations with other people, are gainfully employed, and have positive expectations for the future.

Findings such as those by Werner and Smith (1992) have prompted resiliency researchers to identify key protective processes and factors that are associated with moderating or overcoming severe developmental risks. Protective processes/factors are "traits, conditions, situations and episodes that appear to alter, or even reverse, predictions of [negative outcome] and enable individuals to circumvent life stressors" (Benard, 1991, p. 3). Protective processes/factors include both those that are internal to or can be developed by the individual (e.g., intelligence, self-motivation, sociability, autonomy, being "good at something") as well at those that exist or can be developed in the environment (e.g., promoting supportive relationships, setting and enforcing clear boundaries, providing leadership and other opportunities for meaningful participation).

Resiliency theory offers a conceptual framework that can explain and guide counselors and educators' efforts to develop resiliency and academic, social, and vocational competence in students. In their Resiliency Wheel (see Fig. 1–1), Henderson and Milstein (1996) provide a model that can be used to conceptualize interventions within a strengths-oriented comprehensive counseling program directed at individual students, the school as a whole, or the greater community.

The Wheel addresses six consistent themes identified from research that constitute a six-step strategy for fostering resiliency. Three of the protective factors—(a) prosocial bonding, (b) clear and consistent boundaries, and (c) life skills—focus on mitigating risk factors in the environment. Prosocial bonding involves increasing connections between students and any prosocial person (e.g., a mentor) or activity in the school environment (e.g., participating in interscholastic sports). Research has repeatedly demonstrated that students' need for belonging in the school community significantly affects academic attitudes, beliefs, behaviors, and achievement (see Osterman, 2000 for a review). Implementing school policies that clarify expectations for students coupled with consistently applied consequences constitute clear and consistent boundaries. Life skills involve many of the interventions that typically are offered in comprehensive guidance programs: conflict resolution, assertiveness and communication skills, problem-solving and decision-making skills, and stress management.

The other three factors—providing caring and support, high expectations, and opportunities for meaningful participation—focus on increasing resiliency through building and strengthening protective factors in the environment. Resiliency research consistently indicates that the single most important protective factor, and one which is central to school counseling, is adult caring and support (Henderson & Milstein, 1996). Advisory programs at the middle school level and school-within-a-school programs at the high school level rep-

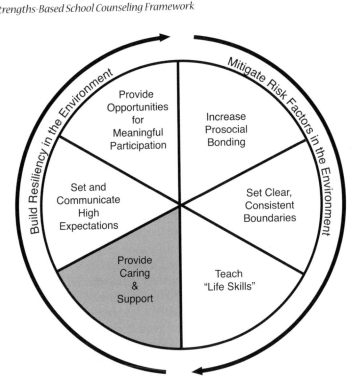

FIGURE 1–1. The resiliency wheel. Henderson, N., Milstein, M. M. *Resiliency in schools: Making it happen for students and educators,* p. 12. Copyright © by Corwin Press, Inc. Reprinted with permisson of Corwin Press, Inc.

resent initiatives to provide students with more opportunities to connect with teachers and other adults in a caring relationship within the school setting. Establishing and communicating high expectations for academic performance is a widely accepted principle in both the resiliency and the education reform-counseling literature (e.g., The Education Trust, 1999). Examples of meaningful opportunities for participation in schools include, giving students some responsibility for problem solving, decision making, planning, and goal setting (e.g., student participation in school governance committees or in student government) and for helping others (e.g., peer tutoring, peer mediation, and student-initiated service learning programs). In short, the Resiliency Wheel provides school counselors with a useful approach for decreasing risk and enhancing protective factors with the at-risk and other students with whom they interact in a direct service (e.g., counseling) capacity. In addition, it provides school counselors as well as other educators a conceptual framework for developing and implementing strengths-enhancing (and risk-reducing) environments for all students.

Competence

The contribution of competence to positive youth development and optimal human functioning has been repeatedly emphasized by researchers and theorists over the years (e.g., Masten & Coatsworth, 1998; White, 1959; Zins & Wagner, 1997). White, for example, defined competence as "an organism's capacity to interact effectively with its environment" (p. 297). As such, the development of competence constitutes another conceptual framework that can inform the practice of the strengths-based school counselor.

In this regard, we focus on the work of Masten and colleagues (e.g., Masten, 2001; Masten & Coatsworth,1998; Masten & Reed, 2002). Masten and Coatsworth asserted that competence refers to:

> A pattern of effective adaptation in the environment, either broadly defined in terms of reasonable success with major developmental tasks expected for a person of a given age and gender in the context of his or her culture, society, and time or more narrowly defined in terms of specific domains of achievement, such as academics, peer acceptance, or athletics. . . . It refers to good adaptation and not necessarily to superb achievement. (p. 206)

Competence results from the child's interactions with the environment and changes as the child develops and as the context changes. Masten and Coatsworth use the developmental tasks associated with different age levels (e.g., infancy to preschool, middle childhood, and adolescence) as the criteria for competence.

Drawing on competence, resilience, and intervention research, three adaptive systems are asserted as fostering competence in both favorable and unfavorable environments. Among these are relationships with caring adults, especially parents, which begin with the mother-infant attachment and extend to relationships with other adults throughout childhood. The ability to self-regulate attention, emotion, and behavior represents the second adaptive system (see chapters 3 and 5 for a discussion of the role of self-regulation in academic development and personal/social development). Once again, the criteria for competence vary according to age with the ability to regulate attention, negative emotions, and compliance to social rules being important in early childhood and social competence with peers and socially appropriate conduct being important in the school years. Cognitive functioning, as represented by academic achievement and IQ, represents the third adaptive system for fostering competence. According to Masten and Coatsworth (1998), the two most widely reported predictors of resilience are relationships with caring prosocial adults and good intellectual functioning. One important implication of Masten and Coatsworth's research for the school counselor is that effective prevention programs involve both fostering competence and preventing problems or reducing risk.

Developmental Assets

Premised on the assertion that the community social infrastructure for raising developmentally healthy young people in this country has eroded, developmental psychologist Peter Benson and his associates at Search Institute (Benson, 1997; Benson, Galbraith, & Espeland, 1998; Benson, Scales, & Mannes, 2003; Scales 2005) have proposed a strengths-based conceptual framework for positive youth development. Through cross-sectional survey research with over 100,000 students (grades 6–12) in over 200 towns and cities in the United States, they have identified 40 developmental assets (see Table 1–3). The assets, which are divided into two groups—20 internal (to the child) and 20 external (within the environment)—are developmental building blocks that enable children to grow up to be healthy, caring, and responsible adults. The internal assets are grouped into the four categories of (a) commitment to learning (e.g., achievement motivation), (b) positive values (e.g., equality and social justice), (c) social competencies (e.g., cultural competence), and (d) positive identity (e.g., positive view of personal future). External assets include the categories of support (e.g., family support), empowerment (e.g., service to others), boundaries and expectations (e.g., school provides clear rules and consequences), and constructive use of time (e.g., youth programs).

Search Institute data consistently indicate that the number of assets experienced by youth is inversely associated with the high risk behaviors of alcohol use, illicit drug use, sexual activity, and violence and directly associated with the positive or thriving behaviors of succeeding in school, valuing diversity, maintaining good health, and delaying gratification (Benson, 1997; Benson et al., 1998; Benson et al., 2003). For example, the percentages of youth who are succeeding in school (defined as getting mostly As on their report cards) is 53% for those reporting having 31–40 assets as compared with 35%, 19%, and 7% for those reporting 21–30, 11–20, and 0–10 assets, respectively. Moreover, high levels of assets seemed to be related to narrowing of traditional equity gaps in achievement (Benson et al., 2003). Conversely, the percentage of youth violence (three or more acts of fighting, hitting, injuring a person, carrying a weapon, or threatening physical harm in the past 12 months) is 61% for those reporting having 0–10 assets as compared with 35%, 16%, and 6%, respectively, for those with 11–20, 21–30, and 31–40 assets. Although experiencing 31–40 assets is associated with especially low levels (e.g., 1–6%) of high-risk behaviors and high levels of positive attitudes and behaviors (53–88%), only 8% of youth experience that many assets. The research also indicates that (a) boys on the average experience fewer assets than girls, (b) older youth tend to experience fewer than younger youth, (c) students whose mothers have a higher level of education experience more assets than those whose mothers have less education, (d) assets are relevant across race and ethnicity, and (e) 62% of all youth experience fewer than 20 assets.

TABLE 1–3.

40 Developmental Assets

Asset Type	Asset Name	Definition
Support	1. Family support	Family life provides high levels of love and support
	2. Positive family communication	Parents and child communicate positively; child is willing to seek parents' advice and counsel
	3. Other adult relationships	Child receives support from three or more non-parent adults
	4. Caring neighborhood	Child experiences caring neighbors
	5. Caring school climate	School provides a caring, encouraging environment
	6. Parent involvement in schooling	Parents are actively involved in helping child succeed in school
Empowerment	7. Community values youth	Child perceives that community adults value youth
	8. Youth given useful roles	Youth are given useful roles in community life
	9. Community service	Child gives one hour or more per week to serving in one's community
	10. Safety	Child feels safe in home, school, and neighborhood
Boundaries and Expectations	11. Family boundaries	Family has clear rules and consequences; and monitors whereabouts
	12. School boundaries	School provides clear rules and consequences
	13. Neighborhood boundaries	Neighbors would report undesirable behavior to family
	14. Adult role models	Parent(s) and other adults model pro-social behavior
	15. Positive peer influence	Child's best friends model responsible behavior
	16. High expectations	Both parents and teachers press child to achieve
Time	17. Creative activities	Involved in three or more hours per week in lessons or practice in music, theater, or other arts
	18. Youth programs	Involved in three or more hours per week in sports, clubs, or organizations at school and/or community organizations
	19. Religious community	Involved in one or more hours per week
	20. Time at home	Out with friends "with nothing special to do" two or fewer nights per week

External Asset

TABLE 1–3 *(Continued)*

Asset Type	Asset Name	Definition
Educational Commitment	21. Achievement motivation	Child is motivated to do well in school
	22. School performance	Child has B average or better
	23. Homework	Child reports one or more hours of homework per day
	24. Bonding to school	Child cares about his/her school
	25. Reading for pleasure	Child reads for pleasure three or more hours per week
Values	26. Caring	Child places a high value on helping other people
	27. Equality and social justice	Child places high value on promoting equality and reducing hunger and poverty
	28. Integrity	Child acts on convictions, stands up for her/his beliefs
	29. Honesty	Child "tells the truth even when it is not easy"
	30. Responsibility	Child accepts and takes personal responsibility
	31. Restraint	Child believes it is important not to be sexually active or to use alcohol and/or other drugs
Social Competencies	32. Planning and decision making	Child has skill to plan ahead and make choices
	33. Interpersonal competence	Child has empathy, sensitivity, and friendship skills
	34. Cultural competence	Child has knowledge of and comfort with people of different racial backgrounds
	35. Resistance skills	Child can resist negative peer pressure
	36. Peaceful conflict resolution	Child seeks to resolve conflict nonviolently
Positive Identity	37. Personal control	Child feels she/he has control over "things that happen to me"
	38. Self-esteem	Child reports high self-esteem
	39. Sense of purpose	Child reports "my life has a purpose"
	40. Positive view of personal future	Child is optimistic about his/her personal future

Internal Asset (vertical label spanning the Values and Social Competencies rows)

In summarizing their findings across a number of studies, Benson et al. (2003) concluded that the explanatory power of developmental assets is "at least as compelling and probably more so, than that of traditional 'social addresses' such as gender, race and socioeconomic status" (p. 383). With respect to education, "the total number of assets, as well as particular configurations of assets, account for as much or more variance in educational achievement as do more conventional schooling factors such as per-pupil expenditures, curricular requirements, teacher preparation, and leadership" (p. 385). According to Benson, the implications of these findings are clear. Schools and communities need to mobilize efforts to build assets if they expect children to develop into healthy, productive, caring adults, and the Search Institute stresses this notion in its *Healthy Communities*Healthy Youth* approach. Thus, the developmental assets framework provides the school counselor not only with research-based data about the type of attitudes and behaviors to promote in comprehensive guidance programs, but also about the types of environments that shape positive youth development. The school counselor, in turn, can collaborate with others and play an important role in helping students to develop internal assets as well as in fostering school environments that are rich in external assets.

Social Development Model/Strategy

Like the *Healthy Communities*Healthy Youth* approach of the Search Institute, *Communities That Care* (CTC) is a comprehensive community-based prevention program (Catalano & Hawkins, 1996; Hawkins, Catalano, & Associates, 1992; Hawkins, Catalano, & Miller, 1992; Pollard, Hawkins, & Arthur, 1999; Posey et al., 1996; Wong, Burgoyne, Catalano, Chappell, & Hawkins, 1997). It has been used in over 600 communities and has an overall goal to foster positive youth development by mobilizing the resources of the community, school, and family. CTC includes some elements that are quite familiar to school counselors; however, it goes beyond our traditional focus on the individual and small group. It recognizes the need to promote change in the school, family, and community contexts by simultaneously reducing risk and enhancing protective factors at a systemic level. Research has indicated that a variety of adolescent problems behaviors (substance abuse, delinquency, teen pregnancy, school dropout, and violence) are associated with a number of common risk factors at the peer, school, family, and community system levels (see Wong et al., 1997 for a list of these risk factors and their relationship to adolescent problem behaviors).

CTC is based on the social development model (Catalano & Hawkins, 1996) or social development strategy (Wong et al., 1997). The model hypothesizes a similar process for prosocial and antisocial development, is recursive, and specifies submodels for four specific periods of childhood and adolescent development (see Catalano and Hawkins for an in depth discussion). The overall goal of the model is to promote the development of healthy, positive behaviors. The likelihood of that occurring is increased if youth are immersed in environments and communities that consistently communicate healthy beliefs and clear standards. Thus, the context in which a young person develops is viewed as critical to healthy development and is a major focus of intervention.

The model/strategy includes three protective factors (healthy beliefs and clear standards, bonding to prosocial groups, and characteristics of the individual) and three protective processes (opportunities, skills, and recognition) that affect the likelihood of youth developing and exhibiting healthy behaviors (see Fig. 1–2). In the model, individual characteristics of the child—intelligence, gender, sociability, a resilient temperament—impact the child's opportunities to be involved in and contribute to community, school, family, and peer groups in positive ways. In order to take advantage of these opportunities, a child needs to learn and use the necessary emotional (identifying, managing, and expressing feelings; controlling impulses; delaying gratification; and reducing stress), cognitive (self-talk; reading and interpreting social cues; problem solving and decision making; self-awareness; taking the perspective of others; and having a positive attitude), and social skills (nonverbal communications, verbal communications such as assertiveness, and taking action). The child also needs to be recognized for his or her efforts to learn and use these skills and to take advantage of opportunities to contribute in prosocial ways. These protective processes help to bond the child to family, the school, and the community. Bonding involves both attachment (a strong positive relationship) and commitment and makes the child more receptive to healthy beliefs and clear standards in the environment if he or she is consistently exposed to them. Adhering to healthy beliefs and standards, in turn, increases the likelihood of the child engaging in healthy behaviors.

Thus, the social development model/strategy provides the school counselor with a blueprint for facilitating positive youth development. In addition, CTC provides a detailed description of over 100 evidence-based interventions for developing student strengths and strengths-enhancing environments (Posey et al., 1996). The recommended interventions are organized into four areas: (a) family, (b) school, (c) community-based youth programs, and (d) community-focused programs and into six age ranges from prenatal to young adult (age 18). For each strategy, Posey et al. (1996) list the specific risk and protective factors targeted. This specificity enables one to (a) select effective developmentally appropriate strategies, (b) target the needed prevention/intervention foci (e.g., school, etc.), and (c) match prevention/intervention efforts against identified risks.

Positive Psychology

The examples that we have just discussed are reflective of a broader trend to focus increasing attention on a positive rather than a disease-oriented model

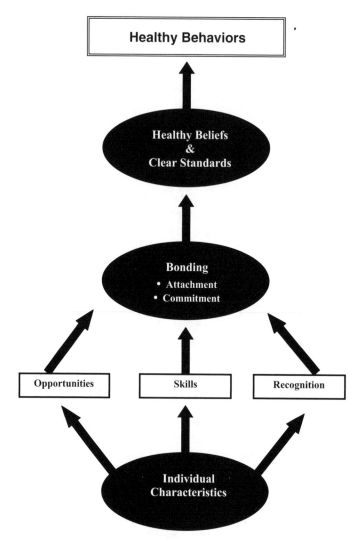

FIGURE 1–2.   The social development strategy. Used with permission from Richard F. Catalano and J. David Hawkins, Social Development Research Group, School of Social Work, University of Washington, Seattle, Washington.

of human functioning (e.g., Larson, 2000; Roberts, Brown, Johnson, & Reinke, 2002; Seligman, 2002; Seligman & Csikszentmihalyi, 2000; Shatté, Seligman, Gillham, & Reivich, 2003; Sheldon & King, 2001). As discussed by Seligman and Csikszentmihalyi (2000), the major strides in prevention of serious problems have come largely from systematically focusing on building competency rather than remediating deficits and weakness. Seligman, Schulman, DeRubeis, and Hollon (1999), for example, reported that building optimism prevents depression.

> We have discovered that certain human strengths act as buffers against mental illness: courage, future-mindedness, optimism, interpersonal skill, faith, work ethic, hope, honesty, perseverance, and the capacity for flow and insight, to name several. Much of the task of prevention in this new century will be to create a science of human strength whose mission will be to understand and learn how to foster these virtues in young people. (Seligman, 2002, p. 5)

Moreover, Fredrickson (2001) summarized research indicating that experiences of positive emotions broaden people's momentary thought-action repertoires and help them to build enduring physical, intellectual, social, and psychological resources. Positive emotions aid in undoing lingering negative emotions, in building psychological resilience, and triggering upward spirals toward improved emotional well-being.

The self-determination theory research program of Ryan and Deci (2000) consistently revealed that social-contextual conditions that enable individuals to satisfy the psychological needs of competence, autonomy, and relatedness facilitate the natural processes of self-motivation and healthy psychological development as reflected by intrinsic motivation, self-regulation, and well being. Conversely, when these needs are thwarted, diminished motivation and well being result.

Finally, research by Good, Aronson, and Inzlicht (2003) demonstrated the power of positive messages in reducing the anxiety-inducing effects of stereotype threat on low-income female and minority adolescents and improving their performance on standardized tests. Their study was based on the assumption that standardized test performance is highly influenced by psychological factors such as stereotypes (e.g., that due to lower intelligence or abilities [e.g., in math for girls] girls and minorities will perform more poorly than males and majority students). College student mentors who worked with low-income seventh graders (63% Hispanic, 15% Black, and 22% White) as part of a computer course encouraged the seventh graders to subscribe to one of three messages that were designed to reattribute their academic difficulties from stable internal causes to temporary, external causes. The messages included (a) the view that intelligence is malleable rather than fixed and that the brain can form new connections throughout life (b) that academic difficulties in the seventh grade are due to the novelty (e.g., the transition) of the educational setting and that most students would overcome these difficulties and reach high levels of achievement, or (c) a combination of (a) and (b). A fourth group (a control) learned about the health effects of using drugs and that drugs could interfere with academic achievement. Results revealed the expected stereotype effect (e.g., boys out perform girls in math) in the control group plus the important findings that (a) girls in three treatment groups earned significantly higher math standardized test scores than girls in the control condition, and (b) scores of girls in the three treatment groups did not differ from the boys' scores in those conditions. Results on the standardized reading tests indicated students (largely minority) in the incremental intelligence and attribution conditions, but not the combined condition, scored significantly higher than those students (largely minority) in the control condition. Overall, the findings suggest that if minority and low-income students receive positive messages about their ability to be successful academically, they are less likely to conform to stereotypes and under perform on standardized tests.

Thus, a number of investigators have called for the development of positive psychology or a science of human strengths (e.g., Larson, 2000; Seligman & Csikszentmihalyi, 2000; Sheldon & King, 2001).

> At the individual level, it [positive psychology] is about positive individual traits: the capacity for love and vocation, courage, interpersonal skill, courage, aesthetic sensibility, perseverance, forgiveness, originality, future mindedness, spirituality, high talent, and wisdom. At the group level, it is about the civic virtues and the institutions that move individuals toward better citizenship: responsibility, nurturance, altruism, civility, moderation, tolerance, and work ethic. . . . Psychologists working with families, schools, religious communities, and corporations need to develop climates that foster these strengths. (Seligman & Csikszentmihalyi, 2000, p. 5)

Two major objectives of positive psychology are (a) increasing understanding of human strengths through the development of taxonomies and psychometrics, and (b) developing and disseminating interventions that build strengths (rather than remediate weaknesses) in children, adolescents, and adults in order to promote life satisfaction and fulfillment in all people (Shatté et al., 2003).

With respect to identifying the specific strengths to be promoted in childhood, Roberts et al. (2002) noted that pathology models of human behavior assume an adult-oriented perspective and assume that the goal of all human development and any intervention is to produce a fully functioning adult. As a result, only adult outcomes are considered to be important in a pathology model. In contrast, they asserted the importance of developmental positive psychology in which improving future (e.g., in adulthood) health and well-being is important as well as addressing the challenges, health, and well-being of the child in her/his current state of development.

> The positive psychology alternative is to focus on the child while a child is in development and to enhance functioning, competence, and overall mental heath at any particular time. . . . Thus, there should be a focus on the health status of children while they are children rather than recognizing children's importance only because the children will become adults in the future. (Roberts et al., 2002, pp. 664 & 671)

The implication of this position is that some of the strengths that the strengths-oriented school counselor will seek to promote are ones that have been empirically related to competent performance in adulthood, while others are strengths that have been shown to be important primarily at a particular point in development.

Thus, the focus of positive psychology is on strengths promotion rather than deficit remediation, and on all people, not just "sick" people. As such, the theory and research that is being generated by positive psychology potentially provide the school counselor with knowledge of the strengths to be promoted in all students as well as the interventions that are effective in facilitating those strengths. With their ready access to children and the major systems that impact them (e.g., schools, peers, and family), school counselors are in an excellent position to enhance both those strengths and the environments that support them.

SUMMARY

SBSC is a new and complementary conceptual framework that can enhance the practice of school counseling in the 21st century as reflected in the comprehensive school counseling programs promulgated by the ASCA National Model (ASCA, 2003). Firmly based in contemporary developmental theory and research, SBSC emphasizes the promotion of holistic positive youth development for all students as the central mission of the school counselor. Within this framework, the school counselor promotes and advocates for student strengths and strengths-enhancing environments that have been shown to be empirically linked to positive development in the academic, personal/social, and/or career development domains. The strengths-oriented school counselor is committed to evidence-based practice.

The conceptual underpinnings of SBSC are rooted in theory and research in a variety of areas, including developmental contextualism, resiliency, competence development, developmental assets, social development theory, positive psychology, and comprehensive school counseling programs. Further, SBSC operationalizes and expands on many of the concepts of ASCA's National Model of School Counseling.

In subsequent chapters, we further articulate theory, research, and practical examples of how SBSC can facilitate academic, personal/social, and career development in students. We also consider assessment from a strengths perspective as well as issues in the education and preparation of strengths-based school counselors. Finally, we conclude with a chapter devoted to questions and limitations of the SBSC framework and a chapter on preparing strengths-based school counselors.

KEY POINTS

Introduction and Overview

- The counselor's main role in Strengths-Based School Counseling (SBSC) is to promote and advocate for positive youth development for all students and for the environments that enhance and sustain that development.
- SBSC emphasizes context-based development, which takes into account environmental and contextual factors in student development and encompasses ethnic and cultural differences.
- It utilizes a strengths-based perspective to identify and enhance evidence-based strengths of students while developing additional competencies that will contribute to academic, personal/social, and career success.
- SBSC promotes the development of strengths-enhancing environments through collaboration, advocacy, and system-level interventions. These evidence-based environments reinforce and help sustain the student strengths that counselors are trying to promote. Strengths-enhancing environments are characterized by factors such as warm and friendly adult-student relationships, consistency with respect to schoolwork instructions, rules for behavior, supervision, and opportunities to learn with support and praise.
- The focus of SBSC is the promotion of social, emotional, behavioral, and cognitive development rather than remediation and prevention. Thus, problem behaviors are prevented as students proactively acquire new skills.
- SBSC utilizes best practices and evidence-based counseling interventions. Outcome data on the effectiveness of interventions can be found within a variety of disciplines relevant to school counseling. However, it is the responsibility of the school counselor to assess the impact of an intervention by collecting school-specific outcome data.
- Advocacy efforts within SBSC focus primarily on lobbying for system policies and environments that enhance development for all students at the building and district levels. Secondarily, the school counselor will focus on identifying and removing barriers such as regulations or policies that impede academic, personal/social, and career development opportunities for all individuals or specific student populations.

Relationship of Strengths-Based School Counseling to Current School Counseling Models

- SBSC builds on contemporary school counseling models and attempts to operationalize important concepts found in those models.
- SBSC expands the focus of a comprehensive guidance program by prioritizing promotion and proactive functioning as more important than remediation and prevention. SBSC also focuses on promoting outcomes, evidence-based student strengths, and strengths-enhancing environments, in a flexible manner rather than assigning fixed percentages of time to specific counseling functions. Leadership is also more integral to the strengths-oriented school counselor's role.
- The Transforming School Counseling Initiative (TSCI) is compatible with many objectives of SBSC. TSCI stresses outcome data, systemic level change, advocacy,

leadership, and the belief that all students can succeed academically; however, development is viewed more holistically and contextually in SBSC. In addition, academic goals in SBSC are addressed in context with personal/social and career goals as interventions in one domain are interrelated to development in the other domains.

- The three domains of the ASCA National Model are incorporated into the SBSC framework. SBSC enhances the National Model by explicitly recognizing that the academic, personal/social, and career domains are interrelated and contextually based. Also, SBSC expands the National Model by stressing the importance of evidence-based strengths, strengths-enhancing environments, and the implementation of evidence-based interventions in each of the domains.

Conceptual Foundations of Strengths-Based School Counseling

- Numerous theories have contributed to the conceptual foundation of SBSC..
- Developmental contextualism is a meta-theory that asserts the holistic nature of development, emphasizes the importance of contextual factors in development, endorses a life-span developmental perspective, and incorporates both strengths and deficits within its framework to account for the risk and resilience of students.
- Resiliency theory strives to identify key protective processes and factors that are associated with overcoming developmental risks. The Resiliency Wheel identifies six such factors: (a) prosocial bonding, (b) clear and consistent boundaries, (c) life skills, (d) high expectations,(e) opportunities for meaningful expectations, and (f) providing caring and support.
- The development of competence is another important conceptual framework for the strengths-oriented school counselor. Relationships with caring adults, the ability to self-regulate attention, emotion, and behavior, and cognitive functioning represent the three adaptive systems that foster competence in students.
- The developmental assets framework identifies 40 assets for students that will help them grow into healthy, caring adults. Internal and external assets are identified so the school counselor is able to promote specific behaviors and attitudes as well as create school environments that support positive youth development. A high level of assets is associated with low levels of high-risk behaviors and high levels of positive attitudes and behaviors.
- The Social Development Model/Strategy strives to promote the development of healthy, positive behaviors. Environments and communities are as seen as critical to positive youth development. The model includes three protective factors and three protective processes that affect the likelihood of developing healthy behaviors. Healthy beliefs and clear standards, bonding to prosocial groups, and individual characteristics are the three outlined protective factors. Opportunities, skills, and recognition by others are the three outlined protective processes.
- Positive Psychology focuses on strength promotion rather than deficit remediation, and on all people rather than "sick" people. The objectives of positive psychology are to increase understanding of human strengths through the development of taxonomies and psychometrics and to disseminate interventions that build strengths in people of all ages at many different points in development.

2

Implementing the Strengths-Based School Counselor's Role

OUTLINE

The Traditional Role of the School Counselor

The Contemporary Role of the School Counselor

The Strengths-Based School Counselor's Role

Direct Services and the Strengths-Based School Counselor

Counseling • Assessment • Classroom Guidance

**Indirect Services or System-Level Functions
and the Strengths-Based School Counselor**

Consultation • Coordination and Collaboration • Leadership • Accountability

Visual Aids

*Common Descriptions of Services or Functions Provided by the School Counselor •
Cowger's (1997) Framework for Assessment • Examples of Standardized Measures
of Personal Strengths or Environments • Summary of CASEL's 22 Select Social
and Emotional Learning Programs • Kahn's (2000) Solution-Focused Model
of Consultation for School Counselors*

Summary

Key Points

THE TRADITIONAL ROLE
OF THE SCHOOL COUNSELOR

Although school counseling has emerged as a profession, many school counselors still define their role by the functions they perform or the services they offer rather than in terms of a contemporary vision (e.g., ASCA, 2003). Those functions/services are typically referred to as "the three Cs"—counseling, consultation, and coordination (Erford, House, & Martin, 2003)—or, in the case of the elementary-school counselor, counseling, consultation, and classroom guidance.

For these school counselors, counseling, typically individual rather than group, involves direct service to students, occupies a substantial portion of time, and is often remedial in focus. At the high-school level, counseling frequently consists primarily of supplying information about colleges and discussing the college-application process. At the elementary level, school counselors often provide classroom guidance, which is a direct service to students, but that service often lacks clear objectives and a programmatic focus. Many times classroom guidance is instituted primarily at the insistence of the principal in order to provide busy teachers with a planning period rather than to provide students with integrated skills that are developmentally relevant. Consultation, if it is performed at all, and coordination are indirect services or system-level functions/interventions (e.g., those directed at changing the classroom or school environment rather than an individual student). Traditionally, consultation focuses primarily on remediation and helping teachers, parents, and/or administrators change how their behaviors impact students. Coordination often consists of scheduling and course placement and frequently results in the school counselor being involved in tracking and other educational practices that have denied rather than extended educational opportunities to certain groups of students. Thus, much of the traditional role of the school counselor consists of providing these services, along with any other duties that are assigned by the principal.

THE CONTEMPORARY ROLE
OF THE SCHOOL COUNSELOR

The traditional role of the school counselor involved providing reactive services to a relatively small percentage of the student population. In contrast, recommendations (e.g., ASCA, 2003; Education Trust, 1999; Gysbers & Henderson, 2000, 2001) for the role of the contemporary school counselor include an organized comprehensive developmental program that (a) is integral to education, (b) is based on a developmental framework, (c) serves the entire student population and includes special provisions for the needs of minorities and other traditionally underserved student groups, and (d) is concerned with demonstrating accountability.

As noted by Erford et al. (2003), the three Cs in the traditional role were too limiting and failed to provide enough breadth and depth as a basis for serving all students. In contrast, recommendations about the role for the contemporary school counselor include a variety of new or additional functions—advocacy, collaboration and teaming, and leadership. Contemporary recommendations also suggest guidelines with respect to how school counselors should allocate their time across these services. In the National Model, for example, it is recommended that a school counselor devote 80% of his or her time to direct services. In Gysbers and Henderson's model as we have seen in chapter 1, the recommended percentage of time devoted to specific functions/services varies according to school level (elementary, middle, or high). Table 2–1 includes some common definitions from the contemporary school counseling literature for the functions/services that the school counselor performs. In the table, we have attempted to differentiate the services by indicating who directly receives the service, who is an indirect recipient, and what other individuals might be involved in providing the service.

THE STRENGTHS-BASED SCHOOL COUNSELOR'S ROLE

Although the "newer counseling functions" are clearly important to the role of the contemporary school counselor, an emphasis on functions is not without limitations. Among the main limitations are the multiple meanings that have been assigned to each of the functions, the resulting confusion generated in attempting to distinguish among them, and the practical realities of routinely attempting to implement all of them in their many forms.

For instance, advocacy is clearly a key counselor function. "One might go so far as to treat *school counselor* and *advocate* as synonymous" (Borders, 2002, p. 184). We have discussed several types of advocacy, including client advocacy; social/political advocacy; and advocacy focused at the school, school district, community, and state levels. In addition, the importance of advocating for one's school counseling program (ASCA, 2003) and advocating for the school counseling profession (Myers, Sweeney, & White, 2002) have also been asserted. While each of these types of counselor advocacy is clearly important, we believe that promotion-oriented client and system developmental advocacy at the school-building level should constitute the majority of the school counselor's advocacy efforts.

In addition to the various forms of advocacy, it is frequently difficult to differentiate advocacy from leadership. For example, Stone and Clark (2001) called for school counselors to demonstrate leadership through advocacy.

Table 2–1.
Some Common Descriptions of Services or Functions Provided by the School Counselor

School Counselor Functions/Services	Definition	Direct Recipients of This Service	Indirect Recipients or Beneficiaries of This Service	Others Involved in This Service
Advocacy	Helping clients challenge institutional and social barriers that impede academic, career, or personal-social development.[1] School counselors advocate for students' educational needs.... School counselors work proactively with students to remove barriers to learning.[2]	Teachers, Parents, Administrators	Students	Community Agencies, Social Workers, School Psychologists
Collaboration and Teaming	Collaboration is a direct helping process involving two or more team members engaged in interactive, planning, decision-making, or problem-solving.[3] School counselors work with all stakeholders, both inside and outside the school system, to develop and implement responsive educational programs that support the achievement of the identified goals for every student. School counselors build effective teams by encouraging genuine collaboration among all school staff to work toward the common goals of equity, access, and academic success for every student.[4]	Teachers, Parents, Administrators	Students	School Psychologists, Social Workers, Community Agencies
Consultation	A problem-solving process involving two or more persons (often professionals) with respect to a client or clients. It is an indirect helping process that empowers the consultee to work with the client.[5]	Teacher, Parents, Administrators	Students	School Psychologists, Social Workers, Community Agencies

	Consultation refers to school counselors' collaborative work with other school staff or parents (consultees) to improve consultees' interactions with students.[6]	Teachers, Parents, Students	Students, Administration	School Psychologists, Social Workers, Community Agencies
Coordination	Coordination activities are vital to a viable, cost-effective school counseling program. . . . [T]ypically . . . [these coordination activities] include organizing and managing regular program activities (e.g., classroom guidance units, student appraisal, peer facilitation training, student orientation, student advising, scheduling and placement, student records, resource center) and special events (e.g., College Night, Career Fair). School counselors also coordinate the work of support staff, volunteers, and program committees (e.g., steering committee and school-community advisory committee), and write and revise policies and procedures. Often, they coordinate services for exceptional students, including diagnostic assessments, placements, record maintenance and review, and IEP meetings. The student referral system also is established and maintained by the counseling staff. Program evaluation activities are critical responsibilities that require much coordination. Finally, because of their access to student information and their schoolwide perspective, school counselors can compile informative summary reports for teachers, administrators, parents, and even students. These reports can be useful inc curriculum planning and evaluation. . . . Coordination activities should lead to efficient management of the counseling program and should allow counselors to spend the majority of their time providing direct and indirect services to students.[7]			

(continued)

Table 2–1 (*Continued*)

School Counselor Functions/Services	Definition	Direct Recipients of this Service	Indirect Recipients or Beneficiaries of This Service	Others Involved in This Service
Counseling	A relationship between two people who meet so that one person can help the other resolve a problem. One of these persons, by virtue of training, is the counselor; the person receiving the help is the client.[8]	Students	Teachers, Parents, Administrators	
	Counseling is a collaborative effort between the counselor and client. Professional counselors help clients identify goals and potential solutions to problems which cause emotional turmoil; seek to improve communication and coping skills; strengthen self-esteem; and promote behavior change and optimal mental health. Through counseling you examine the behaviors, thoughts, and feelings that are causing difficulties in your life. You learn effective ways to deal with your problems by building upon personal strengths. A professional counselor will encourage your personal growth and development in ways that foster your interest and welfare.[9]			
Leadership	School counselors provide leadership in four contexts: Structural Leadership—leadership in the building of viable organizations. Schools Counselors do this by building a comprehensive school-counseling program.	Administrators, Parents, Community	Students, Teachers	Community
	Human Resource Leadership—leadership via empowering and inspiring others to follow. School counselors do this by believing in people, communicating that belief, being visible and accessible, and empowering others.			

Political Leadership—leadership in the use of interpersonal and organizational power. School counselors do this by assessing the distribution of power within the building and district, by forming links with important stakeholders such as parents and school board members, and by using the power of persuasion and negotiation.

Symbolic Leadership—leadership via the interpretation and re-interpretation of the meaning of change. School counselors lead in this context by having a relationship with their community and by being effective models in their efforts to meet student needs, and by inspiring others to follow their example.[10]

School counselors serve as leaders who are engaged in systemwide change to ensure students success. They help every student gain access to rigorous academic preparation that will lead to greater opportunity and increased academic achievement. . . . School counselors become effective leaders by collaborating with other professionals in the school to influence systemwide changes and implement school reforms.[11]

[1]Lee, C. C. (1998a, pp. 8–9). Counselors as agents of social change. In C. C. Lee & G. R. Walz (Eds.), Social action: A mandate for counselors, (pp. 3–16). Alexandria, VA: American Counseling Association.

[2]ASCA National Model: A Framework for School Counseling Programs (2003, p. 24).

[3]Brown, D., Pryzwansky, W. B., and Schulte, A. C. (2001, p. 8). Psychological Consultation: Introduction to Theory and Practice (5th Ed.). Neeham Heights, MA: Allyn & Bacon.

[4]ASCA National Model (2003, p. 25).

[5]Brown, Pryzwansky, and Schulte (2001, p. 8).

[6]Borders, L. D. and Drury, S. M. (1992, p. 492). Comprehensive school counseling programs: A review for policymakers and practitioners. Journal of Counseling & Development, 70, 487–498.

[7]Borders and Drury (1992, p. 492)

[8]Thompson, C. L. and Rudolph, L. B. (2000). Counseling Children (5th Ed.). Belmont, CA: Brooks/Cole.

[9]American Counseling Association (2003) website; http://www.counseling.org/site/PageServer?pagename=resources_faqs.

[10]Dollarhide, C. T. (2003). School counselors as program leaders: Applying leadership contexts to school counseling. Professional School Counseling 6, 304–308.

[11]ASCA National Model (2003, p. 24).

When a school counselor advocates for educational policies that make gifted and talented programs and honors and advanced placement courses more accessible to minority students, isn't that counselor also exercising leadership? More importantly, does it really matter whether that effort is classified as advocacy, leadership, or something else altogether as long as it produces the intended result? Further, when a school counselor leads an orientation program for the transition into middle school, that counselor is advocating for educational policies and practices that help students adjust to new settings.

Similarly, it can be difficult to distinguish between coordination and leadership. Dollarhide and Saginak (2003, p. 213) stated that "coordination is a *counselor initiated leadership process* in which the counselor helps *organize* and *manage* the comprehensive guidance program and related services." Further, Bemak (2000) called for school counselors to provide leadership in educational reform through facilitating interagency and interdisciplinary collaboration.

Differentiating consultation and collaboration can also be difficult at times. According to Friend and Cook (2003), consultation is a process, and collaboration is the style of interaction within the process. The defining characteristics of collaboration are that it (a) is voluntary; (b) requires parity among participants; (c) is based on mutual goals; and (d) depends on shared responsibility for decision making, shared resources, and shared accountability for outcomes. Keys, Green, Lockhart, and Luongo (2003) describe two related forms of consultation: collaborative-dependent and collaborative-interdependent. Collaborative-dependent consultation involves a single consultant and is helpful when seeking change for an individual client, family, or single organizational system related to normal developmental problems. Collaborative-interdependent consultation, on the other hand, is recommended for the type of complex, multicausal, and multicontextual problems often presented by at-risk students. The goals of collaborative-interdependent consultation may be very similar to those of the school-based student-support teams in which many counselors participate or lead. In this form of consultation, a group of people (e.g., school personnel, representatives from community agencies or other members of the community, or family members) come together to generate creative solutions to mutually defined problems. In the process, each of the group members may, at times, share information, as well as serve as a consultant, an advocate, or a leader. Thus, in contrast to collaborative-dependent consultation, collaborative-interdependent consultation may incorporate several different school counseling functions.

Another problem is that counseling functions/services, at times, appear to be treated as ends in themselves rather than being seen as means to our ends. When we prescribe the percentage of counselor time that is to be devoted to each function at different grade levels, for example, we run the risk of being concerned more about what we are doing than about the results that we are achieving. "Although it is certainly important to know what services are provided for students (process data), this doesn't provide the complete picture. . . . Results data answer the question, "So what?" (ASCA, 2003, p. 16).

In Strengths-Based School Counseling (SBSC), the school counselor's role is to promote evidence-based developmental student strengths and to promote and advocate for environments that have been shown to enhance those strengths. In that endeavor, the school counselor employs the function or combination of functions which appear to be most likely to achieve the desired outcome. Thus, in SBSC, the school counselor's role does not revolve around a prescribed set of specific services/functions. Whenever possible, the choice of function/services is based on student and school needs, existing theory, and outcome (e.g., research) data that have been shown to be related to developmental promotion and enhancement of the school environment. Further, a number of the traditional counselor functions/services have a somewhat different focus or emphasis in a strengths-based approach to school counseling. These differences for both direct and indirect services are detailed next.

DIRECT SERVICES AND THE STRENGTHS-BASED SCHOOL COUNSELOR

As the school counselor's role evolved out of teaching, the direct service functions of individual counseling and classroom guidance dominated. The most common forms of teacher-student contact (e.g., with whole classes, individual students, or a few students who are experiencing a common problem) still reflect how school counselors spend much of their time. Even in the new ASCA National Model (ASCA, 2003), it is recommended that the school counselor spend 80% of his or her time in direct services to students, in part to protect the counselor from the imposition of clerical and other non-counseling duties. As we have said, direct services are important components of SBSC, but they have a unique emphasis in this framework.

Counseling

In SBSC, we emphasize approaches to individual and group counseling that focus on promoting student strengths for all students, rather than on simply reducing student deficits. We recognize that helping students to overcome problems and deficits is an important and necessary part of what school counselors do. However, strengths-oriented school counselors attack problems primarily by attempting to build assets and protective factors. Counseling for problem reduction can not occupy a substantial amount of the school counselor's time if she expects to be able to serve all students. While counseling and psychotherapy in general can benefit from a strengths orientation, students with significant biological and psychological needs (e.g., medication or alternative placement) require intensive treatment. Even with ideal student-counselor ratios, student concerns that require a long-term, one-on-one relationship with a therapist are better served through referral to and, when appropriate, collaboration with community agencies and private practitioners.

In addition, the strengths-based school counselor employs empirically supported or evidence-based counseling interventions (e.g., Sexton, 2001; Whiston & Sexton, 1998) whenever possible and attempts to document the effectiveness of those interventions. With respect to the former, a variety of sources on evidence-based counseling interventions for pathology and problem reduction with children and adolescents are currently available. These include several books (Christophersen & Mortweet, 2001; Fonagy, Target, Cottrell, Phillips, & Kurtz, 2002; Kazdin & Weisz, 2003) as well as a special issue of the *Journal of Clinical Child Psychology* (June 1998, volume 27, issue 2) and a recent journal article (Eder & Whiston, 2006). In the special journal issue, for example, empirically supported psychosocial interventions are presented for a variety of problems experienced by children and adolescents including depression, autism, phobias and anxiety disorders, conduct disorders, and attention-deficit hyperactivity disorder. In many instances, the school counselor will not be the primary treatment professional for students who exhibit these problems, because these students will need to be referred. However, access to knowledge about best practices for these problems is invaluable to the counselor in making referrals and linking children and families to needed resources as well as in collaborating with other professionals who are providing the primary treatment.

Clearly, there are some data about the effectiveness of counseling and psychotherapy interventions for problem reduction. What is not evident in these data is the active ingredients of these interventions (see Wampold, 2001 for an extended discussion of this issue) and how they are relevant to the school counselor. Seligman (2002) argued that positive psychology and building strengths may be a common effective ingredient in all of these problem-reduction approaches. He hypothesized that embedded in the so-called "placebo" or "nonspecific effects" of all forms of counseling are *deep strategies* which are techniques of positive psychology. According to Seligman, these strategies help clients to build hope[1] and other "buffering strengths" such as courage, interpersonal skill, rationality, insight, optimism, honesty, perseverance, realism, capacity for pleasure, putting troubles in perspective, future-mindedness, and finding purpose rather than just healing damage. Moreover, he asserted that, if these positive psychology techniques can be targeted and honed, even more effective counseling interventions may result.

Consistent with Seligman's recommendations, problem-reduction approaches to counseling and psychotherapy that incorporate aspects of positive

---

[1]See Snyder and Taylor (2000) for discussion of the role of hope in counseling and psychotherapy, and Snyder, Feldman, Shorey, and Rand (2002) for a school counselor's guide to hope theory.

psychology are beginning to be developed and tested with adults (e.g., Fava & Ruini, 2003; Pesechkian & Tritt, 1998). In Fava and Ruini's (2003) approach, for example, enduring client change is seen as resulting from alleviating the negative **plus** engendering the positive. A variety of cognitive-behavioral interventions familiar to school counselors, including cognitive restructuring of automatic or irrational thoughts; scheduling of mastery, pleasure, and graded task activities; assertiveness training; and problem solving are employed in eight counseling sessions. These interventions are directed toward increasing six dimensions of psychological well-being: autonomy, personal growth, environmental mastery, purpose in life, positive relations, and self-acceptance.

Approaching counseling from a strengths perspective in social work, Saleebey (1997) recommends asking survival, support, exception, possibility, and esteem questions in order to identify client strengths. "How have you managed to survive or thrive thus far?" and "Which people have given you special understanding or guidance?" represent survival and support questions, respectively. A typical exception question asks, "What is different about your behavior, your thinking, or your relationships when things are going well for you?" Examples of possibility questions include "What do you want out of life?" and "What are your hopes and dreams?" Finally, "What are people likely to say when they say good things about you?" represents an esteem question.

Gelso and Woodhouse (2003) also discussed modifications in traditional counseling and psychotherapy approaches that are needed in order to incorporate a positive or strengths perspective. These modifications include the way in which the counselor conceptualizes the client as well as what the counselor actually does in counseling. With respect to the former, the strengths perspective needs to be prominent in both assessment and case conceptualization. Key questions that need to be answered focus on assessing client strengths and include such issues as the areas of life in which the client does well, and the client's psychological assets, capacity for self-insight, adaptability, relationship strengths, and social supports. Moreover, Gelso and Woodhouse stressed the importance of understanding client strengths from a cultural perspective.

The implication of these recommendations for what a school counselor actually does in providing individual counseling is the need to focus more attention (a) on explicitly noting a student's strengths; (b) on confrontations that are based in student strengths, rather than in student deficits; (c) on commenting on small steps that a student is making to develop strengths; (d) on not reinforcing a student's negative view of self by making comments that a particular difficulty is a stable characteristic; and (e) on not dwelling on negative patterns of behavior. Gelso and Woodhouse (2003) also recommended that counselors reframe apparent weaknesses as strengths and attend to strengths that are embedded in defenses. As an example of reframing, the authors cited a student who claimed that she had no control over turning in assigned papers late. A discussion revealed that she was consistently turning them in two days late, thereby indicating that she was specifically choosing the two-day delay and actually had complete control over this behavior pattern. With this realization and a discussion of similar patterns in other areas of her life, she was subsequently able to employ her strengths of choice and control in a productive manner, and turned the assignments in on time.

Yet another change in individual counseling that school counselors need to consider is the amount of attention devoted to negative, as compared to positive, emotions in counseling. Frederickson (2000, 2001, 2002) has proposed and provided empirical support for the broaden-and-build theory of positive emotions. This hypothesis asserts that experiencing positive emotions such as joy, interest, contentment, pride, and love broadens people's momentary thought-action tendencies, which are their tendencies to play, to explore, to savor and integrate, or to envision future achievement. Positive emotions widen the range of thoughts and actions that come to mind—and, in working with students in counseling, widening the range of thoughts and actions in which they habitually engage is often essential if change is to be effected. In contrast, negative emotions, although they may have survival value for the human species, narrow an individual's momentary thought-action repertoire (e.g., fear is associated with the urge to flee, and anger with the urge to attack).

Take, for example, a student who feels angry at a teacher for perceived mistreatment. That student tends to be unwilling or unable to consider more promising forms of behavior with the teacher while he/she is focused on anger. The anger tends to narrow the focus of the student's thought pattern to revenge or getting even almost to the exclusion of more productive ways of interacting with the teacher. Under those circumstances, if a counselor can induce a more positive emotion (e.g., through positive imagery or recalling positive interactions with the teacher in the past) in the student, the hold that the anger has on thoughts and behavior will be decreased. Consequently, the student's ability to reframe the situation with the teacher and to consider an alternative interaction pattern with the teacher will be enhanced.

Thus, by broadening the momentary thought-action tendencies, positive emotions can loosen or undo the hold that negative emotions have on individuals' tendency to think and act in a habitual and, at times, dysfunctional manner. Frederickson presented data indicating that these broadened mindsets, in turn, serve to build psychological resilience and enduring personal resources, which may include physical, intellectual, social, and psychological resources. This process occurs in the following way: through thinking and acting in new ways, individuals acquire new personal resources that can last well beyond the duration of the positive emotional state that fostered it. Finally, through the enhancement of psychological resilience and other enduring personal resources, positive emotions can trigger upward spirals toward emotional well-being for an individual.

Frederickson hypothesized that a number of current counseling approaches may be effective because they induce positive emotional states in clients, thereby undoing negative emotions that clients experience as well as allowing the clients to broaden and change the ways in which they typically think and act. For example, various relaxation and positive-imagery techniques are viewed as inducing contentment. Cognitive-therapy assignments that engage depressed clients in pleasant activities counteract the effects of depression and increase the likelihood of a client finding positive meaning in daily life. Similarly, cognitive approaches that teach optimistic thinking styles and coping strategies despite adversity might also be effective because they induce positive emotional states that allow clients to think and/or act differently and more effectively.

An important demonstration of the implications of Frederickson's work for counseling is provided by research with suicidal young adults (Joiner et al., 2001). The premise of their study was that suicide crises are time limited and, in the course of therapy with these individuals, some positive moods occur. Following Frederickson's broaden-and-build hypothesis, these positive moods represent opportunities for problem-solving skill acquisition. Accordingly, Joiner et al. found that those suicidal individuals who were more prone to positive moods displayed more positive problem-solving attitudes following 10 days of treatment (problem solving) for suicidal symptoms than those who were less prone to such moods. Moreover, support was obtained for the hypothesis that reductions in suicidal symptoms were partly a function of the gains in problem solving achieved by the participants who were more prone to positive moods. The implications of these results are that the chances of achieving successful treatment outcomes are improved if skill-building interventions are presented during windows of positive mood for the client rather than in times of crisis.

Now consider the implications of Joiner et al.'s (2001) finding in a situation that is more frequently encountered by school counselors: a student who is referred to counseling immediately following an incident for which he has been disciplined or is about to be disciplined. The student is extremely angry and unwilling to engage the counselor in a discussion of the incident, let alone in constructive problem-solving designed to prevent similar incidents in the future. Clearly, delaying counseling until the student is in a more positive emotional state would increase the likelihood of a successful counseling outcome. An alternative course of action is to attempt to engage the student in relaxation, imagery, or other strategies that are capable of inducing positive emotions. Cultivating more positive emotions can broaden the student's thought-action tendencies and increase the likelihood of the student being willing to think about functioning in a new and more adaptive manner. Such an approach potentially could be used when counseling students who experience any strong negative emotion that blocks more adaptive ways of viewing the situation or behaving in the situation.

To date, strengths-oriented counseling theories such as wellness (Myers, Sweeney, & Witmer, 2000, 2001), hope theory (Lopez, Floyd, Ulven, & Snyder, 2000; Snyder, Feldman, Shorey, & Rand, 2002), and counseling at-risk youth (Smith, 2006) are only beginning to be developed, and we are not aware of any evidence-based theories that were designed for strengths-promotion counseling in the school setting. As such, school counselors who currently endeavor to conduct one-to-one and group counseling from a strengths perspective must rely on modifying existing theories to guide their work.

Although it was not developed initially in a school context and, to date, only has a limited base of empirical support in that setting (Littrell, Malia, & Vanderwood, 1995), Solution-Focused Brief Counseling (SFBC) (Metcalf, 1995; Murphy, 1997; Murphy & Duncan, 1997; Sklare, 1997) is one theory that can partially guide the school counselor's efforts. With its emphasis on (a) the power of brief counseling (de Shazer, 1985) to effect change (e.g., one to six sessions, and often just one or two in the school setting), (b) increasing what is positive about students and what is working for them, as well as (c) helping students to change how they view situations in order to focus on what is going well as opposed to what is not, SFBC is compatible with many of the guiding principles of SBSC. As is the case with SBSC, SFBC is concerned with helping students to set and achieve approach goals which consist of trying to do or achieve something that is positive. Making new friends and completing and turning in more homework assignments are examples of approach goals. When students are working to achieve approach goals, they are always moving closer to success (Snyder et al., 2002). In contrast, in counseling approaches in which students set avoidance goals (e.g., not to talk out in class, or not to get in fights), they are constantly working to maintain the status quo, a condition which would appear to be considerably less motivating.

However, Solution-Focused Brief Counseling is not without its limitations. As we have previously mentioned, one of those is the lack of extensive empirical support for its effectiveness in the school setting. Another is the fact that it relies heavily on helping the client discover exceptions, either in the way he or she has previously viewed problematic situations, or has behaved in them. These exceptions are viewed as solutions (or at least partial solutions) or times in which the student has been at least somewhat successful in correcting the problem or making it somewhat less intrusive. Once these exceptions/solutions have been discovered, the client is encouraged to do more of them. In instances in which a student is unable to identify exceptions, however, he or she may actually need to learn more adaptive ways to behave in the situation and/or to reframe how that situation is perceived. At these times, techniques designed to teach new behavioral and/or cognitive skills drawn from a broad-based behavioral (e.g., Hughes, 1993) or cognitive-behavioral (e.g., Craighead, Craighead, Kazdin, & Mahoney, 1994) approach will serve the strengths-oriented counselor well. Moreover, extensive data supporting the effectiveness of these approaches (e.g., Durlak, Fuhrman, & Lampman, 1991; also see Sexton, Whiston, Bleuer, & Walz, 1997 for a summary) are available.

Finally, although the school counseling research is mixed on the effectiveness of group, as opposed to individual, counseling (see Sexton et al., 1997), group counseling allows the strengths-based school counselor to reach a much larger percentage of students than individual counseling. It also enables the counselor to use modeling, group process, and practice in skill building to facilitate student development. In addition, group counseling is designed to activate prosocial behavior and to promote bonding, belonging, and attachment to peers, which are some of the important developmental assets and protective factors necessary for positive youth development that we discussed previously.

Once again, research on the effectiveness of Solution-Focused groups in schools is limited (LaFountain, Garner, & Eliason, 1996), but this group-counseling approach (Banks, 1999; LaFountain, Garner, & Boldosser, 1995; Metcalfe, 1995) is in accord with a strengths orientation. On the other hand, there is substantial support for the effectiveness of relaxation groups, cognitive-behavioral approaches to groups, and group interventions for social-skills training, family adjustment issues, and discipline problems (Whiston, 2003).

At this time, the pressures of a high-stakes testing environment that prevail in many of today's schools often make it difficult to arrange group-counseling meeting times that are acceptable to teachers. As such, conducting group-counseling sessions during after school programs, at lunch, and immediately prior to the start of school are options that a school counselor will need to explore.

Assessment

In school counseling, as in counseling and psychotherapy generally, assessment and intervention have been driven by a problem-reduction tradition. Assessment and assessment instruments have been focused overwhelmingly on inadequacies rather than on strengths and on persons rather than environments (Cowger, 1997; Lopez, Snyder, & Rasmussen, 2003; Snyder et al., 2003; Wright & Lopez, 2002). The results of these assessment emphases have been to target individuals as "the problem" and virtually to ignore the contribution of the environment and personal strengths to human functioning. A variety of explanations for these assessment biases have been provided (Lopez et al.; Wright & Lopez). Among these are (a) that counselors and mental-health professionals are oriented toward treating (and assessing) persons and not environments and reducing dysfunction rather than optimizing functioning; (b) that persons are more salient than environments; (c) the influence of the insider versus outsider perspective in which insiders (e.g., clients) are more likely to know and to take situation factors into account, while to outsiders (e.g., counselors) the person's problems more or less tend to stand alone; (e) the greater salience of negative as opposed to positive information; and (f) the fundamental negative bias that, if something is salient, negative and if its context is vague, then the negative value of the phenomenon (e.g., the client's expressed concerns) will be a major factor in guiding perceptions and thinking about the phenomenon.

A more balanced approach to assessment, however, requires attention to strengths as well as deficits and to environmental and contextual factors as well as factors focused on the individual. Cowger (1997), for example, has proposed an assessment framework that revolves around two axes. The horizontal axis consists of environmental factors at one end and personal factors at the other, while the vertical axis involves strengths at one pole and obstacles (deficits) at the other. For conceptual purposes, the axes can be enclosed to form four assessment quadrants: environmental strengths, environmental obstacles (deficits), personal (psychological [cognition, emotion, motivation, coping, and interpersonal] and physiological) strengths, and personal (psychological and physiological) obstacles (See Fig. 2–1). In assessing personal strengths (e.g., psychological strengths), for example, Cowger identified five important areas: cognition (e.g., does the client see the world in the way most other people in her/his culture see it?), emotion (e.g., is the client in touch with her/his feelings and able to express them appropriately?), motivation (e.g.,

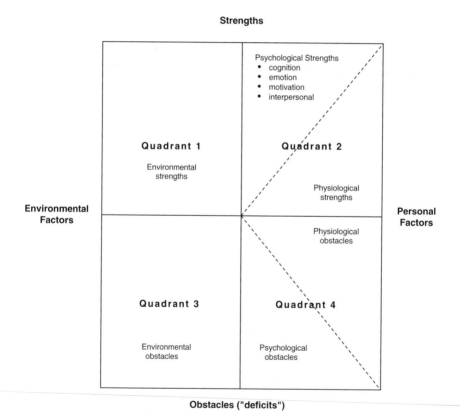

FIGURE 2–1.   Cowger's framework for assessment. Cowger C. (1997). Assessing client strengths: Assessment for client empowerment. In D. Saleebey (Ed.), *The strengths perspective in social work* (2nd ed.) (pp. 59–73). White Plains, NY: Longman. Published by Allyn and Bacon, Boston MA. Copyright © by Pearson Education. Reprinted by permission of the publisher.

when having problems, does the client hide from, avoid, or deny them?), coping (e.g., does the client prepare for and handle new situations well?), and interpersonal (e.g., is the client cooperative and flexible relating to friends?).

The four-front approach to assessment proposed by positive psychologists represents a similar perspective (Snyder et al., 2003; Wright & Lopez, 2002). It involves assessment for four cells of a 2 (CONTENT: liabilities, assets) × 2 (LOCUS: person, environs) matrix. Assessment involves attending to (a) deficiencies and undermining characteristics of the person; (b) strengths and assets of the person; (c) deficiencies and destructive factors in the environment; and (d) resources and opportunities in the environment.

In school counseling, Keys and Lockhart (1999) proposed a multisystemic approach to assessment, noting the importance of assessing the individual's strengths and weaknesses as well as those of the multiple systems (e.g., environments) surrounding the individual. Keys and Lockhart focus on four key systems—family, school, peer, and community—in which the student is embedded.

In Strengths-Based School Counseling (SBSC), the emphasis is on promoting personal strengths and strengths-enhancing environments, while, at the same time, not overlooking the role of personal deficits and environmental obstacles. As such, the four-front assessment framework, multisystemic assessment, and the emphasis of positive psychology to *"develop the strengths and manage the weaknesses"* are all congruent with our framework (Clifton, 2003, p. xiii).

However, the focus of our current assessment discussion will be on assessing personal strengths and the environment. The reason for this emphasis is that information about assessing environments and personal strengths is of special relevance to SBSC. For example, information about the environment is particularly important when the school counselor is engaged in consultation, advocacy, and other systems-level services to increase the strengths-enhancing capacity of a classroom or a school.

> Many of the problems presented by students in today's schools, however, are much too complex and multidimensional to be solved by interventions that only target the individual. Effective problem solving in such cases requires a more systemic-ecological assessment that defines problems by the multiple contexts in which students grow and develop and derives solutions from multisystemic intervention plans. (Keys & Lockhart, 1999, p. 101)

Moreover, in contrast to information about assessing deficits, information about assessing strengths merits special attention because it is not commonly discussed in the school-counseling literature. Also, information about assessing deficits is readily accessible.

Table 2–2 provides examples of some of the standardized instruments that have been developed to date to assess either a student's environmental context or personal strengths. As we have discussed, instrument development and validation in these areas for the most part is a more recent development and generally is not as advanced as it is for instruments that assess personal deficits (e.g., anxiety, depression, etc.). As a result, the school counselor may find in

Table 2–2.
Some Examples of Standardized Measures of Personal Strengths and/or Environments

Measure (Source)	Age/Grade	Personal Strength Area Assessed	Environment Assessed	Construct Assessed
Developmental Assets Profile (DAP) (http://www.search-institute.org/surveys/dap.html)	Ages 11–18	Academic Personal/Social	Family School Community	Eight developmental asset categories (four internal [commitment to learning, positive values, social competencies, positive identity] and four external [support, empowerment, boundaries and expectations, constructive use of time]) within five social contexts (personal assets, social assets, family assets, school assets, and community assets)
The School Success Profile (Bowen & Richman, 2001)	Grades 6–12	Academic Personal/Social	Neighborhood School Friends Family	Risk and protective factors with respect to a Social Environment profile of 14 dimensions (neighbor support, neighborhood youth behavior, neighborhood safety, school satisfaction, teacher support, school safety, friend support, peer group acceptance, friend behavior, family togetherness, parent support, home academic environment, parent education support, school behavior expectations) and an Individual Adaptation Profile of 8 dimensions (social support use, physical health, happiness, personal adjustment, self-esteem, school engagement, trouble avoidance, grades).
The Social Skills Rating Scale (Gresham & Elliott, 1990)	Elem. form, grades 3–6; Secondary form, grades 7–12	Academic Personal/Social	N/A	Teacher and parent forms provide scores on three scales— social skills (cooperation, self-control, empathy, and assertion), problem behaviors (externalizing, internalizing, and hyperactivity), and academic competence.

Measure	Grade/Age	Domain	Setting	Description
The Behavioral and Emotional Rating Scale (Epstein & Sharma, 1998)	Ages 5–18	Academic, Personal/Social	Family School	Completed by adults on the behavioral and emotional strengths of children/adolescents. Provides overall strength quotient and assesses five dimensions—interpersonal strengths, family involvement, intrapersonal strength, school functioning, and affective strength.
Academic Competence Evaluation Scales (DiPerna & Elliott, 1999)	Grades 1–6	Academic	N/A	Academic skills, interpersonal skills, academic motivation, participation, study skills
Homework Motivation and Preference Questionnaire (Hong & Milgram, 2001)	Grades 7–12	Academic	Home	Twenty-one component scores organized in six homework motivation (source, strength) and preference (organizational, surroundings, perceptual-physical, interpersonal) categories
Problem Solving Inventory (Heppner, 1988; Heppner, Manley, Perez, & Dixon, 1994)	Versions with ninth grade and fourth grade reading levels available	Personal/social	N/A	Problem-solving confidence, approach-avoidance style, personal control
Values in Action Inventory of Strengths for Youth (Dahlsgaard, K., Peterson, C., & Seligman, M. (2001). *VIA Inventory of Strengths for Youth (VIA-Y)*. Available on the World Wide Web: http://www.authentichappiness.org/perl/Children.pl)	Ages 10–17	Personal/Social	N/A	Twenty-four character strengths (creativity, curiosity, open-mindedness, love of learning, perspective, bravery, persistence, integrity, vitality, love, kindness, social intelligence, citizenship, fairness, leadership, forgiveness and mercy, humility and modesty, prudence, self-regulation, appreciation of beauty and excellence, gratitude, hope, humor, and spirituality)

(continued)

Table 2-2 (Continued)

Measure (Source)	Age/Grade	Personal Strength Area Assessed	Environment Assessed	Construct Assessed
The Occupational Questionnaire (O'Brien, 2003; Teresa, 1991)	High School	Career	N/A	Career self-efficacy in each of 31 separate occupations as well as in female-dominated, male-dominated, and gender-balanced occupations
Classroom Environment Scale (Trickett & Moos, 1995)	Middle and High School	N/A	Classroom	Relationship (involvement, affiliation, teacher support), personal growth (task orientation), and system maintenance and change (order and organization, role clarity) social climate domains
Comprehensive Assessment of School Environments (National Association of Secondary School Principals, 1904 Association Dr., Reston VA. 22091-1148, 1-800-253-PRIN)	Primarily secondary schools	N/A	School	Student, teacher and parent scores for 10 climate subscales (teacher-student relationships, security and maintenance, administration, student academic orientation, student behavioral values, guidance, student-peer relationships, parent and community-school relationships, instructional management, student activities); also parent satisfaction survey (9 scores), teacher satisfaction survey (9 scores), and student satisfaction survey (8 scores)

some instances that she is unable to find a well-developed instrument for measuring a specific student strength or an environmental context or that she may have to rely on an interview or a non-standardized assessment procedure. In that regard, we will discuss a few assessment procedures that may prove helpful.

In working with students, school counselors conduct many of their assessments within the counseling interview. In these interviews, the counselor might incorporate some of the type of assessment questions suggested by Gelso and Woodhouse (2003) and Saleebey (1997) that we discussed earlier. Gelso and Woodhouse, for example, recommended assessing areas in life in which a client does well, the client's psychological assets, capacity for self-insight, adaptability, relationship strengths, and social supports, while Saleebey recommended asking survival, support, exception, possibility, and esteem questions in order to identify client strengths.

Another assessment framework that can be helpful is the Developmental Assets model discussed in the previous chapter (see Table 1–3). A strength of that model is that it directs a school counselor to look for the presence of *both* personal strengths (internal assets) and environmental supports (external assets). Thus, a school counselor can use the four internal (educational commitment, values, social competencies, positive identity) and four external (support, empowerment, boundaries and expectations, time) asset categories as an assessment framework with students. As needed, definitions of the individual developmental assets (see Table 1–3) can be used to formulate specific assessment questions. With respect to the internal-asset category of educational commitment, for example, a counselor might ask the following type of questions: "What kind of work do you want to do when you grow up?" "How important is what you learn in school for helping you to be able to do that kind of work when you grow up?" "What grades did you get on your last report card?" "How do you feel about school?" "On the average night, how much time do you usually spend on your homework?" "During a typical week, how much time would you say you spend reading something just for the fun of it?" Of course, these questions would be interspersed within the interview rather than asked in rapid-fire manner. In addition, the counselor may not need to ask all of them in order to determine the educational commitment level of a student.

As an alternative, a school counselor might consider using Search Institute's Developmental Asset Profile (DAP, 2004). The DAP was designed for use with students aged 11–15. It consists of 58 items, but it was not designed to measure the presence or absence of each of the 40 developmental assets. Rather, it provides an individual assessment within the context of the four external (support, empowerment, boundaries and expectations, constructive use of time) and four internal (commitment to learning, positive values, social competencies, positive identity) asset categories and for five social contexts (personal assets, social assets, school assets, family assets, community assets).

The School Success Profile (SSP) (Bowen & Richman, 2001; Bowen, Woolley, Richman, & Bowen, 2001) contains 220 multiple-choice items. The SSP is intended as an instrument for planning brief and solution-focused interventions with middle- and high-school students. It taps both risk and protective factors and can yield profiles for both individual students and groups of students, including classrooms and entire schools. The SSP assesses 22 core dimensions, of which 14 constitute a Social Environment Profile and 8 represent an Individual Adaptation Profile. The Social Environment Profile is made up of Neighborhood (neighbor support, neighborhood youth behavior, neighborhood safety), School (school satisfaction, teacher support, school safety), Friends (friend support, peer group acceptance, friend behavior), and Family (family togetherness, parent support, home academic environment, parent education support, school behavior expectations) dimensions. Individual Adaptation dimensions include Personal Beliefs and Well-Being (social support use, physical health, happiness, personal adjustment, self-esteem), School Attitudes and Behavior (school engagement, trouble avoidance), and Academic Performance (grades). An elementary version of the SSP is currently being developed.

In using standardized instruments in assessment, cost can become a prohibitive consideration. Assessing school climate or classroom climate for a large number of classrooms is one example of where cost prohibitions might occur. In that regard, Freiberg (1998, 1999) discussed a number of alternative formal and informal procedures that the school counselor might consider using. Among these are student concern surveys and entrance and exit interviews.

Similarly, Henderson and Milstein (1996) offer a variety of informal tools to assess the extent to which schools foster resiliency in students. The Assessing School Resiliency Building instrument, for example, focuses on perceptions of school climate and addresses the six areas of the Resiliency Wheel—prosocial bonding, clear and consistent boundaries, teaching life skills, caring and support, high expectations, and opportunities for meaningful participation—that were discussed in the previous chapter. The instrument contains six statements for each area—two about students, two about staff, and two about the school as a whole. For prosocial bonding, the following are examples of the three different statement types: students have a positive bond with at least one caring adult in the school; staff engages in meaningful interactions with one another; and the physical environment of the school is warm, positive, and inviting. Statements are responded to on a four-point scale with lower scores indicating a more positive (resilient) climate. This instrument yields a total score as well as six subscale scores. One way of using it would involve the school counselor distributing it to teachers, administrators, and other colleagues to complete at a faculty meeting. At a subsequent faculty meeting, the results could be presented, and the staff could discuss implications of the results and decisions about possible future steps to take.

Additional examples of instruments for assessing individual strengths and environmental characteristics are presented in Table 2–2. Given the newness of these assessment targets, school counselors should expect to have far greater access to standardized measures in these areas in the next few years.

Classroom Guidance

Classroom guidance, or the "school-guidance curriculum" as it is referred to in the National Model (ASCA, 2003, p. 40), "consists of a written instructional program that is comprehensive in scope, preventative and proactive, developmental in design, coordinated by school counselors and delivered as appropriate, by school counselors and other educators." Classroom guidance is designed to reach every student and to promote knowledge, attitudes, and skills in three content areas: academic achievement, career development, and personal/social development. As noted in the National Model, the counselor's responsibilities include planning, designing, implementing, and evaluating the guidance curriculum.

In contrast to what has been recommended in the National Model, it has been our experience that the guidance curriculum at all levels invariably is the sole responsibility of school counselors rather than something which the school counselor coordinates and administers along with teachers and other educators. Moreover, it is rare to encounter a school system in which the guidance curriculum has been organized and sequenced developmentally over the entire K–12 grade span in order to help students acquire the knowledge, attitudes, and skills needed for success in school and life. In order to accomplish that goal, school counselors representing K–12 grades in conjunction with other educators and educational stakeholders would need to plan a research-based, developmental curriculum that meets the needs of local students.

It is more typical, however, for school counselors to initiate classroom guidance in response to expressed teacher needs, such as for help in teaching students study skills. All too often, the school counselor handles this classroom-guidance responsibility in one of two ways. First, she or he may purchase an attractive, commercially-available classroom guidance curriculum that appears to be relevant to the expressed need. In most instances, that curriculum has probably not been empirically tested. Then the counselor administers it more or less intact and with unknown results. Alternatively, she or he may copy a variety of what appear to be relevant and interesting classroom-guidance activities from several different texts, websites, or other sources in order to create a unit that hopefully will engage students and result in some sort of unspecified student growth or change. In many instances, the most that results from the counselor's effort is that students enjoy the experience, and the classroom teacher enjoys a brief respite from her daily routine, yet little documented transfer of learning occurs or is sustained from the classroom-guidance unit to students' everyday functioning.

It has also been our experience that classroom guidance is provided much less frequently by middle- and high-school counselors than by elementary counselors. We suspect that one reason for this is the emphasis on "teaching content" rather than "teaching students" that occurs at this level partially in response to the pressures of the high-stakes testing environment for teachers at the secondary level. In order to implement and sustain an effective classroom-guidance curriculum, especially at the middle- and high-school levels, the school counselor, in conjunction with other educators, may need to (a) demonstrate how the guidance curriculum is capable of enhancing student academic development, (b) show how it can be integrated into the academic curriculum rather than added on to it, and (c) demonstrate that research has shown that it has resulted in desired student developmental outcomes.

Lapan, Gysbers, Hughey, and Arni (1993) demonstrated one way that effective classroom guidance could be offered by English teachers and counselors who worked cooperatively to produce a unit in which high-school juniors developed writing skills while exploring career issues. The unit effected improvements in both vocational identity and English grades. In chapter 4, we propose a similar collaborative approach between teachers and counselors to teach study skills. Collaboration with teachers and administrators appears to be essential, especially at the secondary level, if the school counselor is to fulfill the responsibility for coordinating a classroom-guidance curriculum that impacts all students. An example of such an approach to implementing a school-wide guidance curriculum was described by K. R. Hall (2003) who involved all teachers and administrators in her junior high school as well as parents and community members in developing, instituting, and evaluating the program.

Reviews about the effectiveness of classroom guidance as conducted by school counselors have been mixed (Borders & Drury, 1992; Sexton et al., 1997; Whiston, 2003; Whiston & Sexton, 1998). At the elementary level, for example, the research is not particularly supportive of the effects of classroom guidance on measures of self-esteem. However, the situation is somewhat different for the relation between classroom guidance and achievement as four studies have demonstrated that several kinds of classroom-guidance interventions improved academic achievement with elementary students (Carns & Carns, 1991; Hadley, 1988, Lee, 1993; Wilson, 1986). Unfortunately, the reviewers were unable to identify clear research trends for classroom-guidance activities at the middle-school and high-school levels because of the limited number of studies conducted at those levels.

Another point that school counselors need to consider is that there is considerable doubt about whether short-term (e.g., less than one year) classroom-based social competence programs are even capable of promoting behavioral improvements that endure beyond a very brief period of time (Weissberg et al., 1991). Research suggests that multiyear classroom-based skills-training programs that also impact the students' environments may be essential to producing long-term effects (Greenberg et al., 2003; Weissberg et al., 1991).

In most cases, short-term preventive interventions produce short-lived results. Conversely, multiyear, multicomponent programs are more likely to foster enduring benefits. When classroom instruction is combined with efforts to create environmental support and reinforcement from peers, family members, school personnel, health professionals, other concerned community members, and the media, there is an increased likelihood that students will adopt positive social and health practices (Greenberg et al., 2003, p. 470).

A number of national reports on education including *Turning Points: Preparing Youth for the 21st Century* (Carnegie Council on Adolescent Development Task Force on the Education of Young Adolescents, 1989) agreed that academic learning is possible only after students' social, emotional, and physical needs have been met. Moreover, a study by Wang, Haertel, and Walberg (1997) estimated the relative influence on learning of 30 different categories of educational, psychological, and social variables. Results indicated that social and emotional variables exerted the most powerful influence on performance.

With respect to this last point, consumer-oriented ratings for eighty[2] nationally available classroom-based programs for social and emotional learning are provided by The Collaborative for Academic, Social, and Emotional Learning (CASEL, www.CASEL.org) through its publication, *Safe and Sound*. Social and emotional learning (SEL) is the process of developing the ability to recognize and manage emotions, develop caring and concern for others, make responsible decisions, establish positive relationships, and handle challenging situations effectively (CASEL, 2003, p. 1).

SEL involves five groups of skills on which programs were rated: (a) self-awareness (recognizing one's emotions and identifying and cultivating one's strengths and positive qualities); (b) social awareness (understanding the thoughts and feelings of others and appreciating the value of human differences); (c) self-management (monitoring and regulating one's emotions and establishing and working toward achieving positive goals); (d) relationship skills (establishing and maintaining healthy, rewarding relationships based on cooperation, effective communication, conflict resolution, and an ability to resist inappropriate social pressure); and (e) responsible decision making (assessing situational influences and generating, implementing, and evaluating ethical solutions to problems that promote one's own, and others', well-being).

Programs included in the review had to satisfy four main criteria: (a) being school based with sequenced lessons for a general student population; (b) having at least eight lessons in one of the program years; (c) having either lessons for at least two consecutive grades or grade spans, or a structure that promotes lesson reinforcement beyond the first program year; and (d) having a nationally available program. *Safe and Sound* provides information about program description, costs, grades covered, evidence of effectiveness, and the quality of staff development and support provided.

Of the 80 programs reviewed, 22 were singled out for "Select" status because they provided outstanding coverage of the five essential SEL skill areas, demonstrated effectiveness in at least one rigorous, well-designed evaluation study or had received the highest designation in one or more of six federal reviews, and provided professional development for the individuals who conducted them. Table 2–3 summarizes the 22 "Select SEL programs" that provide developmentally and culturally appropriate instruction. These are multiyear,

---

[2]CASEL initially examined 242 health, prevention, and positive youth development programs.

Table 2–3.
A Summary of CASEL's 22 Select Social and Emotional Learning Programs

Program	Grade Level(s)	Focus of the Program	Documented Behavioral Impact
Caring School Community (Child Development Project) www.devstu.org	K–6	The *Caring School Community* program is a practical, flexible way of creating a climate of caring at school and deepening connections among students, teachers, and families. The program builds a caring community in the classroom, in the school at large, and between home and school using the following materials:	Academic Substance Abuse Prevention Other Social Behaviors
		Ways We Want Our Class To Be is a guide for using class meetings to build your students' commitment to learning and to responsibility and kindness.	
		That's My Buddy! provides guidance for establishing and maintaining a successful cross-age buddy program.	
		Home-side Activities are parent-involvement activities—short conversational activities (in English and Spanish) that students do at home with their parent or caregiver.	
		At Home in Our Schools offers 15 school-wide events and activities that strengthen a school-wide ethos of caring.	
Community of Caring (Growing Up Caring) www.communityofcaring.org	K–12	Through training for teachers, values discussions, student forums, parent involvement and service learning, *Community of Caring* addresses destructive attitudes that lead to early sexual involvement, teen pregnancy, substance abuse, delinquent behavior, and dropping out of school. The five values are articulated and demonstrated in relation to real-life, tough situations where students find themselves without guideposts for sound decision-making. In this way, students develop an understanding of the five values and how they affect life choices and behavior.	Academic Substance Abuse Prevention

High/Scope Educational Approach for Preschool and Primary Grades www.highscope.org	preK–3	The *High/Scope* educational approach for preschool, elementary, and adolescent programs is a set of guiding principles and practices which adults follow as they work with and care for children and youth. These principles are intended as an "open framework" that teams of adults are free to adapt to the special needs and conditions of their group, their setting, and their community. "Active learning"—the belief that children learn best through active experiences with people, materials, events and ideas, rather than through direct teaching or sequenced exercises—is a central tenet of the High/Scope approach for all age levels.	Academic Healthy Sexual Development Other Social Behaviors
I Can Problem Solve (ICPS) www.researchpress.com	preK–6	ICPS serves as an effective violence prevention program by helping children think of nonviolent ways to solve everyday problems. ICPS for Preschool contains 59 lessons. Based on 25 years of meticulous research, ICPS has proven to be extremely effective in helping young children learn to resolve interpersonal problems and prevent antisocial behaviors. ICPS teaches children *how* to think, not *what* to think. It is a self-contained program that involves the use of games, stories, puppets, and role plays to make learning enjoyable.	Academic Other Social Behaviors
Know Your Body www.kendallhunt.com	K–6	*Know Your Body* (KYB) is a comprehensive, skills-based school health promotion program for grades K–6. This curriculum addresses all of the health education content areas recommended by the Centers for Disease Control. Through its cross-curricula matrix, KYB can easily be integrated into programs such as science, math, social studies, language arts, and physical education. Performance assessments accompany each module of the KYB school health education program. They are written to give students an opportunity to demonstrate how well they	Substance Abuse Prevention General Health Promotion

(continued)

Table 2–3 (Continued)

Program	Grade Level(s)	Focus of the Program	Documented Behavioral Impact
		understand health concepts and how effectively they can apply health skills in real life situations. KYB uses five life skills to form the core of its health curriculum: decision making; self-esteem building; goal setting; effective communication; and stress management. KYB content areas include: Nutrition; Dental Health; Alcohol and Drug Use and Prevention; Safety; Skill Builders; Conflict Resolution/Violence Prevention; HIV/AIDS; Consumer Health; Growth and Development; Tobacco Prevention; Exercise and Fitness; Social and Emotional Health; Environmental Health; and Disease Prevention.	
Learning for Life www.learning-for-life.org	K–12	*Learning for Life* is designed to support schools and other youth-serving organizations in their efforts toward preparing youth to successfully handle the complexities of today's society and to enhance their self-confidence, motivation, and self-worth. *Learning for Life* also helps youth develop social and life skills, assists in character development, and helps them formulate positive personal values. It prepares youth to make ethical decisions that will help them achieve their full potential. *Learning for Life* enhances teacher capacity and increases youth learning.	Academic Other Social Behaviors
Lions-Quest ("Skills" series) www.lions-quest.org	K–12	Lions-Quest provides curricula, products, training, and services to support adults in helping young people deal with the complex issues they face every day. Programs are provided for grades K–12 in the following areas: Life Skills; Character Education; Drug Prevention; Service-Learning; and Conflict Resolution.	Academic Substance Abuse Prevention Other Social Behaviors

Michigan Model Comprehensive Health Education www.emc.cmich.edu	K–12	The Michigan Model Comprehensive Health Education is a planned, sequential, K–12 curriculum that addresses the physical, mental, emotional and social dimensions of health. The curriculum is designed to motivate and assist students to maintain and improve their health, prevent disease, and reduce health-related risk behaviors. It allows students to develop and demonstrate increasingly sophisticated health-related knowledge, attitudes, skills, and practices. The comprehensive curriculum includes a variety of topics such as: Safety & First Aid Education; Nutrition Education; Family Health; Consumer Health; Community Health; Growth & Development; Substance Use & Abuse; Personal Health Practices; Emotional & Mental Health; and Disease Prevention & Control.	Substance Abuse Prevention
PATHS (Promoting Alternative Thinking Strategies) www.preventionscience.com	K–6	PATHS is a violence-prevention curriculum that builds the problem-solving and other social and emotional competency skills required for positive relationships today—and throughout students' lives. PATHS program integrates into any K–6 school curriculum.	Academic Violence Prevention Other Social Behaviors
Peace Works (Peace Education Foundation) www.peaceeducation.com	preK–12	The Peace Education Foundation offers grade-level specific classroom-tested curricula for Pre-K through grade 12. These user-friendly materials incorporate activities that foster school norms of cooperation and problem solving rather than violence and aggression. Through role plays, group work and other interactive techniques, students are taught pro-social skills such as anger management, perspective taking, peer resistance, effective communication and problem solving.	Academic Violence Prevention Other Social Behaviors

(continued)

Table 2–3 (Continued)

Program	Grade Level(s)	Focus of the Program	Documented Behavioral Impact
Productive Conflict Resolution Program: A Whole School Approach www.schoolmediationcenter.org	K–12	The "whole-school" approach to conflict resolution education is for schools that want to dramatically change their culture. The School Mediation Center's program incorporates eight components synergistically: bullying prevention (emphasizing no put-downs), conflict resolution skills for staff, curriculum instruction and integration, peaceable classrooms, peer mediation and youth leadership, positive discipline systems, parent and community involvement, and diversity/bias awareness. The program seeks to align the whole culture of the school community with the principles and practices of productive conflict resolution.	Substance Abuse Prevention Violence Prevention Other Social Behaviors
Project ACHIEVE http://modelprograms.samhsa.gov/pdfs/FactSheets/Project%20ACHIEVE.pdf http://cecp.air.org/teams/greenhouses/projectachieve.htm	preK–8	Project ACHIEVE is a research-proven school reform and school effectiveness program developed for use in preschool, elementary, and middle school. The program uses school-wide training and classroom-based interventions to maximize the academic, and social, emotional, and behavioral progress and outcomes of all students. The *Stop & Think Social Skill Program* is a major part of Project ACHIEVE's curriculum for teaching students appropriate behavior and self-management skills.	Program selected because it received highest designation in one or more of six Federal reviews.
Quest (Violence Prevention series) www.kquest.cc/index.htm	K–12	Knowledge Quest distributes top-quality programs in a comprehensive range of Educational subjects as well as in the areas of health, guidance, violence prevention and wellness. Topics include: Conflict Resolution, Family Violence, Teen Violence, and Youth Violence.	Academic

| Reach Out to Schools: Social Competency Program (Open Circle Curriculum)

www.open-circle.org | K–5 | The core of the Program is the *Open Circle Curriculum*, which integrates research findings in child development with the best teaching practices. The curriculum's holistic approach involves training the adult role-models in a child's life to teach and embody principles of communication, responsibility, cooperation, respect and assertiveness. These principles are essential for helping children foster healthy relationships, become engaged, thoughtful citizens, and enjoy productive, fulfilling lives. | Violence Prevention
Other Social Behaviors |
| Resolving Conflict Creatively Program (RCCP)

www.esrnational.org | K–8 | The *Resolving Conflict Creatively Program* (RCCP) is a well-evaluated, K–8 program in character education and social and emotional learning. It is the nation's largest and longest running school program with a special focus on conflict resolution and intergroup relations. RCCP helps children in grades K–8 develop the skills to reduce violence and prejudice, form caring relationships, and build healthy lives. The RCCP model provides extensive teacher training and coaching to implement curriculum-based skill instruction, classroom management, and instructional practices. Their aim is to teach children self-management, cooperation, and problem-solving skills and promote interpersonal effectiveness and intercultural understanding. RCCP helps staff to establish peer mediation programs and other school-wide initiatives that build student leadership in conflict resolution and intergroup relations. In addition, RCCP provides training for administrators, counselors, support staff, and parents so that they are able to model and reinforce what students are learning in their classrooms. | Other Social Behaviors |

(continued)

Table 2–3 (*Continued*)

Program	Grade Level(s)	Focus of the Program	Documented Behavioral Impact
Responsive Classroom www.responsiveclassroom.org	K–6	The *Responsive Classroom* is an approach to teaching and learning that fosters safe, challenging, and joyful classrooms and schools, kindergarten through eighth grade. Developed by classroom teachers, it consists of practical strategies for bringing together social and academic learning throughout the school day. The *Responsive Classroom* approach includes the following main teaching strategies and elements: Morning Meeting; Rules and Logical Consequences; Guided Discovery; Academic Choice; Classroom Organization; and Family Communication Strategies.	Academic Other Social Behaviors
Second Step www.cfchildren.org	preK–9	*Second Step* program teaches social and emotional skills for violence prevention. The program includes research-based, teacher-friendly curricula, training for educators, and parent-education components. Classroom use of the *Second Step* program helps provide children with the skills they need to create safe environments and become successful adults. Based on more than 15 years of classroom application and the most current academic, social, and emotional research, the *Second Step* curriculum focuses on the three essential competencies—empathy, impulse control and problem solving, and anger management.	Violence Prevention Other Social Behaviors

Program	Grade	Description	Categories
Skills, Opportunities, and Recognition (SOAR) http://modelprograms.samhsa.gov/print.cfm?pkProgramid=169 http://www.channing-bete.com/positiveyouth/pages/SOAR/SOAR.html	K–6	SOAR is a scientifically-tested comprehensive, school-based program designed to promote positive youth development and academic success. The program is a school-wide, school climate program for elementary schools that promotes the healthy development of young people by increasing skills for successful participation in the family, school, peer group and community; opportunities for active involvement in family and school; and consistent recognition for effort and improvement. A SOAR school provides social skills training for elementary students, training for their teachers to improve methods of classroom management, and instruction on providing developmentally sequenced parenting workshops for parents. The long-term results indicate that students in SOAR classrooms are more committed to school, have better academic achievement, and less misbehavior in the school and the community.	Academic Substance Abuse Prevention Violence Prevention Healthy Sexual Development
Social Decision Making and Problem Solving Program www.umdnj.edu/spsweb	K–6	The *Social Decision Making and Problem Solving Program* (SDM/PS) provides teachers with training and curricula for grades K through 8 to assist students in the acquisition of social and decision-making skills, and to develop their ability to effectively use those skills in real-life and academic situations.	Academic Substance Abuse Prevention Violence Prevention Other Social Behaviors
Teenage Health Teaching Modules www.thtm.org	6-12	*Teenage Health Teaching Modules* (THTM) is a successful, nationally used, and independently evaluated comprehensive school health curriculum for grades 6 to 12. It provides adolescents with the knowledge and skills to act in ways that enhance their immediate and long-term health. The evaluation of THTM concluded that the curriculum produced positive effects on students' health knowledge, attitudes, and self-reported behaviors. The following essential health skills are highlighted in each of the modules: risk assessment, self-assessment, communication, decision making, goal setting, health advocacy, and healthy self-management.	Substance Abuse Prevention Violence Prevention General Health Promotion Other Social Behaviors

(continued)

Table 2–3 (Continued)

Program	Grade Level(s)	Focus of the Program	Documented Behavioral Impact
Tribes TLC: A New Way of Learning and Being Together www.tribes.com	preK–12	*Tribes* is a step-by-step process to achieve specific learning goals. Four agreements are honored: attentive listening; appreciation/no put downs; mutual respect; and the right to pass. Students learn a set of collaborative skills so they can work well together in long-term groups (tribes). The focus is on how to: 1) help each other work on tasks; 2) set goals and solve problems; 3) monitor and assess progress; and 4) celebrate achievements. The learning of academic material and self-responsible behavior is assured because teachers utilize methods based upon brain-compatible learning, multiple intelligences, cooperative learning and social development research. The teachers and administrators in a Tribes school or district also work together in supportive groups. They too enjoy the participatory democratic process and creative collegiality.	Academic
Voices: A Comprehensive Reading, Writing, and Character Education Program http://www.voicespublishing.com/ http://www.casel.org/about_sel/voicesdesc.php	K–6	*Voices* is an integrated, multicultural literature-based, comprehensive reading and character education curriculum. It focuses on six core social skills and values: identity awareness; perspective taking; conflict resolution; social awareness; love and freedom; and democracy. The program provides broad coverage of violence prevention and citizenship.	Academic

Names of the 22 select programs taken from: Collaborative for Academic, Social, and Emotional Learning. (2003). *Safe and sound: An educational leader's guide to evidence-based social and emotional learning (SEL) programs.* Chicago, IL: Author. © 2003 by the Collaborative for Academic, Social, and Emotional Learning (CASEL).

sequenced programs for general-education classrooms, are especially effective and comprehensive in their SEL coverage, have documented impacts, and provide staff development. The "Select" programs focus on a variety of target areas, including problem solving, achievement, social competency, health, a caring school community, character education, conflict resolution, and violence prevention, and span a variety of grade levels. Some are person-focused. Some are focused on the environment, and some have multiple components and approaches. Of the 22 "Select" programs, 14 produced documented behavioral effects in the academic area in addition to effecting some changes in other areas as well (e.g., social behaviors, general health, substance abuse, violence prevention, and/or healthy sexual development). Once again, this type of information can be invaluable to the school counselor, who seeks to function as an educational leader by helping administrators and faculty select effective interventions at the classroom level.

However, even using an evidence-based classroom-guidance program that is listed in *Safe and Sound* does not guarantee that desired student developmental outcomes will automatically be achieved. The school counselor needs to ensure that the program (a) addresses local contextual and cultural factors that may affect its implementation, (b) is competently and consistently applied, and (c) has its actual effects in the local setting evaluated.

INDIRECT SERVICES OR SYSTEM-LEVEL FUNCTIONS AND THE STRENGTHS-BASED SCHOOL COUNSELOR

One of the major shifts in contemporary school counseling is toward a more indirect services model of school counseling (Green & Keys, 2001) or an increased emphasis on such indirect services or system-level functions as consultation, advocacy,[3] collaboration, and coordination. That shift has been prompted in part by the challenge to meet the more complex needs of the increasingly diverse student population that school counselors are encountering (Green & Keys, 2001). While the importance of indirect services or system-level functions in meeting this challenge is clearly evident in the ASCA National Model (ASCA, 2003), its 80%-direct-service charge appears inconsistent with current trends toward a greater emphasis on indirect services.

As we have discussed, the role of the strengths-based school counselor involves promoting the evidence-based environments and social contexts that foster the knowledge, skills, and attitudes associated with positive youth development for all students. In order to promote and maintain such an environmental context, the counselor must also be able to function effectively at

---

[3]The reader is referred to chapter 1 for our discussion of promotion-oriented developmental client advocacy.

the systems level, but the percentage of time devoted to indirect services is affected by a variety of factors (e.g., student needs) and cannot be prescribed. We now turn to a discussion of how these indirect services or system-level functions are manifested in SBSC.

Consultation

As is true for counseling theories, theories of consultation were developed almost exclusively from a problem-reduction perspective rather than from the strengths-promotion perspective that is emphasized in SBSC. Not surprisingly, teachers and parents often seek consultation services only as problems with students arise. As a result, this approach tends to reinforce a remediation philosophy of consultation-service delivery (Terjesen, Jacofsky, Froh, & DiGiuseppe, 2004). In contrast, Terjesen et al. proposed that consultation be employed to foster a system-wide program that reinforces positive child development which, in turn, may help in the long-term in reducing referrals for academic and behavioral problems. Thus, consultation efforts with teachers and parents would be focused on helping to foster student potential and already existing strengths and would be redirected from reducing specific target negative behaviors to increasing specific positive strengths or attributes.

In addition to their focus on remediation and problem reduction, existing consultation theories rarely take into account important contextual features of the school setting, namely the time limitations on school counselor and others, the fact that consultation sessions in schools typically are very brief (often less than 20 minutes), and that the practical realities of the school setting make it unlikely for consultation to extend beyond one or two sessions. Because of these contextual factors, the strengths-based school counselor should favor consultation approaches that are time sensitive yet promote student strengths and strengths-enhancing environments.

Although its effectiveness has yet to be evaluated empirically, Solution-Focused consultation (Kahn, 2000; Metcalf, 1995) is one approach that is compatible with SBSC. Solution-focused consultation emphasizes the positive by helping consultees use their strengths and past successes to formulate desired goals. Kahn described a five-step approach to solution-focused consultation (see Table 2–4). This approach also tends to fit well with the limited amount of time which teachers, parents, and administrators often have available to devote to consultation with the school counselor, and it is congruent with Terjesen et al.'s (2004) concern for incorporating a "positive mentality" into school. As was the case for solution-focused counseling, the consultation application of this theory is also limited with regard to teaching new positive behaviors that consultees may need to employ. In these instances, the strengths-based counselor will often find it effective to draw upon interventions from the older and better-researched behavioral approach to consultation (e.g., Bergan & Kratochwill, 1990; Kratochwill & Bergan, 1990; Martens, 1993).

Table 2–4.

Kahn's (2000) Solution-Focused Model of Consultation for School Counselors

Step 1. Presession and Initial Structuring
  (a) Orient the consultee to a Solution-focused approach using a pre-session questionnaire.
  (b) Help the consultee identify strengths/resources she/he brings to consultation.
  (c) Have consultee identify initial goals for self and client.
  (d) Have consultee scale change in need for consultation since the time consultation was requested.

Step 2. Examining Consultation Goals
  (a) Do minimal problem exploration before establishing consultation goals.
  (b) Help consultee choose goals for self and client in consultee's own words.
  (c) Define goals as the *presence* (positive)of an observable, measurable behavior, not the absence (negative) of a behavior.

Step 3. Examining Attempted Solutions and Exceptions
  (a) Examine attempted solutions tried by the consultee.
  (b) Review exceptions (when the problem does not occur or occurs less).
  (c) If can't find exceptions, try one of the following:
    (i) give assignment to look for exceptions in coming week;
    (ii) ask consultee (e.g., teacher) to recall/imagine how a master teacher would handle the problem; or
    (iii) observe in classroom and provide feedback about exceptions.

Step 4. Helping Consultees Decide on a Solution
  (a) Help consultee decide on a solution (defined behaviorally and concretely) based on:
    (i) "if it aint' broke, don't fix it;"
    (ii) "once you know what works, do more of it;" or
    (iii) "if it does not work, don't do it again; do something different."
  (b) Move emphasis of change from the student's behavior to the consultee's (i.e., the teacher's) behavior.

Step 5. Summarizing and Complimenting
  (a) Summarize goals and chosen solutions for the consultee.
  (b) Compliment consultee for successful past exceptions and for what consultee (e.g., teacher) did to foster them.
  (c) If consultation sessions continue, repeat basic steps with continual goal re-evaluation and examination of exceptions.

Table developed from Kahn, B. B. (2000). A model of solution-focused consultation for school counselors. *Professional School Counseling, 3,* 248–254.

Akin-Little, Little, and Delligatti proposed a preventative model of teacher consultation that is strengths-oriented. The model draws upon principles of mental health and behavioral consultation and concepts from positive psychology. With respect to mental-health consultation, the consultant focuses initially on helping teachers to develop and foster positive psychological characteristics such as optimism, happiness, and positive coping strategies in themselves. Reinforcement and other behavioral and cognitive-behavioral strategies are employed in this endeavor. Thus, the consultant's first step in this model is to enhance a teacher's own personal positive psychology through routine meetings with teachers at the beginning of the year. The second and final step is to encourage and help teachers through behavioral principles to use positive psychology in the classroom. The rationale for this step is based on the premise that "positive environments that evoke and reinforce positive behaviors are necessary in order to shape and maintain the optimal human experiences" (p. 160). In this step, teachers are encouraged and helped to reinforce children's prosocial activities and other positive behaviors as well as to develop, implement, and evaluate a plan to help each student reach optimal development.

In chapter 4, we discuss conjoint behavioral consultation (Sheridan, 1997) which is another consultation approach that is compatible with SBSC. Unlike the previous approaches, conjoint behavioral consultation simultaneously targets intervention at two systems—home and school—that impact students rather than at either system alone. As we will discuss, initial research suggests that intervention in multiple systems that affect a child's development produces results superior to those that target only a single system. Thus, this type of consultation represents an important systemic intervention that nicely complements some of the more recently recommended indirect service functions such as collaboration, leadership, and advocacy.

Coordination and Collaboration

Coordination and collaboration are two other overlapping indirect services that loom as larger components of the school counselor's role in the comprehensive school counseling programs of the 21st century. Contemporary education is challenged by what have been referred to as "the new morbidities"—poor nutrition, unsafe sex, drugs, teenage pregnancy and parenting, lack of job skills, inadequate access to health care, and homelessness (Walsh, Howard, & Buckley, 1999)—all of which markedly impact students' ability to be successful in school and life. To address these difficult challenges successfully and to foster the types of school, family, and community contexts that research has indicated support healthy development requires counselors to coordinate their services and to work effectively with other professional groups and organizations within the school and community. Much of the speculation about effective school counseling in the 21st century suggests that collaboration and coordination will be intertwined services in comprehensive counseling programs that are characterized by strong school-community partnerships (Adelman & Taylor, 2001; Bemak, 2000; Porter, Epp, & Bryant, 2000; Taylor & Adelman, 2000).

Coordination involves the focusing and management of resources to either prevent or resolve the difficulties of client groups as well as to foster student strengths and strengths-enhancing environments. School counselors frequently coordinate services that impact all three areas of student development:

academic, personal/social, and career. Typical counselor coordination efforts in the academic area include information fairs about college and other post-secondary opportunities, scholarships, new student orientation and school transition programs, high-stakes testing, and peer tutoring. School-to-work programs, career days, job shadowing, and internship programs are examples of coordination activities that influence career development for students, while, in the personal/social area, peer mediation, advisory programs, substance abuse and violence prevention programs, and referrals to mental health and other community services are frequently coordinated by the school counselor. Of all the counseling services, Gerler (1992) argued that coordination needs to come first if counselors are to influence the educational and personal development of students, and Keys et al. (1998) asserted that it is the most important one for serving at-risk students.

An important coordination function for the strengths-oriented counselor is linking students to programs and activities, both in and outside the school setting, which enhance personal strengths in the academic, career, and personal/social areas. One type of program to which school counselors commonly link students is after-school and summer-school programs intended to promote academic development and achievement. But are these programs actually effective? A recent meta-analysis (a statistical review of the research literature) of the effects of out-of-school-time (OST; e.g., after-school and summer-school) programs for K–12 at-risk students in reading and/or mathematics indicated that they are effective (Lauer et al., 2006). Both elementary and secondary students benefited from programs for improved reading, although the benefits for mathematics achievement occurred primarily in the secondary grades. In addition, larger effects in reading occurred for programs that involved individual tutoring. Whether OST programs took place after school or during the summer did not make a difference in effectiveness. Moreover, results indicated that OST programs need not focus solely on academic activities as programs which included both academic and social activities also produced increases in achievement. Finally, OST programs needed to deliver strategies for a minimum amount of time to be effective (e.g., at least 45 hours), but longer programs were not necessarily more effective.

School counselors also link students to more generic extracurricular activities, although they do not typically coordinate these activities. Rather, as we have seen, school counselors coordinate activities such as peer mediation, peer mentoring, and student-ambassador programs which engage such resiliency and protective factors as enhancing meaningful participation and bonding and attachment. But, as we shall discuss, extracurricular activities also enhance protective factors such as meaningful participation and school engagement. As such, encouraging participation in, and helping students link to, extracurricular activities is an important coordinating function.

Extracurricular activities are discretionary activities that are physically or mentally stimulating to the individual and contain some structured parameters

(Larson & Verma, 1999). They include nonacademic programs during or after school in the building, and community programs. These activities are distinguished from leisure, as extracurricular activities require effort and provide a forum to express an identity and passion.

School counselors need to be more knowledgeable about the relationship between after-school/out-of school activities and to share this information with teachers and parents. In their review of research on the relationship between structured extracurricular activities and adolescent development, Gilman, Meyers, and Perez (2004) noted that discretionary activities account for 40–50% of an adolescent's waking hours. Although the relationship was not a linear one, time spent in structured extracurricular activities (SEAs) was found to be associated with higher academic achievement, higher self-concept and life satisfaction, and a decreased likelihood of dropping out of school. SEAs were defined as highly structured, voluntary activities that emphasize skill building under the guidance of competent non-parental adults and have supportive social networks that establish a school identity. SEAs included school athletics, fine arts, and academic clubs. In contrast to the findings for SEAs, time spent in solitary, non-structured, non-cooperative pursuits, often without adult supervision was associated with negative psychosocial outcomes. The authors caution that the likelihood of a successful outcome for students from participating in an SEA is compromised by a variety of factors including whether it (a) is not chosen voluntarily; (b) is perceived as uninteresting or of low social status; (c) is not supported by the student's peer network; and (d) fails to provide adequate supervision by a competent, supportive adult.

Similarly, Feldman and Matjasko (2005) reviewed the research on school-based extracurricular activities on adolescent development. Extracurricular activities were defined as those that were organized and supported by schools and primarily occurred on school grounds. They concluded that:

> School-based, structured, extracurricular activity participation, in contrast to participation in unstructured activities (sometimes including school-based activities), is associated with positive adolescent developmental outcomes, namely (a) higher academic performance and attainment; (b) reduced rates of dropout; (c) lower (to a degree) rates of substance use; (d) less sexual activity among girls; (e) better psychological adjustment, including higher self-esteem, less worry regarding the future, and reduced feelings of social isolation; and (f) reduced rated of delinquent behavior, including criminal arrests and antisocial behavior. (Feldman & Matjasko, p. 193)

Taking a somewhat broader view of student involvement in activities, Cooper, Valentine, Nye, and Lindsay (1999) reviewed the relationship between five after-school activities and academic achievement for students in grades 6–12. Generally, more time in extracurricular activities and other structured groups and less time in jobs and television viewing were associated with higher test scores and class grades. Not surprisingly, more time spent on home-work was also associated with better grades.

> Thus, it seems safe to conclude that parents and educators can profitably focus on student after-school activities as a potentially important influence on achievement. Activities that relate directly to learning or that foster positive school identity can improve achievement, whereas activities that displace learning or replace school identities with other identities diminish achievement. (Cooper et al., 1999, p. 377)

In addition, students, especially those at high-risk, who are involved in school extracurricular programs have been shown to be less likely to drop out of school and less likely to be involved in delinquent activity (Mahoney, 2000; Mahoney & Cairns, 1997). Moreover, the benefits of extracurricular participa-tion have also demonstrated a positive influence even beyond formal school years (Gholson, 1985; Mahoney, 2000) as consistent participation in extracur-ricular activities across adolescence was positively linked to educational status at young adulthood (Mahoney, Cairns, & Farmer, 2003). In fact, Zaff, Moore, Papillo, and Williams (2003) found that consistent participation in extracur-ricular activities in eighth through twelfth grade predicted academic achieve-ment and prosocial behaviors (e.g., voting, volunteer work) in young adulthood, even after controlling for individual, peer, parent, and school process variables.

Most likely, participating in extracurricular activities enhances student strengths by engaging a number of the internal and external assets and protec-tive factors that we have been discussing. Thus, extracurricular activities can appeal to student interests, encourage peer interaction, promote cooperation, build student-adult relationships, provide structure and challenge, and connect students to school (Holloway, 2002). In their comprehensive review of ex-tracurricular and out-of-school activities, Eccles and Templeton's (2002) sug-gest that common elements of successful extracurricular programming include social support from adult and peers, inclusive social networks/organization, strong and clear social norms, intentional learning experiences, motivational scaffolding, and opportunities to experience a sense of mattering (e.g., mean-ingful participation or making a meaningful contribution to one's environment) and leadership. In short, by engaging in coordinating activities to link students to prosocial extracurricular activities, the school counselor can markedly in-crease the impact she has on positive development of all students. Moreover, in schools where the extracurricular program is limited, the school counselor can also advocate extending the program and incorporating the elements which research has shown to be associated with positive youth development.

Collaboration consists of forming coalitions with professionals and others in the school and community to better serve students. Previously, we discussed Friend and Cook's (2003) defining characteristics of collaboration, which in-clude that it (a) is voluntary; (b) requires parity among participants; (c) is based on mutual goals; and (d) depends on shared responsibility for decision making, shared resources, and shared accountability for outcomes. Keys and Green (2005) observed that two pieces of federal legislation—the Individuals with Disabilities Education Act (IDEA; U.S. Department of Education, 1997) and the No Child Left Behind (NCLB) Act of 2001 (NCLB; U.S. Department of Education, 2001a)—foster collaboration between school counselors and other professionals within the school setting. The IDEA requires that every student with an identified physical or learning disability must have an Individualized Education Program (IEP) of goals, objectives, and services. By law, the IEP must be developed by a team of professional educators which often includes the school counselor. Similarly, the NCLB Act with its requirement that schools achieve adequate yearly progress (AYP, as measured by performance on standardized tests) toward academic outcomes will require collaborative efforts among counselors and others if this requirement is to be met.

Besides these examples, Bemak (2000) identified three domains for collaboration for school counselors: within schools, with community agencies, and with families. Within their schools, counselors can interpret data on school performance to administrators in order to identify and help remove obstacles to achievement and student development. They can also work with teachers to help them understand cultural learning styles and coordinate services with other support-service personnel such as school psychologists and school social workers. In addition, they can work with community agencies to link students to needed outside services, to bring community services into the schools, and to mutually develop prevention/intervention and promotion programs. Collaboration with families can take a variety of forms, including working with other professionals to develop family-advocacy programs to improve communication between families and school staff or skill-training programs in areas such as parenting skills, parents' rights, and tutoring skills.

To date a variety of school-community collaboration models have been proposed. Recently, however, Adelman and Taylor (Adelman & Taylor, 2001; Taylor & Adelman, 2000) have raised concerns about these efforts.

> Such restructuring requires more than outreach to link with community resources (and certainly more than adopting a school-linked services model), more than coordinating school-owned services with each other and with community services, and more than creating Family Resource Centers, Full Service Schools, and Community Schools. Policymakers must realize that, as important as it is to reform and restructure health and human services and link them to schools as much as feasible, the focus is too limited. (Taylor & Adelman, 2000, p. 299)

Adelman and Taylor (2001) believe that current collaboration approaches fragment and marginalize efforts to remove barriers to learning and that what is needed is a new type of school-community collaborative that meshes or weaves together community services and programs with school-operated programs in a single, unified effort rather than co-locating or coordinating services. Such a comprehensive effort would be characterized by shared resources, responsibilities, and decision making, would be multifaceted, and would function in six areas: classroom-focused programs, support for transitions, student and family assistance, community outreach, crisis response and prevention, and home improvement in schooling. In such an effort, the counselor would have an important leadership role to integrate school and community programs and to ensure that the efforts to address learning barriers are well-integrated with instructional and management efforts. At this time, it probably is too soon to know whether coordination of school and community-based services, collaboration between and co-location of school and community-based services (e.g., independent school and community services located at the school and collaborating with each other), or an actual integration of school and community-based services will be most effective. However, it is clear that the strengths-based school counselor will need to draw on a broad set of resources in order to promote healthy student development in the 21st century.

Leadership

"A review of the school counseling literature reveals that there are as many definitions of leadership as there are authors on the subject . . ." (Phillips, Sears, Snow, & Jackson, 2005, p. 216) To that, we would add that there are even more areas in which a leadership role has been proposed for the school counselor than there are authors on the subject. Among the proposed leadership roles/areas for the school counselor are:

- facilitating academic success, staff development, social reform, and institutional decision making;
- identifying and removing barriers to high academic achievement and increasing learning opportunities;
- being the key person in the school who maintains a focus on understanding the needs of all students;
- closing the achievement gap;
- collaborating with other professionals in the school to influence system-wide changes and implement school reforms;
- promoting educational reform and meeting national and state educational objectives inclusive of creating healthy, safe school environments, partially by playing a major role in facilitating interagency and interdisciplinary collaboration;
- developing portfolios and authentic assessment for students;
- championing students, families, issues of social justice, schools, and, most of all, the developmental agendas of students and families;
- promoting staff development, school reform, multicultural awareness, mentoring programs, and political involvement;

- promoting, planning, and implementing programs, career and college activities, course selection and placement activities, social/personal management and decision-making activities;
- providing snapshots of student outcomes, showing accomplishments and achievement gaps, and providing leadership for the school to view things through the equity lens;
- arranging one-to-one relationships with adults in school setting for additional support and assistance in reaching academic success; and
- defining and carrying out the guidance and counseling function.

While we would certainly agree that most, if not all, of the above are worthy of leadership by the school counselor, practical realities make it imperative that the strengths-based school counselor focus and prioritize leadership efforts.

Leadership is "the process of influencing others to create a shared commitment to a common purpose," (Phillips et al., 2005, p. 216), which, in this case, involves fostering optimal academic, personal/social, and career development for all students by enhancing the environments and systems which impact their development. As such, leadership in SBSC stems from a clear role and identity. Moreover, we believe that there are some clearly *focused* leadership activities which are compatible with a strengths orientation that the school counselor should emphasize.

As a first priority, the school counselor has the leadership responsibility for developing and maintaining an effective comprehensive school-counseling program in conjunction with other stakeholders. That task represents no small leadership responsibility considering the multiple management tasks (e.g., establishing and maintaining an advisory council, conducting needs assessments, monitoring student programs, conducting a program audit) listed in the National Model (ASCA, 2003) for a comprehensive, data-driven school-counseling program.

In addition, the strengths-based school counselor is more broadly conceptualized as a school leader. Through varied contacts with students, peer groups, classrooms, teachers, parents, and administrators, the counselor is in an excellent position to evaluate the climate of a school and how its policies, procedures, and programs are impacting student development. From this vantage point, the counselor is able to forge a partnership for school improvement and positive youth development not only with the principal (Stone & Clark, 2001) but also with key stakeholders (e.g., teacher leaders, parents, other community members) and systems (e.g., community mental health, juvenile justice). In SBSC, the main focus of the counselor's school leadership efforts is directed at building-level issues. In this regard, the counselor engages in a variety of leadership activities both individually and in collaboration with others.

Among these additional leadership activities are analyzing and disaggregating data (e.g., according to race and ethnicity, gender, ESL) with respect to academic (see Dimmit, 2003; and Hayes, Nelson, Tabin, Pearson, & Worthy, 2002 in chapter 4 for examples), personal/social, and career development. Once the implications of these data are understood, support for enhancing identified developmental areas needs to be enlisted from teachers and other stakeholders, decisions have to be made regarding policy changes or programs to be implemented, implementation needs to occur and be monitored, and results need to be evaluated. The strengths-based school counselor plays a variety of important leadership roles in this process.

One of these roles is structural leadership (Bolman & Deal, 1997; Dollarhide, 2003; Dollarhide & Saginak, 2003). Knowing what programs and policies actually have been shown to foster positive youth development in the academic, career, and personal/social areas and knowing where to find these programs is an important decision-making consideration. Greenberg et al. (2003) noted that, despite the availability of evidence-based programs, many schools still do not use them. We suspect that one of the reasons for this failure is that many principals and other educational leaders do not know where to find information about these programs. The strengths-based school counselor can find much of the current information about exemplary programs and best practices for school, family, and community settings in the Web sites, professional journals, and other sources cited in Tables 1–2, 2–3, and 4-4, and in the section on comprehensive school reform in chapter 4. Being able to supply information about effective programs to decision-making sessions by teachers, administrators, parents, and other educational stakeholders is an important leadership contribution. In the past, it has been rare for school counselors to be equipped with such broad-based knowledge, let alone for them to have been involved in and brought that knowledge to the decision-making table. As such, accessing and being able to use this knowledge is an important training issue for school-counselor educators and is discussed in chapter 8.

Being able to evaluate the effects of the programs and policies that ultimately are implemented is yet another form of structural leadership that the strengths-based school counselor can provide. The school counselor is one of the few professionals at the building level who is equipped with even basic knowledge of needs-assessment and program-evaluation procedures. In a results-based, high-stakes testing environment, this expertise positions the school counselor for leadership responsibility.

Finally, symbolic, political, and human-resource leadership at the building level are all important forms of leadership for the strengths-based school counselor to demonstrate. The counselor articulating an identity and a vision of a strengths-oriented environment in which all students can experience success and positive development (symbolic leadership) is a radical notion in many school settings. Empowering and inspiring others to implement such a context (human resource leadership) and mobilizing the necessary teacher, administrator, parent, and community support (political leadership) to make needed changes is no small task in most schools, let alone in a low-performing school in which morale and energy are low or nonexistent.

Accountability

A variety of educational reform initiatives such as *A Nation at Risk* (National Commission on Excellence in Education, 1983) and the *No Child Left Behind Act* (2001) have made accountability the central topic in education. In education, accountability has come to mean demonstrating that the services provided make a difference in (e.g., improve) the academic success of all students, and, in particular, that they reduce and ultimately eliminate the achievement gap between White students and minority students. Correspondingly, ASCA's National Model (2003) has connected school counseling with current educational reform efforts and aligned the counselor's role more closely with the school's academic mission.

But accountability is by no means a new function for school counselors (e.g., Krumboltz, 1974; Wheeler & Loesch, 1981). The importance of this function, however, and the acknowledged pressure to demonstrate that school counseling programs are accountable has increased dramatically (ASCA, 2003; Dahir & Stone, 2003; Isaacs, 2003; Myrick, 2003). In addition, the accountability focus has shifted in recent years from an emphasis on program inputs such as what services school counselors provide and how they spend their time (e.g., Fairchild & Seeley, 1995) to an emphasis on outputs (e.g., outcomes) such as how students are different or better off because of the school counseling program (e.g., ASCA, 2003). In the past, for example, tallying how many study-skills sessions counselors provided might have constituted an acceptable type of accountability data. Now counselors would be expected to collect accountability data about the extent to which these sessions were subsequently associated with improved test performance by the students who participated in them or by particular sub-groups who participated in them, such as Hispanic students or those on free and reduced school lunch.

The ASCA National Model (ASCA, 2003) provides a number of important recommendations with respect to demonstrating accountability for school-counseling programs. All of these recommendations emphasize the use of data in the school-counseling program either to monitor student progress or to evaluate program effectiveness. Counselors are to inspect data not only for students overall (e.g., aggregated data), but also disaggregated for different sub-groups of students. Data may be disaggregated in a variety of ways including by gender, ethnicity, both gender and ethnicity, free- and reduced-lunch status, educational track, language spoken at home, grade level, teacher, etc. Disaggregating data provides the counselor and other stakeholders with a more informed sense of which students are making what kind of progress or what effect a particular program intervention is having on which students. Thus, it is important to know that 75% of fifth graders are performing at or above grade level in reading, but it may be more informative, for example, to know whether Hispanic or African-American students are performing at or above grade level at the same rate as White students as this information may raise equity or special-needs issues that need to be addressed in a school.

With respect to monitoring student progress, three categories of data are specified: achievement data, achievement-related data, and standards- and competency-related data (ASCA, 2003). Examples of achievement data include grade-point averages, standardized and end-of-course/grade test scores, graduation rates, and number of students passing all subjects. Achievement-related data are those that have been shown to be related to (e.g., associated with) achievement such as attendance rates, course enrollment patterns, disciplinary referrals, homework completion rates, and participation in extracurricular activities. With respect to standards- and competency-related data, the National Model specifies nine student standards—three each for the academic, career, and personal social-development domains—together with a series of student competencies (knowledge, skills, and attitudes) for each domain that students will acquire through the school comprehensive-guidance program. ASCA's examples of standards- and competency-related data are the percentage of students (a) with four-year plans on file, (b) who have participated in job shadowing, (c) who have set and attained academic goals, and (d) who can apply conflict resolution skills. As we discuss in subsequent chapters, the empirical basis for these standards and competencies is unclear. In SBSC in contrast, we present data (e.g., strengths and environments) in the academic (chapters 3 and 4), personal/social (chapter 5), and career (chapter 6) that have been shown empirically to be associated with positive youth development in one or more of the three domains.

The impact of the school counseling programs is demonstrated through program evaluation data. In this regard, the National Model (ASCA, 2003) identifies three types of data: process, perception, and results. Process data provide a record of what was done and for whom (e.g., four-year planning sessions were held with 240 eighth-grade students). Perception data measure attitudes and beliefs, perceptions, and what people think they know. Examples of perception data include (a) 80% of the 240 eighth-grade students said that the planning sessions gave them a clearer idea of what to expect in high school, (b) 90% of the fourth-grade teachers in the district perceive that the conflict resolution program provided by counselors has reduced disagreements among students on the playground, and (c) 95% of fourth-grade students can successfully recite the steps in conflict resolution. Results data are concerned with the impact of a program or intervention on student achievement or behavior. Improvements in grades, test scores, attendance, and graduate rates are examples of results data.

The National Model (ASCA, 2003) also specifies three time frames for data collection: immediate, intermediate, and long-term. Immediate data measure knowledge, skills, and attitude change (e.g., pre-post change) at the conclusion of a counseling intervention/activity. Intermediate data assess application of that knowledge, skills, and or attitude change over a short period of time. For example, data on the effect of a study-skills intervention on spelling-test performance or the percent of homework completed and turned in after a homework-completion intervention represent examples of intermediate-data collection. Finally, year-to-year data on student attendance and graduation are examples of long-range data that may be relevant to the evaluation of a school-counseling program.

Although the data (e.g., variables) mentioned above are important ones to consider with respect to the accountability of counseling and other educational programs, school counselors need more guidance about (a) how to analyze those data, (b) what data school counselors can realistically expect to impact with their interventions, and (c) the level of confidence that counselors can have in concluding that their interventions as opposed to some other factors were responsible for the pre-post changes they are reporting.[4] While some have asserted that school counselors do not have to be skilled statisticians to meaningfully analyze data and that simple percentages can often convey what is happening in a school (ASCA, 2003), school counselors do need to be able to disaggregate data, to compute means, medians, and other descriptive statistics, as well as correlations and an occasional inferential statistical test, in order to draw more informed conclusions from the data. The Web site of the National Center for School Counseling Research at The University of Massachusetts, Amherst (http://www.umass.edu/schoolcounseling/) is a useful resource for school counselors for data analysis and other accountability issues. With respect to data analysis for example, EZAnalyze (http://www.ezanalyze .com/) is a free, downloadable software program designed to help school counselors analyze data. It is available from the Center's website. EZAnalyze is an Excel "Add In" that works on both Macintosh- and Windows-based computers. Excel is a computer program that is commonly bundled with those computers. According to the program description, EZAnalyze does not require you to type in a formula, nor does it require you to know anything about the math involved with the analyses. It does descriptive statistics (e.g., median, mean, standard deviation); disaggregates data; and can compute correlations, chi square, t-tests, and single factor analyses of variance.

Recognizing which phenomena a school-counseling program can realistically be expected to change is another important aspect of accountability that needs to be addressed. If counselors promise or expect to effect change in areas over which they exercise little control, it is likely not only that they will fail in those efforts but also that they will be frustrated and tempted to abandon their accountability efforts overall.

---

[4] See Ware and Galassi, 2006 for an example analyzing student achievement data.

> Counselors can play a role in helping students adjust to school and perform better in classrooms. It's difficult to claim credit for improved performance on state or national tests. Teachers work every day with students on their academic skills, whereas counselors work with students briefly and periodically. It is hard to make a case that academic performance on state standardized tests was due to a counselor intervention. Brief counseling can make a difference in terms of student attitudes, classroom skills, or working relationships with teachers. Class grades or grade-point averages may be too broad and inclusive to be of much value in a counselor-accountability study. On the other hand, improvement in learning behaviors related to school achievement might be a goal and the focus of individual or group counseling sessions—if, as a result of a counselor intervention, a learning behavior is improved, then the intervention might be deemed effective and useful. (Myrick, 2003, pp. 177–178)

We are not saying that counselors should not track test scores, class grades, etc., before and after they provide counseling interventions. Rather they should not expect that their interventions will directly or invariably impact these variables. Instead, counselors should focus their accountability efforts on variables that (a) their interventions are likely to change and (b) have been shown empirically to be related to positive development in the academic, personal/social, and/or career areas (see Chapters 3–6 for these variables). For example, homework completion, which is discussed in chapter 4, has been shown to be highly related to academic achievement for high-school students, and a number of interventions have been shown to be effective in increasing homework-completion rate. A counselor might administer a homework-completion intervention for students in a math class with those students who had initially low rates of homework completion and low math grades. Before and after the intervention is administered, a variety of accountability data could be collected, including homework-completion rate (e.g., percent of completed homework assignments turned in, percent of homework problems done correctly on each assignment), math test grades, and math course grade. The most direct measure of the effectiveness of the intervention is change in students' homework completion rate as that was the focus of the intervention. Improvement in math test grades would hopefully occur as well, but math test grades are a less direct measure of the effectiveness of the intervention. Moreover, math test grades are affected by factors other than homework completion (e.g., test anxiety, whether the students studied effectively prior to the test, etc.). Finally, overall grade in the math course is the least directly affected accountability measure with respect to the intervention, and the most difficult one to change as well. It is affected by even more factors, such as homework grade in the course, math test grades, math project grades, extra-credit assignments, make-up work, and perhaps even class attendance, or classroom behavior. The point is that counselors need to select appropriate and realistic accountability measures.

Although pre-post improvements following a counseling intervention represent important accountability data to collect, school counselors need to exercise caution in concluding that their interventions, as opposed to some other factors, were responsible for those changes. For example, the improvements in math grades may not have been due to the homework intervention but to a change in the teacher's grading policy as a result of parents complaining to the principal that the teacher was being too hard on students. In general, pre-post data derived from a single group of students who receive an intervention provide a weak basis for demonstrating the effectiveness of that intervention. In these situations, there are a number of equally plausible alternative explanations for the changes that cannot be ruled out in the absence of a no-treatment or a wait-list control group of similar students who did not receive the intervention (Shadish, Cook, & Campell, 2002). In most circumstances, it is not realistic to expect the school counselor to be able to employ even a wait-list group of students just to be able to increase confidence that the counseling intervention was responsible for the students' improvement. As an alternative, single-subject research designs hold promise for measuring change and the effectiveness of counseling interventions for both individual students and groups of students (Foster, Watson, Meeks, & Young, 2002; Galassi & Gersh, 1991; McDougall & Smith, 2006). But these designs also have limitations such as the practical and ethical considerations of withdrawing/withholding an intervention even for a short period of time. Overall, we believe that important steps toward more accountable school-counseling programs will be taken if counselors routinely collect relevant pre-post (e.g., results) data for their interventions and then are cautious in how they interpret the results that they have obtained.

Lastly, several very useful sources of information and models of program evaluation and accountability are available for school counselors. We have already mentioned the Web site of the National Center for School Counseling Research (http://www.umass.edu/schoolcounseling/). In addition to EZAnalyze, the site contains information about a variety of accountability issues for school counselors, including construction of counseling surveys, action research, and data usage. The Accountability Bridge Model (Astramovich & Coker, in press), results-based comprehensive guidance (Lapan, 2001), MEASURE (Stone & Dahir, 2004), data-driven decision making (Isaacs, 2003), and the Transformative Individual School Counseling Model (Eschenauer & Chen-Hayes, 2005) are alternative accountability models that merit the school counselor's consideration.

SUMMARY

In Strengths-Based School Counseling (SBSC), the role of the counselor is to promote and advocate (a) evidence-based students' strengths that are associated with positive youth development in the academic, personal-social, and/or career areas, and (b) those environments that have been empirically shown to be associated with or which nurture those strengths. In implementing that role, the school counselor is less concerned about how much time is being devoted to a particular professional function or service (e.g., counseling, consultation, etc.) and more concerned with whether that function or service is producing the desired outcomes.

In SBSC, some of the standard professional functions or services have different emphases than in traditional and recent school-counselor role statements. Counseling, both individual and group, emphasizes strength promotion rather than deficit reduction. Classroom guidance, while coordinated by the school counselor, is implemented by the school's professional staff and revolves around organized, evidence-based programs for the K–12 sequence. In more indirect, systemic efforts, promotion-oriented developmental advocacy at the school level is emphasized. Consultation focuses on increasing the strengths-enhancing capacity of the environment for positive youth development rather than on problem reduction. Coordination activities link students to programs and activities, both in and out of school, that foster personal strengths in the academic, career, and personal social areas. Moreover, the strengths-based school counselor collaborates with other professionals and community members, and engages in leadership activities that promote and advocate the development of student strengths and strengths-enhancing environments. School counselors must be responsive to accountability concerns with respect to the services they provide. Specifically, they need to demonstrate that, as a result of counseling services received, students acquire or improve targeted strengths in the academic, personal/social, and/or career domains which are associated with positive youth development.

KEY POINTS

The Traditional Role of the School Counselor

- The traditional role of a school counselor focuses on the services of counseling, consultation, and coordination (the three Cs). Classroom guidance often replaces coordination at the elementary level. Typically, the services are remedial in nature, lack clear objectives, are not programmatic, and are inefficient because they target individuals rather than groups. Additional duties assigned by the principal may also be included in the traditional role of a school counselor.

The Contemporary Role of the School Counselor

- The role of a contemporary school counselor includes an organized comprehensive developmental program that is integral to education, is based on a developmental framework, services the entire student population, and is concerned with demonstrating accountability.
- The contemporary role includes the additional functions of advocacy, collaboration and teaming, and leadership.

- It is recommended that school counselors devote 80% of their time to direct services in the contemporary role.

The Strengths-Based School Counselor's Role

- In SBSC, advocacy is clearly a key counselor function. Many types of advocacy are discussed, but promotion-oriented developmental client and system advocacy at the school-building level should constitute the majority of the school counselor's efforts.
- The strengths-based school counselor's role includes leadership, advocacy, coordination, collaboration, and consultation, but it does not revolve around a prescribed percentage of time allotted for each of these functions. The functions often overlap and are hard to differentiate. Instead, the choice of functions or services are based on student and school needs, existing theory, and outcome data that have been shown to be related to developmental promotion and enhancement of the school environment.

Direct Services of the Strengths-Based School Counselor

- School counselors can employ strengths-oriented counseling by incorporating and modifying existing theories such as wellness, hope therapy, the broaden-and-build theory of positive emotions, positive psychology, Solution-Focused Brief Counseling, and cognitive-behavior therapy.
- Individual and group counseling focuses on promoting student strengths for all students, rather than on simply reducing negative emotions and remediating student deficits. Strengths-based school counselors attack problems primarily by building assets and protective factors.
- Specifically in individual counseling, counselors use a strengths perspective and incorporate positive psychology to help students. Counselors focus more attention on explicitly noting client strengths and confrontations that are based in client strengths rather than client deficits, commenting on small steps the client is making to develop strengths, not reinforcing clients' negative views by associating difficulties with a stable characteristic, and not dwelling on negative patterns of behavior in clients.
- Strengths-oriented school counselors also devote more attention to positive emotions rather than negative emotions in individual counseling based on the broaden-and-build theory of positive emotions. Increased positive emotions encourage broadened mindsets and problem solving, which helps build psychological resilience and enduring personal resources.
- Group counseling should be utilized to reach a larger percentage of students and to enable group process, modeling, and skill building. School counselors should explore conducting group sessions during lunch, in after-school programs, or before school to ensure that the school staff is supportive of the groups.
- Student concerns that require intensive treatments are served through referral to and collaboration with community agencies and private practitioners. Even in cases where students are referred, strengths-based school counselors should have knowledge of best practices for general problems experienced by children and adolescents so that referrals and collaborations are successful.

- Counselors employ empirically-supported or evidence-based counseling interventions whenever possible and attempt to document the effectiveness of these interventions.
- Assessment within SBSC requires attention to strengths as well as deficits and to environmental and contextual factors as well as to factors focused on the individual. A four-front assessment framework for SBSC is congruent with the positive-psychology framework, although the assessment of personal strengths and environment is of especial relevance.
- Assessment of student strengths and the school environment can be achieved using many formal and informal instruments. If cost is a prohibitive consideration for standardized measures, school counselors can use alternatives such as student-concern surveys and entrance and exit surveys. As strengths-based assessment receives more emphasis in the coming years, school counselors will have far greater access to standardized measures.
- School counselors should implement classroom guidance in a purposeful, effective manner. They may need to demonstrate how the guidance curriculum can enhance student development and show how classroom guidance can be integrated into the academic curriculum rather than added on to it. Although the results of research on traditional classroom guidance as conducted by the school counselor have been mixed, research on classroom-based social and emotional learning programs suggests that multiyear, multicomponent programs are more likely to foster enduring benefits for students.
- School counselors must collaborate with teachers and administrators to coordinate a classroom guidance curriculum that will impact all students.
- In all levels, the school counselor must ensure that a classroom guidance program addresses local contextual and cultural factors that may affect its implementation, is competently and consistently applied, and has its actual effects in the local setting evaluated.

Indirect Services or System-Level Functions of the Strengths-Based School Counselor

- Emphasis on indirect services such as consultation, advocacy, collaboration, coordination, and accountability has increased in an attempt to meet the complex needs of an increasingly diverse student population in schools.
- The strengths-based school counselor will engage in consultation efforts with teachers and parents that are time sensitive and focus on helping to foster student potential and already existing strengths as well as strengths-enhancing environments. Solution-Focused consultation and conjoint behavioral consultation are two consultation approaches that are compatible with SBSC. Conjoint behavioral consultation simultaneously targets two systems—home and school—and has been shown to be more effective than a single-system intervention.
- School counselors will participate in coordination activities by linking students to programs and activities, both in and out of the school setting, which enhance personal strengths in the academic, career, and personal/social areas. This coordinating function is especially important because time in structured extracurricular activities has

been found to be associated with higher academic achievement, higher self-concept and life satisfaction, a decreased likelihood of dropping out of school, and future prosocial behaviors in young adulthood.

- School counselors can collaborate within schools as they interact with administrators and teachers, with community agencies as they link students with needed outside services, and with families as they conduct a multitude of skill training or advocacy programs.

- The main focus of the school counselor's leadership efforts is directed at building-level issues. The school counselor can display leadership by developing and maintaining an effective comprehensive school-counseling program in conjunction with other stakeholders. As a leader, the school counselor is also able to evaluate the school climate and how its policies, procedures, and programs are impacting student development.

- The school counselor should analyze and disaggregate data with respect to the three domains (academic, career, and personal/social) in order to elicit support for appropriate policies and programs. The counselor can then engage in structural leadership to implement evidence-based programs and policies that have been shown to foster positive youth development. Upon implementation, the counselor will evaluate these programs and policies to ensure positive outcomes.

- Symbolic, political, and human-resource leadership at the building level are other forms of leadership that the strengths-based school counselor will display. Symbolic leadership involves articulating a strengths-oriented vision for all students within a school, political leadership deals with mobilizing staff and community support to make needed changes, and human resource leadership refers to empowering and inspiring others to implement a strengths-oriented environment.

3

Promoting Academic Development: Basic Principles

OUTLINE

The Traditional Role of the School Counselor in Academic Development

The Contemporary Role of the School Counselor in Academic Development

The Strengths-Based School Counselor's Role in Academic Development

Academic Strengths to Promote

Self-regulated Learning • *Effective Learning and Study Strategies* • *Intrinsic and Extrinsic Motivation* • *Goal Orientation* • *Self-efficacy* • *Attributions*

Academic Enablers

Motivation and Study Skills • *Academic Engagement* • *Interpersonal Skills*

Strengths-Enhancing Academic Environments

Satisfy Basic Needs • *Promote Cooperation* • *Stimulate Situational Interest* • *Encourage Complementary Roles of Home, School, and Community*

Visual Aids

Two Approaches to Promoting Academic Strengths • *Types of Learning and Study Strategies* • *The Self-Determination Continuum* • *Two Goal Orientations and Their Approach and Avoidance Forms* • *Characteristics of People with Learning Versus Performance Goals* • *Characteristics of Strengths-Enhancing Environments* • *Teacher-mediated and Peer-mediated Learning: Potential Advantages and Disadvantages*

Summary

Key Points

THE TRADITIONAL ROLE OF THE SCHOOL
COUNSELOR IN ACADEMIC DEVELOPMENT

School counselors have always had an ancillary role in the academic mission of schools and in student academic development. Depending on the schooling level, that role has included a variety of responsibilities. Among these are (a) scheduling academic courses; (b) placing students in academic courses or tracks; (c) educational and career counseling coupled with advising regarding course selection; (d) placing students in internship or work-study sites required by particular courses of study; (d) maintaining academic records; (e) teaching study and test-taking skills; (f) administering tests; (g) and/or coordinating testing programs.

Perhaps unknowingly, historical factors appear to have impacted today's school counselors as they function to facilitate student academic development. The number of school counselors in this country was increased tremendously as a result of funds provided by the National Defense Education Act (NDEA) of 1958. The NDEA was a response to the Soviet Union having placed a satellite in Earth's orbit before the United States and to the associated fears regarding our national defense that the event spawned (Herr, 2003). An important purpose of the NDEA was to encourage more students to go to college, to major in the "hard" sciences, and, ultimately, to find employment in defense and defense-related fields. The NDEA required states to submit plans for how they would test secondary students so that the most capable could be encouraged to go to college and study the hard sciences (Herr, 2003). A key element in the NDEA was the preparation of a large number of secondary-school counselors. These counselors would then test students, identify those capable of majoring in the sciences in college, and encourage them to follow that path (Herr, 2003).

This test and select orientation, coupled with the tendency of many school districts to use tracking as an approach to educating students has influenced, often unwittingly, how school counselors have functioned up to now. It placed a major focus on the academic development of a small percentage of students (e.g., the college bound), deprived or failed to encourage optimal academic development for a large number of students, and seriously underestimated student potential. In addition, it typically resulted in school counselors serving as the gatekeepers to academic success—allowing access to some and keeping others out—rather than as the facilitators and advocates of academic success for all (Hart & Jacobi, 1992).

Over the years, school counselors have also been directed to work with failing or underachieving students. Much of this work, however, has taken the form of arranging for remedial instruction or providing supportive counseling in an effort to help these students catch up to their peers academically. Once again, the school counselor's role in student academic development was restricted in scope and confined to only a portion of the student population.

THE CONTEMPORARY ROLE OF THE SCHOOL COUNSELOR IN ACADEMIC DEVELOPMENT

A number of factors are resulting in a redefinition of the role and functions of school counselors with respect to student academic development. Educational reform initiatives, the high-stakes testing movement, the No Child Left Behind (NCLB) Act, the Education Trust and Dewitt-Wallace-Reader's Digest Fund National Initiative for Transforming School Counseling (The Education Trust, 1999), The American School Counseling Association (ASCA) National Standards for School Counseling Programs (Campbell & Dahir, 1997), and The National Model for School Counseling Programs (ASCA, 2003; Bowers & Hatch, 2002) are among the most salient of these factors.

Two primary concerns have driven much of the current reform efforts in education (Erford, House, & Martin, 2003). On the one hand, there is the demand to produce a well-educated and knowledgeable workforce for an increasingly technologically based economy that must compete in an international marketplace. On the other hand, is the educational system's challenge to respond to the complex and multifaceted needs of an increasingly diverse student population that includes greater numbers of low-income, minority, and immigrant families.

Both of these concerns have been manifested in initiatives designed to raise educational standards and to hold students, educators, schools, and school districts accountable for student academic achievement by evaluating their performance on high-stakes achievement tests and imposing penalties or rewards for results. Cimbricz (2002), for example, noted that 48 states have a statewide assessment program aligned with specific state educational standards. Moreover, with the passage of the No Child Left Behind Act on January 8, 2002, the federal government decreed that (a) states create their own standards for what a child should know and learn for all grades; (b) states must test every student's progress toward those standards by using tests aligned with the standards; (c) every state, school district, and school will be expected to make adequate yearly progress toward meeting those state standards as measured by disaggregating test results for students who are economically disadvantaged, from racial or ethnic minority groups, have disabilities, or have limited English proficiency; (d) school and school district performance will be publicly reported in district and state report cards; and (e) districts or schools that continually fail to make adequate yearly progress toward the standards will be held accountable and subject to various sanctions such as state takeover or the hiring of a private-management contractor (No Child Left Behind; USDOE, 2001a).

Educational reform, in turn, has impacted school counselors in a variety of ways. As an example, school counselors are increasingly being called upon to demonstrate their value in bolstering student achievement. In many instances, these demonstrations have required them to assume extremely time-consuming test-coordination responsibilities in their state's high-stakes program (Brown, Galassi, & Akos, 2004; Burnham & Jackson, 2000). Typically, these responsibilities do not capitalize on their professional skills and involve tasks such as arranging for testing modifications for students with special needs, recruiting and training test proctors/administrators, and distributing, collecting, and counting materials (e.g., pencils, calculators, rulers), achievement tests, and answer sheets.

However, more substantial and professional-level responsibilities have been recommended for school counselors in student academic development. The Education Trust Initiative (1999), for example, defined the school-counseling profession in direct relation to student academic success.

> School counseling is a profession that focuses on the relations and interactions between students and their school environment with the expressed purpose of reducing the effect of environmental and institutional barriers that impede student academic success. The profession fosters conditions that ensure educational equity, access, and academic success for all students K–12.

Advocacy, leadership, teaming and collaboration, counseling and coordination, assessment, and use of data are essential school-counselor functions in the Education Trust's new vision for the profession.

The ASCA National Standards for School Counseling Programs (Campbell & Dahir, 1997) and its National Model for School Counseling Programs (ASCA, 2003; Bowers & Hatch, 2002) assert enhancement of student achievement as the primary goal of the school counseling program. In the National Standards and the National Model, school counselors are encouraged to become catalysts for educational change, assume a leadership role in educational reform, and serve as advocates for students as they strive to meet school demands and prepare for transition to options after high school. Given that the purpose of a school counseling program is to promote and enhance the learning process for all students, ASCA advances three academic standards:

> Standard A: Students will acquire the attitudes, knowledge, and skills that contribute to effective learning in school and across the life span.
>
> Standard B: Students will complete school with the academic preparation essential to choose from a wide range of substantial postsecondary options, including college.
>
> Standard C: Students will understand the relationship of academics to the world of work, and life at home, and within the community. (Campbell & Dahir, 1997, p. 20)

Each standard is accompanied by a list of student competencies and a set of indicators that define the specific knowledge, skills, and attitudes that students should demonstrate as a result of participating in a school counseling program. "The competencies are not exhaustive; however, they represent the student attitudes, knowledge, and skills suggested by professionals participating in field reviews" (Dahir, 2001, p. 324). Thus, the National Model (ASCA; Bowers & Hatch, 2002) provides a valuable source of direction for school counseling programs, and, as we will discuss, Strengths-Based School Counseling (SBSC) augments that direction.

THE STRENGTHS-BASED SCHOOL COUNSELOR'S ROLE IN ACADEMIC DEVELOPMENT

With its emphasis on promoting strengths, SBSC further articulates how school counselors can operationalize their emerging role in enhancing academic success for all students. The ASCA National Standards outline a set of student competencies for academic development, and SBSC specifies both the research-documented strengths and strengths-enhancing environments that are actually associated with academic success. Moreover, SBSC identifies examples of the research-documented counseling interventions for academic development that school counselors need to guide their practice.

In this chapter, we discuss those research-identified academic strengths that school counselors need to promote through direct-service and systemic-level interventions (see Table 3–1). Historically, school counselors have typically focused more on the personal and social development of students rather than on their academic development (The Education Trust, 1999). As such, the graduate education of school counselors in basic principles that impact student academic development (e.g., learning, motivation, self-regulation, and classroom management) have not tended to be as strong as in the area of principles that impact student personal and social development (e.g., personality theory, counseling theory). Given that school counselors must play a key role in student academic development, it is imperative that they have a firm grasp of those related principles. At the same time, we recognize that a number of these principles and concepts may be new and unfamiliar to many readers and

TABLE 3–1.
Two Approaches to Promoting Academic Strengths

Self-Regulated Learning	*Academic Enablers*
Learning/study strategies	Study skills
Motivation	Motivation
Goal Orientation	Academic engagement
Self-efficacy	Interpersonal skills
Attributions	

that it will take time to integrate them into practice. However, knowledge of those principles will enable school counselors to function more effectively as consultants to teachers with respect to learning, performance, and classroom-management issues as well as to provide their own successful classroom guidance to students. Moreover, the school counselor's focus on the role of developmental factors in student academic success nicely complements the teacher's focus on (teaching) knowledge and content. Therefore, we will also discuss some of the basic principles that facilitate the development of research-identified student academic strengths and the interventions that school counselors can use to enhance those strengths.

We will also review the type of environments that have been documented to enhance student academic success. In addition to advocating for systemic change to remove barriers to academic success for minorities and other traditionally underserved groups of students (e.g., The Education Trust, 1999), school counselors must take the additional step to articulate strategies to cultivate environments and policies that nurture achievement. They must also partner with other educators, parents, and community members to develop and sustain these strengths-enhancing academic environments for all students.

A key issue in that regard is for 21st-century counselors to collaborate with educators and others to eliminate academic achievement gaps (Sink, 2005).

> Without question, the number one challenge facing American public education today is the achievement gaps among different students. Achievement gaps exist when groups of students with relatively equal ability do not achieve in school at the same levels; in fact, one group often far exceeds the achievement levels of others. Gaps in achievement exist across the nation and can be found based upon race/ethnicity, language background, disability status, and gender. (NEA, 2006)

In both this chapter and in Chapter 4, we discuss the strengths and strengths-enhancing environments that counselors can use to promote academic development for all students. In addition, we highlight some of the resources regarding interventions and environments that are especially relevant to racial/ethnicity-based achievement gaps (e.g., http://www.aypf.org/publications/rmaa/index.html) as well as to achievement gaps more broadly defined (www.achievementgaps.org). We now turn to a consideration of the specific individual strengths that all students need for academic success.

ACADEMIC STRENGTHS TO PROMOTE

Sink (2005) asserted that school counselors can influence student academic development and performance, but that their influence is largely secondary or tertiary to other educational activities in the school. Rather than having an *immediate* impact on academic outcomes, most counseling interventions are likely to have an *intermediate* effect on these outcomes as a result of having a more immediate impact on student learning. Thus, these interventions can enhance the learning skills students need to master subject matter in different classrooms, which, in turn, can impact such academic outcomes as grades and test scores. One of the most important sets of these skills is self-regulated learning.

Self-regulated Learning

In conjunction with students, teachers, and parents, school counselors have an important role to play in facilitating students' academic development as self-regulated learners (Lapan, Kardash, & Turner, 2002). In his review of research on what middle-school counselors can do to foster student academic development and learning, Sink (2005) identified the critical role in academic development and performance of interventions that help students self-regulate their learning.

Zimmerman (2000) reported that students who have trouble self-regulating their academic studying perform more poorly in school (Zimmerman & Martinez-Pons, 1986, 1988) and present more behavior problems for their teachers (Brody, Stoneman, & Flor, 1996). In contrast, self-regulated learners set higher academic goals, learn more effectively, and achieve at higher levels in the classroom (Ormrod, 1999).

Although there are several theories of self-regulated learning (Zimmerman, 2001), Pintrich (2000) proposed a common working definition:

> Self-regulated learning is an active, constructive process whereby learners set goals for their learning and then attempt to monitor, regulate, and control their cognition, motivation, and behavior, guided and constrained by their goals and the contextual features in the environment. These self-regulatory activities can mediate the relationships between individuals and the context, and their overall achievement. (p. 453)

As self-regulated learners, students evaluate the results of their learning and adjust their efforts accordingly. Self-motivation, goal setting, planning, attention control, application of learning strategies, self-monitoring, and self-evaluation are all elements of self-regulated learning (Ormrod, 1999). As we shall see in the next chapter, school counselors can help students to develop or enhance their capabilities in each of these areas either through direct-service interventions such as counselor-teacher co-led study-skill interventions or indirectly, for example, through consultation efforts with students' teachers and parents directed at homework completion.

For Zimmerman (2000), self-regulation involves three cyclical phases: (a) forethought, (b) performance/volitional control, and (c) self-reflection.

Each phase includes several important processes (see Zimmerman for a detailed description). *Forethought* involves processes related to one's motivation and analysis of the task (e.g., "What does the task require me to do, and how much do I want to do it?"). Goal setting (e.g., deciding to solve the set of long division problems assigned for homework), strategic planning to accomplish the task (e.g., deciding how, where, and when to complete the assignment), judging the likelihood of completing the task successfully (self-efficacy), and assessing the personal desirability of doing so are among the self-regulatory processes and beliefs that comprise the forethought phase. The second phase, *performance or volitional control*, involves self-control processes such as self-instruction that enable students to focus on the task and optimize their effort (e.g., systematically guiding oneself through each of the steps needed to solve the problems). It also involves attention-focusing and self-observation processes to track performance (e.g., monitoring whether one is focusing on the task and reminding oneself to avoid distractions). In the final or *self-reflection* phase, students judge the adequacy of their performance (self-evaluate) against a standard or goal (e.g., checking whether one followed all of the long division steps correctly and avoided making careless mistakes), make attributions (e.g., due to effort, ability, luck, etc.) about the cause of a successful or unsuccessful performance (e.g., "I got it right because I am smart.") and react to themselves (e.g., with self-satisfaction or dissatisfaction) with regard to their performance (e.g., "Well, I'm not happy with myself for getting it wrong. Next time, I need to be more careful about following all of the steps, and I will get it right.").

Acquiring self-regulatory competence is a developmental process that involves inducing the necessary skills or strategies through observing a model(s) perform them followed by emulating the general pattern of the model's performance, often with assistance, feedback, and reinforcement (Zimmerman, 2000). The school counselor seeks to facilitate this developmental process by increasing exposure to self-regulated learning in the classroom, in small groups, and individually. As we will discuss later, research indicates that a counselor (or teacher) who teaches study skills by actually modeling or demonstrating those skills (e.g., test taking) will be more effective than one who merely explains those skills. Independent practice of self-regulatory skills under conditions similar to those in which they have been learned (e.g., practice test-taking sessions) helps to hone these skills further. At the most advanced level of development, individuals can systematically adapt their self-regulatory skills to changing personal and contextual conditions (e.g., test-taking conditions that differ in some way from practice sessions).

At this point, we will highlight some of the key self-regulatory processes that research has shown to be associated with academic achievement. In addition, we will consider what counselors and others can do to enhance students' use of these strategies. Specifically, we will discuss effective learning and study strategies, motivation, goal orientation, self-efficacy, and attributions.

Effective Learning and Study Strategies

"Effective study skills are associated with positive outcomes across multiple academic content areas and for diverse learners" (Gettinger & Seibert, 2002, p. 350). A number of research-supported or evidence-based study skills or study strategies that facilitate learning and retention have been identified (Gettinger & Seibert, 2002; Ormrod, 1999). Unfortunately, students often fail to use these strategies for a variety of reasons, including being uninformed or misinformed about them, not knowing when to apply them, having low confidence (self-efficacy) about their ability to learn, and believing that too much effort is required to apply the strategies (Ormrod, 1999). Instruction in study skills, however, has been associated with improved academic performance across a variety of academic areas (Harvey & Goudvis, 2000).

Current approaches to study skills tend to be based on information-processing models and are premised on the assumption that students process or manipulate information to be learned in order to facilitate learning and retention (Gettinger & Seibert, 2002). There are a variety of research-documented, effective study-skills strategies. The more elaborate the strategy, the deeper the level of processing. Ormrod's (1999) list of effective study skills (see Table 3–2), for example, includes both overt and covert strategies.

Among the overt strategies is note taking, which has been shown to be positively correlated with student learning and facilitates encoding of material for retention. Reorganizing and elaborating on notes also enhances understanding and retention. Outlining and writing summaries are two additional overt strategies. Outlining, concept mapping, and graphical representation of material all serve to help students to internally organize and make connections within new material, thereby facilitating understanding and retention.

TABLE 3–2.
Types of Learning and Study Strategies

Ormrod (1999)		Weinstein and Mayer (1985)
Overt	Covert	
Note taking/reorganizing	Meaningful learning	Repetition or rehearsal-based strategies
Outlining	Elaboration	Procedural or organization-based study strategies
Writing summaries	Identifying important information	Cognitive-based study strategies
Concept mapping	Comprehension monitoring	Metacognitive-based study strategies
Graphical representation	Mnemonics	

A concept map is a diagram of the concepts or main ideas of a unit often consisting of various-sized circles linked together by lines indicating how their relationships to each other (e.g., a genealogy chart of the relationships in a step- or extended family), while graphical representation can involve a variety of visual displays of information (e.g., a map, a flowchart, pie chart, a matrix). Writing summaries of lectures and readings also helps students to integrate and retain what they are learning, because it increases their involvement in manipulating the information to be learned.

Meaningful learning and elaboration, identifying important information, comprehension monitoring, and mnemonics are covert strategies that enhance learning and studying. Meaningful learning involves relating new material to prior knowledge. In this instance, the new material is made more meaningful by linking it to something similar with which the student is already familiar rather than treating it as an isolated fact to be memorized. When students find meaning in the information that they are to learn, they have a much easier time in recalling that information because meaningfulness appears to facilitate information retrieval from long-term memory. Ormrod (1999) provided a very simple example that illustrates this point. Asking students to memorize and subsequently recall a list of the following 15 letters— MAIGUWRSENNFLOD—is a relatively difficult task, but when the same 15 letters are reorganized—MEANINGFULWORDS—into a form that is already familiar to the students, it becomes an easy task.

Elaboration, on the other hand, consists of using prior knowledge to interpret and expand on new material. Once again, the objective is to attempt to relate what is already known to what is to be learned in order to increase meaningfulness, understanding, and retention. In learning new information, people tend to impose their own interpretation or draw inferences about the information and then learn those interpretations with the actual information that has been presented. Strategies such as having students put ideas in their own words, developing their own examples of ideas that have been presented, and drawing inferences from the new information are all examples of elaboration, and elaboration tends to facilitate recall of information as compared to mere verbatim memorization (Ormrod, 1999).

Teaching students to recognize signals such as italicized words in texts, chapter summaries, or ideas or objectives of the lesson written on the chalkboard helps them to identify the most important information to be learned. In comprehension monitoring, students periodically check whether they are absorbing what they are reading or learning in class. Comprehension monitoring involves students asking themselves questions as they are reading or listening in class. Some of these questions, which are designed to check for understanding, may have been formulated prior to beginning a reading assignment and are answered as the student proceeds through it (e.g., "What is the main idea of this story?" "How is the situation in Iraq for American soldiers similar to what they faced in Vietnam?" "In what major ways, do the two wars differ?"). Students would also formulate other comprehension-monitoring questions to periodically check for understanding as they progress through a reading assignment or a class period (e.g., "How do the views of race relations in America that my teacher is expressing compare to the author's views?")

Mnemonics are "memory tricks" that facilitate the learning and recall of information (Ormrod, 1999). They include a variety of memory devices based on mechanisms such as verbal mediation, visual imagery, superimposed meaningful structure, and external retrieval cues that enhance learning and retention. *The principal is my pal* is a verbal mediation mnemonic that is commonly used by teachers to help students remember the correct spelling for the school administrator (e.g., princi*pal* rather than princi*ple*) (Ormrod, 1999).

A variety of mnemonic devices are based on visual memory. With a path mnemonic (or method of loci), for example, key places or landmarks along a well-traveled route such as a student's path to school are associated with items to be memorized (e.g., a list of the first ten presidents in order of their term of office). For example, the student leaves his or her house and goes to wait for the school bus at a place where there is a large tree (the first landmark). The tree is then associated with George Washington, the first president, who once cut down a cherry tree. The student then gets on the bus, which passes a restaurant (the second landmark). This restaurant serves beer. Adams is a type of beer that the student has seen advertised on television, so the student associates John Adams, the second president, with the restaurant. The bus then passes a bank (the third landmark); banks have Jefferson nickels. Thus, the student associates Thomas Jefferson, the third president, with the third landmark, the bank. The student then proceeds to pair additional landmarks in a meaningful way with the remaining list of presidents to be learned.

Other mnemonic devices are based on superimposed meaningful structure including acronyms and acrostics (sentences). HOMES is an acronym for learning and recalling the names and order of the great lakes—Huron, Ontario, Michigan, Erie, and Superior. As a music student, the combination of an acronym, FACE, and an acrostic, Every Good Boy Does Fine, enabled the first author of this text to remember the order of the space (FACE) and line (EGBDF) notes of the treble clef.

The discussion of study skills by Gettinger and Seibert (2002) incorporates Weinstein and Mayer's (1985) information-processing classification framework and specifies four clusters of study strategies. Repetition- or rehearsal-based study strategies are the simplest to use and are most typically taught to young students to facilitate learning/retention tasks such as spelling words (e.g., repeatedly spelling a list of words) and multiplication facts (e.g., flash cards). These strategies involve minimal processing of information, emphasize rehearsal, and incorporate mental imagery in the case of certain mnemonic devices. Procedural or organization-based study skills represent the second category. Managing time effectively, developing study schedules, and organizing materials and notebooks are examples of these skills. Cognitive-based study skills, the third category, are intended to engage students in appropriate thinking about the information to be learned. Cognitive organizers in the form of concept or semantic maps, generating (and answering) questions about the material to be learned, and generative summarization (using the student's own words to summarize new materials and concepts) are cognitive-based strategies. Their purpose is to make the new learning meaningful, in part, by integrating it with existing knowledge and organizing it to facilitate retention. The final category is meta-cognitive-based study skills. How students select, use, and monitor their learning and how they adjust their studying to varying task and environmental demands are the focus of these skills. Instruction in meta-cognitive strategies involve teaching students to ask questions to check for understanding, to check on which study strategies to use in order to solve a problem, to assess the effectiveness of a particular strategy, and to check whether a change in strategy is needed, and so forth. Table 3–2 summarizes the types of learning and study strategies that we have discussed.

Research indicates that study-skills programs are especially effective for low-ability students and that effective programs tend to be multifaceted and include a number of the strategies just discussed (Ormrod, 1999). In implementing study-skills programs or in coordinating teacher-led programs, school counselors would do well to include a variety of the known, evidence-based learning strategies that we have just discussed. In addition, Ormrod presented a number of research-based recommendations that school counselors can use in consulting with teachers about helping students employ more effective learning strategies or in conducting their own classroom guidance sessions on study skills. Among these are that instruction about effective learning strategies is more effective when: (a) it occurs in the context of a specific academic course or task (e.g., during a history class or lecture); (b) students are shown through teacher modeling and "thinking aloud" rather than told how to use the strategy (e.g., actually shown how to take notes and what notes to take for the history lesson); (c) students have a number of opportunities to practice the specific strategies with a variety of tasks (e.g., during a few history classes in which they receive feedback on notes taken and then later in science class); (d) students learn the situations in which each strategy is appropriate; (e) students are provided with graduated support (scaffolding) in initial attempts to use strategies with difficult tasks (e.g., in-depth feedback on their notes initially and abbreviated feedback/reminders in new subject areas or assignments); and (f) when students develop procedures for monitoring and evaluating their own learning (e.g., asking themselves questions such as, "Am I consistently using the note-taking procedure?" "Am I consistently taking down main ideas rather than every word?").

The recommendations just cited above raise doubts about whether the traditional forums in which counselors have taught study skills (e.g., in classroom guidance units or in individual and small group counseling sessions) represent the most effective approaches to helping students acquire and use these skills. In both instances, study skills tend to be taught outside of the learning tasks and contexts in which they will subsequently be used. As a result, students are faced with the often difficult task of having to transfer or adapt the generic study skills to the specific learning tasks with which they are confronted.

Given these limitations, the strengths-based school counselor may want to try a different approach such as working as a collaborator and co-leader with the classroom teacher in study-skill instruction. The counselor and classroom teacher can incorporate study-skills instruction in the context of language arts, mathematics, or any other academic subject. Incorporating this instruction within the academic curriculum has a number of potential benefits. It provides students with opportunities to learn and practice study skills directly within the contexts in which they will be used and with the support needed to apply them to realistic learning tasks. Moreover, these new skills should enhance student academic achievement in the short term and facilitate their academic development in the long term. In addition, this collaboration should help teachers and administrators to view the school counselor as an essential partner in fostering student academic development.

Admittedly, this proposal has not been empirically evaluated. However, such collaboration is not without precedent. Lapan, Gysbers, Hughey, and Arni (1993) evaluated a program in which high-school counselors and teachers worked together to provide an opportunity for students to develop academic skills while exploring career issues within the language arts curriculum. English teachers presented instruction on how to write a research paper that included selecting and using references, organizing information for personal use, summarizing information, and using various sources of information, while the counselors emphasized connecting self-understanding to possible occupational and educational alternatives, exploring several occupational areas, and developing tentative postsecondary plans. The collaboration resulted in significant increases in vocational identity for students and in significantly higher English grades for girls.

Of course, there are examples of successful traditional counselor-led study-skill interventions. Brigman's (Brigman & Campbell, 2003; Brigman & Goodman, 2001) student success skills (SSS) group counseling and classroom guidance employs school counselor-led study skills along with several other interventions. The SSS program consists of a minimum of three classroom guidance lessons plus eight weekly group sessions and four monthly group booster sessions. Three sets of skills that research has shown to be associated with children and adolescents developing academic and social competence are involved. These are (a) cognitive and meta-cognitive skills such as goal setting, making outlines and cognitive maps, chunking key ideas into small groups, picking out the most important ideas to study, making and reviewing note cards, progress monitoring, and memory skills; (b) social skills such as interpersonal skills, social problem solving, listening, maintaining several study buddies, and teamwork; and (c) self-management skills such as managing attention, motivation, and anger. The SSS intervention has been shown to improve school social behavior of treatment students in grades 5, 6, 8, and 9 and to result in significant gains in their reading and math scores on standardized tests as compared to no treatment comparison group students (Brigman & Goodman, 2003). Moreover, these results have largely been replicated in two other studies (Campbell & Brigman, 2005; Webb, Brigman, & Campbell, 2005) and make the SSS a promising academic intervention for the strengths-based school counselor to consider.

Another program involving study skills that shows promise is Solution Shop (Cook & Kaffenberger, 2003). It consists of study-skills instruction, Solution-Focused group and individual counseling, and individualized tutoring. Fifty-seven percent of 35 seventh- and eighth-grade students (largely Hispanic and African American) who had more than two core grades of F improved their grade point average (GPA) after nine weeks in the program. Only two students (5.7%) had a lower GPA, but the program has not been evaluated against a wait-list comparison group.

Intrinsic and Extrinsic Motivation

Research has shown that children's academic motivation, attitudes toward school in general, and toward specific subject areas declines over time (Hidi & Harackiewicz, 2000). A student's academic achievement is unquestionably affected by motivation to learn, and, as such, the goal of facilitating the development of self-regulated learners is especially important.

Self-regulated learners are, to a large degree, intrinsically motivated. Intrinsic motivation is ". . . the inherent tendency to seek out novelty and challenges, to extend and exercise one's capacities, to explore, and to learn" (Ryan & Deci, 2000, p. 71). Individuals who are intrinsically motivated perform an activity for the satisfaction inherent in the activity. In contrast, extrinsic motivation involves performing an activity in order to attain an outcome (e.g., a reward) that is separate from the activity itself. People with intrinsic as opposed to extrinsic motivation have more interest, excitement, and confidence, which in turn is manifested as enhanced performance, persistence, creativity, heightened vitality, self-esteem, and general well-being, even when the two groups evidence the same level of perceived competence (self-efficacy) for an activity (Ryan & Deci).

With respect to learning, individuals who are intrinsically motivated are more likely to pursue a task on their own initiative, keep their attention focused on it, to learn meaningfully, and persist at the task or assignment in the face of failure (Ormrod, 1999). External rewards may even have adverse effects on learning and undermine intrinsic motivation for engaging in an activity. This undermining can occur under a variety of circumstances including when external rewards are (a) perceived as controlling or manipulating behavior rather than providing information about progress; (b) perceived as communicating that the task is not worth doing for its own sake; (c) interpreted as bribes or perceived as limiting an individual's freedom; (d) involve threats and deadlines; and (e) involve surveillance and evaluation of performance by other people (Ormrod).

Therefore, whenever possible, counselors, teachers, and parents should attempt to encourage the development of intrinsic motivation toward learning in students as one approach to enhancing academic achievement. In consulting with teachers, for example, counselors could suggest that, when possible, they allow students to pick assignments or projects based on personal interests. Also, counselors could encourage student participation in school clubs or extracurricular activities that develop academic interests (e.g., Odyssey of the Mind, Science Olympiad, school newspaper).

However, extrinsic motivation is not always to be shunned. Providing an extrinsic reward contingent on performance may be useful and even essential when (a) students begin a new and difficult or frustrating task; (b) encounter a task in which they have no initial interest; (c) are academically unmotivated; or (d) when a desirable behavior may not occur without it. Hidi and Harackiewicz (2000), for example, noted that a combination of intrinsic rewards and external rewards, particularly those that provide performance feedback, may be required to maintain students' engagement during especially difficult periods of learning. When students first begin to learn to read, many find it to be quite difficult, and providing tangible (e.g. stickers) and social (e.g., verbal praise) reward for sounding out words can often enhance performance and persistence in the activity. As they become more proficient, students often find the stories that they read enjoyable and seek more of them as intrinsic interest in reading increases. At this point, the external rewards for reading are no longer necessary, and, in some cases, their extended use may even decrease students' interest in reading. Extrinsic rewards can also promote student achievement when they are provided on a group rather than an individual basis, for example, as where each member contributes to obtaining a reward such as in cooperative learning. (Fantuzzo & Ginsburg-Block, 1998). Thus, when counselors and teachers use extrinsic rewards to motivate students to complete difficult or low-learning tasks, they should emphasize the use of group contingencies in which each student's performance influences whether the group achieves its learning goal. In these instances, group cohesion will tend to augment or enhance the motivation of individual students.

In general, Harter and Jackson (1992) found that children showed three different patterns of motivation with respect to school learning. Some children displayed extrinsic motivation in some subjects and intrinsic motivation in other subjects, while other children displayed either extrinsic or intrinsic motivation in all subjects. The implication of this finding is that a school counselor would want to identify a student's current motivation (e.g., extrinsic or intrinsic) in an academic subject area prior to developing either a consultation or a direct service intervention to enhance academic accomplishment in that area. Some ways of doing that include observing and/or talking with the student about that subject and obtaining teacher and/or parent feedback about the student's interest and performance in that subject area.

Ryan and Deci (2000) offered a substantial revision and extension of the intrinsic-extrinsic view of motivation. They proposed a self-determination continuum of motivation that ranges from nonself-determined, amotivated (e.g., the state of lacking the intention to act), non-regulated behavior at one end to self-determined, intrinsically motivated, internally regulated behavior at the other end (see Fig. 3–1).[1] Thus, a student who functions at the left end of the continuum either does not act (e.g., does not study) or simply "goes through the motions" of studying. Amotivation may result from not valuing an activity, not feeling competent to do it (e.g., low self-efficacy) or not expecting it to yield a desired outcome (e.g., low-outcome expectancy). Although Ryan and Deci do not offer specific interventions for school counselors who work with academically amotivated students, we can speculate on counseling-related interventions that might have potential for addressing each of the proposed causes, such as (a) a career-related work or internship experience that would connect the importance of studying to obtaining a desired job; (b) tutoring to build academic skills and self-efficacy in an academic area; (c) cross-aged mentoring by older student role models who indicate how studying has been linked to obtaining more immediately desired outcomes (e.g., participation in interscholastic sports or extracurricular activities) for them.

As the figure demonstrates, promoting academic motivation is more involved than many counselors might presume. Within the continuum, Ryan and Deci (2000) identified four types of extrinsic motivation. These types of extrinsic motivation become less externally and more internally regulated as one proceeds through the continuum. In other words, the individual rather than circumstances outside of the individual increasingly controls his of her own actions as one proceeds from left to right along the continuum.

External regulation, the first type, involves performing a behavior solely to obtain an external reward (e.g., reading for stickers), satisfy an external demand, or avoid a punishment (e.g., reading to avoid losing recess time) and represents extrinsic motivation as previously discussed. Introjected regulation is a second form of extrinsic motivation. In this instance, an individual performs a behavior to avoid guilt or anxiety or to maintain pride or feelings of self-worth (e.g., doing well academically to obtain parental praise or to avoid disappointing parents). The individual is internally regulating the behavior in accord with some perceived external standard or rule, but the individual doesn't fully accept the regulation (e.g., the rule) as his or her own. Next, in

---

[1]It should be noted, however, that Ryan and Deci do not see it as a developmental continuum in the sense that individuals must progress through each stage in order to reach the next stage.

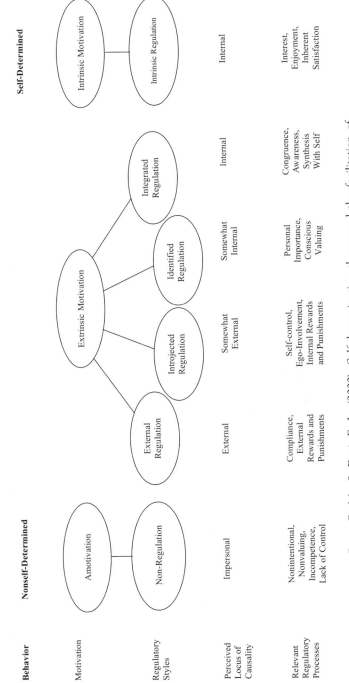

FIGURE 3–1. The self-determination continuum showing types of motivations with their regulatory styles, loci of causality, and corresponding processes.

Ryan, R. M., & Deci, E. L. (2000). Self-determination theory and the facilitation of intrinsic motivation, social development, and well-being. *American Psychologist, 55,* 68–78. © American Psychological Association. Reprinted with permission.

identified regulation, the individual has accepted not only the regulation of the behavior but also sees the behavior as being personally important. In this instance, a student values learning and academic success because it is perceived as a way to improve his or her lifestyle and future standard of living (e.g., getting good grades in order to go to college and obtain a higher-paying job). Integrated regulation is the fourth and most autonomous form of self-regulation within the extrinsic motivation portion of the continuum. Integrated regulation involves fully accepting the desirability of certain behaviors as well as integrating them with one's other needs and values. Thus, a student devotes a great deal of time to studying science because he/she wants to become a doctor in order to further his or her self-concept of a person who improves the well-being of others. The student's actions are still somewhat extrinsic in that they are done to attain separable outcomes rather than for inherent enjoyment.

For our purposes, the extrinsic motivation portion of the continuum is especially important to understand because research cited by Ryan and Deci (2000) indicates that the more autonomous forms of extrinsic motivation are associated with more engagement, better performance, lower dropout, higher-quality learning, and better teacher ratings. Thus, the more autonomous forms of extrinsic motivation are likely to yield academic development and achievement outcomes that approximate those from behavior that is intrinsically motivated, intrinsically regulated, and self-determined. For school counselors and teachers then, the key task may be to assist most students in developing increasingly autonomous levels of extrinsic motivation rather than to shift from primarily extrinsically motivated to primarily intrinsically motivated academic behavior.

But how can this shift toward more integrated, internally regulated motivation in students be accomplished? Traditionally, school counselors are likely to think in terms of individual counseling, group counseling, and classroom guidance interventions such as those that attempt to get students to explore personal values with respect to long-range plans and to connect what they are supposed to be learning in school with their career goals (e.g., through internships, service learning, virtual reality, or other simulated learning experiences). Moreover, these interventions may prove to be effective with a number of students. However, as far as Ryan and Deci (2000) are concerned, the answer to this question for most students lies at the system or environmental level and involves the extent to which the learning conditions in the environment (e.g., the classroom and the school) meet three basic needs in students: (a) relatedness, (b) competence, and (c) autonomy.

In the environment section of this chapter, we will review the role of these needs in learning as well as some of the environmental conditions that (a) satisfy those needs, (b) enhance internalized and intrinsic motivation, and (c) support academic achievement.

Goal Orientation

Understanding how students orient themselves to goals can help counselors and teachers predict strategies that will motivate these students to achieve academically. Researchers have identified two main types of goal orientations involved in academic achievement motivation. These orientations have been discussed under a variety of designations including learning versus performance goals (Dweck & Leggett, 1988), mastery versus performance goals (Ames, 1992), and task-involved versus ego-involved goals (Nicholls, 1984). Goal orientations have also been differentiated in terms of whether they are directed toward securing something desirable such as good grades (approach focus) or avoiding something negative (avoidance focus) such as parental disapproval.

For the purposes of our discussion, we have adopted Pintrich's (2000) two-way classification system in which goals are classified based on whether they exemplify a mastery (learning) or performance orientation on the one hand, coupled with an approach or avoidance focus on the other. Using these designations, mastery goals involve attempts to improve competence, knowledge, skills, and learning based on self-referenced standards (e.g., "I really want to learn how to read."), while performance goals consist of efforts to demonstrate superiority over others in order to demonstrate ability and self-worth (e.g., "I want to be a better reader than anyone in the first grade in this school."). An approach focus leads individuals to move toward more positive ends (e.g., "If I learn how to read, then I can read the stories that I like all by myself."), whereas an avoidance focus leads them to move away from or to try to prevent negative outcomes (e.g., "If I'm the best reader in the first grade in this school, then my parents won't be mad at me."). Thus, a mastery-approach focus to learning would involve attempts to master an assignment, gain new knowledge, and improve understanding (e.g., "I like learning to read because it's fun, and you learn new things."), and, in contrast to a performance-avoidance focus to learning which would involve attempts to not look stupid or dumb in comparison to other students ("If I don't learn to read better than anyone else in the first grade in this school, my parents are going to think I'm dumb."). Table 3–3 presents Pintrich's classification system, the standards for each goal orientation, and the other terms that have been used in the literature to refer to each goal orientation. With respect to the table, Pintrich noted that it is unclear whether the mastery-avoidance goal exists, and no research has been conducted on it.

Most of the existing research on goal orientation has been conducted on the mastery-performance (learning-performance) distinction and indicates that students who adopt a mastery-approach goal orientation engage in more self-regulated learning than students who do not (Pintrich, 2000). Mastery goals are more likely to be associated with a variety of beneficial learning outcomes such as students monitoring and controlling their cognitions and attributions (e.g., their beliefs about the causes of success and failure), their motivation,

TABLE 3–3.
Two Goal Orientations and Their Approach and Avoidance Forms

	Approach Focus	Avoidance Focus
Mastery orientation	Focus on mastering task, learning, understanding	Focus on avoiding misunderstanding, avoiding not learning or not mastering task
	Use of standards of self-improvement, progress, deep understanding of task	Use of standards of not being wrong, not doing it incorrectly relative to task
	(Also referred to as learning goal, task goal, task-involved goal)	(Rarely referred to in the literature)
Performance orientation	Focus on being superior, besting others, being the smartest, best at task in comparison to others	Focus on avoiding inferiority, not looking stupid or dumb in comparison to others
	Use of normative standards such as getting best or highest grades, being top or best performer in class	Use of normative standards of not getting the worst grades, being lowest performer in class
	(Also referred to as performance goal, ego-involved goal, self-enhancing ego orientation, relative ability goal)	(Also referred to as performance goal, ego-involved goal, self-defeating ego orientation)

Reprinted from Pintrich, P. R. (2000). The role of goal orientation in self-regulated learning. In M. Boekaerts, P. R. Pintrich, & M. Zeidner (Eds.), *Handbook of self-regulation* (p. 477). San Diego, CA: Academic Press © with permission from Elsevier.

and behavior. In addition, these students tend to use learning strategies such as comprehension monitoring, deeper-processing strategies (e.g., paraphrasing and summarizing) and organizational strategies (e.g., outlining) (Pintrich), while performance goals are more likely to be associated with negative outcomes and withdrawal of effort. "Generally, the research shows that adopting a mastery (learning) goal has positive implications for self-efficacy, task value, interest, attributions, and affect" (Pintrich, 2000, p. 482). In contrast, "research suggests that students who adopt performance goals avoid challenge, use superficial and effort-minimizing learning strategies, and experience impaired problem-solving," and that these effects are more evident for individuals low in perceived competence (Hidi & Harackiewicz, 2000, p. 161).

Table 3–4 presents a summary of the learning-related differences associated with mastery (learning) and performance-goal orientations (Ormrod, 1999). The clear implication of these findings is that counselors, teachers, and parents should encourage and facilitate a mastery orientation in students. In consulting about student performance with teachers and parents, for ex-

TABLE 3–4.
Characteristics of People with Learning Versus Performance Goals

People with Learning Goals	*People with Performance Goals*
Believe that competence develops over time through practice and effort	Believe that competence is a stable characteristic (people either have talent or they don't) and think that competent people shouldn't have to try very hard
Choose tasks that maximize opportunities for learning	Choose tasks that maximize opportunities for demonstrating competence and avoid tasks that might make them look incompetent
React to easy tasks with feelings of boredom or disappointment	React to success on easy tasks with feelings of pride or relief
Are more likely to be intrinsically motivated to learn course material	Are more likely to be extrinsically motivated, that is, motivated by expectations of external reinforcement and punishment
Invest considerable effort in tasks	Invest the minimal effort needed to succeed
Use learning strategies that promote true comprehension of course material (e.g., meaningful learning, elaboration, and comprehension monitoring)	Use learning strategies that promote only rote learning of course material (e.g., repetition, copying, and word-for-word memorization)
Seek feedback that accurately describes their ability and helps them improve	Seek feedback that flatters them
Evaluate their own performance in terms of the progress they make	Evaluate their own performance in terms of how they compare with others
View errors as a normal and useful part of the learning process and use their errors to help improve performance	View errors as a sign of failure and incompetence
Are satisfied with their performance if they try hard and make progress, even if their efforts result in failure	Are satisfied with their performance only if they succeed
Interpret failure as a sign that they need to exert more effort	Interpret failure as a sign of low ability and therefore predictive of continuing failure in the future
Persist in the face of failure	Give up easily when they fail and avoid tasks that have previously led to failure
View a teacher as a resource and guide to help them learn	View a teacher as a judge and as a rewarder or punisher
As students, are more likely to be enthusiastic about, and become actively involved in, school activities	As students, are more likely to distance themselves from the school environment

Ormrod, Jeanne Ellis, *Human learning*, 3rd Edition, © 1999, p. 437. Reprinted by permission of Pearson Education, Inc., Upper Saddle River, NJ.

ample, counselors should stress the importance of encouraging students, especially in the elementary grades, to focus primarily on effort, acquiring skills, and self-improvement. Deemphasizing the importance of grades and focusing attention more on the process of learning rather than on the products/outcomes of learning are ways to encourage student mastery goals in young students.

But is a performance orientation necessarily detrimental to academic achievement? The research on performance goals and self-regulated learning is not as clear-cut as it is for mastery (learning) goals, but it does suggest that there may be some positive aspects of a performance-approach orientation (Pintrich, 2000). Midgley (1993) has shown that junior-high and middle-school classrooms are more performance oriented than elementary classrooms which tend to be more mastery oriented, and Hidi and Harackiewicz (2000) reported that evidence is beginning to accumulate that performance goals can have positive effects in high-school contexts. In addition, a recent meta-analysis (a statistically based review of the literature) indicated that performance-approach goals can have positive effects on intrinsic motivation comparable to those of mastery goals (Rawsthorne, & Elliot, 1999). Pintrich (2000) reached a similar conclusion: "Students who are somewhat more competitive and trying to best others can engage tasks in a manner that involves some adaptive aspects of cognition (more use of strategies) and motivation (increased interest and value)" (p. 489).

In contrast, research revealed that a performance-avoidance goal is not an adaptive approach to learning (Pintrich, 2000). Therefore, a focus on outperforming others in order to avoid punishment would not be useful.

Finally, mastery goals and performance goals are not mutually exclusive. Although there are some circumstances in which the two orientations are incompatible, students can have both kinds of goals at the same time. In some studies, the two goal orientations have even been found to be related (e.g., positively correlated), while, in other studies, they were not related (e.g., uncorrelated), (see Hidi & Harackiewicz, 2000). In addition, Hidi and Harackiewicz summarized research indicating that students who strongly endorsed both types of goals had higher levels of self-regulation and grades than students who identified with only one type of goal or with neither goal. Similarly, Zimmerman and Kitsantas (1999) found that interest and skill development were maximized on an academic writing task with a combination of mastery and performance goals. In another example of the combined effects of mastery and performance goals, Barron and Harackiewicz (2001) revealed that the combination was more effective than a single mastery and a single performance-goal condition with respect to interest and intrinsic motivation on a math learning activity.

In summary, research clearly supports the importance of school counselors, teachers, and parents encouraging a mastery-approach orientation in students, especially when students face new learning challenges or are of low ability.

Using a variety of meaningful and challenging tasks in the classroom such as hands-on, applied activities in math and science rather than worksheets and relating learning in school to things outside school is one way to foster a mastery-approach orientation (Linnenbrink & Pintrich, 2002). Parents might encourage a student to engage in an activity such as learning to play chess in order to develop the type of cognitive and organizational skills that are related to academic success. As students develop more academic skills (e.g., in high school), they may need to learn to combine mastery-approach and performance-approach goals in order to achieve academic excellence. Helping students developmentally to achieve a workable combination of these goal orientations may be especially important for academic success later in school given that research has shown that achievement motivation and attitudes toward school decline over time. Counselors, for example, can make students aware of extracurricular academic opportunities such as chess teams, spelling bees, science fairs, art competitions, geography challenges, and college-bowl-type team competitions in which students further develop their cognitive and academic skills and are motivated to demonstrate the quality of those skills in comparison to those of their peers.

Self-Efficacy

People tend to engage in an activity when they (a) perceive that it is worthwhile or valuable and (b) expect that they can perform it successfully (perceived self-efficacy in the activity) with a reasonable amount of effort (Ormrod, 1999). Self-efficacy is an individual's conviction about her or his ability to perform a specific behavior required to produce certain outcomes (Bandura, 1977). In turn, successful performance of that behavior tends to increase the individual perception of her or his self-efficacy in that situation. Thus, successful academic performance (e.g., on an academic assignment or a test), in turn, tends to increase a student's perceived competence or self-efficacy with regard to academics. As self-efficacy increases, a student is likely to be interested in and receptive to more difficult academic tasks, willing to devote more time to them, to perform better on these tasks, and show more persistence in the event of occasional failure or poor performance (Bandura, 1986). Self-efficacy has been shown to be positively related to higher levels of achievement and learning with students from a variety of age groups (Bandura, 1997; Pintrich & Schunk, 2002) and to decisions to take or continue to take more difficult (e.g., advanced math) courses in school (Eccles, Wigfield, & Schiefele, 1998).

Providing opportunities for students to succeed on academic tasks and assignments within their range of competence as well as tasks that develop new skills best enhances academic self-efficacy. For example, low achievers will feel more efficacious if they begin to learn new concepts with simple tasks that build to more difficult learning. At the same time, students must value or feel engaged in an academic activity. For students with low academic self-efficacy, it will be especially important to frame or embed new learning in a context that is meaningful to them (e.g., learning fractions based on pizza slices). Embedding new learning in more familiar contexts for students is more likely to invoke the belief (e.g., self-efficacy) that mastering the new challenge is within their abilities and lead to greater persistence if they find the challenge to be difficult. Finally, research has indicated that praise that is inaccurate and/or not associated with task accomplishment does not foster self-efficacy (Linnenbrink & Pintrich, 2002).

Thus, the self-efficacy literature has at least three direct implications for the strengths-based school counselor as a learning consultant to teachers and parents. School counselors need to advise their consultees to (a) sequence learning tasks hierarchically in terms of difficulty (e.g., less to more difficult) and not to make large leaps in difficulty from one task to another; (b) embed new learning in more familiar contexts whenever possible; and (c) provide praise for persistence and task accomplishment. Adhering to these principles is likely to result in students who perform better academically, are more interested in learning, more confident in their ability to be successful academically, more willing to tackle new and more difficult course work, and more persistent in the face of academic difficulty or failure.

Attributions

Whether self-efficacy increases following a successful academic performance and whether persistence is demonstrated in the face of difficulty or failure is also affected by the student's beliefs or attributions about the cause of success and failure. What students attribute the consequences of their academic efforts to influences not only the long-term effects that these consequences have on learning, but also how students feel about themselves. If they generally attribute academic successes to their own ability and effort and failures to bad luck, they will tend to be positive about themselves and their academic pursuits.

Weiner (1986) identified five dimensions on which attributions can vary: (a) locus of control, (b) temporal stability, (c) cross-situational generality, (d) controllability, and (e) intentionality. With respect to locus of control, students can either attribute their academic successes and failures to internal (e.g., their own effort) or external causes (e.g., efforts of others). In addition, they can explain these successes and failures in terms of either stable (e.g., inherited ability) or unstable (e.g., illness) temporal factors. They may also see their academic performance as reflecting a general or consistent pattern (e.g., "I'm a poor student and that's why I did poorly on the test.") or as a specific, isolated incident (e.g., "I did poorly on the test because I didn't study enough this time."). Students' also vary in the extent to which they view their academic successes and failures as being the result of controllable (e.g., effort) or uncontrollable (e.g., teacher attitudes) factors and to things we either meant (intentional) or did not mean (unintentional factors) to do. Of course any explanation for either successful or unsuccessful academic performance can incorporate a number of these attributional dimensions. The explanation, "I did well on the test because I decided to study hard this time, and it paid off," reflects an internal, unstable, controllable, specific, intentional attribution. In turn, a less beneficial explanation for success would be, "I did well on this test because the teacher was feeling generous when she graded it," which reflects an external, unstable, uncontrollable, specific attribution.

Ormrod (1999) noted that students tend to exhibit a developmental pattern in their attributions. When they enter school, they tend to view ability as a function of effort and, therefore, as unstable but controllable, but, as they get older, they are more inclined to view ability as an inherited characteristic and therefore as stable and uncontrollable. Older students who have not experienced a great deal of academic success are likely to conclude that they lack ability and reduce their academic efforts accordingly. As such, it is important for teachers, counselors, and parents to increasingly impart messages to students that academic success is strongly influenced by hard work and the use of effective learning and study strategies. In addition, boys tend to attribute academic success to ability and failure to lack of effort, while girls tend to show the reverse pattern, attributing success to effort and failure to lack of ability (Ormrod). Therefore, in working with girls or with students who tend to display this second pattern it is important to help them to develop alternative explanations for a less-than-successful academic performance. If students believe that failure is due to lack of effort and that they have the necessary ability, they are more likely to persist with difficult academic tasks and to expend effort in the future. On the other hand, if they believe that they lack the ability, they are more likely to give up.

In addition to the fact that children's attributions exhibit a developmental pattern, a number of experimental studies have demonstrated that attributions can be changed so that they are more adaptive and that these changes are accompanied by greater persistence in the face of failure and/or improved performance (e.g., Andrews & Debus, 1978; Chapin & Dyck, 1976; Dweck, 1975; Fowler & Peterson, 1981; Schunk, 1983). Dweck, for example, had learned-helpless[2] children solve arithmetic problems under either a success-only condition or one in which they occasionally failed. When they failed, they were given effort-attributional feedback (e.g., told that they should have tried

---

[2]Learned helplessness is the belief in one's own powerlessness which makes efforts to learn futile or extremely difficult. Learned helplessness theory was developed based on Martin Seligman's http://www.psych.upenn.edu/~seligman/experiments with animals. Animals were repeatedly exposed to inescapable shocks in one condition. They were then placed in another condition in which they could avoid or escape the shocks if they simply jumped over a low barrier. However, they either failed to learn to jump over the barrier in the second condition or took an exceedingly long time to learn that they could escape the shocks by jumping over the barrier. Thus, it appeared that the prior exposure to inescapable shock had interfered with their ability to learn in a situation in which avoidance or escape was possible.

harder). Results indicated that following training students in the attributional group maintained or improved their performance following failure, while the performance of those in the success-only group deteriorated. In addition, students in the effort attributional group showed an increase in the degrees to which they emphasized insufficient motivation versus ability as a determinant of failure. Schunk (1983), on the other hand, studied the impact of success attributions (effort and ability) with low subtraction-skill third-graders. All students received three 40-minute subtraction-training sessions over a three-day period. In the ability-attribution-feedback condition, students were told periodically during training, "You're good at this," whereas students in the effort feedback condition were told, "You've been working hard." Students in a combined ability-effort treatment group received both types of feedback ("You're good at this; you've been working hard." or "You've been working hard, and you're good at this."). Students given only ability feedback demonstrated the highest subtraction skill and self-efficacy (perceived competence). The effort-only and ability-plus-effort groups did not differ from each other, but each outperformed a no-feedback condition.

In general, the results of attributional research suggest that counselors, teachers, and parents should encourage students to explain their academic successes in terms of a combination of both stable and unstable internal factors (e.g., that they have the ability, have worked hard, and have employed effective learning strategies). In addition, students need to learn to explain subpar performances in terms of internal, unstable, and controllable factors (e.g., that they have the ability but they may not have worked hard enough and/or may not have employed effective study strategies) (Ormrod, 1999). Thus, in working with a student who feels badly about him- or herself because of poor performance on a math problem-solving test, a counselor might ask the student to evaluate the extent to which his or her performance was the result of inadequate preparation rather than insufficient ability. Attributing failure to bad luck (unstable, uncontrollable, external) can also be adaptive because it suggests that the reasons for failure are not likely to recur (Linnenbrink & Pintrich, 2002). These adaptive attributions have been linked to deeper cognitive processing and better learning and achievement (Pintrich, 2000). However, Ormrod cautions that, if students have expended a great deal of effort on academic tasks but have not been successful, they are prone to attribute failure to lack of ability and to reduce their academic efforts in the future. In this instance, attributing lack of success to choice of learning strategies rather than to effort would constitute a more functional attribution. Similarly, if a teacher praises students for success on easy academic tasks, the students may (a) perceive that they weren't expected to succeed, (b) conclude that the teacher thinks that they have low ability, and (c) reduce their subsequent efforts (Ormrod).

As a school counselor, systemic-level change could be achieved in this area by conducting workshops to train teachers how to use feedback in their classrooms and encourage adaptive attributions in their students for academic performance. A direct service application by counselors would involve classroom guidance or study-skills groups in which students are taught to employ adaptive attributions with regard to test taking.

ACADEMIC ENABLERS

Up to this point, our discussion has focused on the concept of students as self-regulated learners. DiPerna and colleagues (DiPerna & Elliott, 2002; DiPerna, Volpe, & Elliott, 2002), however, have presented an alternative empirically based conceptual model focused on promoting student academic development. Their emphasis is on academic enablers, which, as we shall see, overlap with some of the constructs that have been used to characterize self-regulated learners.

In this model, the skills, attitudes, and behaviors that contribute to academic competence fall into one of two categories: (a) academic skills and (b) academic enablers. Academic skills (e.g, reading, mathematics, critical thinking) are the traditional focus of teachers and schooling. Academic enablers, on the other hand, are nonacademic skills that have been shown to contribute to academic success, many of which have been the focus of school counselors and other student support personnel. Academic enablers ". . . are attitudes and behaviors that allow a student to participate in, and ultimately benefit from, academic instruction in the classroom" (DiPerna & Elliott, 2002, p. 294). Four categories of academic enablers have been identified: (a) motivation, (b) study skills, (c) engagement, and (d) interpersonal skills.

Motivation and Study Skills

Motivation refers to a student's approach, persistence, and level of interest regarding academic subjects (DiPerna & Elliott, 1999). The motivation academic enablers—self-efficacy, attributions, intrinsic motivation, achievement goals (e.g., mastery and performance) (Linnenbrink & Pintrich, 2002)—as well as study skills are topics that we have already discussed.

Academic Engagement

Academic engagement or engagement in academic responding refers to a variety of specific classroom behaviors, such as writing, participating in assigned classroom tasks, reading aloud, reading silently, talking about academics, and asking and answering questions (Greenwood, Horton, & Utley, 2002). Teachers and counselors have been and will continue to be heavily involved in devising and implementing interventions to increase student academic engagement. (See the next section of this chapter and the next chapter for examples.)

Interpersonal Skills

Interpersonal skills involve the communication and cooperation behaviors necessary to interact with peers and adults (DiPerna & Elliott, 1999) and include skills that enable the student to get along with others, correct behavior, accept suggestions, and listen to others. Of course, enhancing students' interpersonal and social skills has been a traditional focus of school counseling. For example, Sink (2005) identified counselor-directed activities in social problem solving, listening, and teamwork for fostering academic development and learning in middle-school students.

Wentzel and Watkins (2002) summarized research that demonstrates a relationship between these skills and academic achievement. Specifically, high levels of peer acceptance and popular peer status have been found to be consistently related to academic achievement. In addition, prosocial displays of behavior (e.g., helping, cooperating, and sharing) have been linked to peer acceptance and popularity and to achievement, while aggression and antisocial displays of behavior have been associated with peer rejection and academic problems. Thus, enhancing positive student interpersonal skills represents one potentially useful approach for school counselors in promoting student academic development. As Wentzel and Watkins note, peer relationships can provide students with a sense of social relatedness and belongingness that can motivate positive engagement in the social and academic activities of the classroom. In Chapter 5, we review a number of evidence-based interventions that school counselors and other educators can implement in order to improve interpersonal skills and relationships, and in a later section of this chapter, we discuss the role that cooperative learning and peer tutoring can play in enhancing student learning and academic success.

Although the academic enablers conceptual framework is a useful one for school counselors, it is not without its limitations (Christenson & Anderson, 2002; Keith, 2002 for discussions). One of the more important limitations is that it locates the factors related to academic competence and success (e.g., academic enablers) largely within the student and devotes little attention to the influence of context (e.g., school, peers, family) on the development and application of these enablers (Christenson & Anderson). It is to a discussion of environmental influences on the development of academic competence that we now turn.

STRENGTHS-ENHANCING ACADEMIC ENVIRONMENTS

In recent years, ecology or the child's environment has been increasingly recognized as an important developmental influence (Bronfenbrenner, 1979). For example, Finn (1993) reported that fewer parental discussions about school and fewer academic resources such as dictionaries and books at home were associated with academic disengagement for at-risk ethnically diverse eighth-grade students. Sink (2005) asserted that the middle-school counselor should collaborate with all educators and adopt a systemic orientation to fostering student academic development and learning. The strengths-based school counselor employs indirect and systemic-level interventions not just to remove barriers to successful development (e.g., The Education Trust, 1999) but, more importantly, to foster strengths-enhancing environments for the academic development of all students. Moreover, the characteristics of these strengths-enhancing environments have been identified by empirical research.

What are the characteristics of classrooms, schools, and homes that encourage the development of self-regulated learning, of mastery-approach goals, internalized motivation, adaptive attributions, or academic enablers? In this section, we review some of the key environmental characteristics that research has shown to be associated with these qualities and with academic performance. Table 3–5 summarizes some characteristics of these environments.

Satisfy Basic Needs

Through research, Ryan and Deci (2000) identified three basic needs that appear to be essential for facilitating optimal human functioning: (a) autonomy, (b) competence, and (c) relatedness. Autonomy refers not to independence but to the belief that behavior is chosen or self-determined (e.g., an internal, perceived, locus of causality). Competence involves a feeling of ability and mastery, and relatedness refers to a sense of belongingness. Strong links have been demonstrated between intrinsic motivation and satisfaction of autonomy and competence needs, and, to some extent, relatedness (Ryan & Deci).

TABLE 3–5.
Some Characteristics of a Strengths-Enhancing Academic Environment

Characteristic
Satisfies Basic Needs
Autonomy
Competence
Relatedness (belongingness)
Promotes Cooperation
Cooperative/collaborative learning
Peer tutoring
Stimulates Interest
Personal
Situational
Encourages Complementary Roles—Home, School, Community

In addition, satisfying basic needs is important for facilitating student movement along the motivation continuum and helping them achieve a more internally regulated form of extrinsic motivation (Ryan & Deci, 2000). Many of the academic tasks required of students are not inherently interesting to them and are performed to satisfy adults to whom they feel attached. It is difficult to make all instruction interesting to all students. As such, the need for belongingness (e.g., relatedness) is important for internalizating the value of academic behaviors and for regulating these behaviors. Ryan, Stiller, and Lynch (1994) have shown that children who have more fully internalized the regulation of school-related behaviors were those who felt more securely connected to teachers and parents. Similarly, perceived competence is also important to internalization as students are not likely to adopt and value academic activities for which they do not feel competent. Finally, autonomy is important both for internalizing and incorporating (integrating) the activity into a student's system of needs and values (Ryan & Deci, 2000). In that regard, Grolnick and Ryan (1989) found more internalization of school-related values among students whose parents were more supportive of autonomy and relatedness. Moreover, research summarized by Ryan and Deci demonstrated that teachers who are autonomy supportive (in contrast to controlling) stimulate greater intrinsic motivation, curiosity, and desire for challenge in their students in contrast to more controlling teachers whose students tend to lose initiative and learn less effectively, especially when learning requires conceptual, creative processing.

The school counselor can incorporate these research findings in classroom consultation sessions with teachers about students displaying low academic motivation. Providing a brief rationale about the positive effects that choice has been shown to have on learning, the strengths-based counselor can encourage teachers to give students choices, whenever possible, in the types of tasks or projects that they can complete in order to satisfy a particular assignment or learning objective. Permitting greater choice in learning can capitalize on or stimulate key personal and situational interest factors that we discuss later in this chapter.

Adopting the social cognitive perspective of Ryan and Deci (2000), Osterman (2000) reviewed the research on students' need for belongingness (a sense of community [relatedness]) in school. Osterman noted that, because of the nationwide emphasis on standardized achievement test performance, there is little attention to students' affective need for belonging or relatedness. Belonging is the need to feel securely connected with others in the environment and to experience oneself as worthy of love and respect. Osterman also commented that there is a (mistaken) belief that belonging is not a precondition for academic engagement.

In her extensive review of the research literature, however, Osterman (2000) assembled an impressive body of evidence demonstrating that satisfying students' need for belongingness is associated with a host of desirable academic outcomes and correlates. Notably, belongingness was (a) associated with a positive orientation toward school, class work, and teachers; (b) associated with achievement motivation and intrinsic academic motivation; (c) an important factor in participation in school activities, school engagement, and dropout (e.g., dropping out is associated with low relatedness); (d) most strongly related to student engagement with teacher support being a particularly important factor; and (e) impacted achievement through its effects on engagement. Moreover, popular status among peers and high levels of acceptance have been shown to be related to successful academic performance, whereas low levels of acceptance and rejection by peers is related to academic difficulties (Wentzel & Watkins, 2002). Belongingness is important at all levels from preschool through high school, and middle school seems to be a crucial time particularly for boys (Osterman).

Research indicates that three aspects of classroom practice—method of instruction, teacher support, and authority relations—impact students' sense of belonging and that this effect is mediated through altering the frequency and nature of classroom interactions (Osterman, 2000). It will be especially important for the school counselor to incorporate the findings about effective classroom practices in consultation sessions with teachers who complain about student bickering and cliques in their classrooms.

Cooperative learning, which will be discussed later, and dialogue, the opportunity to express personal opinions, constitute two instructional strategies that impact belongingness, apparently by affording students an opportunity to discover that others care. Class discussions or dialogue can facilitate student learning in a variety of ways including (a) helping students to organize their thoughts so that they can explain them to others; (b) showing them that they need to enhance their knowledge or information; and (c) presenting them with new information or opinions that they may need to integrate into their current conceptualization.

Feeling that they are cared about and worthy of respect from teachers is also an important factor that enhances belongingness for students. Unfortunately, and not surprisingly, research (e.g., Gamoran & Berends, 1987; Osterman, 2000) indicates that teachers' supportiveness of students is differentially affected by a variety of student variables including ability, engagement, academic performance, and tracking. Students assigned to high-ability groups, for example, experience more supportive teacher relationships than their peers.

The third classroom practice that is related to belongingness is the extent to which teachers are autonomy-supportive as opposed to controlling in their classroom-management approach. Teachers who are autonomy supportive provide students with enough information to guide learning, while allowing opportunities for student initiative, choice, and creativity. In contrast, controlling teachers demand that students follow a detailed, rigid format, use words like "should" and "must," and pressure students to learn. Deci, Vallerand, Pelletier, and Ryan (1991), for example, reported research indicating that students with autonomy-supportive teachers displayed more intrinsic motivation, perceived competence, and self-esteem than did students in classrooms with controlling teachers. Unfortunately, however, reviews (e.g., Eccles, Midgley et al., 1993) indicate that, while adolescents' need for autonomy increases, opportunities for student autonomy in the typical middle- and junior-high-school classroom tend to be more restricted as compared to those in the elementary school. This contextual change in the adolescent's learning environment, therefore, may be one important factor in explaining the previously cited finding that academic motivation and attitudes toward school decline over time.

This last finding has clear implications for the middle-school counselor. Advocating with teachers and administrators for greater student choice in assignments, projects, and other aspects of the learning environment is an important developmental consideration for maintaining and enhancing academic motivation at this level.

Finally, Osterman (2000), citing a review by Anderman and Maehr (1994), pointed out that the overall culture of the school may be even more important than that of individual classrooms in impacting student motivation and learning. For example, tracking or ability grouping and departmentalization (clustering teachers by content area) are two commonly used organizational practices that negatively impact the nature and quality of peer relationships, because they tend to be associated with depersonalization. These types of situations provide school counselors with opportunities for leadership and collaboration with administrators and teachers to eliminate barriers and/or to develop other organizational structures that support relatedness. On the one hand, counselors can advocate for policies that eliminate or minimize tracking, departmentalization, and depersonalization (e.g., The Education Trust, 1999). On the other hand, strengths-based school counselors should also promote structures, such as teaming in a middle school or a school-within-a-school organization within a large high school, that enhance a sense of relatedness for both students and teachers. Additionally, counselors can impact the overall school culture through developing peer mediation and peer tutoring programs that foster a greater sense of belongingness among students.

In summary, Osterman (2000) drew a number of conclusions in her review of research on the role of belonging in academic learning. Among these are (a) that many students do not experience a sense of belonging in schools; (b) their needs for relatedness and autonomy are generally ignored in schools; (c) that addressing those needs may go a long way toward improving motivation, behavior, and learning; and (d) efforts to enhance the school community have tended to focus on teacher-student relationships and have tended to neglect enhancing peer relationships.

With respect to the last point, Wentzel and Watkins (2002) asserted that perceiving positive peer relationships is likely to promote a student's sense of emotional well-being and relatedness, thereby increasing engagement in classroom activities. In addition, they summarized research indicating that students who believe that their peers care about them tend to be more positively engaged in the classroom, pursue academic and prosocial goals more frequently, and earn higher grades than those who do not perceive such support. As such, enhancing a sense of student belongingness through direct service interventions such as classroom guidance and systemic interventions such as consultation about classroom and school peer-climate factors or coordination of peer programs should represent a central focus for the strengths-based school counselor.

Promote Cooperation

Johnson and Johnson (1994) identified three ways students can interact with each other as they learn: (a) cooperatively, (b) competitively, or (c) individualistically. They can work cooperatively with a vested interest in each other's work as well as their own. They can compete to be the best, or they can work toward their own goals without paying attention to each other. Johnson and Johnson believe that it is important for students to learn to interact in each of these three ways. At the same time, they assert that competition is the most dominant perception held by students of the interaction patterns in our current educational system. Competition among students or groups of students can, at times, play a useful role in learning. In addition, as we have seen, performance goals that involve besting others can also have positive effects on academic achievement especially for high achievers and particularly in high school. On the whole, however, research indicates that practices designed to increase levels of cooperation in the classroom (e.g., cooperative learning and peer tutoring) enhance academic performance and motivation (Johnson & Johnson, 1994). To a large degree, these educational practices enhance the student's sense of belonging or relatedness that Osterman's (2000) review of research has demonstrated is so important to achievement motivation. As such, they represent additional ways to enable students to satisfy at least one, if not more, of the three basic student needs identified by Ryan and Deci (2000): (a) autonomy, (b) competence, and (c) relatedness.

In this section, we discuss two approaches—cooperative learning and peer tutoring—that involve varying degrees of peer-assisted or peer-mediated learning and promote student cooperation and academic accomplishment. These approaches represent useful ways to supplement more traditional teacher-directed or teacher-mediated learning. Table 3–6, which is drawn from Topping[3]

---

[3]Strictly speaking, Topping (2001, p. 3) does not include cooperative learning as a type of peer-assisted learning because, in cooperative learning, ". . . typically the participants are working in parallel toward some common goal, rather than primarily, specifically and consciously helping each other's learning." However, we believe that this distinction is overly restrictive, and we consider cooperative to be a type of peer-assisted learning.

TABLE 3–6.
Teacher-mediated and Peer-mediated Learning:
Potential Advantages and Disadvantages

Factor	Teacher	Peer
Engagement	Variable	High
Activity/arousal	Variable	High
Interactivity	Variable	High
Engaged time	Low	High
Noise level		
Communication	Professional, complex	Vernacular, simple
Vocabulary of instruction	Low, mostly verbal generalized	High, also non-verbal
Modeling/demonstration		Concrete, local, specific
Exemplification		
Individualization	Difficult	Less difficult
Differentiation	Variable to low	High
Opportunities to question	Variable to low	High
Opportunities to be questioned	High	Low
Quality of question/answer		
Error* Management	High	Low
Disclosure threshold	Reliable, low contact, low f	Unreliable, high contact, high f
Detection	High quality, low quantity	Low quality, high quantity
Diagnosis	Low	High
Immediacy of correction	High quality, low quantity	Lower quality, high quantity
Nature of correction	Low, delayed	High, immediate
Prompting opportunities	Low, delayed	High, immediate
Self-correction opportunities		
Reinforcement	Few, often delayed	Many, immediate
Encouragement opportunities	Few, often delayed	Many, immediate
Praise opportunities	Usually high	Can be high
Encouragement/praise impact		
Ownership & Metacognition	To teacher	To teacher and peer partner(s)
Accountability/responsibility	Higher	Lower
Dependency on teacher	By teacher, distant	By peer, proximal
Modeling of coping/success	Possible	Possible for helper & helped
Metacognitive development	Lower	Higher
Self-regulation of learning		
Organization	Planning/preparation	P/P & training
Time costs	Lower need, little time available	Higher need, more time available
Quality assurance/monitoring		
Personal/Social Development	Limited effect	Often higher
Social tolerance	Limited effect	Significant effect
Social skills	Limited effect	Significant effect
Communication skills	Variable	Higher
Self-esteem		

*misconception, gap, etc.

Topping, K. (2001). *Peer assisted learning: A practical guide for teachers.* © Cambridge, MA: Brookline Books. Reprinted with permission.

(2001), summarizes some of the potential advantages and disadvantages of peer-mediated learning as compared to teacher-mediated learning.

With respect to the two peer-assisted approaches that we will discuss, Foot and Howe (1998) noted that there is some evidence that a collaborative (cooperative) learning approach is most suitable for problem-solving tasks and tasks that involve manipulating ideas and understanding concepts. In contrast, peer tutoring may be better suited to tasks that involve the learning of rules, the application of principles, and the elaboration of a child's repertoire of skills. Due to these distinctions, these two forms of peer-assisted learning are discussed separately.

Cooperative learning refers to a variety of peer-assisted instructional methods including student-team learning (e.g., achievement divisions, teams-games-tournaments, team-assisted individualization, cooperative-integrated reading and composition), jigsaw, group investigation, and learning together (see Slavin, 1990 for details). In general, cooperative-learning methods involve students spending some of their class time working often in 4–6 member heterogeneous (based on achievement) groups with cooperative-incentive structures in which they can earn recognition, reward, or grades based on the academic performance of their groups (Slavin, 1983, 1990). The methods consist of structured, systematic, instructional strategies that can be used at any grade level and with most academic subjects (Slavin, 1985).

As an example, student team learning encompasses a variety of instructional strategies in which students work together to learn something as a team rather than to do something. It is based on three concepts: (a) team rewards, (b) individual accountability, and (c) equal opportunities for success (Slavin, 1990). Teams may earn certificates or other rewards if they meet or exceed a set criterion, and all teams may achieve the criterion. Individual students contribute to the team by improving on their past performance (equal opportunities for success). The team's success depends on the individual learning (individual accountability) of all members, and, members help each other to prepare for quizzes or other forms of assessment that they take individually. Thus, students are responsible for their own learning as well as the learning of their teammates.

In effective cooperative learning, the teacher provides the group with a well-defined learning goal or goals to achieve and a structure or set of steps to follow with guidelines on how to behave in the group. The teacher then serves as a resource and a monitor of group process. Frequent use of relevant interpersonal and small-group skills and frequent and regular group processing of current functioning to improve the group's future effectiveness are an essential part of cooperative learning. Of course, the latter are fundamental areas in which school counselors are prepared and for which they can serve effectively as trainers and consultants to teachers who endeavor to use cooperative learning.

Research results have typically been supportive of the effectiveness of cooperative learning. Slavin (1990), for example, reviewed 60 studies on cooperative learning that met strict methodological requirements. The studies compared the effects of various cooperative-learning methods to those of control groups studying the same materials. Because the studies involved multiple cooperative-learning methods, a total of 68 comparisons of cooperative learning and control methods were involved. With respect to gains in achievement, 72 % cooperative learning, and only 12 % the control groups. Moreover, Ormrod (1999) noted that students of all ability levels show higher academic achievement with cooperative learning, and females, minorities, and students at-risk for failure were especially likely to show increased achievement. Within cooperative learning, those methods that emphasize group goals and individual accountability (principally student-team learning methods) had the most consistent effects on increasing achievement as reflected not only by both curriculum-related measures but also by standardized achievement tests not directly related to the curriculum (Slavin, 1990).

In addition to gains in academic achievement, research results indicate that cooperative learning has produced positive changes in a variety of social- and class-climate variables. These changes included (a) positive outcomes in race relations (increases in cross-racial friendships); (b) acceptance of mainstreamed handicapped students; (c) gains in student self-esteem; (d) increases in internalized motivation; (e) peer support for academic achievement; and (f) increases in some aspects of cooperative and altruistic behavior (Ormrod, 1999; Slavin, 1990).

Johnson and Johnson (1994) performed a meta-analysis (a statistical review of research) of 375 studies conducted during the past 90 years of the effects of cooperative, competitive, and individualistic learning methods on academic achievement, interpersonal attraction, social support, and self-esteem. The studies used a large number and variety of student outcome measures at all school-age levels, in almost every curriculum area, and with a wide range of students from many different countries. Relative to competitive and individualistic methods, cooperative learning increased learning, resulting in more higher-level reasoning, more frequent generation of new ideas and solutions, and greater transfer of what is learned within one situation to another. Cooperative learning promoted considerably more connectedness among students regardless of differences in ability level, sex, disability, ethnic membership, social-class differences, or task orientation. Students in cooperative-earning conditions were also more supportive of each other and had higher levels of self-esteem. In particular, a study by Widaman and Kagan (1987) revealed that competitive classrooms did not benefit African and Mexican American minority students, who tend to hold cooperative rather than competitive social orientations. Alternatively, cooperative-classroom situations were associated with positive educational outcomes for these students.

Like cooperative learning, peer tutoring is a form of peer-assisted learning. Counselors are often instrumental in coordinating or providing training for peer-tutoring programs and in consulting with teachers in order to enhance cooperative or other learning formats. Peer tutoring is characterized by specific role-taking in which someone has the role of the tutor whereas the other person(s) has the role of tutee, has a high focus on curriculum content, and often targets skill gains (Topping & Ehly, 1998). In their review, Topping and Ehly noted that there have been 28 previous reviews and meta-analyses of peer tutoring. In general, these reviews have found (a) strong evidence of cognitive gains for tutees and tutors; (b) some evidence for improved attitudes and self-image; (c) that training and structured procedures improved outcomes; and (d) that same-age tutoring was as effective as cross-age tutoring. In his review, Bloom (1984) concluded that tutoring by a skilled peer was more effective than both teacher lecture-based instruction and student-regulated mastery learning. In mastery learning, students received conventional lecture-based teaching plus formative tests for feedback, followed by corrective instruction and retesting to determine the extent to which they mastered the subject matter. Tutoring produced improvements that were far superior to those produced by lecture-based teaching and better than those by mastery learning.

Peer tutoring can be applied successfully (a) at almost any age level (Foot & Howe, 1998); (b) with a range of students, including urban and minority, English language learners, low achievers, handicapped students, students with learning disabilities and academic delays, students with autism, and students with attention deficit hyperactivity disorders (Arreaga-Mayer, Terry, & Greenwood, 1998; Fantuzzo & Ginsburg-Block, 1998; Foot & Howe, 1998; Maheady, 1998); and (c) across a variety of curriculum areas, including mathematics, reading, spelling, writing, and vocabulary. In addition, research summarized by Maheady indicated that peer tutoring resulted in a number of social and interpersonal benefits, including increased frequency of positive social interactions, reduced levels of inappropriate behavior, decreased truancy and tardiness rates, improved self-concepts and attitudes toward school, and enhanced racial relations. Finally, Maheady reported that a cost-effectiveness study of instructional interventions revealed that peer tutoring produced the greatest gain in achievement per dollar spent as compared to three well-known reform strategies: (a) reduced class size, (b) computer-assisted instruction, and (c) a longer school day.

There are a variety of peer-tutoring procedures, including paired reading, classwide peer tutoring, peer-assisted learning strategies, reciprocal peer tutoring, cued spelling, and paired writing. Many of these procedures are highly structured and well researched. Some of them (e.g., reciprocal peer tutoring and classwide peer tutoring) have been developed and validated with low achieving and minority students. Classwide peer tutoring (CWPT) represents one interesting and well-researched approach (Greenwood, Carta, Kamps, & Hall, 1988). Developed for instruction with children who are challenging to teach, CWPT involves same-age, intraclass peer-assisted instruction. It has been applied successfully to a variety of subjects (reading, language arts, science, mathematics, and social studies) with a range of students (regular education, special education, low achievers, and English-language learners) from kindergarten through high school, and research has demonstrated that students are able to learn more in less time using CWPT when compared to conventional forms of teacher-directed instruction (Arreaga-Mayer, Terry, & Greenwood., 1998). Depending on the situation, students are either paired randomly or matched by ability for tutoring. All tutoring pairs are assigned to one of two teams that compete for the highest point total resulting from daily sessions in which individual students earn points for performance. Student roles (tutor-tutee) are switched (e.g., reciprocal tutoring) within daily tutoring sessions, and content, teams, and tutoring pairs are changed on a weekly basis. Tutoring sessions for the entire class occur at the same time. The teacher's role in CWPT is to organize tutoring content, prepare tutoring materials, train students in tutoring procedures, and monitor the process (Arreaga-Mayer, Terry & Greenwood).

Knowledge of effective peer-tutoring models is essential for the school counselor in consulting with teachers and administrators. In addition, advocating for peer-tutoring programs, training peer tutors, and coordinating these programs are all valuable services that the strengths-based school counselor can provide in the effort to enhance student academic development and school success. For example, a school counselor could develop, implement, and co-ordinate CWPT-type procedures as part of the structured portion of an after-school program at an elementary or a middle school. The counselor would train the students in the tutoring procedures and then after-school teachers or parent volunteers that the counselor also trained would oversee the program with the counselor serving as its coordinator.

We now turn to stimulating student interest, a third characteristic of strengths-enhancing academic environments that school counselors can help promote.

Stimulate Situational Interest

Students frequently comment that academics simply are not interesting to them and that is why they are not motivated to learn and achieve in school. From a common sense perspective, it follows that, if academic activities could be made more interesting, then engagement and subsequently academic achievement should improve. Not surprisingly, research has substantiated the influence of interest on academic performance across individuals, knowledge domains, and subject areas (Hidi & Harackiewicz, 2000).

Theorists often distinguish two types of interests: (a) individual or personal on the one hand and (b) situational on the other (Hidi & Harackiewicz, 2000; Linnenbrink & Pintrich, 2002; Ormrod, 1999). Personal interests, which are relatively stable over time, involve finding a topic intriguing and engaging and representing one form of intrinsic motivation. Personal interests tend to sustain involvement in an activity over time, to promote more effective information processing, increased recall, and greater likelihood of building on learned information in the future. In addition, interested students demonstrate high academic achievement (Ormrod, 1999). As mentioned previously, allowing students to pick topics for class projects or reports is one way to capitalize on personal interests.

Situational interests, on the other hand, involve some aspect of the environment (e.g., something new, unusual, or surprising) or task that focuses attention at least temporarily and may evoke an affective response. Although we would clearly prefer students to have a strong personal interest in school and in academics, situational interests may be easier to pique in many situations, can play an important role in learning, and may be especially significant with academically unmotivated children (Hidi & Harackiewicz, 2000). By enhancing situational interests in a topic, a teacher can increase the likelihood of engaging student involvement, stimulate more enduring personal interest and intrinsic motivation, and increase academic motivation. In addition to selecting more stimulating texts, research indicates that teachers can increase situational interest by: (a) increasing student self-determination through providing more choices in the instructional process; (b) involving them in work with other students; and (c) teaching them strategies to make boring tasks more interesting (Hidi & Harackiewicz, 2000).

With respect to the last point, Sansone and Smith (2000) found that people often engage in strategies to make their performance on uninteresting tasks more interesting. Students can be taught to generate strategies such as making a game out of an initially boring task or setting higher goals to make the task more challenging. In doing so, they are endeavoring to control their effort and increase their persistence and interest in the task. In addition, if they are provided with a reason to value the activity, then their generation and use of strategies tends to be enhanced (Sansone & Smith).

Finally, Mitchell (1993) found that different factors were involved in triggering situational interest as opposed to maintaining it. Although group work, puzzles, and computers (e.g., novel approaches) were able to "catch" students' interest in math, they were unable to "hold" it over time. Meaningfulness (to students in their personal lives because it empowers them to achieve their personal ends) and involvement (experienced as absorbing, active participation in learning) proved to be variables that sustained the students' interest. Small-group work and discussions constitute activities that are more likely than lectures to encourage active student involvement. Hidi and Harackiewicz (2000) speculated that different processes may be involved in triggering and maintaining situational interest, with attentional factors being more important in triggering ("catching") it and affective or motivational processes being more salient for maintaining ("holding") it. Thus, it appears that novel instructional approaches (e.g., an exciting experiment or a captivating computer program or Web site) that stimulate situational interests need to be coupled with procedures that actively involve students in learning and evoke personal meaning if long-term interest in the activity is to be sustained. Helping students connect the activity to an interest outside of school (e.g., computing free-throw percentages in basketball) or to future goals may help to increase the "hold" factor of the situational interest.

Once again, the school counselor can incorporate these research findings into consultation sessions with individual teachers about "reaching" students who display low academic motivation. In these sessions, the potential contributions of interventions such as (a) allowing more student choice in learning assignments; (b) incorporating peer-assisted learning into classroom instruction; and (c) implementing brief class discussions about how a particular topic connects with students' current interests and future goals can be considered. These interventions address students' need for autonomy, belonging, and competence respectively and, as we have discussed, impact academic engagement and achievement. In addition to consulting with individual teachers, the school counselor can coordinate-team or school-wide workshops in which teachers share novel approaches that they have used to stimulate situational interests in students and discuss how they subsequently connected to students' personal interests and stimulated learning. This last approach is a systemic-level intervention that can help foster a more strengths-enhancing academic environment for all students.

But students are affected by a variety of environmental systems (e.g., home, school, community) that impact their academic development. We now consider how these systems can mutually foster academic success.

Encourage Complementary Roles of Home, School, and Community

Christenson and Anderson (2002) asserted that the roles of parents and teachers are complementary. They do not need to perform the same tasks with respect to children's learning, but they need to work on shared mutual goals with respect to learning. Children are embedded in a dynamic social system of family, school, and community, and the messages that they receive about learning need to be congruent.

According to a review of over 200 studies of family, school, or community influences on positive indicators of school success (Christenson & Peterson, 1998), there is a common set of contextual influences important for learning regardless of the child's immediate microsystem (e.g., home or school). Six factors emerged that reflect the complementary nature of family-school-community roles for academic success: (a) standards and expectations, (b) structure, (c) opportunity to learn, (d) support, (e) climate and relationships, and (f) modeling.

Standards and expectations refer to the level of expected performance held by adults and communicated to students. Structure is concerned with the learning routine and monitoring processes employed by families and schools. Access to learning materials such as reading materials and computers, academically related clubs and organizations, and time to acquire or master new skills constitute examples of opportunity to learn. Praise and regular explicit feedback about academics, frequent discussions about school, and autonomy-supportive academic environments represent sources of support from family, school, and community. Warmth and friendliness, praise and recognition, and positive and respectful adult-youth relationship are indicative of climate and relationships with key adults that support student success. Finally, teachers who establish academically challenging classrooms and parents and other adults who read, discuss the importance of education, and set long-term goals represent the type of modeling that is related to school success for students.

> The degree of continuity in messages between home and school to the student about such things as the value of school and learning, use of time, and persistence in the face of challenging tasks must be considered . . . consensus between home and school about the goals of education . . . [is] essential to counter information from competing sources, such as television and peers . . . discontinuities between families and schools compromise the effectiveness of either parents or educators as socializing agents. (Christenson & Anderson, 2002, p. 388)

Through consultation, parent education, and parent-educator committees, school counselors clearly have a key opportunity to facilitate supportive and complementary roles for families and educators in educating youth. One example of an important systemic-level service that the strengths-based school counselor can provide is to coordinate discussion sessions in which parents, teachers, counselors, and administrators brainstorm how home and school can more effectively work together to support student success. These sessions could be conducted at the class, team, grade, and/or school level.

SUMMARY

School counselors have always had a role in the academic development of students and the academic mission of schools. In the past, that role has often involved serving in a secondary-support capacity to classroom teachers and other instructional personnel for low achievers and inadvertently as gatekeepers to academic success for a small percentage of students rather than acting as facilitators of academic success for all students. Today, the emerging conception of the school-counseling program is for school counselors to play a more direct and central role in academic development for all students, to implement a variety of interventions and new services, and to participate in and influence education-reform efforts.

The strengths-based school counselor implements this role by promoting the individual student strengths and strengths-enhancing environments that research has shown to be related to academic accomplishment. Those strengths include self-regulated learning and academic enablers. Environments that foster student academic achievement satisfy basic student needs, promote cooperation, stimulate personal and situational interest, and encourage complementary educational roles for home, school, and community. Through direct service and systemic interventions, the school counselor promotes those student academic strengths and strengths-enhancing environments.

KEY POINTS

The Traditional Role of the School Counselor in Academic Development

- A test-and-select orientation as well as the tendency of many school districts to track students within the educational process have influenced how school counselors have functioned in the traditional role. These tendencies placed a major focus on the academic development of a small percentage of students, such as those who are college bound.

- Remedial instruction and supportive counseling have been encouraged in the traditional role as school counselors have targeted underachieving students. School counselors have failed to encourage the optimal developmental of a majority of students, and student potential has been underestimated.

- The traditional role of a school counselor has typically resulted in school counselors serving as gatekeepers to academic success rather than as facilitators and advocates of academic success for all.

The Contemporary Role of the School Counselor in Academic Development

- The demand to produce a well-educated and knowledgeable workforce as well as an increasingly diverse student population that presents complex challenges has driven current reform efforts in education.

- Many initiatives have been introduced to hold schools accountable for academic progress. Most notably, the federal government's No Child Left Behind Act (2002) has been passed to ensure that students make adequate yearly progress (AYP) toward state standards. School and school district performances are publicly reported in district and state report cards and those schools that continually fail to make AYP will be subject to sanctions by the federal government.

- Educational reform initiatives have impacted the school counselor's role. School counselors are increasingly being called upon to demonstrate their effectiveness in increasing student achievement. As a result, many school counselors have been required to assume time-consuming test-coordination responsibilities.

- The Education Trust has included advocacy, leadership, teaming and collaboration, counseling and coordination, and assessment and use of data as essential to increasing academic success for all students.

- The ASCA National Model asserts enhancement of student achievement as the primary goal of the school counseling program. The Model proposes three academic standards as well as indicators within each standard that define specific knowledge, skills, and attitudes students should acquire.

The Strengths-Based School Counselor's Role in Academic Development

- SBSC specifies research-documented strengths and strengths-enhancing environments that are associated with academic success. Strengths-based school counselors should have knowledge of the basic principles that facilitate the development of research-identified student academic strengths. They should also be aware of the types of environments that have been documented to enhance student academic success.

- Strengths-based school counselors facilitate the acquisition of self-regulated learning in students. Self-motivation, goal setting, planning, attention control, application of learning strategies, self-monitoring, and self-evaluation are all elements of self-regulated learning. Counselors and teachers can teach self-regulations skills by exposing students to self-regulated learning in the classroom, in small groups, and individually. Also, counselors or teachers can model the skills of a self-regulated learner to students and allow them to hone self-regulatory skills independently in practice sessions.

- Strengths-based school counselors promote the acquisition of effective learning and study strategies. Overt strategies such as note taking, outlining, writing summaries, and concept maps as well as covert strategies such as mnemonic devices, meaningful learning, elaboration, and comprehension monitoring are utilized with students. Evidence-based learning strategies are incorporated into study-skills programs, and research-based recommendations are used when consulting with teachers.

- School counselors should consider collaborating or co-leading study skills instruction with classroom teachers as research has demonstrated that study-skills programs are most effective when they occur in the context of a specific academic course or task.

- Student Success Skills (SSS), a traditional study skills program utilizing group counseling and classroom guidance has been used effectively to increase academic achievement.

- In SBSC, school counselors encourage students to develop intrinsic motivation toward learning. Counselors encourage students to participate in school clubs or extracurricular activities that develop academic interests. Also, counselors encourage teachers to allow students to focus assignments or projects on individual interests so that students will have increased academic motivation.

- Although strengths-based counselors prefer the development of intrinsic motivation, extrinsic motivation should be used when students begin a new and difficult or frustrating task, when students encounter a task in which they have no initial interest, when students are academically unmotivated, or when a desirable behavior may not occur without extrinsic motivation.

- They should assess a student's current extrinsic or intrinsic motivation level in an academic subject prior to developing an intervention to enhance academic achievement. The self-determination continuum of motivation, which ranges from nonself-determined, amotivated, non-regulated behavior at one end to self-determined, intrinsically motivated, internally regulated behavior at the other end can aid in identifying a student's motivation level.

- School counselors should assess a student's goal orientation when considering strategies to enhance academic achievement. Students can exemplify a mastery or performance orientation coupled with an approach or avoidance focus.
- Generally, a mastery-approach focus to learning is associated with positive outcomes as students engage in self-regulatory learning and develop intrinsic motivation. A performance-avoidance focus is associated with negative outcomes and withdrawal of effort. However, it is suggested that there may be some positive aspects of a performance-approach orientation, especially in high-school environments. School counselors should help students achieve a workable combination of both goal orientations in order to achieve academic excellence.
- Strengths-based school counselors should encourage student self-efficacy, the students' belief about his or her ability to perform a particular task. Self-efficacy can be increased by providing opportunities for students to succeed on academic tasks within their range of competence, embedding new learning in a meaningful context, and accurately praising students on specific task accomplishments.
- School counselors should encourage adaptive attributions in their students, so that students may show improved performance and/or greater persistence in the face of failure. Students should be encouraged to explain their academic successes in terms of a combination of both stable and unstable internal factors. Students should explain sub-par performances in terms of internal, unstable, controllable factors.

Academic Enablers

- Strengths-based school counselors also focus on academic enablers—motivation, study skills, engagement, and interpersonal skills—to increase academic competence in students. These nonacademic skills have been shown to contribute to academic success.
- Effective study skills and intrinsic student motivation should be encouraged by the school counselor. Levels of self-efficacy, appropriate attributions to successes and failures, and goal orientation and approaches are all components of a student's motivation.
- Strengths-based school counselors should implement interventions to increase student academic engagement in class. Writing, participating in assigned classroom tasks, reading aloud, reading silently, talking about academics, and asking and answering questions are examples of specific classroom behaviors that increase academic engagement.
- Counselors should enhance positive student interpersonal skills to promote academic development. High levels of peer acceptance and popular peer status have been found to be consistently related to academic achievement.

Strengths-Enhancing Academic Environments

- Strengths-based school counselors employ indirect and systemic-level interventions to remove barriers to successful development and foster strengths-enhancing environments that promote the academic development of all students.
- Autonomy, competence, and relatedness or belonging are three needs that are essential for facilitating optimal human functioning in students. Academic environ-

ments should strive to satisfy these basic needs as desirable academic outcomes are associated with these characteristics.

- Notably, belongingness is associated with achievement motivation and intrinsic academic motivation as well as a positive orientation toward school, class work, and teachers. It is also an important factor in participation in school activities, school engagement, and a decreased dropout rate. Belongingness is strongly related to student engagement with teacher support being an important factor, and belongingness impacts achievement through its effects on engagement.

- School counselors can advocate for policies and organizational structures that support belongingness. They can also promote the enhancement of peer relationships, which is positively associated with academic engagement and achievement. Currently, tracking and departmentalization detract from a sense of belongingness by depersonalizing peers and their teachers.

- Strengths-based school counselors support incorporating cooperative learning in the academic environment. Cooperative learning utilizes the concepts of team rewards, individual accountability, and equal opportunities for success to increase academic achievement. Research results also indicate that cooperative learning produces positive changes in a variety of social and class climate variables such as increased cross-racial friendships, increased student self-esteem, and increased internal motivation.

- Peer-tutoring programs are another form of peer-assisted learning that school counselors should promote to create strengths-enhancing academic environments. These programs can be applied successfully with a wide range of students and provide social and interpersonal benefits as well as academic benefits. Paired reading, reciprocal peer tutoring, classwide peer tutoring, cued spelling, and paired writing are all examples of peer-tutoring approaches.

- School counselors can promote the enhancement of situational interest to create strengths-enhancing academic environments. Situational interest can be increased by involving students in work with other students, teaching students specific strategies to make boring tasks more interesting, and increasing student self-determination by providing more instructional choices. Although novel instructional approaches increase situational interest, meaningfulness and involvement in school work should also be encouraged to maintain personal interest.

- School counselors can encourage the complementary nature of family-school-community roles in six key areas with student: (a) standards and expectations, (b) structure, (c) opportunity to learn, (d) support, (e) climate and relationships, and (f) modeling. Through consultation, parent education, and parent-educator committees, they can help to foster complementary roles between families and educators and create strengths-enhancing academic environments.

4

Promoting Academic Development: Interventions

OUTLINE

TRADITIONAL SCHOOL COUNSELING INTERVENTIONS FOR ACADEMIC DEVELOPMENT

As we discussed in the previous chapter, school counseling and school counselor education have been criticized (e.g., The Education Trust, 1999) for focusing on the mental-health concerns of a small percentage of students rather than on the academic development of all students. The school counseling services that traditionally have impacted all students—class scheduling and placing students in academic/career tracks—have been viewed as primarily administrative tasks rather than developmental interventions. Moreover, criticism has been leveled that these services have actually limited, rather than enhanced, academic development for many students, especially those of color, by denying them access to honors, advanced placement, and other college-preparatory classes.

Other traditional academic services provided by school counselors, such as coordinating the school's testing program and maintaining academic records/transcripts, are largely clerical tasks, and their relationship to fostering academic development is somewhat vague and remote at best. When school counselors have attempted to apply a developmental focus to academic services, those services have tended to be limited to a small percentage of the student body and often appear to be more remedial in nature. Typical services have included arranging for tutoring for failing or low-performing students, teaching study skills to underachieving students, and meeting with failing students for individual or small-group counseling sessions in an effort to motivate them to "try harder."

CONTEMPORARY SCHOOL COUNSELING INTERVENTIONS FOR ACADEMIC DEVELOPMENT

Recently, the focus in education has shifted from what is being taught in schools to what is being learned by students.

> Today's school counselor is envisioned to be a school leader who advocates the academic, career, social, and personal success of every student. In doing so, the new-vision school counselor demonstrates a fundamental belief in the capacity of all students to achieve at high levels on rigorous and challenging academic course content when provided with the necessary encouragement and supports to ensure their success. Consistent with the new mission of education, the contributions of the new-vision school counselor to the academic success of all students are evaluated against a set of performance standards. (Paisley & Hayes, 2003, p. 199)

The No Child Left Behind (NCLB) Act (USDOE, 2001a) and other reform efforts require all educators, including school counselors, to focus more attention on student achievement and accountability. Increasing student achievement for all students, eliminating the achievement gap between Caucasian and minority students, ensuring that every student remains in school until graduation, and ensuring equity and access to educational programs and supports that lead to academic success are all key expectations of today's school counselor. School counselors are being called upon to move from a service-centered emphasis for some students to a program-centered emphasis for every student, and from a focus on what counselors are doing to a focus on how students are different and have improved academically as a result of the school counseling program (ASCA, 2003; Paisley & Hayes, 2003). Similarly, school counseling educators can be expected to place increasing emphasis on preparing future school counselors to deliver interventions and services that demonstrably promote academic competencies and success for all students (CACREP, 2001).

The pressures of the high-stakes testing environment in which school counselors are employed can easily result in equating academic development with academic achievement and, even more narrowly, to successful performance on standardized tests. Demonstrating that school counseling can positively impact achievement is clearly an important part of facilitating student academic development, but it is by no means the entire or only goal. Helping students to be prepared for a wide range of postsecondary options, to acquire skills for lifelong learning, and to understand the relationship of academics to work and to life are other important aspects of student academic development (ASCA, 2003). Furthermore, school counselors do not teach core content and therefore can be most effective in impacting other aspects of academic development rather than subject-specific test scores. In this chapter, we articulate some of the evidence-based interventions school counselors can implement to demonstrate accountability in promoting student academic strengths and strengths-enhancing academic environments.

STRENGTHS-BASED SCHOOL COUNSELING INTERVENTIONS FOR ACADEMIC DEVELOPMENT

In this chapter, we chose three primary academic issues that illustrate how school counselors can enhance student academic development. We demonstrate how they can provide a variety of counseling interventions in that capacity to promote both academic strengths in students and the strengths-enhancing capacity of their academic environments. These particular examples were chosen because they illustrate a number of the theories and principles discussed in the previous chapter. Table 4–1 summarizes the intervention examples that we present, the strengths that they attempt to enhance, and their environmental focus.

TABLE 4–1.
Selected Interventions for Fostering Academic Development

Intervention	Type of Service/Function Performed by Counselor	Strength Promoted	Environment Addressed	School Level
High-Stakes Testing Programs	Leadership Collaboration	Test-Taking Abilities	Classroom School	Elementary High
School Homework Policy	Leadership Collaboration	Self-Regulated Learning, Motivation	School Home	All
Homework Motivation and Preferences Questionnaire	Classroom Guidance	Self-Regulated Learning, Motivation	Home	High Middle
Homework Motivation—Parents	Small Group or Classroom Guidance—Parent Workshop	Self-Regulated Learning, Motivation	Home	High Middle
TIPS Interactive Homework	Leadership Advocacy	Self-Regulated Learning, Motivation	Home	Middle
Conjoint Behavioral Consultation for Homework	Consultation	Self-Regulated Learning, Motivation	Home-School Partnership	Middle Junior High
Developmentally Appropriate Homework	Consultation Advocacy	Self-Regulated Learning, Motivation	Classroom	Elementary
School Transition Environment Project	Collaboration Counseling Consultation		School	Middle High

We begin by discussing high-stakes testing. The counselor's roles as a leader and collaborator in high-stakes testing is illustrated by both an elementary- and a high-school program that have been successful in increasing student achievement scores. We chose to discuss high-stakes testing first due to the emerging emphasis placed on achievement tests in relation to the NCLB legislation. The examples we provide illustrate both promoting student test-taking strengths and enhancing the test-taking environment.

Second, we focus on services that the counselor can offer with respect to homework completion and propose that the strengths-based counselor can provide both direct and indirect (e.g., system-level) services to promote academic development. Specifically, we outline systemic-level interventions in leadership and/or collaboration with teachers, administrators, and parents in formulating research-informed, developmentally appropriate homework practices that support academic success for all students. We chose homework as an example because it (a) clearly illustrates the importance of developing self-regulated learning skills (see Chapter 3) that are important for life-long learning, (b) illustrates the SBSC emphasis on development as the school counselor's primary guiding principle, (c) has generated the depth of research findings necessary to clearly inform practice, and (d) is an area in which counselors are frequently called upon for assistance and one in which they can clearly make a major contribution to students' academic development and achievement.

At the high-school level, we review a one-session classroom guidance unit to help students become more effective self-regulated learners by more fully accommodating their learning preferences in homework completion. We also review a parent workshop designed to support students (e.g., to enhance the homework environment) in this endeavor. At the middle-school level, we present an interactive homework approach that increases family involvement (e.g., strengthens the home learning environment) in their children's education and enhances communication between parents and teachers (e.g., encourages complementary home and school system roles) as well as a consultation intervention that simultaneously targets both the family (e.g., parents) and school (e.g., teacher) systems in order to increase student homework completion and accuracy. A consultation-advocacy approach with individual teachers that emphasizes developmentally appropriate homework is illustrated at the elementary level.

Next, our focus shifts to middle- and high-school transitions and a systemic-level intervention to restructure the school environment to foster more successful academic transitions. Then we briefly consider the effects of comprehensive school reform initiatives. Comprehensive school reform represents the most overarching effort to improve academic performance through modifying the school as a system. It is also a topic that is not frequently addressed in school counselor preparation. Finally, we conclude by touching upon a variety of other interventions that promote academic strengths and strengths-enhancing environments. In each example, we also highlight how evidence of promoting strengths and strengths-enhancing environments particularly benefits minority and other traditionally underserved groups of students.

HIGH-STAKES TESTING

High-stakes testing is one aspect of current educational reform efforts that was generated, in part, in response to the publication *A Nation at Risk* (National Commission on Excellence in Education, 1983). High-stakes testing involves using scores on standardized tests to measure the effectiveness of instructional efforts. Accountability measures in the form of tests are presumed to promote higher educational standards and ensure equitable opportunities to quality education for all students (Riley & Cantu, 2000). High-stakes testing is one method that many state departments of education and legislatures are using to set standards of achievement, individually for students and collectively for schools and school districts. The results of these tests for individual schools and districts are made public and often carry rewards, in the form of monetary bonuses for school personnel, and punishments, such as loss of jobs or seizing of control of local schools by state departments of education. For students, the consequences of low performance may include retention and not graduating from high school.

As we discussed in Chapter 3, the NCLB Act (USDOE, 2001a) has made high-stakes testing a national mandate. Results from some research, however, have suggested that high-stakes testing often has a negative impact on teaching and learning and may not produce the desired effects for which it was intended (Amrein & Berliner, 2002; Cimbricz, 2002). At this time, it may be too early to have a complete picture of the impact of high-stakes testing, but the nation is committed to it for the foreseeable future. What then is the current school counselor's typical role in high-stakes testing?

Surprisingly, there has been relatively little research on high-stakes testing and the school counselor. Burnham and Jackson (2000) reported that 87.5% of a convenience sample of 80 school counselors in two southeastern states revealed that they served as testing coordinators for their schools. Brown et al. (2004) reported two studies with 141 and 139 school counselors in North Carolina in which 81% and 83% respectively indicated that either they or another counselor functioned as the testing coordinator for their school. Many of the duties of the test coordinator are largely clerical rather than professional and involve activities such as counting, distributing, packaging, and manipulating test materials; securing test administrators and proctors; and arranging modified testing arrangements for students with special needs.

Serving as testing coordinator is not compatible with professional conceptualizations of the school counselor's role (e.g., ASCA, 2003; Gysbers & Henderson, 1994, 2000, 2006). Moreover, although counselors noted some positive effects of the high-stakes testing program, they overwhelmingly reported that it negatively impacted their ability to provide counseling services and their relationships with students, teachers, and administrators, and that serving as test coordinator consumed a considerable percentage of their time (Brown et al., 2004).

To the extent that serving as test coordinator interferes with the school counselor's ability to provide a comprehensive school counseling program, it may also negatively impact student school success. Research has demonstrated that students enrolled in middle and high schools, which more fully implemented comprehensive guidance programs reported more positive outcomes, including higher grades, better relationships with teachers, and greater feelings of safety at school than students in schools in which these programs were less fully implemented (Lapan et al., 2001; Lapan, Gysbers, & Sun, 1997). In addition, a study using actual achievement-test scores of elementary students in Washington state revealed that, controlling for SES differences, over time third- and fourth-grades students in schools with a comprehensive school counseling program (CSCP) do better on a variety of norm-referenced and criterion-referenced tests than peers in schools without a CSCP in place (Sink & Stroh, 2003). Although the strength of effects of the results was modest in these studies, they do suggest that comprehensive school counseling programs are associated with positive student academic achievement and personal development. As such, serving as a test coordinator may negatively impact student academic achievement if it impairs the counselor's ability to provide students with a comprehensive school counseling program.

In summary, the role of testing coordinator within this high-stakes educational environment is neither an appropriate nor a productive one for the school counselor. What then is an effective role for the counselor in high-stakes testing?

Enhancing Student Test-taking Strengths and the Testing Environment: The Counselor as Leader and Collaborator in High-Stakes Testing

Many counselors and counselor educators have exhorted school counselors to become educational leaders and reformers (ASCA, 2003; Dollarhide, 2003; Education Trust, 1999; House & Hayes, 2002; House & Martin, 1998; Lennon, Blackwell, Bridgeforth, & Cole, 1996). More specifically, Stone and Clark (2001) urged that the leadership role be in collaboration and partnership with the principal in an effort to move schools toward rigorous academic achievement for all students. Perhaps the most pressing concern for principals in today's educational environment is the performance of students in her or his school on high-stakes tests. One principal (Hoover, 2002) identified a dozen ways to raise students' test performance. Several of these ways involved implementing a test-taking skills program, an area which potentially taps into the school counselor's professional and leadership skills. But to what extent are these programs effective? In addition, what contributions could the counselor make to the program, and what responsibilities would that counselor have?

Several meta-analyses (e.g., statistical, reviews of the research literature) of the effects of test-taking skills programs on performance on standardized achievement tests have been reported (e.g., Bangert-Drowns, Kulik, & Kulik, 1983; Samson, 1985; Scruggs, White, & Bennion, 1986). Samson, for example, reviewed 24 studies of the effectiveness of training programs in test-taking skills on elementary and secondary achievement. He reported that the average student in the test-taking skills group scored at the 63rd percentile on achievement tests, relative to the 50th percentile for the average student in the control group. Most of the studies he reviewed provided training in general test-taking skills such as following directions, proper use of time, and instruction in the use of answer sheets and in checking answers. Many studies also included discussion of guessing strategies and deductive-reasoning strategies. There were no differences between these general test-taking skills treatments and those that included additional treatment components such as motivational techniques, provision of incentives, test-anxiety reduction, or coaching for a specific test. Average achievement gains were significantly greater for programs that lasted five weeks or longer as compared to those conducted for shorter periods of time. Bangert-Drowns et al. also reported that length of training was positively related to achievement-score gains and that the effects of training were essentially the same for elementary and secondary students.

The Scruggs et al. (1986) review focused exclusively on elementary students and covered a larger number of studies than the two previous reviews. Scruggs et al. drew a few different conclusions. First, they found a much smaller overall effect of test-taking skills programs on achievement-test scores of elementary students. In agreement with the previous reviews, longer treatments (four hours or more) did have a significantly greater effect on achievement-test scores than those that were less than four hours in length. Overall, test-taking skills interventions had a much greater impact on students in the upper elementary (fourth to sixth) grades as compared to the primary (first to third) grades. In addition, treatments of less than four hours had no effect or even a slightly negative effect for primary-grade students, but there was no difference in the effects on upper- and lower-grade-average achievement if the treatment lasted four hours or more. Thus, it may take more test-taking skills training before there are observable benefits on achievement tests for younger students. In addition, with higher levels (four or more hours) of treatment, students from low socioeconomic backgrounds benefited more than twice as much as students who are not from low socioeconomic backgrounds. Finally, and as is the case for the previous reviews, the available data do not provide information to determine what specific type of test-taking skills programs are most effective.

As the "testing expert" and testing coordinator at the building level, the school counselor is often consulted by teachers, parents, and administrators about how to improve students' test-taking skills and enhance their success in today's high-stakes testing environment. As such, the counselor needs to be knowledgeable about interventions that improve student performance on standardized tests. Two recent test-taking skills programs—one at the elementary-school level (Smith, 2000) and one at the high-school level (Weller & Weller, 1998)—illustrate interventions that have been used successfully to improve student test scores. Both programs involve enhancing the test-taking skills of students as well as their test-taking environments.

The elementary program (the Standardized Timed Curriculum or STC) was a school-wide effort conducted in a K–6, Title 1 school and yielded consistent and dramatic improvements (e.g., with scores at or well above the national average) in performance of third- through sixth-grade students over a four-year period as measured by the Iowa Tests of Basic Skills (ITBS) (reading, language, and mathematics). The STC consisted of school-wide strategies, procedures, and materials developed by the staff. It incorporated a variety of interventions both to modify the school-wide environment with respect to testing and to provide students with test-taking skills.

Specifically, it involved (a) discussions to develop positive attitudes toward testing within the faculty and to recognize the importance of test-taking skills; (b) learning about the test; (c) developing an initial strategy to achieve quick, school-wide results (focus on a single curriculum area [mathematics computation]) that can be easily taught and measured; (d) aligning and timing the curriculum with the test; and (e) focusing on raising class average scores. A variety of procedures used to motivate students to try hard included (a) student certificates signed by the principal for "passing-off" (completing) a learning objective; (b) class rewards when every student in the class passed-off a specific grade-level learning objective; (c) posting of class and student progress on bulletin boards outside classroom doors; (d) trophies for every student who passed all the objectives for his or her grade level; (e) intercom recognition for individual students and classes; and (f) an award ceremony for students receiving "math master" certificates, indicating that they demonstrated significant achievement beyond all of the learning objectives for their grade level. The principal served as a cheerleader and encouraged learning and high performance by visiting classes, commending student accomplishments, and encouraging students to work hard. Parent understanding and cooperation with the program was enlisted through meetings and information sessions, and parents were encouraged to assist in their children's homework. Consistent with the research-based recommendations in the previous chapter, test-taking skills and strategies were taught in the context of the regular school curriculum. In addition, special instructional materials were developed to help students master the necessary academic skills. Students were given practice tests that contained similar problems to those on the ITBS, asked in similar ways, using similar answer bubble sheets and the same time limits as on the ITBS. Finally, students were taught test-taking skills relevant to the mathematics, reading, and language sections of the ITBS. Some of the test-taking skills included helping students organize their desks, reminding students to complete as many problems as possible, instructing them to circle lightly the problems they skipped, providing them with scratch paper with numbered boxes, encouraging them to stop guessing, and explaining what to do if they got out of order on the answer sheet.

The test-taking skills program was similarly successful at the high-school level. Gains were demonstrated on both state (Georgia High School Graduation Test and Grade Eleven Tests of Achievement and Proficiency) and national (SAT) tests. The program employed teacher and administrator teams and a continuous improvement framework (Weller & Weller, 1998) to remove barriers inhibiting student outcomes on tests, improve student learning through improving the total high-school program and its curriculum, and monitor and maintain the improvement process. The program had both short- and long-range goals focusing on the environment, test-taking skills, and knowledge of students and teachers. Environmental modifications included using parent volunteers for proctoring tests, providing food for students being tested, giving tests in the morning, and moving the testing location away from the school site to a quiet location. School counselors made phone calls and sent letters to parents about the testing program, how the results would be used, and what parents could do to help ensure that students came to school ready for the test. Trained teachers provided preparation courses on the math and verbal sections of the SAT, and all teachers were trained on reading strategies for use across the curriculum. Teachers also used practice questions in daily lesson plans and gave students practice sessions on essay writing. As was the case in the elementary program, teachers also aligned curriculum with the tests. In addition, they rearranged the grades in which certain courses were offered to better fit the state testing sequence. Finally, the school used a leadership team that consisted of department heads, at-large teachers, and administrative staff to focus on continuous improvement in all areas of the school program.

There are a variety of leadership functions, both individually and in collaboration with a school principal, which a school counselor can provide to programs designed to increase performance on high-stakes tests. Based on her or his graduate education in research, the school counselor is able to critically evaluate results of studies on enhancing test performance and to recommend promising programs and practices for teachers and administrators to consider implementing. Drawing on previous training in data analysis, the counselor is also able to assist administrators and teachers to disaggregate high-stakes testing data for her or his school according to the various subgroups (e.g., economically disadvantaged students, racial or ethnic minority groups, or students with disabilities or limited English proficiency) targeted by the NCLB Act. By disaggregating the data, teachers and administrators can determine the academic progress of different student groups and the effects that test-taking and other instructional interventions are having on them. Often we think of disaggregating data only in order to determine whether a particular group (e.g., racial or ethnic minority) is not performing as well as the majority of students and whether we and other educators need to work toward removing barriers to the academic development of these students. In Strengths-Based School Counseling (SBSC), we are also concerned about disaggregating scores within that racial or ethnic minority group in order to identify students who are performing well. By doing so, we can begin to determine the strengths they are evidencing that we need to promote among their peers. In addition, we may be able to identify the supports and strengths-enhancing they are experiencing in their environments that we need to foster with other students.

There also are several other types of leadership that the school counselor can provide with respect to high-stakes testing interventions. Based on work by Bolman and Deal (1997), Dollarhide (2003) described four general leadership contexts that can be applied. *Political leadership* involves the use of interpersonal and organizational power. In partnership with the principal, the school counselor can use her or his interpersonal, team-building, and persuasive skills to forge the linkages among individual teachers and different teacher factions needed for effective collaboration to develop, implement, refine, and maintain a comprehensive program to increase test performance of all students. *Human resource leadership* involves empowering and inspiring others. Improving test scores can be a complex, difficult, lengthy task. In order to be successful and to sustain their efforts with this task, teachers and others need to believe that they can be successful (e.g., have a strong sense of self-efficacy with respect to the goal) and that they have the power to make the instructional and curriculum changes that seem necessary along the way. By being able to discuss teacher concerns about the process, by providing support, and by continuously expressing encouragement and confidence in the faculty's ability to reach the desired goal, the school counselor can provide critical human-resource leadership that empowers teachers in this effort. *Symbolic leadership* involves interpreting and reinterpreting the meaning of change. In order to comply with the requirements of NCLB, educators and others must have a vision that all students can succeed. Together with the principal and other instructional leaders, the counselor can help to communicate and reinforce this vision as well as to make sure that it is the central focus of all instructional and other efforts undertaken by faculty, students, parents, and other stakeholders. Finally, *structural leadership* involves building viable organizations. The two successful high-stakes testing-skills programs that we reviewed were complex, had multiple intervention components, and involved a number of different team efforts. The school counselor can team with administrators and teacher-leaders to develop and maintain the organizational structure needed to increase student performance on standardized tests and to maintain it at a high level.

As we discussed, the objectives of high-stakes testing are concerned with measuring and improving academic performance for all students and eliminating the achievement gaps between minority, ESL, and other traditionally under-served students as compared with Caucasian students. Our discussion revealed several testing-related ways to reduce these gaps, including (a) a specific test-taking program that raised average scores of a Title 1 school at or well above the national average, (b) the fact that longer test-taking programs (e.g., more than four hours in length) are much more effective for students from lower socioeconomic backgrounds, (c) the need to disaggregate data in order to determine the progress that different groups of students are making on tests, and (d) the importance of counselors and administrators continuously reinforcing faculty expectations that all students can learn and be successful on high-stakes achievement tests. Finally, we reviewed a number of leadership roles that the school counselor can play in directly addressing the achievement gaps associated with high-stakes testing.

Not surprisingly, however, the strengths-based counselor's primary response to this challenge should not focus on testing per se. Rather it should focus on promoting the student academic strengths and strengths-enhancing environments that have been empirically shown to be associated with academic achievement and especially with the academic achievement of minority and low-performing students. Before leaving this section, we want to note some alternative approaches that can be employed to reduce and/or eliminate achievement gaps. In Chapter 1, for example, we provided links to evidence-based resources (see Table 1–2) that included the American Youth Policy Forum's compendium of 38 programs and practices that successfully raised minority academic achievement. In Chapter 3, we reviewed in depth two additional evidence-based strategies—cooperative learning and peer tutoring—for reducing these gaps. Both strategies promote specific student academic skills as well as enhance the overall class and school learning climate for all students, and especially for minority students.

A review of the research literature (Thompson & O'Quinn, 2001) revealed other ways to reduce achievement gaps. Many of these ways involve school counselors' influence at the systemic level through providing leadership, advocacy, consultation, and related services. These ways include reducing class size in the early grades, adopting sound and equitable grouping practices in elementary schools, assuring that African American and other minority students are equitably represented across curriculum tracks in high schools, and desegregating programs within schools. Historically, school counselors have had a major role in assigning students to classes, programs, and academic tracks and have been criticized for exercising a gate-keeping function that often restricted the opportunities for minority students to access more academically challenging courses and, as a result, widened the achievement gap. Thompson and O'Quinn's review indicated that students from impoverished minority families gain even more academically from small class sizes (e.g., fewer than 18 students) in grades K–3 than white and middle-class students. As such, elementary counselors who frequently work with principals in assigning students to classes at the beginning of the school year would do well to advocate smaller class sizes in these early grades. The review also revealed that black students are underrepresented in upper-level high-school tracks. Moreover, there is evidence that requiring students to take more challenging, college-oriented courses does raise test scores (e.g., narrows the achievement gap) but does not increase dropout rates or harm minority or low-income students (Thompson & O'Quinn, 2001). The authors noted that minority and low-income students may benefit more than white and other middle-class students from more rigorous course requirements. The implications of these findings for the strengths-based school counselor are clear. The counselor must function as an advocate for increased minority and low-income student representation in more challenging academic environments as these environments will enable them to acquire skills needed to eliminate the achievement gap. Our discussion now turns to another evidence-based strategy, homework completion, which also has potential for reducing the achievement gap and enhancing academic development for all students.

HOMEWORK COMPLETION

In the previous chapter, we reviewed the development of self-regulated learning skills and the role that these skills play in fostering academic achievement. We also considered the importance of motivation and environmental or contextual factors in learning. Homework completion is a prime example of an area in which the influence of self-regulated learning, motivation, and environmental considerations are all clearly manifested. Through homework interventions, the school counselor can make important contributions to facilitating academic development and student success if she or he employs the principles from these areas that we have already discussed as well as from the research findings and best practices that we will now consider.

Homework Completion: Some Basic Findings

Homework is defined as "tasks assigned to students by schoolteachers that are intended to be carried out during nonschool hours" (Cooper, 2001, p. 3). Teachers assign homework for a number of reasons, including practice, preparation (for the next lesson), participation (to increase involvement in learning), personal development (to increase perseverance, self-confidence, and study skills), parent-child relations (e.g., so parents can reinforce the importance of learning), parent-teacher communications (e.g., so parents are aware of what is being taught and how their child is doing), peer interactions, policy (to comply with school or district policy), public relations (to demonstrate high standards), and punishment, with the last purpose being an inappropriate use of homework (Epstein & Van Voorhis, 2001).

In the United States, homework is a low-cost, fundamental instructional strategy in education. It accounts for an estimated 20% of a child's total academic-engaged time (Cooper & Nye, 1994). Homework is also a frequent battleground for students and parents, students and teachers, and parents and teachers. During the 20th century, controversies about homework—e.g., too much versus too little—have followed a 30-year cycle, with public outcries for more or less homework occurring about 15 years apart (Cooper, 2001). An understanding of research results about (a) the influence of homework on academic performance, (b) guidelines for assigning homework, and (c) parental involvement in homework will better enable the school counselor to implement homework interventions that facilitate student academic development.

Homework completion and academic achievement.   Students who consistently fail to complete homework are commonly referred to school counselors by disgruntled teachers and parents who think the counselor's role is to magically "fix the problem" and send back academically responsible, self-regulated learners who are internally motivated to turn in high-quality, completed homework assignments in a timely manner. What services might the counselor offer with respect to homework completion, and to what extent is homework completion related to academic achievement? As we shall see, the answers to both questions are affected by development and student grade level. Not surprisingly, individual student characteristics and skill level also play an important role. For example, if a student lacks the academic skills (e.g., the reading level of the assignment is too high, or the student hasn't mastered short division and is being asked to complete long division problems), then a homework-completion intervention will not be successful if the skill deficit continues. The homework-completion intervention may even increase the student's frustration and unwillingness to learn. As such, assessing whether academic-skill deficits are impacting homework completion is an important consideration for the school counselor. If academic-skill deficits are not a factor, then a homework-completion intervention is appropriate.

But what relation, if any, is there between homework and academic achievement, and what implications does this have for the school counselor? Much of the research about this relationship was summarized by Cooper and colleagues (Cooper, 1989, 2001; Cooper, Lindsay, Nye, & Greathouse, 1998). Cooper (1989, 2001) reviewed 17 studies about the relationship between homework (or no homework) and achievement as measured by class tests/grades and standardized achievement tests and drew the following conclusions:

- About 70% of the studies indicated a positive effect for homework. The average student doing homework had a higher achievement score than 55% of students not doing homework. The average high-school student in a class doing homework would outperform 75% of the students in a no-homework class.

- The effect varies markedly by grade levels. The effect was very small to nonexistent in the primary grades. For junior-high students, it was twice as large as for elementary (grades four to six) students. The effect was largest for high-school students, e.g., twice as large as for junior-high-school students.

- The effects of homework were not different for males or females, or for students of different intelligence levels.

- Homework has neither a general positive nor a negative effect on students' attitudes toward school, teacher, or subject matter, except in one case. Cooper et al. (1998) reported that the amount of teacher-assigned homework was negatively related to student attitudes toward homework in the lower grades (two and four).

Noting the work of Walberg (1986) and Lipsey and Wilson (1993) that compared the effects of homework on student achievement to that of other instructional strategies (e.g., ability grouping, cooperative learning, advance organizers, higher-level cognitive questions), Cooper concluded that "homework's effect on achievement of elementary school students could be described as *very small*. . . . Although the overall impact of homework on achievement might be labeled *small to average*, it was clearly not small for students in secondary school" (2001, p. 22).

The effects of doing homework were also compared to some form of in-school supervised study (e.g., teachers sat and monitored the session or moved around the room and engaged students about their work) as reported in eight studies. The average student in the homework condition outperformed 53.6% of the in-school supervised-study students. However, supervised study had a more positive effect on the elementary students (grades five and six), whereas homework was more effective for older students. According to Cooper (2001), younger children have more limited study skills and a more limited ability to tune out distractions. These developmental differences as compared to older students may well explain the limited relationship between homework and achievement in elementary students and the greater relationship between supervised study (rather than homework) and achievement for them.

Homework completion is also a part of many after-school programs. Unfortunately the design of these programs makes it difficult to determine their impact on academic achievement, although there is some evidence that these programs serve a protective function for ESL and other students at risk of school failure (Cosden, Morrison, Albanese, & Macias, 2001). Students in these programs may experience a boost in self-confidence because they are more likely to complete assignments.

At this point, it is clear that doing homework (as opposed to not doing it) is associated with achievement for high-school students. There is also evidence that not doing homework is a key factor in course failure for high-school students. Collaborating on a study about the reasons high-school students received a D or F in a course, school counselors and counselor educators found that the students (61%), their teachers (70%), and their parents (73%) all independently identified not doing homework as the number one reason for the D and F grades (Dimmitt, 2003).

As we have seen, research findings on the relation between homework completion and academic achievement have different implications for school counselors depending on the developmental level of the students they are serving. At the high-school level and to a lesser extent at the middle/junior-high school level, providing interventions and fostering environments that increase homework completion is an important counseling service for enhancing student academic development. We will present some examples of these interventions and environments later in the chapter. At the elementary level and particularly for the primary grades, focusing on homework completion does not increase academic achievement and may even result in negative student attitudes toward homework, learning, and school. Instead, elementary-school counselors may want to encourage teachers and administrators to consider greater use of in-school supervised study as one way to increase student achievement and the development of academic skills and self-efficacy.

Time spent on homework and academic achievement: Research-based guidelines.   What is the relation between the amount of time spent doing homework and academic achievement? Is devoting more time to homework associated with higher achievement? Studies show that, within limits, spending more time on homework is associated with improved skills and achievement over time. Keith (1982) reported that high-school students, regardless of initial ability level, who regularly did their homework, received higher report-card grades than did other students. Moreover, with race, family background, prior ability, and high-school curricular-track statistically controlled, low-ability students who did 10 hours of homework or more per week had as good report card grades as high-ability students who did no homework.

In 50 studies that correlated the amount of time spent on homework and achievement levels, Cooper (2001) reported that 43 correlations indicated that students who spent more time on homework had better achievement-test scores or class grades, whereas seven indicated the opposite effect. Although causality was not unequivocally demonstrated, Cooper concluded that there is a positive association between time spent on homework and measures of academic achievement or attitude. Thus, the more time students spent on homework, the higher their scores on measures of achievement and vice versa. However, this association was strongest for high-school students and nearly nonexistent for elementary (grades three to five) students. In addition, Cooper et al. (1998) reported little relationship between the amount of teacher-reported assigned homework and student achievement in both lower (two to five) and upper grades (six to twelve), but a positive relationship at both grade levels between the portion of homework completed and achievement. The relationship between homework completed and achievement applied even when the amount of homework assigned or the use of homework in determining grades was statistically controlled.

Probing deeper, homework time and achievement may be related in a curvilinear fashion (e.g., the relationship between homework time and achievement is strongest for a moderate amount of time spent on homework and drops off when student puts in either very little time or a great deal of time). In the studies he reviewed, Cooper found a negative relation between homework time and achievement when one or less hours per week was spent on homework by high-school students. A positive relationship between the two appeared and strengthened for the high-school students as their study time increased from one to ten or more hours per week. In contrast, the strength of the positive relationship between time spent on homework and achievement for junior-high students increased steadily from zero to 5–10 hours per week and then deteriorated above the 5–10 hour interval.

Based on his review of the literature and the relationships between amount of homework and achievement, Cooper recommended the following guidelines for frequency and duration of homework assignments:

> Grades 1 to 3—one to three assignments per week, each lasting no more than 15 minutes
>
> Grades 4 to 6—two to four assignments per week, each lasting 15 to 45 minutes
>
> Grades 7 to 9—three to five assignments, each lasting 45 to 74 minutes
>
> Grades 10 to 12—four to five assignments per week, each lasting 75–120 minutes (Cooper, 1989, p. 52)

In addition, Cooper recommended that homework should have different purposes developmentally: to foster positive attitudes, habits, study skills, and character traits, and to reinforce simple skills learned in class for younger students and facilitate knowledge acquisition in specific topics for older students.

As we have discussed, the purpose of homework, whether homework should be assigned, to whom it should be assigned, and how much should be assigned are questions that are debated, disagreed about, and "fought over" by students, parents, and educators. Moreover, the school counselor is frequently called upon by these stakeholders either to offer an opinion or to answer these questions. Although there are no definitive answers, Cooper's research-based recommendations do provide elementary-, middle-, and high-school counselors with age-related homework guidelines that are associated with positive academic development.

The parents' role in homework. School counselors are frequently questioned about the appropriate role for parents in homework. Cooper et al. (1998) reported that positive parental attitudes toward homework in the upper grades (six through twelve) are positively associated with both student attitudes toward homework and student grades. A similar relationship between positive parental attitudes and positive attitudes about homework and school learning has also been found with African-American adolescents (Sanders, 1998) and students from other cultural groups (Hong, Milgram, & Perkins, 1995). More positive student attitudes, in turn, are related to decisions about time and effort to be spent on homework, personal responsibility for learning, and persistence in completing assignments (Hoover-Dempsey et al., 2001).

With respect to the type of parental involvement in homework, Hoover-Dempsey, Battiato, Walker, Reed, DeJong, & Jones (2001) reported studies indicating that more structured (e.g., task-centered efforts to help the child with assignments) approaches to parent involvement in homework have been associated with poorer student performance, and that less structured (more informal, student-responsive) have been associated with better student performance. Similarly, Cooper, Lindsay, and Nye (2000) investigated dimensions of parenting style and homework involvement. Although the styles that are helpful may be influenced by how well the student is doing in school, the researchers reported that, as parental support for autonomy increased, so did student achievement as measured by standardized tests, grades, and completed homework. Autonomy support consisted of valuing and using techniques that encourage the child in independent problem solving, choice, and participation in homework decisions. Parents in higher grade levels reported giving students more homework autonomy. Conversely, when direct parental involvement in homework increased, student achievement decreased, as measured by test scores and class grades, especially for elementary-school students. Direct parental involvement concerned the extent to which parents took an active part in their children's homework assignments. They noted that some of the relationship may be developmental in nature. For older students, providing autonomy support, refraining from providing help that actually interferes with their children's studying, and creating an environment that facilitates student self-study appear to be productive homework roles for parents. Although an active teaching role for parents may be appropriate for parents of students in early grades who are experiencing difficulty in school, "studies examining whether there are positive effects to casting parents in the role of teacher suggest this will be of limited success" (Cooper, 2001, p. 62). In general, research suggests that the primary role for parents with respect to homework is to create a home environment that facilitates self-study. Parents' involvement in homework:

> influence not only child achievement, but students' development of learning pertinent attributes, including positive attitudes toward learning tasks, positive perceptions of personal competence and ability, productive attributions about the causes of successful performance, and knowledge of personally effective learning strategies. In their influence on such proximal outcomes, parents' homework involvement activities develop student attributes directly associated with school success. (Hoover-Dempsey et al., 2001, p. 206)

In summary, the research literature provides school counselors with some guidelines about the appropriate role for parents in homework. In general, a more informal, student-responsive role to homework (e.g., encouraging independent homework completion by students coupled with providing assistance when requested) should be recommended to parents in preference over a more formal, structured (e.g., parents are involved in a daily teaching role in homework) role. In addition, positive parent attitudes toward homework are especially important to the academic development of middle- and high-school students.

Homework completion interventions: An overview.　　As we have seen, the results of homework research have important implications for the practicing school counselor in efforts to foster student academic development. It is clear, for example, that homework completion and amount of time spent on homework are especially related to student achievement at the high-school level. As such, it is reasonable for counselors to consider involvement in homework completion efforts as one way to foster academic achievement and to reduce the minority achievement gap.

A variety of counseling interventions have been found to be effective in increasing homework completion. Cooper (2001), for example, reported that studies have shown that providing students rewards for handing in homework can increase completion rates. Other effective interventions have included school-home notes in the form of daily report cards (Dougherty & Dougherty, 1977; Strukoff, McLaughlin, & Bialozor, 1987), having parents sign completed assignments (Holmes & Croll, 1989), self-instruction training (Fish & Mendola, 1986), self-management training (Olympia, Sheridan, Jenson, & Andrews, 1994), and an intervention consisting of self-monitoring, self-evaluation in the form of goal-setting, and self-graphing of completed/turned in assignments (Trammel, Schloss, & Alper, 1995) .

Enhancing the Homework Environment for All Students through Effective Homework Policies: The Counselor as Leader and Collaborator

Based on the results of homework research, the school counselor can assume a systemic-level role as either a leader or a collaborator with parents, teachers, administrators, and other stakeholders to formulate homework policies that support academic success for all students. In addition to providing information about the implications of these research findings, the school counselor can assess current teacher or school homework practices and the effects of those practices on student attitudes and achievement. In the process, school counselors may find it useful to encourage teachers and other decision-makers to compare local homework practices to the research-based homework guidelines (e.g.,

Cooper, 2001) for districts, schools, and classrooms that we have just discussed. In addition to helping teachers and administrators to develop or revise homework policies, school counselors at different grade levels may discover that they need to implement different types of homework interventions. It is to a selection of some of these other developmentally specific interventions that we now turn.

Enhancing Self-Regulated Homework Skills and Motivation in High-School Students through Classroom Guidance

The work of Hong and colleagues (Hong & Milgram, 2000, 2001; Rowell & Hong, 2002) is relevant to homework intervention in general and at the high-school level in particular. Their approach emphasizes student self-regulated learning. Hong and colleagues assumed that "accommodating students' learning preferences [in homework completion] increases the likelihood students' learning potential will be actualized" (Rowell & Hong, 2002, p. 289). This premise is supported by studies indicating that students taught through their learning preferences learn better in school and attain more enjoyment from the learning process (e.g., Dunn & Dunn, 1992, 1993; Sims & Sims, 1995). It is also supported by research demonstrating improved academic performance by college students who did their homework under conditions (e.g., time of day and preference for sound, light, and formal or informal design of furniture) that matched their learning style (Dunn, Deckinger, Withers, & Katzenstein, 1990; Lenehan, Dunn, Inghan, Signer, & Murray, 1994). In their own research, Hong, Topham, Wozniak, Carter, and Topham (2000) compared treatment and control students following a homework intervention. Students in the intervention saw themselves as doing their homework better than those who had not received the intervention, and students who applied their strong preferences in doing homework had more positive attitudes toward homework than those who did not.

Hong and Milgram (2000) developed a model of homework performance that included two categories of conceptual components: motivation and preference (see Table 4–2). There are three sources of motivation for doing homework. A learner may be *self-motivated*, *teacher-motivated* (e.g., motivated to please the teacher by doing homework), and/or *parent-motivated*. Individually or in combination, these sources of motivation activate the process of doing required homework. Referring back to our discussion of the self-motivation continuum in the previous chapter, students who are self-motivated exhibit more intrinsically oriented, internally regulated homework behavior, whereas students who are parent- or teacher-oriented exhibit more extrinsically motivated, externally regulated behavior with respect to homework completion. The strength of the student's motivation to do homework is reflected by *promptness* (e.g., the tendency to do it when assigned and not procrastinate) and *persistence* (e.g., the degree of sustained effort in doing homework).

TABLE 4–2.
Hong and Milgram's (2001) Model of Homework Motivation and Preferences

Motivation	*Preference*
Source	Organizational
Self-Motivated	Structure
Parent-Motivated	Order
Teacher-Motivated	Place
Strength	Time
Promptness	**Surroundings**
Persistence	Sound
	Light
	Temperature
	Design
	Perceptual-Physical
	Auditory
	Visual
	Tactile
	Kinesthetic
	Intake
	Mobility
	Interpersonal
	Alone-Peers
	Authority Figures

The preference category is divided into four subcategories: *organizational, surroundings, perceptual-physical,* and *interpersonal.* There are four *organizational* components: *structure, order, place,* and *time. Structure* refers to the student's preferences for the kinds of instruction the teacher gives (e.g., highly structured, well-defined versus relatively unstructured, open-ended) about how the homework is to be done. The other three *organizational* components refer to the student's preferences with respect to the *order* (e.g., whether the student maintains a stable unchanged order or varies the pattern in which the homework is to be done), as well as to the *place* (variable place or set place) and *time* (variable time or set time) the homework is to be done. *Surroundings* have to do with the student's preferences for *sound* (silence versus background sound), *light* (dim versus bright light), *temperature* (cool versus warm), and/or *design* (formal furniture such as a desk and straight chair versus informal such as an easy chair or thick rug) while doing homework. The *perceptual-physical* category contains six components: *auditory, visual, tactile, kinesthetic, intake,* and *mobility.* Does the student prefer assignments that require listening (e.g., a tape or CD), viewing (e.g., a film), "hands-on" or tactile activities (e.g., preparing an exhibit), first-hand experience and active participation (e.g., a virtual-reality experience), and activities that allow eating and drinking (intake), and/or moving around (versus sitting still)? Lastly, the *interpersonal* preference category has two components: *alone-peers* and *authority figures*. Does the student prefer to do homework alone or with a peer or peers, and with an adult authority figure (e.g., a parent) present or absent?

Hong and Milgram (2001) developed the 63-item Homework Motivation and Preference Questionnaire (HMPQ) that enables students to assess and profile their preferences for each of the 21 homework-motivation and preference components. Rowell and Hong (2002) proposed that the HMPQ be used in a proactive classroom guidance activity with ninth-graders. This activity may be especially useful in assisting students at this grade level to meet the more rigorous academic demands that will confront them as they make the transition from middle school to high school. Research studies have demonstrated that this transition is challenging to students and that academic achievement is often negatively affected in the process (e.g., Alspaugh, 1998). The one-session classroom guidance lesson is preceded by a 10- to 15-minute pre-session in which students complete the HMPQ. With instruction from a counselor or teacher, students then also score the HMPQ and prepare their own homework motivation and preference profiles for use in the classroom guidance session. The actual session includes the following:

> (a) introducing the relationship of homework to success in school; (b) explaining homework motivation—whether students are self-, parent, and/or teacher motivated; (c) explaining homework preferences—organizational issues, physical surroundings, perceptual-physical elements, and interpersonal elements; (c) interpreting the students' individual profiles; (e) encouraging students to be aware of and to utilize their strong preferences; and (f) encouraging students to diversify their preferences. (Rowell & Hong, 2002, p. 288)

During the session, students are encouraged to brainstorm about how they can increase both the sources and strength of homework motivation. In addition, they are asked to share suggestions with each other about how to modify their home environments to more closely approximate their homework preferences, or, in instances when that is not feasible, how to diversify their homework preferences in order to make more effective use of their homework environment. The students could also be asked to discuss the findings with their parents.

Enhancing the Homework Environment for High-School Students: A Parent Workshop

Coupling the classroom guidance lesson with a parent workshop might be an especially useful way to enhance the homework-completion environment for students (Rowell & Hong, 2002). It is also a way of facilitating the type of complementary home-school relations discussed in Chapter 3 that foster student academic development. In addition, if the ninth-grade students and their parents are the target audience, then these activities would seem to be well suited as components of a middle-to-high-school transition program that is presented early in the school year. During the workshop, parents are asked to complete the HMPQ as they think their child would respond. Counselors help them to understand each of the components, and, as research has shown, the importance of providing their children with autonomy-support for homework completion. By comparing how they think their child would complete the HMPQ profile with how their children actually complete it, parents can develop a higher level of awareness of their child's learning preferences. Studies have found that a higher level of parental awareness of a child's homework preference is associated with a child having higher academic achievement and more positive attitudes toward homework (Hong & Lee, 1999; Hong et al., 1995). In the workshop, parents are also encouraged to help their child to implement his or her homework preferences wherever possible as well as to help the child to extend those preferences as needed.

Enhancing Family Involvement in Education and Home-School Communication in the Middle School through "Interactive Homework"

Epstein and her colleagues (Epstein, Salinas, & Jackson, 1995; Epstein & Van Voorhis, 2001) have developed an "interactive homework" approach that improves achievement, increases families' involvement in their children's education, and enhances communication between parents and teachers (i.e, complementary home-school roles). As we shall see, this approach is relevant to middle-school counselors who are interested in impacting student academic development and achievement through homework interventions.

The Teachers Involve Parents in Schoolwork (TIPS) process "encourages students to share interesting things they are learning in class with family members, friends, peers, or others in the community" (Epstein & Van Voorhis, 2001, p. 186). It guides them to conduct conversations and interactions with family members in math, science/health, and language arts. In all instances, the TIPS assignments are the students' responsibility. Parents are not asked to teach skills, but instead to play a supportive role in discussing homework with their children. The TIPS homework may involve students demonstrating math skills, conducting science experiments, gathering parents' memories and experiences, or applying school skills to real life (see Table 4–3 for features of the TIPS process).

Epstein and Van Voorhis (2001) reported three studies of the effects of TIPS interactive homework on students' skills, parents' involvement, and student and parent attitudes' about homework. The approach was applied to three

TABLE 4–3.
Features of the Teachers Involve Parents in Schoolwork (TIPS) Process
(Epstein & Van Voorhis, 2001)

Teachers and principals orient parents and students to the TIPS process.

Teachers send home TIPS activities on a regular schedule (e.g., once a week or twice a month).

Teachers allow extra time (e.g., 2 days or over a weekend) for TIPS homework to accommodate family schedules.

TIPS are designed for two sides of one page and include simple instructions that the student can explain to a family partner.

All activities use readily available materials at home and require no expensive purchases.

TIPS activities include a home-to-school communication for parents to check or comment whether they enjoyed the activity with their child and whether they learned something about what students are learning in class.

Teachers use the same methods for collecting, grading, and discussing TIPS as they use for other homework.

Teachers use family and student feedback for redesigning activities or to contact families who may have questions about their students' work or progress.

From Epstein, J. L., & Vam Voorhis, F. L. (2001). More than minutes: Teachers' roles in designing homework. *Educational Psychologist, 38,* 181–193. Reprinted with permission from Lawrence Erlbaum Associates Publishers.

different subject areas—writing, mathematics, and science—and with middle schools in three different school districts: one with predominantly poor, urban, African-American East Coast families (70% free/reduced lunch), one with a Midwestern middle school with predominantly middle-class white families, and one from an East Coast predominantly middle-class middle-school but with a heterogeneous population.

In the writing study with African American families, the researchers found that, after taking into account initial skill levels and attendance, students who completed more TIPS homework assignments had higher language report-card grades. Over 80% of the students and nearly 100% of the families surveyed agreed that TIPS gave them information about what the children were learning in school. Moreover, the study demonstrated that parents with little formal education could become productively involved in their children's education. The study that focused on mathematics also demonstrated more family involvement in math homework for students in groups with prompts for involvement than for groups without prompts. In the science study, TIPS students had higher science report-card grades and more family involvement in science than did students in non-TIPS classes. Thus, TIPS assignments added significantly to students' report-card grades over and above the general effects of homework.

TIPS is clearly an effective middle-school homework program that increases student achievement and family support of children in education. However, it was designed by teachers and researchers, and its successful use is predicated on teacher input, involvement, and ownership. What possible role can a middle-school counselor have in such a program? Middle-school counselors can play a key leadership and advocacy role with TIPS. They can present examples of TIPS assignments and the research results on TIPS to middle-school administrators and influential teacher team leaders in an effort to build support for implementing TIPS assignments in the school as a whole or in one or more instructional teams. Moreover, they can advocate especially the use of TIPS assignments with minority students. As we discussed, the effects of TIPS assignments on writing with urban, African-American students and their families are particularly promising and suggest that TIPS might be another example of an effective technique for helping educators to eliminate the minority achievement gap by involving minority students and their families more fully in the educational process.

Simultaneously Enhancing Home- and Middle-School Systems for Homework Completion: Conjoint Behavioral Consultation

Conjoint behavioral consultation (Sheridan, 1997) is another approach that has been used to increase homework completion and accuracy at the middle-school level. Conjoint behavioral consultation (CBC) "is a structured indirect form of service delivery in which parents, teachers, and other support staff are joined to work together to address the academic social, or behavioral needs of a student" (Sheridan, Eagle, Cowan, & Mickelson, 2001, p. 362). The approach has been applied successfully with a variety of concerns including behavior disorders, attention-deficit hyperactivity disorder, and learning disabilities (Sheridan et al., 2001). As we discussed in the previous chapter, it is extremely important to promote effective home-school partnerships in order to facilitate student academic development and achievement. CBC operates on the premise that gains in student performance are greatest when interventions focus on the reciprocal relationship between school and home (e.g., a mesosystemic orientation) rather than attending to only one of these systems (e.g., a microsystemic orientation) (Christenson & Sheridan, 2001). Moreover, two studies have supported this principle, demonstrating that CBC produced superior effects to teacher-only consultation (Sheridan, Kratochwill, & Elliott, 1990) and to self-training manuals (Galloway & Sheridan, 1994). Thus, CBC focuses on the interacting systems that affect children and assumes that children, families, and schools have reciprocal and bidirectional influence over each other.

CBC involves parents, teachers, and a consultant[1] (the school counselor) working together simultaneously in a structured problem-solving framework to

---

[1]CBC was originally designed as a consultation intervention for school psychologists.

collect data and intervene on a child's behavior over time and across settings. The model is structured around a four-stage problem-solving process—problem identification, problem analysis, treatment implementation, and treatment evaluation—between a consultant (the school counselor), parent(s), and teacher(s), that is fluid and cyclical.

Weiner, Sheridan, and Jenson (1998) applied CBC and a structured homework program, *Sanity savers* (Olympia, Jenson, & Hepworth-Neville, 1996), on math completion and accuracy with five junior-high-school students (three girls and two boys) who demonstrated noncompliant behavior in this area. The consultation sessions were generally conducted with participant pairs (e.g., parent-teacher). The consultant (a school psychologist) and consultees each participated in three interviews: conjoint problem identification, conjoint problem analysis, and conjoint treatment evaluation. The problem-analysis interview also included the student, in part, in order to discuss individualized reinforcement preferences.

Sanity savers (Olympia et al., 1996), which is a homework-compliance and behavioral reinforcement program, was implemented across the classroom and home settings. This intervention included a school component with self-recording, a home program with homework structure and supervision, and positive reinforcement provided across settings. The school component involved students recording their assignments in a planner each day and the teacher initialing the assignment to indicate to students and parents that it was recorded correctly. When the assignment was returned, the teacher corrected it, computed completion and accuracy percentages daily, and provided verbal feedback to the students. The home program included five rules that parents followed to increase homework compliance: having homework done in only one place (preferably not the student's bedroom), making sure the workspace was equipped with appropriate materials (e.g., pencils and paper), limiting access to the study area during homework, keeping noise to a minimum, and starting homework the same time every day. Students and parents together determined the most appropriate homework time and place. Parents also checked the day planner for the assignment, confirmed that the student had begun working on the assignment, and recorded the amount of time spent on math homework each night, the location in which the homework was done, and the number of items completed. Teachers designed each assignment to be completed within approximately 20 minutes by an average student. Tangible reinforcers were provided both at home and at school. The consultant provided the reinforcers at school. In order to receive the nightly reinforcer, the student had to meet the criteria of 20 or more minutes spent on the assignment and 100% of the assignment completed, as checked by the parents. Weekly reinforcement (e.g., gift certificates for pizza, music, and movies) was provided by the consultant and delivered by classroom teachers via a lottery system. Long-term reinforcers were also used and were delivered by parents based upon overall accuracy percentages (e.g., 70% or greater average accuracy percentage on math homework assignments at the end of the intervention).

As a result of the intervention, four of the five students improved their completion rates during the treatment; accuracy rates increased as well, but to a lesser degree. At follow-up, three of the students maintained or improved their gains, and one, who had not improved during treatment, showed improvement at follow-up. Another student was unable to maintain the gains made during treatment. In summary, this small-sample study, one of the few consultation studies with middle-grade/junior-high-school students, demonstrated how a consultant can work simultaneously and effectively with both parents and teachers to improve student math-homework performance. In the study, the consultant was a school psychologist, but a school counselor could have provided this service as well.

Establishing Developmentally Appropriate Homework Environments for Elementary-School Students through Consultation and Advocacy

In an elementary school, the issues regarding homework are not the same as those in middle and high school. As we have seen, the relationship between homework and achievement is much weaker than in the upper grades. In addition, the amount of homework assigned and the purpose of homework are also different. The elementary-school counselor needs to be attuned to whether homework assignments are facilitating the development of both a strengths-enhancing academic environment within the school and of individual student academic strengths. If not, then the counselor has to decide whether intervention on the individual and/or systemic level is warranted.

For example, an elementary-school counselor may be seeing a number of second-grade students from the same class who are upset about the amount of homework that they are being given each night and about the fact that their assignments necessitate learning difficult concepts and material on their own. In addition, the counselor may also have had complaints from parents that the amount of homework is excessive and that it is disrupting family life. The counselor concludes that the student and parent concerns have merit and needs to decide on a course of action. On the one hand, the counselor might consider working with the students individually or in small groups to reduce their anxiety level. The counselor might also attempt to find tutors or homework help for the students in an after-school program.

On the other hand, that same counselor might consider implementing a more systemic-level approach, adopting a combined consultation-advocacy intervention with the classroom teacher. Thus, the counselor would discuss with the teacher his or her homework assignment objectives, the school or district homework policy if one has been adopted, the type of homework being assigned, and the difficulties that the students and families are experiencing with the assignments. The counselor would then share his or her knowledge about what has been learned from the homework research and, if necessary, advocate that the teacher adopt a homework policy that is more informed by this research. Thus, sharing knowledge about (a) the negative effects of a large amount of assigned homework on student attitudes toward homework in the early grades, (b) the limited relationship between doing homework and student achievement in the early grades, (c) the superior effects of supervised in-school study as opposed to homework on achievement in the early grades, (d) the research-based recommendations about appropriate amounts of homework at different grade levels, and (e) the use of homework in the early grades to build study skills and positive attitudes could provide a convincing rationale for encouraging the teacher to use homework in a manner that more effectively enhances the class environment for the academic development of all students.

While homework presents one type of challenge to student academic development, the transition from one level of schooling to another, which also tends to increase homework demands on students, presents a different and far more complex set of challenges. We now turn to a discussion of these school-transitions issues. As we shall see, the strengths-based school counselor can be instrumental in facilitating smoother, less stressful school transitions, thereby fostering academic development for all students.

SCHOOL TRANSITIONS

The transitions from elementary to middle school and from middle school to high school represent significant milestones in students' academic development. These transitions present changes and challenges for all students, and many find them difficult to negotiate. The elementary to middle/junior-high school transition, for example, has been found to be associated with a variety of negative effects on adolescents including declines in achievement (Alspaugh, 1998), decreased motivation (Harter, 1981; Simmons & Blyth, 1987), lowered self-esteem (Eccles, Wigfield et al., 1993; Wigfield, Eccles, Mac Iver, Reuman, & Midgley, 1991), and increased psychological distress (Chung, Elias, & Schneider, 1998; Crockett, Peterson, Graber, Schulenberg, & Ebata, 1989). Similarly, the transition to high school has also been accompanied by negative consequences for some students, including achievement loss (Alspaugh, 1998) and dropping out shortly after they enter high school or falling behind and failing to graduate on time (Mizelle & Irvin, 2000). Given that (a) school transitions are associated with an increased likelihood of not completing high school, (b) Hispanic and black students are more likely than white students to leave school prior to graduation (USDOE, 2001c), and (c) students from low-income families are more likely to drop out than students from middle- and high-income families (USDOE, 2001b), effective school-transition programs may be especially important in fostering these students' academic development and reducing the minority achievement gap.

Recognizing the challenges that school transitions present, many schools provide transition programming for students and parents. This programming is often conducted as a team effort by counselors, teachers, and administrators. The content of the programming has tended to evolve from an event rather than a process conception of the transition experience. As such, one-shot interventions such as guided tours of the school, information/orientation sessions for students and parents, open-house nights, and course-registration sessions for students conducted by the school counselor are the most common components. Recently, however, counselors have begun to take a more informed look at the needs of students during school transitions and at school transition programming (e.g., Akos, 2002; Akos & Galassi, 2004a, 2004b; Akos, Queen, & Lineberry, 2005; McCall-Perez, 2000) with the view that a more comprehensive approach may be needed.

Restructuring School Ecology for Successful Middle- and High-School Transitions through Collaborating and Teaming

Felner et al. (1993) described the year-long School Transition Environment Project (STEP), and, as we will see, the school counselor can play an important role in systemic efforts to restructure environments to be more supportive for students involved in school transitions. The STEP project was based on a transactional-ecological model of prevention and employed a school restructuring and transformation approach to prevent the deleterious effects of school transitions and to create school environments that are developmentally enhancing. STEP is viewed as an inexpensive, but effective, contextually focused, developmentally informed, preventive intervention for facilitating middle/junior-high and high-school transitions. It is based on assumptions that are highly compatible with Strength-Based School Counseling, namely to (a) modify or remove risk conditions in the environment that interfere with successful school transitions, and (b) enhance developmental conditions that increase the probability that students will "naturally" acquire the strengths associated with successful school transitions (see Henderson and Milstein's Resiliency Wheel in Chapter 1). Moreover, STEP capitalized on the critical environmental factors (see Chapter 3) of relatedness (Ryan & Deci, 2000) and belongingness (Osterman, 2000) between teachers and students and among students that are associated with positive academic development.

The project involved facilitating successful adaptation to the transition by reducing the adaptation demands imposed by the transitions and increasing coping resources available to students. STEP employed two primary types of interventions. First, the school social system was reorganized in order to reduce the complexity and degree of flux that ninth graders experienced. Smaller learning environments were created within the larger school to provide students with a stable and consistent set of classmates. These changes were accomplished by assigning 60–100 ninth graders to a STEP team and then assigning students to classes so that each STEP academic core class was composed of the same STEP team. In addition, all STEP classrooms were located in close physical proximity to each other so as to reduce the size and complexity of the environment and to reduce the likelihood that the incoming ninth graders would be exposed to social pressure or intimidation from older students. Second, the project resulted in a restructuring of the homeroom teacher's role and in increasing teacher support for students. STEP students were assigned to a homeroom. Homerooms consisted of 20–30 STEP students, and the homeroom teacher conducted a teacher-advisory program with them. The homeroom teacher assumed a number of guidance-like responsibilities, including helping students choose classes, discussing students' school and personal problems, and checking on student absences and following up with family members. In addition, all STEP teachers met several times a week (at times with school counselors) to identify students who needed additional assistance or other services. There were four goals for these changes in teachers' roles:

1. to make the transitional task of acquiring and reorganizing formal support less difficult and to increase the amount of support students receive and perceive as being available from school staff;

2. to reduce the difficulty with which students can gain access to important information about school rules, expectations, and regularities;

3. to increase students' sense of accountability and belongingness and reduce their sense of anonymity; and

4. to increase the extent to which teachers are familiar with students and to reduce the overload that teachers often experience in gaining familiarity with large numbers of entering students. (Felner et al., 1993, p. 113)

Felner et al. (1993) reported two studies about the effects of STEP on students. The first study was conducted with entering ninth graders in a large, urban high school that served primarily low SES and/or minority students whose families were largely on public assistance. By the end of the first project year (e.g., ninth grade), matched control-group students showed marked decreases in grades, attendance, and self-concept, whereas STEP students exhibited stable levels of academic performance (e.g., grades), attendance, and self-concept. In addition, STEP students perceived the school environment as more stable, understandable, well-organized, involving, and supportive in contrast to the controls who exhibited systematic declines in ratings of school climate and staff support. A five-year follow-up revealed that the 43% dropout rate for control-group students was almost twice that (24%) of STEP students. In addition, grade-point average of STEP students was significantly higher than for control students at the end of ninth and tenth grade years but did not differ significantly for the 11th- and 12th-grade years, perhaps because of greater drop-out in the control group (e.g., more students who were doing poorly dropped out). Finally, absences were significantly lower for STEP students across all four high-school years. Thus, it appears that a one-year (ninth grade) transition program that modified the school environment was associated with enduring effects on grades, absences, and drop-out rates for high-school students long after the program had concluded.

In a second study reported by Felner et al. (1993), the STEP program was implemented with either middle- or junior-high-school students in four STEP and four non-STEP comparison schools that represented a wide range of geographic (e.g., urban, suburban, and rural), demographic (SES), and structural (e.g., varying sizes and number of feeder schools) characteristics. During the transition year, students in STEP schools reported more positive school experiences and better adjustment outcomes across academic (grades), socioemotional (e.g., depression, anxiety, stress), and behavioral measures (e.g., teacher ratings of acting out, moodiness/shyness) than non-STEP students.

The STEP results would appear to have clear implications for school counselors with respect to middle/junior-high and high schools. Large school environments can be restructured in order to increase the likelihood of successful academic and social transitions by incoming students. School counselors can advocate, collaborate, and team with teachers, administrators, parents, and other educational stakeholders to bring about this type of environmental change. Once the change has occurred, they can then provide their more traditional services (e.g., counseling and consultation) to support students during the transition process.

COMPREHENSIVE SCHOOL REFORM

As we have discussed, STEP represents an effort to reform and restructure school ecology for the purpose of facilitating school transitions. In these initiatives, the strengths-based school counselor can engage in a variety of direct service and systemic-level functions, including counseling, advocacy, collaboration, coordination and teaming, consultation, and training. But a number of more general and extensive school reform efforts are also underway, and the strengths-based school counselor has an important part to play in these efforts as well (Adelman & Taylor, 2002; Herr, 2002; House & Hayes, 2002). "Counselors must no longer operate from the educational sidelines; instead, they need to assume leadership in this area, first by assisting with school reform in their buildings and districts . . ." (Sink, 2005, p. 133).

Comprehensive school reform (CSR) or "whole school" reform is the term for major federally-funded initiatives that seek to alter educational environments to increase student academic achievement. The Comprehensive School Reform (CSR) Program began in 1998 and was authorized as Title 1, Part F of the Elementary and Secondary Education Act, which was signed into law on January 8, 2002. "CSR focuses on reorganizing and revitalizing entire schools rather than on implementing a number of specialized and potentially uncoordinated school improvement initiatives" (Borman, Hewes, Overman, & Brown, 2002, p. 2). In order to qualify as a CSR program, the U.S. Department of Education specifies 11 specific components that the program must include. Among these are (a) proven methods and strategies based on research; (b) measurable goals and benchmarks for student achievement; (c) support within the school by teachers, administrators, and staff; (d) meaningful parent and community involvement; (e) high-quality professional development for teachers and staff; and (f) significant improvement or demonstration of strong evidence that it will improve the academic achievement of students (U.S. Department of Education, 2002).

Such comprehensive reform efforts as *Accelerated Schools* (http://www.acceleratedschools.net/), *Success for All* (http://www.successforall.net/), and *High Schools That Work* (http://www.sreb.org/programs/hstw/HSTWindex.asp) are heavily financed by federal and other funding agencies, have been implemented in thousands of schools, and affect millions of students. As such, the school counselor needs to be knowledgeable about the extent to which the various CSR efforts have led to developmentally more effective strengths-enhancing environments for students. Descriptions of the major CSR initiatives are available on the World Wide Web through the Northwest Regional Educational Laboratory's National Clearinghouse for Comprehensive School Reform (http://www.nwrel.org/scpd/catalog/aboutnccsr.shtml) and in Appendix B (http://www.csos.jhu.edu/CRESPAR/techReports/report59AppendixB.pdf) of the review by Borman et al. (2002).

The extent to which CSR initiatives impact student achievement as measured by test scores was addressed by a recent meta-analysis, a statistical review of the empirical literature (Borman et al., 2002). Twenty-nine of the most widely implemented CSR models were studied. Results indicated that schools implementing CSR models for five years or more showed particularly strong effects on student achievement, and schools of higher- and lower-poverty levels benefited equally. Furthermore, the reviewers classified the 29 models into four categories based on the evidence of demonstrated effectiveness: (a) Strongest Evidence, (b) Highly Promising Evidence, (c) Promising Evidence, and (d) Greatest Need for Additional Research.

The strongest evidence was found for three models: *Direct Instruction* (K–6) (http://www.nifdi.org/), *School Development Program* (K–12) (http://www.comerprocess.org/), *and Success for All* (preK–8) (http://www.successforall.net/). *Expeditionary Learning Outward Bound* (K–12) (http://www.elob.org/), *Modern Red Schoolhouse* (K–12) (http://www.mrsh.org/), and *Roots and Wings* (K–6) (http://www.successforall.net/elementary/index.htm) fell into the second-highest category, highly promising evidence of effectiveness, while the evidence for *Accelerated Schools* (K–8) (http://www.acceleratedschools.net/), *America's Choice* (K–12) (http://www.ncee.org/acsd/acindex.jsp?setProtocol= true), *ATLAS Communities* (pre K–12) (http://www.atlascommunities.org/), *Montessori* (preK–8) (http://www.montessori-namta.org/NAMTA/index.html), *Paideia* (K–12) (http://www.paideia.org/), and *The Learning Network* (K–8) (http://www.rcowen.com/TLNpgs.htm) was judged to be promising. Specific costs for implementing these programs as well as the components that constitute them vary substantially. Counselors, educators, and other stakeholders are encouraged to review them carefully and with respect to local needs and conditions before advocating and selecting among them. It is clear that a number of these school-restructuring initiatives positively impact student achievement. To be an effective school leader and systemic-change agent, the school counselor needs to be knowledgeable about these comprehensive school-reform initiatives.

OTHER INTERVENTIONS TO BUILD ACADEMIC STRENGTHS AND STRENGTHS-ENHANCING ENVIRONMENTS

In this chapter, we have provided several examples of the type of evidence-based, direct-service and systemic-level interventions that the strengths-based school counselor can employ or advocate in order to foster student academic development. Of course, a host of other interventions are available. We will briefly discuss two of these (disaggregating achievement data and mentoring programs) and then alert the reader to an evidenced-based compilation of successful programs for raising academic achievement.

Acting in a school-leadership role, counselors can use their research skills to disaggregate data in order to better understand the levels of achievement of different groups of students and to advocate practices that increase the likelihood of academic success for all students. Dimmitt (2003) reviewed the pattern of failures (D and F grades) in a high school, whereas Hayes et al. (2002) analyzed high-school dropouts for a cohort of eighth graders through the time that they were scheduled to graduate from high school. In the Dimmitt study, for example, one important finding was that almost half of the students who failed a class said that they sometimes or often spoke another language besides English at home. Also, as we noted earlier, the study revealed that teachers, students, and parents all agreed that the number one reason why students received D or F grades was not doing homework. These two findings, in turn, spawned a variety of changes in homework practices and policies—holding after-school tutoring sessions in English-writing skills, translating a pamphlet about the importance of homework into several languages, editing the students' handbook to more clearly state the grading process and the role of homework, and daily written (rather than verbal) homework assignments handed out to students—to better meet the learning needs of these students and to foster academic success.

Previously we discussed the role of structured extracurricular/out-of-school activities on academic achievement and the importance of looking beyond the school to community-based programs and resources that also facilitate positive youth development. For students who lack sustained relationships with positive adult role models outside of school, counselors should consider establishing linkages with effective mentoring programs. The Big Brothers/Big Sisters program is an example of a community-based mentoring program that has been empirically demonstrated to enhance academic and other aspects of youth development, especially for poor and minority students (Tierney, Grossman, & Resch, 1995). In the Tierney et al. study, 60% of the students in the program were minority-group members (predominantly African-American and Hispanic), and more than 40% received food stamps or public assistance. This research was conducted at eight sites across the country and involved 959 youths aged 10–16. The youth were matched with trained adult mentors based on backgrounds, preferences, and geographic proximity. Mentors were required to commit several hours, two to four times a month, for at least a year.

Compared to students on an 18-month, wait-list control group, mentored students increased perceived ability to complete schoolwork, skipped classes or school less often, and showed modest gains in grade-point averages. In addition, mentored minority girls' scholastic competence scores were 10% higher than those of control-group minority girls, and Caucasian boys showed a significant (7%) increase in their scholastic competence scores. Mentored youth also demonstrated significant differences in other important areas of development—they became less likely to use drugs and alcohol, hit people, or lie to their parents, and they improved parental (trust) relationships. The reduction in likelihood to initiate drug use was especially pronounced (67.8%) for minority boys.

Benard (1999, p. 94) noted that authors of the mentoring study reported that:

> . . . sustained relationships were those in which the mentor saw him/herself *as a friend, not as a teacher or preacher*. . . . While most developmental volunteers ultimately hoped to help their youth improve in school and be more responsible, they centered their involvement and expectations on developing a reliable, trusting relationship and expanded the scope of their efforts only as the relationship strengthened.

Benard commented that the effective relationships were grounded in the mentor's belief in the importance of meeting the developmental needs of youth and providing supports and opportunities which the youth did not currently have.

The volunteers placed top priority on making the relationship enjoyable and fun to both partners. Furthermore, they were "there" for the young person; listened non-judgmentally; looked for the youth's interests and strengths; and incorporated the youths into the decision-making process, giving them "voice and choice" around their activities (p. 94).

According to the resiliency perspective discussed in Chapter 1, the mentors provided at least three protective factors: a caring relationship, positive expectations and respect, and ongoing opportunities for participation.

In general, advocating programs that enhance the academic development of minority, ESL, and other traditionally underserved groups of students requires school counselors to be knowledgeable about effective programs and to exercise a leadership role in this regard. Although most school counselors have probably had little exposure to information about these programs in their graduate studies, they can use the literature and computer-search skills that they have acquired in order to locate and share this information with administrators, teachers, and other educational stakeholders. For example, an ERIC search revealed that the American Youth Policy Forum (Jurich & Estes, 2000) published a report on 20 successful (evidence-based) programs for raising academic achievement for all students. Table 4–4 provides a list of these programs. Almost all of them serve youth who are at high risk for academic failure due to poverty, immigrant status, minority background, and so forth (also see AYPF's review of programs for raising minority achievement, at http://www.aypf.org/rmass/pdfs/Book.pdf).

The evaluations of these programs included multiple measures of academic achievement, including standardized test scores, grades, attendance and dropout rates, school graduation rates, and college enrollment and retention. Success was defined as improving the academic achievement of participants compared to a similar group of students or against baseline data. Using qualitative analyses of the program components, the authors identified 80 features that they believe contribute to program success. The 80 features were consolidated into five overarching strategies shared by most of the programs:

1. The program demonstrated high expectations for youth, program, and staff (academically challenging content, the expectation that all students have the ability to succeed, clear well-defined education goals, ongoing staff training, rigorous program evaluation).

2. The program provided personalized attention (small learning environments, individual help and support, extra services such as referral to health care and social services, career exploration, mentors, assistance filling out college applications and financial assistance forms, and financial assistance).

3. The program was characterized by innovative structure/organization (using research findings to improve outcomes, keeping flexible hours of

TABLE 4–4.
The American Youth Policy Forum's List of Twenty Successful Programs
for Raising Academic Achievement (Jurich & Estes, 2002)

Youth Organization	Website
The Academic Bilingual and Career Upgrading System (ABACUS) and Auxiliary Services for High Schools (ASHS): New York City	www.aypf.org/RAA/01abacus.pdf
Advancement Via Individual Determination (AVID)	www.aypf.org/RAA/02avid.pdf www.avidonline.org
Boys & Girls Clubs	www.aypf.org/RAA/03bgca.pdf www.bgca.org
Career Academies: California	www.aypf.org/compendium/C2S03.pdf www.ncrel.org/sdrs/areas/issues/envrnmnt/stw/sw3caree.htm
Career Academies: Junior ROTC	http://www.aypf.org/RAA/05ca.pdf
College Bound	www.aypf.org/forumbriefs/2002/fb110802.htm www.ge.com/community/fund/grant_initiatives/education/collegebound.html
Gateway to Higher Education	www.aypf.org/RAA/07gate.pdf www.edc.org
High Schools That Work	www.aypf.org/pressreleases/pr08.htm www.sreb.org/programs/hstw/hstwindex.asp
Hoke County High School	http://www.aypf.org/RAA/09hoke.pdf www.sreb.org
I Have A Dream: Chicago, IL	www.aypf.org/RAA/10ihad.pdf www.ihad.org
Maryland's Tomorrow	www.aypf.org/compendium/C1S45.pdf www.howard.k12.md.us/lrhs/departments/mdtomorrow/MDT%20webpage
Quantum Opportunities	www.aypf.org/RAA/12quant.pdf www.oicofamerica.org/programs.html
Sponsor-A-Scholar	www.aypf.org/RAA/13spons.pdf
Student Support Services	www.aypf.org/RAA/14sss.pdf
Success for All/Exito Para Todos	www.aypf.org/RAA/15exito.pdf www.successforall.net
Tech Prep: Texas	www.aypf.org/RAA/16tech.pdf http://www.techpreptexas.org/techpreptexas/index.htm
Turner Technical Arts High School: Florida	www.aypf.org/RAA/17turner.pdf www.education-world.com/a-issues/issues041.shtml
Union City School District: New Jersey	www.aypf.org/RAA/18union.pdf http://www2.edc.org/cct/projects-summary.asp?numprojectId=774
Upward Bound	www.aypf.org/RAA/19ub.pdf www.ed.gov/offices/OUS/PES/higher/upward.pdf
Youth River Watch: Austin, Texas	www.aypf.org/RAA/20youth.pdf www.angelfire.com/ri/riverwatch/

Jurich, S., & Estes, S. (2000). *Raising academic achievement: A study of 20 successful programs.* Washington, DC: American Youth Policy Forum.

operation, extending the school year, using the summer months and after-school time, involving team teaching and teachers in program design, and involving family, businesses, and community).

4. The program included experiential learning (demanding academic course-work integrated with career preparation, internships, community service, technology training, leadership training, and cultural experiences).

5. The program provided long-term support (one to five years, continues from grades 9–12, focus on academic transitions, post-graduation support).

The key to the success of these programs is not any one of the strategies, but rather a mix of elements from the five strategies. (Jurich & Estes, 2000).

SUMMARY

In this chapter, we noted some of the academic services—class scheduling, placing students in academic/career tracks, test coordination, maintaining academic records, "motivational" discussions with failing students or poten-tial dropouts, arranging for tutoring, and providing remedial interventions to underachievers—that school counselors have traditionally provided to stu-dents. These services (a) are often administrative or clerical rather than de-velopmental in nature, (b) are frequently directed at only a relatively small percentage of students, and (c) may even restrict or impede the academic development of some groups of students by depriving them of the opportunity to enroll in more academically rigorous courses of study.

In contrast, contemporary approaches to school counseling focus on iden-tifying and removing obstacles and policies that thwart student academic de-velopment, and providing a comprehensive developmental program to address the academic needs of all students. In SBSC, we emphasize, in addition, how the school counselor can enhance academic achievement and foster academic development by promoting academic strengths and the strengths-enhancing environments that have been empirically shown to be associated with aca-demic success. Our discussion focused primarily on examples of interventions and environments in three areas that affect all students: high-stakes testing, homework completion, and school transitions. While our examples are not ex-haustive, we demonstrated how a variety of counseling services including lead-ership, advocacy, collaboration, coordination, counseling, classroom guidance and consultation can be used successfully to enhance student academic de-velopment. In addition, we discussed the impact of national comprehensive school reforms efforts on student academic development and achievement. The strengths-based school counselor needs to be knowledgeable about the potential relevance of these efforts to the local issues of student academic development that their schools face.

KEY POINTS

Traditional School Counseling Interventions for Academic Development

- Traditionally, school counselors have focused on academic services that are largely administrative or clerical, such as scheduling classes, placing students in academic/career tracks, coordinating the school's testing program, and maintaining academic records or transcripts.
- When school counselors have attempted to apply a developmental focus to their academic services, their interventions have mainly focused on low-performing or underachieving students. The relationship between the traditional school counselor and academic development has been vague and remote at best.

Contemporary School Counseling Interventions for Academic Development

- Today, school counselors focus more attention on student achievement and accountability due to the No Child Left Behind (NCLB) Act and other educational reform initiatives. School counselors are being called to move from a service-centered emphasis for some students to a program-centered emphasis for every student.
- Due to the high-stakes testing environment in which school counselors work, it is easy to equate academic achievement with academic development. However, impacting academic achievement is not the only role of the contemporary school counselor. Helping students to be prepared for a wide range of postsecondary options, to acquire skills for lifelong learning, and to understand the relationship of academics to work and to life are all important aspects of student academic development.

Strengths-Based School Counseling Interventions for Academic Development

- School counselors can employ a variety of counseling services to promote academic strengths in students and the strengths-enhancing capacity of their academic environments. Three primary academic areas that can be impacted are high-stakes testing, homework completion, and transitions to middle or high school.
- Due to the emerging emphasis on student-achievement tests in schools, school counselors should focus their attention on academic interventions in this area. Promoting student test-taking strengths and enhancing the test-taking environment are ways to impact every student's academic development.
- Homework completion is an area of increased focus for school counselors because it clearly illustrates the importance of developing self-regulated learning skills that are important for lifelong learning. The school counselor can use leadership and collaboration in an effort to formulate evidence-based, developmentally appropriate homework practices that support academic success for all students.
- The school counselor can impact students during school transition by implementing systemic-level interventions. These interventions would restructure the school environment to foster more successful academic transitions.

High-Stakes Testing

- School counselors often are assigned the role of testing coordinator, which is not compatible with professional conceptualizations of the school counselor's role. School counselors overwhelmingly report that high-stakes testing has negatively impacted their ability to provide counseling services and their relationships with students and staff. In contrast, research has demonstrated in middle and high schools that more fully implemented comprehensive guidance programs are associated with positive student outcomes such as higher grades, better relationships with teachers, and greater feelings of safety at school.

- To have a more effective role within high-stakes testing, the school counselor can take on a variety of individual and collaborative leadership functions to implement programs that are designed to increase performance on high-stakes tests. The counselor is able to critically evaluate results of research studies on enhancing test performance and recommend successful programs such as test-taking skill instruction to school staff. Also, the counselor can assist in disaggregating school-specific test data to evaluate whether testing interventions are successful with all subgroups within the school.

- School counselors can employ four types of leadership when implementing high-stakes testing interventions: political leadership, human resource leadership, symbolic leadership, and structural leadership.

- Political leadership involves the use of interpersonal and organizational power. The school counselor can use his or her interpersonal, team building, and persuasive skills to link all teachers and teacher factions needed for effective collaboration. Thus, a comprehensive program can be developed, implemented, and maintained to increase test performance for all students.

- Human-resource leadership involves empowering and inspiring others. School counselors can provide critical human-resource leadership by being able to discuss teacher concerns about the process, by providing support, and by continuously expressing encouragement and confidence in the faculty's ability to reach the desired goal.

- Symbolic leadership consists of interpreting and reinterpreting the meaning of change. Together with key leaders of the school staff, the school counselor can help communicate and reinforce the NCLB vision that all children can succeed. The school counselor can also ensure that this vision is the central focus of all instructional efforts and other efforts undertaken by faculty, parents, students, and other stakeholders.

- Structural leadership involves building viable organizations. The school counselor can team with administrators and teacher-leaders to develop and maintain the organizational structure needed to increase student performance on standardized tests and to maintain it at a high level.

- The school counselor should be increasingly focused on the academic achievement of minority and other groups of low-performing students so that achievement gaps can be eliminated. Previously discussed interventions of cooperative learning and peer tutoring have been shown to reduce achievement gaps. Also, test-taking programs that are more than four hours in length have proven to be more effective with students from lower socioeconomic backgrounds.

- More broadly, the school counselor can reduce achievement gaps through systemic-level functions such as leadership, advocacy, consultation, and related services. These system-wide changes include reducing class size in early grades, adopting sound and equitable grouping practices in elementary school, assuring that minority students are equitably represented across curriculum tracks in high school, and desegregating programs within schools.

Homework Completion

- Homework is a fundamental instructional strategy for American children. However, the relationship between homework completion and academic achievement depends on a student's individual characteristics and skill level. School counselors should assess whether academic skill deficits are affecting homework completion before implementing a homework-completion intervention.

- School counselors should be knowledgeable about the appropriateness of homework at different grade levels. In a review of 17 studies on the relationship between homework and achievement, 70% of the studies indicated a positive effect for homework. The effect varies with grade levels. The overall effect of homework on elementary students' achievement is very small, whereas it is much greater for students in secondary school.

- In general, the time students spend on homework is related to increased achievement, especially with high-school students. However, achievement levels deteriorate if too much time is spent on homework. Therefore, guidelines for frequency and duration of homework assignments have been provided through research. Also, homework should serve different developmental purposes: fostering positive attitudes, habits, study skills, and character traits, and reinforcing the learning of simple skills learned in class for younger students and facilitating knowledge acquisition in specific topics for older students.

- School counselors should be knowledgeable about the appropriate parent role in homework. Positive parental attitudes are positively associated with student attitudes toward homework and student grades in grades six through twelve. Also, less-structured approaches to parental involvement in homework and increased parental support for student autonomy are associated with increased student achievement. In general, the primary role for parents with respect to homework is to create a home environment that facilitates self-study.

- Due to these positive research results, the school counselor should consider involvement in homework-completion efforts as one way to foster academic achievement for all students and to reduce the minority achievement gap. Providing student rewards for homework completion, sending school-home notes in the form of daily reports cards, having parents sign completed assignments, and advocating self-monitoring or self-graphing of completed assignments are all examples of effective interventions.

- The school counselor can also assess current teacher or school homework practices and policies and the effects of those practices and policies on student attitudes and achievement. The school counselor can encourage school decision-makers to compare local homework practices to research-based homework guidelines for districts, schools, and classrooms.

- Research indicates that high-school students who complete homework according to their learning styles have improved academic performance. Therefore, Hong and Milgram (2000) developed a model of homework performance that included two categories of conceptual components: motivation and preferences.
- A student may be self-motivated, teacher-motivated, and/or parent-motivated. The strength of the student's motivation to do homework is reflected by promptness and persistence. Student preferences can be divided into four categories: organizational, surroundings, perceptual-physical, and interpersonal. Each category is further subdivided into categories that help define student preferences. By identifying these preferences in a classroom guidance session using the Homework Motivation and Preference Questionnaire, school counselors can help students create personal profiles. Then, students can brainstorm about ways to modify their home environments or diversify homework preferences to increase academic success.
- The school counselor can conduct parent workshops so that the homework-completion environment can be enhanced for high-school students. Parents can be instrumental in helping their child implement or extend homework preferences.
- The use of "interactive homework" is another approach that school counselors can utilize to increase academic achievement in students. Teachers Involve Parents in Schoolwork (TIPS) is a middle-school homework program that increases family involvement in a student's education and increases communication between parents and teachers. School counselors can build support for implementing evidence-based interventions such as TIPS.
- Conjoint behavioral consultation (CBC) is another evidence-based intervention that has been proven effective at the middle-school level. CBC focuses on the interacting systems that affect children and assumes that children, families, and schools have a reciprocal and bidirectional influence over each other.
- In contrast to middle and high school, school counselors must be aware of the relationship between homework and achievement at the elementary level. The amount of homework assigned and the purpose of the homework is different at this level. Therefore, school counselors must advocate homework policies that are developmentally appropriate for elementary students.

School Transitions

- The elementary to middle-school transition has been found to be associated with a variety of negative effects on adolescents including declines in achievement, decreased motivation, lowered self-esteem, and increased psychological distress. Similarly, the transition to high school has also been accompanied by negative consequences such as declines in achievement, dropping out, or failing to graduate on time. As black, Hispanic, and low-income students have higher dropout rates, an effective school-transition program may be especially important in fostering these students' academic development and reducing the minority achievement gap.
- School counselors can implement school-wide programs such as the School Transition Environment Project (STEP) that restructures the school environment to reduce its complexity for students and to create smaller learning environments. Programs such as STEP increase the likelihood of successful academic and social transition of incoming students.

Comprehensive School Reform

- Comprehensive school reform (CSR) is the term for major federally-funded initiatives that seek to alter educational environments to increase student academic achievement. A review of 29 of the most widely implemented CSR models indicated that implementing certain CSR efforts such as Success for All, Direct Instruction, and School Development Program especially for five or more years resulted in strong effects on student achievement. School counselors should be knowledgeable about CSR efforts across the country and their effectiveness in creating strengths-enhancing environments for students as they determine their local needs.

Other Interventions to Build Academic Strengths and Strengths-Enhancing Environments

- School counselors should disaggregate achievement data to identify groups of students whose academic development requires special attention.
- For students who have lacked relationships with positive adult role models, community-based mentoring has been shown to foster positive academic and personal/social development.
- School counselors should seek out evidence-based programs that offer personalized attention to student; have an innovative structure or organization; provide experiential learning; offer long-term support; and create high expectations for youth, program, and staff. These five overarching strategies have been identified in many successful programs that target high-risk students, especially minority, ESL, and traditionally underserved students.

5

Promoting Personal and Social Development

OUTLINE

THE TRADITIONAL ROLE OF THE
SCHOOL COUNSELOR IN PERSONAL
AND SOCIAL DEVELOPMENT

Supporting and facilitating personal and social development of students has been an important focus of school counselors for many years, even though truly comprehensive developmental counseling programs have rarely been implemented (Paisley & Borders, 1995). On the other hand, some people would say that personal and social development has had too prominent a focus in school counseling. In recent years, school counselors have been increasingly criticized for taking the personal/social issues and the mental health concerns of a small number of students rather than academic issues and the needs of all students as the *primary focus* of their endeavors (e.g., Education Trust, 1999; Erford, House, & Martin, 2003). As we have discussed earlier, school counselors' efforts in the personal/social area have tended to consist of providing one-to-one counseling services and, to a lesser extent, small group counseling. These activities were usually driven by a clinical model of service provision that emphasized eliminating or reducing student problems (e.g., reducing deficits) and returning students to a more "normal" mode of functioning so that instruction could be more effective with them. One result of this focus is that school counselors have occupied an ancillary or supportive role in schools as compared to the more central role played by classroom teachers and other educators.

THE CONTEMPORARY ROLE OF THE
SCHOOL COUNSELOR IN PERSONAL
AND SOCIAL DEVELOPMENT

Some contemporary reforms efforts in school counseling (e.g., Education Trust, 1999; Erford et al., 2003) appear to view the counselor's role as being focused primarily on the academic development of students and only secondarily on their personal and social development. However, student development is actually a holistic process in which development (e.g., personal/social) in one area impacts development in other areas (e.g., academic and career). Moreover, as we have previously discussed, an exclusive focus on academic issues can actually impede or even be counterproductive to academic development if students' personal and social needs for autonomy, competence, and relatedness are not met (Ryan & Deci, 2000).

While recognizing the primacy of student academic development, the role of the school counselor in facilitating students' personal and social development was recently reaffirmed by the American School Counselor Association in the National Standards for School Counseling Programs (Campbell & Dahir, 1997) and the National Model for School Counseling Programs

(ASCA, 2003); however, in this instance, the role is conceptualized from a developmental perspective in which all students are the focus and in which the program provided by school counselors is central to schooling.

"Standards in the personal/social area guide the school counseling program to implement strategies and activities to support and maximize each student's personal growth" (Campbell & Dahir, 1997, p. 28). ASCA advances three standards in the personal/social development domain:

> Standard A: Students will acquire the knowledge, attitudes, and interpersonal skills to help them understand and respect self and others.
>
> Standard B: Students will make decisions, set goals, and take necessary action to achieve goals.
>
> Standard C: Students will understand safety and survival skills. (Campbell & Dahir, 1997, p. 28)

In turn, each of these standards is accompanied by student competencies and a set of indicators that define the specific knowledge, skills, and attitudes that students should demonstrate as a result of participating in a school counseling program.

THE STRENGTHS-BASED SCHOOL COUNSELOR'S ROLE IN PERSONAL AND SOCIAL DEVELOPMENT

Thus, the National Standards (Campbell & Dahir, 1997) and National Model (ASCA, 2003) provide intuitively valid standards, competencies, and indicators to the school counselor for promoting the personal and social development of all students. SBSC complements the National Model by providing examples of the personal and social strengths that have actually been shown to be associated with positive youth development. In addition, the type of research-documented environmental contexts that facilitate the acquisition and nurturance of those strengths are identified. Finally, detailed examples of evidence-based counseling interventions that promote those strengths are presented. As was the case for the academic domain, the role of the strengths-based school counselor is to emphasize promotion of strengths and strengths-enhancing environments in the personal/social domain over problem reduction and problem prevention.

In Strengths-Based School Counseling, moreover, we view personal/social, academic, and career development as interrelated and overlapping. As such, interventions directed to one domain may facilitate development not only in that domain, but in one or both of the other domains as well. Similarly, barriers to development in one domain may very well constitute barriers to development in the others.

Unlike our treatment of academic development, in this chapter we discuss *both* the basic principles and the interventions for fostering students' personal/social strengths and strengths-enhancing environments. We have combined the two topics—principles and interventions—because we believe that the factors impacting personal and social development are much more familiar to school counseling students and school counseling educators than are those affecting academic development. In addition, we provide a number of examples of interventions and environments at different grade levels that reflect a strengths-based framework. As such, our discussion of them is fairly lengthy. Therefore, the reader may want to focus primarily on those interventions and strengths-enhancing environments that reflect the grade levels with which he or she will be working. Tables 5–3 and 5–6 provide information about the grade levels to which our examples apply. We now move to a consideration of the research-identified personal and social strengths of youth that school counselors need to foster.

PERSONAL AND SOCIAL STRENGTHS
TO PROMOTE

In Chapter 1, we discussed the importance of strengths-based school counseling and promoting strengths in all students (for example, see Development Assets in Table 1–3 and the Resiliency Wheel in Fig. 1–1). We also noted that what we refer to as strengths are sometimes described in the literature by a variety of other terms such as developmental assets, protective factors, protective processes, resiliency, competence, and indices of well-being. More importantly, these strengths have been shown to be associated with positive youth development in the personal/social, academic, and/or career development domains. In fact, research and theoretical advances from a variety of disciplines are increasingly converging on the specific strengths and strength areas that school counselors should promote.

A prime example is the work of The Committee on Community-Level Programs for Youth of the National Research Council and Institute of Medicine (Eccles & Gootman, 2002). Although the committee was concerned with programs for youth development primarily in community rather than in school or strictly educational settings, its findings apply to educational settings as well. The Committee reviewed studies of resilience and adolescent development, programs that target young people ages 10 to 18. Three sources of information were consulted: (a) theory, (b) practical experience, and (c) qualitative and quantitative research data, including seven published literature reviews and meta-analyses (e.g., statistical reviews of research). The Committee found substantial convergence across the three information sources and compiled a list of personal and social assets that promote the healthy development and well-being of adolescents and facilitate a successful transition from childhood through adolescence and into adulthood.

These assets are viewed as universally applicable, but their exact manifestations will vary depending on cultural context. For example, what constitutes effective coping skills for resisting peer pressure for students of color in an inner-city, urban environment might be somewhat different from what are regarded as effective coping skills in a middle-class, White-suburban context. The assets, which were organized around four general categories—(a) physical health, (b) cognitive development, (c) psychological and emotional development, and (d) social development—are presented in Table 5–1. As can be seen, these personal and social assets are relevant not only to ASCA's (2003) personal/social development domain, but also to its academic and career domains. We will discuss the type of environments that foster these assets, and we will provide examples of some of the interventions that promote these assets (strengths) in subsequent sections of this chapter.

The positive psychology perspective of Martin Seligman and his colleagues (e.g., Seligman & Peterson, 2003; Peterson & Seligman, 2004; Shatté, Seligman, Gillham, & Reivich, 2003) represents another approach to identifying and measuring personal/social strengths. These researchers have focused on developing a classification of character strengths and virtues that (a) make the good life possible, (b) buffer against misfortune and psychological disorders, and (c) help to build resilience. To be included, each character strength had to satisfy a variety of criteria such as having some generality across situations and stability across time (e.g., be trait-like), be recognized and valued in almost every major subculture, be celebrated when present and mourned when absent, and be cultivated by parents within their children. Twenty-four character strengths organized into six core moral virtues comprise the resulting classification system devised by Seligman and his colleagues (see Table 5–2). These strengths are measured by the Inventory of Strengths for Youth that we discussed in Chapter 2. School counselors are frequently responsible for delivering character education programs, and Peterson and Seligman's (2004) Classification of Character Strengths presents an empirically based approach for determining which character traits to include in these programs.

Lastly, a variety of strengths have been advanced from the wellness/well-being literature (e.g., Bornstein, Davidson, Keyes, & Moore, 2003; Myers et al., 2000). For example, Ryff (1985) and Ryff and Singer (2003) have proposed and developed instruments to assess a multidimensional model of well-being in adults that includes six dimensions: (a) self-acceptance, (b) purpose in life, (c) personal growth, (d) environmental mastery, (e) autonomy, and (f) positive relations with others. Zaff et al. (2003) have discussed child development and dimensions of physical, social emotional, and cognitive well-being and their interrelationships.

TABLE 5–1.
Personal and Social Assets that Facilitate Positive Youth Development

Physical Development
- Good health habits
- Good health risk management skills

Intellectual Development
- Knowledge of essential life skills
- Knowledge of essential vocational skills
- School success
- Rational habits of mind—critical thinking and reasoning skills
- Good decision-making skills
- In-depth knowledge of more than one culture
- Knowledge of skills needed to navigate through multiple cultural contexts

Psychological and Emotional Development
- Good mental health including positive self-regard
- Good emotional self-regulation skills
- Good coping skills
- Good conflict resolution skills
- Mastery motivation and positive achievement
- Confidence in one's personal efficacy
- "Planfulness"—planning for the future and future life events
- Sense of personal autonomy/responsibility for self
- Optimism coupled with realism
- Coherent and positive personal and social identity
- Prosocial and culturally sensitive values
- Spirituality or a sense of a "larger" purpose in life
- Strong moral character
- A commitment to good use of time

Social Development
- Connectedness—perceived good relationships and trust with parents, peers, and some other adults
- Sense of social place/integrations—being connected and valued by larger social networks
- Attachment to prosocial/conventional institutions such as school, church, nonschool youth programs
- Ability to navigate in multiple cultural contexts
- Commitment to civic engagement

Reprinted with permission from *Community programs to promote youth development* © 2000 by the National Academy of Sciences, Courtesy of the National Academy Press, Washington, D.C.

In a classic article, Emory Cowen (1994), a leader in prevention research, proposed five major strands that can act alone or in combination to enhance or pose threats to psychological wellness. Some of these are developmental factors, while others are more concerned with the environmental context. In infancy, a warm, secure early attachment relationship with the primary care-giver is a key to wellness. In early childhood, acquiring age-appropriate cognitive and interpersonal skills at home and in school is paramount. In that

TABLE 5–2.
Peterson and Seligman's (2004) Classification of Character Strengths

Wisdom and knowledge—cognitive strengths that entail the acquisition and use of knowledge
- Creativity (originality, ingenuity)
- Curiosity (interest, novelty-seeking, openness to experience)
- Open-mindedness (judgment, critical thinking)
- Love of learning
- Perspective (wisdom)

Courage—emotional strengths that involve the exercise of will to accomplish goals in the face of opposition, external or internal
- Bravery (valor)
- Persistence (perseverance, industriousness)
- Integrity (authenticity, honesty)
- Vitality (zest, enthusiasm, vigor, energy)

Humanity—interpersonal strengths that involve tending and befriending others
- Love
- Kindness (generosity, nurturance, care, compassion, altruistic love, "niceness")
- Social intelligence (emotional intelligence, personal intelligence)

Justice—civic strengths that underlie healthy community life
- Citizenship (social responsibility, loyalty, teamwork)
- Fairness
- Leadership

Temperance—strengths that protect against excess
- Forgiveness and mercy
- Humility/Modesty
- Prudence
- Self-regulation (self-control)

Transcendance—strengths that forge connections to the larger universe and provide meaning
- Appreciation of beauty and excellence (awe, wonder, elevation)
- Gratitude
- Hope (optimism, future-mindedness, future orientation)
- Humor (playfulness)
- Spirituality (religiousness, faith, purpose)

Abbreviated from Table 1–1 from Peterson, C., & Seligman, M. E. P. (2004). *Characters, atrengths, and virtues: A handbook and classification*, New York: Oxford University Press. By permission of Oxford University Press, Inc.

regard, Strayhorn (1988) listed 62 key skills organized into nine clusters (e.g., handling frustration, delaying gratification, celebrating good things, and feeling pleasure), with most of these skills being formed in the preschool years. Acquiring the ability to cope effectively with life stress represents another of Cowen's developmental factors. Finally, settings that promote empowering conditions such as those that offer people justice, hope, and opportunity or a sense of controlling one's own fate are important environmental factors favoring wellness. We discuss these strengths-enhancing environments later in this chapter.

STRENGTHS-BASED INTERVENTIONS
TO PROMOTE PERSONAL AND
SOCIAL DEVELOPMENT

In this section, we present interventions that exemplify the basic principles of Strengths-Based School Counseling (SBSC). Specifically, these interventions promote some of the evidence-based strengths that research has shown are associated with positive youth development. In addition, the interventions are evidence-based themselves; that is, empirical research has demonstrated that they are effective. These interventions tend to emphasize promotion over problem prevention and problem reduction although, in many cases, they have been shown to impact prevention and problem reduction as well. Many of them are relevant to the principle of context-based development as well. Because we already discussed individual counseling from a strengths-based perspective in Chapter 2, we have chosen not to present any interventions specific to one-to-one counseling in this section.

We present two types of interventions. First, we discuss interventions that enhance students' ability to regulate their behaviors and emotions. As was the case with academic development, we have again chosen to discuss self-regulation interventions. Research in such areas as developmental assets and competence, and research reviews (e.g., Eccles & Gootman, 2002) have repeatedly identified self-regulation as a strength that plays a key role in positive youth development in the personal and social domains. Interventions that focus on enhancing cultural identity and multicultural competence are the second type that we discuss. Once again, research (e.g., developmental assets) and literature reviews (e.g., Eccles & Gootman, 2002) have demonstrated the importance of helping students to develop these type of assets. Moreover, these strengths will become even more important in the future as the cultural diversity of our society continues to increase. School counselors need to play a central role in helping students to develop these strengths.

Table 5–3 presents the specific interventions that we discuss. The interventions are organized according to level (e.g., elementary, etc.) so that a reader who is interested in counseling primarily at one particular level may choose to focus primarily on interventions for that level.

Enhancing Behavioral and
Emotional Self-Regulation

In Chapter 3, we discussed the central role that self-regulated learning plays in the academic development of all students. Being able to regulate one's thoughts, behaviors, and emotions plays a similarly important role in students' personal and social development. With respect to emotions, for example, Halle (2003) noted that emotions affect the successful development of individuals in a number of ways. Positive emotions are not always associated with optimal

TABLE 5-3.
Selected Interventions for Promoting Personal and Social Strengths in Students

Intervention	Type of Service/Function Performed by Counselor	Strength Promoted	Environment Addressed	School Level
ICPS	Advocating for the program, coordinating, training, possibly classroom guidance	Problem solving	Classroom	Elementary
Anger Coping Program	Group Counseling	Anger management	N/A	Upper elementary and middle
Peacemakers	Advocating for the program, coordinating, training, possibly classroom guidance	Conflict resolution and mediation	Classroom School	Elementary, middle, and high
Penn Prevention Project	Group counseling	Attributional thinking and interpersonal problem solving	N/A	Upper elementary and middle
Life Skills Training Programs	Advocating for the program, coordinating, training teachers and/or junior and senior to lead the program	Resistance skills, decision making, self-directed behavior change, anxiety coping, and social skills	N/A	Middle–ninth grade
Teen Outreach Program	Advocating for the program, collaborating, training teachers, coordinating, classroom guidance	Empowerment through opportunities for meaningful participation.	N/A	High
Research-Based Model Partnership Education Program	Advocating for the program, collaborating, coordinating, training, providing group counseling	Ethnic identity	N/A	Elementary, middle, and high
Bicultural Competence Skills Approach	Group counseling	Ethnic identity, resistance skills	N/A	Elementary, middle

outcomes for individuals, and negative emotions are not always associated with nonoptimal outcomes. Rather, it is "the ability to regulate the overt expression of one's emotional responses (in terms of intensity, duration, and social appropriateness) that leads to optimal outcomes" (p. 131), and "the factors that influence the promotion of emotion regulation are primarily elements of cognitive development" (p. 132). The examples that follow present different types of interventions at different school levels that have been empirically shown to increase students' ability to regulate behaviors and emotions, thereby enhancing personal and social development, and, in many instances, academic development as well (see Table 5–3). Many of the following interventions demonstrate that "a systemic school-based approach to developing the skills of emotional competence will enhance a school's ability to help students reach educational goals" (Buckley, Storino, & Saarni, 2003, p. 177).

The I Can Problem Solve Program (ICPS).   The I Can Problem Solve (ICPS) program is an interpersonal cognitive problem solving program designed for classroom instruction of children ages 4–12 (e.g., Shure, 1996, 2000, 2001). ICPS is relevant to the reduction and prevention of high-risk behaviors such as aggression, inability to wait and cope with frustration, social withdrawal, and poor peer relations that predict later and more serious problems such as violence, substance abuse, and depression. All of these behaviors involve self-regulation skills, the absence of which results in many students being referred to school counselors who are asked to work in a remedial capacity with regard to these deficits. ICPS teaches several cognitive problem-solving skills that are important to self-regulation and which were found to be lacking or less common in the thinking of impulsive adolescents (Spivack & Levine, 1963) and less well-adjusted as compared to more well-adjusted fifth graders (Shure & Spivack, 1972). As such, ICPS is a promotion and prevention-oriented program which affords the elementary school counselor the opportunity to function in a variety of ways, including program advocate, program coordinator, trainer, and provider of classroom guidance.

ICPS is based on over 30 years of research and development with over 1000 students and on implementation efforts with thousands of others. It was originally designed for use with low-income, inner-city, African American four-year olds attending federally funded day care. It has since been extended for use by teachers in classrooms of students up to age 12 and by parents of children ages 4–7. In addition, it has been successfully implemented to serve a variety of other populations including Hispanic and Polish American students and their families, middle- and upper-class (primarily African American and White) populations, and children with ADHD.

There are three versions of the ICPS program: (a) preschool, (b) kindergarten and primary grades, and (c) intermediate elementary grades. The program involves one daily 20-minute lesson and takes about four-months to complete so that the concepts become a part of the child's style of thinking. In the intermediate elementary grades, Shure (2001) indicated that teachers have found it possible to substitute ICPS for language arts for that period of time and that the students do not lose anything academically because standardized achievement tests results have actually increased for ICPS students. In kindergarten and the primary grades, Shure suggested that the program can be implemented during story-time or any time that the children are together in a group. Although four months of daily lessons is a substantial time commitment, it appears to be time well spent given the results that have been achieved with ICPS and the fact that reviews of research have indicated that short-term, non-intensive preventive interventions produce, at best, time-limited benefits, especially with at-risk students (e.g., Catalano, Berglund, Ryan, Lonczak, & Hawkins et al., 2002; Greenberg, Domitrovich, & Bumbarger, 2001). Thus, implementing the ICPS program would appear to have several advantages for the strengths-based school counselor. Among these are the facts that (a) it tends to be more effective than the short-term classroom-guidance interventions that the school counselor is often asked to provide in this area, and (b) it can reach more students and therefore is more efficient than the one-to-one and small-group counseling approaches that the counselor has to provide when students fail to develop these skills.

The focus in ICPS is on teaching children *how* to think, not *what* to think. The purpose is to teach a cognitive problem-solving style that students can use in dealing with everyday problems. In the kindergarten and primary grades version of ICPS, students learn pre-problem-solving and problem-solving skills through sequenced games, pictures, role plays, and dialogues. The pre-problem-solving skills involve teaching a set of word pairs (e.g., same/different, is/is not, some/all, before/after, if/then) that set the stage for later problem solving. A second set of pre-problem-solving skills is an understanding of feeling words such as happy, sad, angry, afraid, frustrated, impatient, worried, and relieved. It also involves understanding that (a) different people can feel differently about the same thing; (b) feelings can change; (c) you can find out how someone feels by listening, watching, and asking; and (d) everyone does not choose the same thing.

The problem-solving thinking skills include developing the view that problems are interpersonal in nature with different people having different motives and perceiving the same situation differently. The skills also include developing causal (cause and effect) thinking. In addition, students learn to generate alternative solutions to interpersonal problems, to anticipate consequences of actions, and then to evaluate whether the choice of a particular solution is a good idea (e.g., to evaluate a solution and likely consequence pair).

A critical challenge for all classroom guidance interventions is to get students to transfer or generalize what they have learned from the guidance lesson into their everyday encounters in the classroom, on the playground, etc. The

ICPS program addresses this challenge through the teachers' use of dialoguing. Instead of sending students to "time out" or telling them what to do differently when they have a conflict, the teacher engages them in the process of thinking about what to do. Dialoguing takes the form of asking the involved students a series of problem-solving questions such as "What do you think the problem is?" "How do you think he felt when you did that?" "How did you feel when he did that back to you?" "What happens when the two of you fight?" "Can the two of you think of a different way to solve the problem so that you won't fight?" Shure (2001) noted that once the students are familiar with the process, dialoguing can be shortened to, "Can you think of another way to solve this problem?" Thus, a key procedure for enhancing transfer is built into the ICPS program because teachers remind students to implement the problem-solving procedures when a conflict is occurring if the students neglect to do so on their own.

The program has repeatedly demonstrated positive effects on behavioral adjustment, as well as changes in cognitive problem solving that include increased generation of solutions to problems and increased thinking about the consequences of one's actions. Among the behavioral effects for African American children who participated in the program over a two-year period (preschool and kindergarten) were the following: (a) greater behavioral adjustment ratings for ICPS children as compared to children in the control group; (b) fewer ICPS children rated as impulsive or inhibited following training as compared to the controls; and (c) fewer impulsive and withdrawn behaviors for ICPS students as compared to control students five years later (e.g., grade 4) (Shure, 1993, 2001). When ICPS was implemented in the upper-elementary grades (5 and 6), changes in cognitive problem solving (e.g., solution and consequential thinking) were immediate following a 4-month exposure to ICPS, as was the case when ICPS was implemented with younger children; however, it required a repeated exposure in both grades 5 and 6 to decrease negative behaviors in low-income African American children as compared to non-trained control students. ICPS also produced increases in prosocial behaviors such as caring, sharing, and cooperating in grade 5, as well as increases in standardized achievement test scores and reading grade book levels (Shure, 2001).

Thus, based on research findings, ICPS is well-suited to promoting personal and social problem-solving strengths (e.g., self-regulation) in elementary—and especially early elementary (e.g., kindergarten and first grade)—aged students. It is a teacher-based, promotion and prevention-oriented classroom guidance program. As such, it provides school counselors, who can prepare teachers to use ICPS, with an extension of classroom guidance resources for students. Shure (2001) recommended that ICPS be implemented initially only with teachers who want to participate in order to minimize resistance. Additional teachers can be prepared later as interest and information about the program's effects spread. With ICPS, school counselors actually have an opportunity to coordinate an effective, evidence-based guidance curriculum that promotes student strengths rather than having to administer the entire curriculum themselves.

The Anger Coping Program.   As we have seen, ICPS is a classroom-based, promotion program (primary prevention) to teach elementary students self-regulation skills for interpersonal problem situations. In contrast, Anger Coping is a small group counseling intervention (secondary prevention) that targets the self-regulation skills of upper-elementary to early-middle-school students whose customary response to interpersonal problems is anger and aggression (Lochman, 1992; Lochman, Burch, Curry, & Lampron, 1984; Lochman, Curry, Dane, & Ellis, 2001; Lochman, Lampron, Gemmer, & Harris, 1987; Lochman, Nelson, & Sims, 1981; Lochman & Wells, 2002). Longitudinal research summarized by Lochman (1992) indicated that aggressive, antisocial behavior in childhood is predictive of drug use, higher levels of conduct disorder, and off-task classroom behavior in middle school. Therefore, the purpose of Anger Coping is to promote better perspective-taking skills, increased awareness of the physiological signs of anger, improved social problem-solving skills, and an increased inventory of responses to problem situations. For elementary and middle school counselors, the Anger Coping Program provides an effective, "traditional" group counseling intervention that not only reduces anger problems for individual students but may also foster a more positive school climate for all students by reducing the overall violence level in schools.

The program has been the subject of research and development since the early 1980s and has consisted of between 12 and 18 small group sessions of 5–7 students led by two co-leaders in a school setting. In Lochman's research, coleading has typically involved professional collaboration between the school counselor and a mental health professional (e.g., community mental health counselor) who has experience with aggressive or oppositional children. Group sessions are approximately 45 minutes to an hour long and are conducted once a week. An expanded 33-session version, the Coping Power Program, includes group sessions and individual counseling for participants, as well as parent training and teacher consultation (Lochman & Wells, 1996).

The program is based on theory and research suggesting that aggressive children exhibit deficits in social-cognitive information processing. Specifically, these children have difficulties encoding social cues, accurately interpreting social events, generating multiple appropriate solutions to problems, considering consequences of solutions, and skillfully carrying out solutions. Furthermore, they selectively attend to hostile cues, perceive hostile intent in ambiguous situations, and generate fewer—and, not surprisingly, more physically aggressive—solutions than other children (Lochman et al., 2001).

The Anger Coping program was designed to improve these social-cognitive skills and incorporates homework and a variety of cognitive and behavioral interventions that are familiar to school counselors. What follows is a brief description of the 18 session program.

Session One

- Get acquainted activities, group rules, point system (individual and group rewards) for cooperative behavior, loss of points for disruptive behavior

Session Two

- Set short- and long-term goals for each student, review goals/progress corroborated weekly by teachers with points awarded

Session Three

- Identify feeling states and anger levels; use of anger thermometer

Session Four

- Practice using coping statements for anger in a self-control game

Sessions Five and Six

- Use stimulus pictures to generate multiple interpretations of problem situations to increase perceptual/cognitive flexibility

Session Seven

- Identify physiological aspects of anger as cues; explore role of self-statements (e.g., "Stop! Think! What should I do?") on angry feelings and behavior

Sessions Eight–Ten

- Learn problem-solving model of anger

Sessions Eleven–Thirteen

- Watch model videotapes of children coping with anger; create videotape demonstrating use of the Anger Coping, problem-solving method

Sessions Fourteen–Eighteen

- Apply model to additional problems; anticipate future obstacles to anger control, identify steps to resolve these problems; choose to make and review more videotapes

Lochman's research on the effectiveness of Anger Coping was conducted with fourth-, fifth-, and sixth-grade boys who were identified as aggressive and disruptive (Lochman et al., 1984; Lochman & Lampron, 1988), with some of these boys being followed for as long as three years after the end of the intervention (Lochman, 1992). Immediately following Anger Coping, boys in the Anger Coping group demonstrated improvements in self-esteem; reductions in observed disruptive-aggressive, off-task classroom behavior; and reductions in parents' ratings of aggression compared to boys assigned to minimal and untreated control conditions. In addition, the boys who showed the greatest reductions in aggressive behavior were the boys who were initially the poorest problem solvers. Improvements in classroom behavior continued to be evident at a seven-month follow-up. At a three-year follow-up, when the boys were about 15 years old, the Anger Coping boys had better problem-solving skills and higher self-esteem than boys in an untreated control condition. They also showed lower levels of substance (alcohol and drug) use than the control students, suggesting a prevention effect in this area, as substance use was not addressed in the Anger Coping program. Also, the treated boys scored in the same range on early substance use as their nonaggressive peers. Unfortunately, continued reduction in off-task behavior at school and parents' ratings of aggression occurred only for boys who received a six-session booster treatment for themselves and their parents in a second school year. Finally, Lochman et al. (2001) reported that the program was equally effective for African American and European American children.

Thus, Anger Coping has been documented as an effective small group counseling intervention that promotes the development of skills to self-regulate anger and aggressive behaviors. As we have seen, however, the intervention does take a substantial amount of time to conduct. A key question that the school counselor needs to consider is whether the likely effects to be gained from Anger Coping are worth the investment of time that is required to implement it. One important factor is the extent to which these students disrupt teaching and learning not only for themselves, but also for their classmates and teachers. A second factor is the clear need for these students to learn self-regulatory skills that will enhance their personal and social development, as well as their own academic development. An additional consideration is the extent to which they increase the overall level of violence in the school, thereby negatively impacting school climate. In most instances, the time invested in the Anger Coping program will probably prove to be worthwhile. For example, if the Anger Coping group is composed of 5–7 aggressive, disruptive students who are drawn from different classrooms, then the gains in improved classroom behavior may well make it a very efficient intervention not only for these students but for their classrooms and for the overall climate of the school as well.

Teaching Students to be Peacemakers. The deadly events that occurred at Columbine High School in 1999, together with other highly publicized examples of school violence in recent years, have propelled the prevention of school violence into the forefront of the minds of parents, teachers, school counselors, and other educators. The results of a 1994 survey (Metropolitan Life Survey of the American Teacher, 1994) estimated that 160,000 students miss class each day due to fear of violence at school. In addition, the National Center for Education Statistics (1997) estimated that approximately 16,000 serious crime incidents occur on a daily basis in our nation's schools. Furthermore, a survey of almost 11,000 middle- and high-school students in a Virginia suburban school district revealed that 5.6% had carried a gun to school during the previous 30 days, 7.7% carried a knife for protection, and 9.9% carried some other weapon for protection (Cornell & Loper, 1998), and the results were even more alarming from a survey of inner-city high schools (Sheley, McGee, & Wright, 1992). Helping students develop skills to prevent school violence is such an important concern for school counselors that *Professional School Counseling* devoted a special issue of the journal (December 2000, volume 4, number 2) to this topic. Absent from that discussion, however, was a consideration of Johnson and Johnson's (1995) evidence-based *Peacemakers* program, a program that should be of considerable interest to strengths-based school counselors at all grade levels.

Peacemakers is a K–12 grade proactive, school-wide approach to violence prevention. Most importantly, the program *promotes* the development of conflict resolution and mediation skills. Ten to twenty hours of initial training is given to all students in a class or school in 30-minute lessons spread out over several weeks. Subsequently, teachers teach at least two 30-minute lessons each week to refine and upgrade students' negotiations and mediations skills (Johnson & Johnson, 1995). Students are taught to be peacemakers in five steps. First, they learn what constitutes a conflict and that conflict can result in positive outcomes if managed properly. Students then learn the six steps to negotiating integrative agreements, meaning that they resolve conflicts by maximizing joint outcomes through

- describing what you want
- describing how you feel
- describing the reasons for your wants and feelings
- taking the other's perspective
- inventing three optional plans to resolve the conflict that maximize joint benefits
- choosing the wisest course of action to implement and formalizing the agreement with a handshake

Third, they learn how to mediate their classmates' conflicts by

- ending hostilities and cooling down disputants
- ensuring disputants are committed to the mediation process

- helping disputants successfully negotiate with each other
- formalizing the agreement

Once students have completed the initial training, teachers implement the *Peacemakers* program by selecting two class members to work in a pair as mediators in the classroom, on the playground, and in the lunchroom. All students work as mediators an equal amount of time during the year. If peer mediation fails, the teacher mediates the conflict. If that fails, the principal mediates the conflict, and if that fails, the principal arbitrates. Finally, as the academic year continues, students receive further training to enhance their negotiation and mediation skills.

A series of 17 research studies conducted from 1988–2000 in eight different schools—rural, suburban, and urban—and two different countries have demonstrated the effectiveness of the *Peacemakers* program for students from kindergarten through the ninth grade (Johnson & Johnson, 2001). The results of the studies showed that *Peacemakers* training was effective in several ways. First, over 90% of trained students were able to recall 100% of the negotiation steps and peer mediation procedures immediately following training. Long-term (one-year) recall of these steps/procedures was demonstrated by over 75% of the students. Also, studies focusing on integrative agreement (e.g., an agreement which both parties liked) and mediation in actual conflict showed that trained students tended to employ learned strategies much more than untrained students. Furthermore, generalization of the training to conflict outside of classroom and school settings was evident in research results that included observation of students and conflict report forms from students. The use of the procedures was reported on the playground, in the lunchroom, in the hallways, and on school buses. Parents even reported that students mediated conflicts at home and in other contexts than school.

The *Peacemakers* program not only resulted in positive effects for general conflict resolution, but also had an impact on other areas outside of this domain. School staff endorsed the program and reported that they spent much less time resolving conflicts throughout the day following training. Specifically, conflicts referred to teachers were reduced by 80%, and the number of conflicts referred to the principal was reduced to zero. Also, the classroom climate became more positive in general, due to improvement in conflict resolution, self-regulation of behavior, and attitudes toward conflict. Results with kindergarten students suggested that *Peacemakers* had an effect on the children's cognitive-social development as their reasoning skills became more sophisticated after training (Stevahn, Oberle, Johnson, & Johnson, 2001).

A particularly intriguing effect was the program's impact on academic achievement. Students were randomly assigned to classes in which *Peacemakers* training was integrated into an English literature academic unit or to classes in which the academic unit was studied without any conflict training. Results indicated that, even though time was taken away from studying a novel, students in the *Peacemakers* condition scored higher on achievement and retention tests than did students who studied the academic unit only (Stevahn, Johnson, Johnson, Green, & Laginski, 1997). The students in the *Peacemakers* condition not only learned the factual information in the academic unit better, but they also were better able to interpret the information in more insightful ways.

Peacemakers affords the school counselor an opportunity to engage in a range of services/functions. These include advocating to administrators and teachers to implement the program, training teachers in classroom guidance skills, coordinating the program, and even providing some of the classroom guidance sessions to students.

The Penn Resiliency or Penn Prevention Project (PPP).

It is estimated that as many as 20% of children will suffer a major depressive episode by the time that they finish high school (Gillham, Reivich, Jaycox, & Seligman, 1995). Children who suffer from depression are at increased risk for depression as adults (Harrington, Fudge, Rutter, Pickles, & Hill, 1990). Furthermore, depression has been linked to many other problems, including academic difficulties, substance abuse, suicidal ideation, and suicidal attempts (Shatté & Reivich, 1997–2003), and each year approximately 13 in every 100,000 American adolescents commit suicide (Lewinsohn, Hops, Roberts, & Seeley, 1996). As such, helping students to acquire the strengths necessary to prevent depressive episodes from occurring and to overcome depression if it is experienced is developmentally significant for all students. It is also the objective of a major positive psychology initiative, the Penn Prevention Project (PPP; Cardemil, Reivich, & Seligman, 2002; Gillham & Reivich, 1999; Gillham et al., 1995; Jaycox, Reivich, Gillham, & Seligman, 1994; Shatté & Reivich, 1997–2003), which more recently has been referred to as the Penn Resiliency Project. As we will see, the program is relevant to the strengths-based school counselor because it involves promoting a more optimistic explanatory style and more effective social skills in students.

PPP interventions are based on two major research findings about children with depressive symptoms. First, these children tend to have a more pessimistic explanatory style for events (e.g., Bodiford, Eisenstadt, Johnson, & Bradlyn, 1988; Nolen-Hoeksema, Girgus, & Seligman, 1986). For example, they are more inclined to attribute internal, global, and stable causes to negative events than children who are not depressed (e.g., "I always do poorly on tests because I am dumb."). As the reader may recall from an earlier chapter, this type of dysfunctional attributional style is also problematic for students with respect to academic development and achievement. Second, depressed children and adolescents are less socially skilled than their nondepressed peers, tend to generate less assertive solutions to interpersonal problems (e.g., Quiggle, Garber, Panak, & Dodge, 1992), and tend to attribute negative interpersonal events to the hostile motives of others (e.g., Dodge & Frame, 1982).

As a result of these findings, the PPP was designed to be composed of two components—cognitive and social problem solving—based on the premise that a more optimistic explanatory style coupled with more effective social skills are strengths that can buffer against depression for all students, as well as reduce the effects of depression for those students who are experiencing it. The PPP is a 12-session small group counseling program, although the core cognitive skills of the program can be implemented in 7 sessions (Shatté & Reivich, 1997–2003). Sessions are conducted weekly by coleaders according to a detailed training manual and range in length from 1–2 hours. Clinical psychology students, teachers, and school counselors have been trained to served as coleaders for groups that have been conducted in both in-school and after-school contexts. Groups are composed of 8–12 students and have been conducted with upper elementary and middle school students (grades 5–8).

The cognitive component of the model is predicated on Ellis' ABC model of dysfunction (Ellis, 1962) and on Beck's cognitive therapy procedures (Beck, 1976). Ellis asserts that it is beliefs (B) about antecedent events, rather than the antecedent events (A) themselves, which are largely responsible for the behavioral, cognitive, and emotional consequences (C) that we experience in life. Cognitive therapy procedures focus on teaching students how to analyze their own thinking. This component involves teaching them to detect inaccurate thoughts generated by their explanatory styles, to evaluate the accuracy of those thoughts, and to reattribute them to more accurate causal beliefs. In this way, students are able to operate with a more accurate view of themselves, their world, and the future. The social problem-solving training focuses more on attempts to solve interpersonal problems and involves assertiveness and negotiation, social skills training, and the application of cognitive skills to the interpersonal domain.

Sessions 1–5 comprise the cognitive component of the program. Session 1 is concerned with establishing rapport, building cohesion, self talk and automatic thoughts, and the link between thoughts and feelings (e.g., the B-C of the ABC model). Thinking styles (optimism and pessimism) are the focus of session 2 as students learn permanent (stable) thoughts through skits. In session 3, a Sherlock Holmes type of story and a game are used to teach students how to evaluate evidence regarding the accuracy of pessimistic automatic thoughts, as well to generate alternative thoughts and explanations. The focus of session 4 is thoughts about the future and de-catastrophizing those thoughts through stories and games. Session 5 is devoted to applying cognitive skills (e.g., learned in sessions 1–4) to attributions about parental conflict (e.g., it's my fault that my parents are fighting/divorcing) as the participants in PPP research were selected in part because of family conflict.

Sessions 6–11 comprise the interpersonal problem-solving component. Students learn and practice assertiveness skills and negotiation skills in the 6th session, while behaviorally-oriented strategies—e.g., muscle relaxation, controlled breathing, and positive visualization—for coping with stressful situations are learned and practiced in session 7. Procrastination and perfectionistic thinking are the focus of the 8th session as students apply the cognitive skills they learned earlier to negative thoughts about projects and chores and to automatic thoughts about meeting new people and making new friends. Sessions 9 is concerned with decision making (e.g., indecisiveness). In the 10th session, students learn to resist attending to hostile cues from others and to resist attributing hostile intent to the behavior of others in ambiguous situations. Instead, they are taught to gather evidence, engage in perspective taking, and to determine their goal in the situation. Sessions 11 and 12 involve students consolidating the skills of social problem solving, applying these skills to interpersonal situations in their own lives, reviewing the entire program, and having a party to mark the conclusion of the group. Additional information about the PPP and about training to run the groups is available from Adaptiv Learning Systems, www.adaptivlearning.com.

The Penn Prevention Program has been implemented in at least four countries—the United States, Australia, Canada, and China—and has been the subject of research for over a decade. Among the findings of that research program are the following:

- Immediately following treatment, students (10–13 years old) who were at-risk based on depressive symptoms and reports of parental conflict, demonstrated improved classroom behavior, reduced depressive symptoms, and were less likely to attribute negative events to stable, enduring causes as compared to peers who did not participate in the program.

- At a six-month follow-up, the PPP participants continued to demonstrate reductions in depression as compared to the control group participants. In addition, parents of PPP participants reported fewer externalizing conduct problems in the treated children as compared to the controls.

- Reductions in depressive symptoms were evident for the PPP participants as compared to the controls at a two-year follow-up, as 44% of those in the control group had suffered clinically significant levels of depressive symptom versus 22% of those in the prevention group. Moreover, the PPP children demonstrated a significantly more optimistic explanatory style (less stable, global, and internal for negative events) during the follow-up period.

- The significant differences in explanatory styles persisted at 30- and 36-month follow-ups (e.g., when the students were eighth- and ninth-graders) even though the differences in depression between the two groups were no longer evident at these time periods.

- When the program was modified for inner-city students, Latino student participants evidenced significant reductions in depression at post-test and at a six-month follow-up as compared to Latino nonparticipants. Treatment also reduced negative thoughts and hopelessness at post-test and follow-up for the Latino students. Similar findings were not found, however, for African American participants, and the reason for these differential effects was not immediately apparent.

In summary, the Penn Resiliency Project provides the school counselor with an effective small group counseling intervention that promotes an optimistic explanatory style and positive social skills in students. These two strengths appear to reduce the likelihood of student depression which, in turn, has been shown to be associated with a variety of other problems such as academic difficulties, substance abuse, and suicide.

The Life Skills Training (LST) Program. Helping students acquire the strengths needed to resist the temptations of alcohol, tobacco, and marijuana is a key developmental task that is especially important in the middle school/junior high school years. Students who use these drugs are at greater risk for using other drugs such as heroine and cocaine, for school dropout, and a variety of negative health consequences. The LST program developed by Botvin and colleagues (e.g., Botvin, 1983; Botvin, 2000; Botvin, Baker, Dusenbury, Botvin, & Diaz, 1995; Botvin, Baker, Filazzola, & Botvin, 1990; Botvin, Baker, Renick, Filazzola, & Botvin, 1984; Botvin & Tortu, 1988) is an evidence-based, cognitive-behavioral substance abuse prevention curriculum that has been the subject of research for more than 20 years. As such, it is a program that holds considerable promise for school counselors and other educators in their efforts to facilitate positive youth development.

The LST curriculum teaches (e.g., promotes) resistance skills within the larger context of acquiring basic life skills and enhancing personal and social competence. The program focuses on preventing use of the gateway substances—tobacco, alcohol, and marijuana—and reducing the motivation to use these substances by enhancing overall personal competence. According to Botvin and Tortu (1988, p. 101), it has the following objectives:

- Provide students with the necessary skills to resist direct social pressures to smoke, drink excessively, or use marijuana
- Decrease students' susceptibility to indirect social pressure to use tobacco, alcohol, and other drugs by helping them to develop greater autonomy, self-esteem, self-mastery, and self-confidence
- Increase students' knowledge of the immediate consequences of smoking by providing them with accurate information concerning the prevalence rates of tobacco, alcohol, and marijuana use
- Promote the development of attitudes and beliefs consistent with non-substance use

The program is 18 sessions in length and may be taught either on a once-per-week basis or concentrated into a minicourse over a 3- to 4-week period. It is designed to start in the 7th grade, although it may begin in the 6th grade. Because the pressure and opportunities to use these substances do not disappear, a 10-session booster curriculum for the 8th grade and a 5-session booster curriculum for the 9th grade have been added to the program. Teacher's manuals are available for all levels of the curriculum.

The program consists of five major components (Botvin & Tortu, 1988). Each component is two to six lessons long and is taught in a prescribed sequence. *Knowledge and information* is the first component which is four sessions in length. Information about the myths and realities of substance (tobacco, alcohol, and marijuana) use, drug prevalence rates, the social acceptability of using these substances, stages of drug use, physiological effects, and the difficulty of breaking these habits is presented.

A four-session component on *decision-making* follows. The first two of these sessions are concerned with making decisions effectively and responsibly and the social influences affecting decision making. Sessions 3 and 4 of this component focus on the techniques used by advertisers to influence consumers' decisions, deceptive advertising, and how to avoid falling prey to appeals to smoke cigarettes and drink alcohol.

Self-directed behavior change is the third component and is two sessions in length. The first of these sessions is concerned with self-image—what it is, how it is formed, and how it can be improved through a self-improvement plan. In the second session, each student selects a skill or behavior to improve or change as well as long-term and short-term improvement goals for that behavior.

The fourth component consists of two sessions devoted to learning to *cope with anxiety*. Students learn to use basic relaxation, a breathing exercise, and mental rehearsal, and are encouraged to use these techniques as coping strategies in their everyday lives. Students also learn about their own anxiety-producing thought sequences and the importance of controlling them.

Social skills, the final component of LST, is also the longest, consisting of six sessions. The first two sessions are concerned with verbal and nonverbal communication and guidelines for avoiding misunderstandings. Sessions 3 and 4 are concerned with overcoming shyness and involve initiating social contacts, giving and receiving compliments, and beginning, maintaining, and ending conversations. The next two sessions focus on opposite sex relationships, including how to initiate and maintain conversations and how to plan dates and social activities. Assertive behavior is the topic of the last two social skills sessions. Special emphasis is placed on applying assertiveness to resisting peer pressures to smoke, drink, or use marijuana.

The effectiveness of the program is supported by an abundance of research ranging from small-scale pilot studies involving a few hundred participants to large-scale prevention trials involving several thousand participants. With respect to the latter for example, Botvin et al. (1995) studied the long-term effects (e.g., six years after baseline) with 3597 students in 56 public schools. Results from this program of research indicated that the LST program implemented in junior high school can produce meaningful and durable reductions in tobacco, alcohol, and marijuana use. Among the specific results obtained by this body of research (Botvin, 2000; Botvin et al., 1984, 1990, 1995) were the following:

- Multiple studies have shown that the program is effective with only the first year component, and that it is enhanced with booster sessions as evidenced by the fact that it reduced smoking by 56% to 67% without booster sessions and by as much as 87% with booster sessions.
- At a six-year (grade 12) follow-up, the strongest effects for teacher-led LST were produced for individuals who received a complete version (e.g., including booster sessions) of the program, resulting in 44% fewer drug users and 66% fewer polydrug (tobacco, alcohol, and marijuana) users.
- In a comparison of the effectiveness of the program as conducted by older peer (11th and 12th grade) leaders versus teachers, there were 40% fewer experimental smokers in the peer-led LST conditions at the end of the program than in the control condition, and 71% fewer students in the peer-led condition reported marijuana use than in the control condition.
- At a one-year follow-up, significantly fewer students in a peer-led booster LST group than the controls were smoking and using marijuana. Results also indicated that teachers were more variable than peer leaders in the quality of program implementation, but that a sample of teachers who implemented the program with reasonable fidelity achieved findings similar to those of the peer leaders.

LST involves school counselors in a variety of functions. In addition to advocating for implementing the program, they can coordinate it, train teachers and/or junior and senior peer leaders to conduct it, and even conduct it themselves.

The Teen Outreach Program.   School failure and teen pregnancy resulting in teen childrearing are two problems that have long-term costs for teenagers, their offspring, and society in general. Allen, Philliber, Herrling, and Kuperminc (1997) noted the annual societal costs of teen parenthood range from $9 to 29 billion dollars. Furthermore, school failure is a major cause of school dropout, and it is estimated that it costs $260 billion in lifetime lost income and taxes for each year's class of dropouts (Allen et al., 1997). Of course, neither of these statistics captures the actual costs of these issues with respect to the personal/social, academic, and career development of the individual teenagers themselves.

These problems also incur costs for school counselors in terms of their time, effort, and overall program impact. Middle- and high-school counselors are commonly called upon to work with school failure and teen pregnancy concerns. Often, however, their involvement begins after the pregnancy has occurred, or when failure is imminent. By necessity, much of their interventions are then focused on reducing the impact that these problems subsequently have on development, rather than on promoting positive youth development. While the need for these services will always exist, the Teen Outreach Program (TOP) is one initiative that can help counselors reduce the amount of time devoted to remedial services and increase the time available for promoting positive development for all students.

The TOP is directed toward reducing rates of teenage pregnancy, school failure, and school suspension (Allen et al., 1997; Allen, Kuperminc, Philliber, & Herre, 1994; Allen, Philliber, & Hoggson, 1990; Edwards, Bell, & Hunter-Geboy, 1996). The program primarily addresses these issues indirectly through a promotion approach. It attempts to provide teenagers with a sense of empowerment. TOP achieves this goal by engaging teens in opportunities for meaningful participation (Henderson & Milstein, 1996) and belonging (Osterman, 2000) in their community and in opportunities that support efficacy and mattering (e.g., feeling that you make a difference) (Eccles & Gootman, 2002). Teen Outreach has an explicit developmental focus to help teens understand and evaluate their future life options and to further progress in the developmental task of establishing competence and autonomy in a context that maintains feelings of relatedness (a sense of being connected) to important adults (Allen et al., 1997).

The academic, year-long program is designed for high-school students (grades 9–12) and has three interrelated components: (a) supervised community volunteer service, (b) classroom-based discussions of service experiences, and (c) classroom-based discussions and activities related to key social-developmental tasks of adolescence. Service activities are selected by the students under the supervision of trained staff and adult volunteers, and include work as aides in hospitals and nursing homes, participation in walkathons, and peer tutoring. Students are required to provide a minimum of 20 hours of service for the year. Classroom discussions are held at least once a week for the academic year and focus on maximizing learning from the service experiences, or on helping students cope with developmental tasks that they faced. The service learning discussions deal with issues—lack of self-confidence, social skills, assertiveness, self-discipline—affecting the service learning experience. Trained facilitators (teachers and school counselors) also cover topics related to developmental tasks—managing family relationships, new academic and employment challenges, and handling close friendships and romantic relationships—using a variety of approaches including structured discussions, group exercises, role-playing exercises, guest speakers, and informational presentations (Edwards et al., 1996). The authors noted that the program actually places very little emphasis on the two target behaviors to be prevented. For example, less than 15% of the curriculum focuses on sexuality, and that material is often not used if it overlaps with other material used in school or conflicts with community values.

The effectiveness of TOP has been evaluated in several studies, the most well-controlled of which (Allen et al., 1997) involved 695 students (grades 9–12) in 25 sites nationwide. The majority (over 80%) of the participants were female minority students, with Black students accounting for two-thirds of the sample and Hispanic students constituting more than 10% of the sample. As compared to control group students at the conclusion of the program, Teen Outreach participants reported significantly lower rates of school suspension, course failure, and, for females, teen pregnancy than their counterparts who did not participate in the one-year program. These results replicated the findings of earlier evaluation studies about preventive effects of the program on these behaviors. In addition, the results of the Allen et al. study indicated that the program did not work significantly better or worse as a function of characteristics of the participants such as household composition, parental education levels, racial or ethnic minority status, student grade in school, or history of prior problems behaviors.

The reasons the program was successful in reducing teen pregnancy and school failure are not entirely clear; however, indications are that community service may be a key component as an inverse relationship between volunteer service and course failure was found (Allen et al., 1997). Students who performed more volunteer service tended to fail fewer courses. In contrast, variations in the amount of class time and how closely facilitators adhered to the Teen Outreach curriculum did not appear to be related to reductions in course failure and teen pregnancy. Thus, these results further support the important role discussed earlier that extracurricular activities can play in strengths development for students (e.g., Cooper, Valentine, Nye, & Lindsay, 1999; Eccles & Templeton, 2002; Zaff et al., 2003).

Moreover, the Teen Outreach program demonstrates how the strengths-based school counselor may often be involved simultaneously in a variety of counseling services/functions. Although serving as discussion facilitator is a direct service (classroom guidance), the majority of the school counselor's participation in TOP is indirect or at the systemic level. Thus, preparing teachers to facilitate classroom discussions and to implement the curriculum involves training, teaming, and coordination, while placing students in volunteer experiences involves collaborating with a school or community-based service learning coordinator.

The Teen Outreach program concludes our discussion of examples of interventions that embody the strengths-based framework and foster students' abilities to regulate their behaviors and emotions. We will now consider another category of interventions that is consistent with Strengths-Based School Counseling.

Enhancing Identity and Developing Multicultural Competence

In Chapter 1, we identified a positive identity and cultural competence as key evidence-based strengths for positive youth development. As such, they constitute important strengths for school counselors and other educators to foster.

Forming a coherent and stable personal identity is an essential developmental task in adolescence (e.g., Erikson, 1968) and is associated with a variety of positive psychological outcomes for individuals including positive self-esteem and a sense of mastery (e.g., Marcia, Waterman, Matteson, Archer, & Orlofsky, 1994). It is also one of the key personal assets for positive youth development (see Table 5–1) identified by The Committee on Community-Level Programs for Youth (Eccles & Gootman, 2002) in its review of the literature.

As we have discussed, context and environmental factors play an important role in all development processes and appear to be especially important for youth who differ by race, culture, and/or ethnicity from the majority group. For these youth, successful identity formation involves achieving a secure sense of their racial, cultural, and/or ethnic[1] identity in order to function in a healthy manner in the face of lower status, restricted opportunities, and the presence of stereotypes and racism (e.g., Gay, 1985; Phinney & Kohatsu, 1997). Ethnic identity is "a complex construct including a commitment and sense of belonging to one's ethnic group, positive evaluation of the group, interest in and knowledge about the group, and involvement in activities and traditions of the group" (Phinney, 1996, p. 145). The ideal outcome of this process for ethnic minority students is a secure sense of one's identity as a member of an ethnic group as well as an acceptance of other groups.

Research indicates that an achieved ethnic identity is associated with positive attributes for ethnic minority students. For example, Phinney and Kohatsu (1997) summarized research indicating a positive association between ethnic identity and self-concept for Asian American, African American, and Hispanic high-school students. In addition, Smith, Walker, Fields, Brookins, and Seay (1999) reported that empirical studies using multidimensional measures have suggested that African American students with positive feelings about their ethnic group are more engaged academically and perform better. Similarly, Chavous et al. (2003) reported that, for African American high-school students, having pride in their racial group is related to having positive feelings about school and positive self-perceptions around academics. In their own study of a multiethnic middle school sample composed primarily of African American students, Smith et al. found that ethnic identity and self-esteem were both related to perceived academic and career self-efficacy, and ethnic identity impacted prosocial attitudes indirectly via self-efficacy. In other re-

---

[1] We have chosen to use the term ethnic identity in this context.

search reviewed by Smith et al., African American and White (e.g., Italian Americans, Irish Americans, etc.) students who had strong ethnic identifications reported fewer behavior problems than students without strong identities (Rotheram-Borus, 1990; Jagers & Mock, 1993). Eccles and Gootman (2002) concluded from their review of the literature that a positive ethnic identity is associated with (a) high self-esteem, (b) a strong commitment to doing well in school, (c) a strong sense of purpose in life, (d) self-efficacy, and (e) high academic achievement.

More recently, Rayle and Myers (2004) studied the relationship of ethnic identity, acculturation, and mattering to six measures of wellness in high school students. Wellness is defined as "a way of life oriented toward optimal health and well-being in which body, mind, and spirit are integrated by the individual to live more fully in the human and natural community" (Myers, Sweeney, & Witmer, 2000, p. 252). For ethnic minority students (mostly African American), ethnic identity was significantly related to five of six areas of wellness: (a) self-direction, (b) schoolwork, (c) leisure, (d) love, and (e) friendship). In contrast, a similar relationship was not found for majority students. This latter finding supported contentions that: (a) ethnic identification plays a less salient role for White students; (b) White students spend far less time exploring their ethnicity; and (c) ethnicity is usually invisible and unconscious for White students because societal norms have been constructed around their cultural frameworks and values (Chávez & Guido-DiBrito, 1999; Holcomb-McCoy, 1997; Phinney & Kohatsu, 1997). As we shall see, however, ethnic identification is by no means unimportant for White students and does affect their interactions with others.

Positive ethnic identification is influenced by a variety of environmental and contextual factors, not the least of which is the ethnic group of which an individual is a member. Moreover, positive ethnic identification is learned and does not happen for all individuals; schools are an important influence on that development (Gay, 1985). Furthermore, school counselors as have an important role to play in ethnic identification development, including (a) educating others in the school about the importance of ethnic identity development; (b) providing multicultural training to teachers and other educators; (c) creating a climate that empowers students to explore their ethnic heritage; and (d) directly aiding students in the ethnic identity development process (e.g., Holcomb-McCoy, 1997; Pedersen, 2003; Rayle & Myers, 2004; Washington et al., 2003).

Ethnic Identity Development Theories

In recent years, ethnic identity development models and theories have been proposed for a variety of ethnic minority groups, and some research on the validity of these models has been generated. Table 5–4 lists some of the most influential models that have emerged. For the most part, these models propose

TABLE 5–4.
Racial/Cultural/Ethnic Identity and Identity Development Theories/Models

African-American/Black	Asian-American	Chicano/Hispanic/Latina/o	Native American	White	Models that Span Multiple Groups
Banks (1981)	Kim (1981)	Arce (1981)	Garrett and Walking	Hardiman (1982)	Atkinson, Morten, and Sue (1998)
Cross (1971, 1991)	Lee (1991)	Ruiz (1990)	Stick Garrett (1994)	Helms (1990)	Helms (2003)
Helms (1984)	Sodowsky, Kwan, and Pannu (1995)	Szapocznik, et al. (1982)		Ponterotto (1988)	Phinney (1990)
Parham (1989)				Katz (1989)	Sue and Sue (2003)
Thomas (1970)				Sabnani et al. (1991)	

a series of invariant stages (usually four to six) through which identity development proceeds. The models proposed by Phinney (1996) and Parham (1989), however, are exceptions to the invariant stage sequence approach. Parham, for example, conceptualized racial identity development in terms of cycles in a lifelong, continuously changing process. School counselors needs to be knowledgeable about the specific issues that affect the identity developmental process of the particular ethnic groups with which they are involved.

For our purpose, which is to link ethnic identity development to the strengths promotion efforts of the school counselor, we focus on some of the common issues affecting the ethnic identity development of students of color as well as issues in White racial identification. With respect to the former, Atkinson, Morten, and Sue (1998) proposed a five-stage Minority Development model that Sue and Sue (2003) elaborated into a Racial/Cultural Identity Model as a way to help counselors understand culturally different clients' attitudes and behaviors. Each of the five stages of development is associated with a specific set of attitudes toward (a) the self, (b) others of the same minority, (c) others of a different minority, and (d) the dominant group. Sue and Sue asserted that this model may be applied to White Identity development as well.

For Phinney and Kohatsu (1997), the process involves four phases (initial, transition, intermediate, and final) rather than invariant stages. It also involves the resolution of three issues: (a) the individual's sense of belonging and commitment to their ethnic or racial group, (b) their minority status in society and the associated effects of racism and discrimination, and (c) their relationship to the dominant culture and to other ethnic groups.

In the initial phase, the meaning and implications of the student's ethnic group have not been examined and evaluated. Ethnic identity may either be of low salience or of little or no concern (a diffused identity), or the student may have fixed notions about her or his identity derived from the majority (White) culture (identity foreclosure). Students in this phase (a) view the dominant culture as a reference group, (b) may express a wish to be White, and (c) may denigrate their own and other ethnic groups. Research has indicated that feelings of low self-esteem, anxiety, and insecurity are associated with attempting to fit into the White world and shunning one's own group (Phinney & Kohatsu, 1997).

The transition phase is characterized by the student beginning to question his or her views of the world and cultural frame of reference, and may be triggered by a variety of factors such as personal experience with racism or discrimination, exposure to positive ethnic role models, or information about one's cultural group. In this phase, the student experiences a state of dissonance with respect to his or her previous views and attitudes, and an identity crisis.

Heightened awareness of racism, prejudice, and discrimination; rejection of White culture; and intense involvement in the student's own ethnic culture are characteristic of minority students who are in the intermediate phase of ethnic identity development (Phinney & Kohatsu, 1997). In the process of rejecting White values, for example, African American students may also perform poorly academically because they associate schooling and education with being White (Fordham & Ogbu, 1986; Ogbu, 1987), despite the fact that Townsend and Patton (1995) contend that excelling academically is consistent with and expressive of African American values, and that to do otherwise is to deny their heritage (see Day-Vines, Patton, & Baytops, 2003).

The final phase is characterized by ethnic identity achievement. That identity includes (a) inner security, (b) a strong, positive feeling about membership in her or his own ethnic group, and (c) commitment to the values and culture of that group. It is typified by more controlled anger about racism, prejudice, and discrimination, and more positive ways of coping with them. It also is characterized by positive appreciation of other ethnic minority groups and openness to—and selective appreciation of—aspects of the dominant culture.

In contrast to ethnic identity development, White racial identity formation is concerned with becoming aware of racism and privilege associated with being White and developing a non-racist White identity (Phinney, 1996). Helms (2003) discussed a White racial-identity development model that occurs via a six-status process: (a) Contact, (b) Disintegration, (c) Reintegration, (d) Pseudo Independence, (e) Immersion/Emersion, and (f) Autonomy. Students exemplifying the Contact status give little or no thought to issues of race and ethnicity and are unaware of the advantages that being White affords them. As the process unfolds, students experience a growing recognition of the advantages of being White and of the inequalities experienced by ethnic minorities. This process can result in feelings of discomfort, guilt, and denial

(Disintegration), and denigration of ethnic minorities and idealization of White people and White culture (Reintegration). The Pseudo Independence status is characterized by an intellectualized awareness of the sociopolitical advantages of being White, and liberalism toward ethnic minority group members; whereas the Immersion/Emersion status involves emotional awareness of the advantages of being White, and anger at oneself and other Whites for maintaining these advantages. Students exemplifying the Autonomy status have abandoned beliefs of White superiority, have a positive sense of self as White, value cultural differences, and appreciate the need to confront racism and oppression.

Interventions to Facilitate Ethnic Identity Development

Because of the developmental importance of ethnic identification, especially for students of color, a variety of educational and counseling-related approaches have been proposed for facilitating this process. Unfortunately, little empirical research has been conducted on the effectiveness of most of these interventions. For example, Gay (1985) and Helms (1994b) have identified interventions for teachers to use in promoting ethnic identification, while Banks (1981) has discussed ideas for curriculum reform using identity models. Strengths-based school counselors can advocate for and collaborate with teachers and administrators to implement these recommendations.

With respect to direct service applications, Washington et al. (2003) proposed the use of Cultural Identity Groups, a seven-session group counseling approach. Cultural identity groups are a developmental model of group counseling for students of color. The groups employ narrative storytelling and cultural maps in an attempt to strengthen individual and group identity to counter prejudice and racism in the schools. An Emotional Climate Scale and a Cognitive Self-Esteem Scale are used to evaluate the results of the group, but we are not aware of research evaluating the effectiveness of these groups at this time. More recently, Bemak, Chung, and Siroskey-Sabdo (2005) proposed empowerment groups for academic success to prevent high school failure for at-risk, urban, African American girls. The groups meet for 45 minutes a week for most of the academic year, are led by co-facilitators, and, although unstructured, involve the members in developing ownership and making choices about discussing personal and social problems (e.g., racial and ethnic differences) that are directly related to school behavior, academic performance, and school attendance. Unfortunately, "hard data" about the effectiveness of these groups are not currently available.

With respect to other interventions, Phinney and Kohatsu (1997) noted that ethnic identity organizations in high school, such as Latin dance clubs and step competition groups, can provide a forum for exploration and discussion around topics of race and ethnicity. School counselors can encourage, mobilize school support for, and facilitate the development of those organizations. More extensive community and school-based programs that include racial identification as an important component are Lee's (1992) *Empowering young Black males*, which involves mentoring by and special attention to the history of African American men, and *Project: Gentlemen on the Move* (Bailey & Paisley, 2004). The latter involves a variety of components such as:

- studying African, African American, and family histories, health-related issues, and tips on enhancing academic excellence
- social development including improvement of self-efficacy, personal and business etiquette training, the importance of giving back to the community, and appreciating and accepting individual differences by being exposed to traditional African American culture, as well as interaction with individuals from other cultures
- Saturday learning institutes, establishing short-term and long-term academic goals, exam lock-in preparation sessions, and rewards for academic progress
- field trips, college visitations, special event opportunities, and community service projects.

Unfortunately, we are not aware of empirical data about the effectiveness of either of these programs. However, data are available for the next program that we discuss.

The Research-Based Model Partnership Education Program (Model Program). The Model Program is a culturally sensitive program that has generated data about its effectiveness (Tucker & Herman, 2002). The program is a community-based, university-school-community partnership designed to empower low-income African American children for academic and social success. It is located in an African American church within a low-income African American community and endeavors to link academic and other success behaviors to students' cultural identities as African Americans. The program is predicated on self-empowerment theory, which is consistent with the self-regulation approach that we have been discussing in this and earlier chapters. Self-empowerment theory holds that prosocial behavior and academic success, as well as behavior problems and academic failure, are significantly influenced by (a) self-motivation to achieve academic and social success, (b) perceived self-control over one's behavior and academic success, (c) self-reinforcement for engaging in social and academic success behaviors, (d) adaptive skills for life success, and (e) engagement in success behaviors.

The Model Program, which was in its 12th year of operation in 2002, is conducted in the education center of an African Methodist Episcopal church (Tucker & Herman, 2002). It operates two days per week for two hours after school and serves parent-referred or school-referred children (in grades 1–12) with low grades in math and/or reading, and mild behavior problems and/or some adaptive skill weakness. Each student participates in the program, at no cost, for only two hours per week. The following components comprise the Model Program: (a) individualized tutoring with trained tutors and homework assistance; (b) a small-group training format with cognitive-behavioral approaches to teach adaptive skills (e.g., communication skills, socialization skills, daily living skills) and skills for managing negative and positive emotions and for engaging in success behaviors; (c) public feedback regarding their effort, progress, and success in learning skills and behaviors for academic, social, and life success, and practice in giving positive feedback to tutors and other staff; (d) monthly parent training to learn the methods used to promote children's academic and social success; and (e) training teachers to used the Model Program's self-empowerment-oriented methods and strategies in their classrooms. Throughout the program, the staff encourage students to publicly identify and praise their own academic and skills development efforts, progress, and success, and reminds the students that engaging in success behaviors is "acting African American" and that it is "cool" to participate in sharing time.

The effectiveness of the program was evaluated with a randomly selected sample of third- and ninth-grade low-income students who had an overall GPA of 2.5 or below and a reading and/or math performance of at least one year below grade levels. After two years of operation, the control group experienced a significant decline in overall GPA; whereas a group that received the intervention, which included tutoring, showed a significant increase in reading GPA (Tucker et al., 1995). Data also indicated that students in the Model Program showed increases in adaptive skills and decreases in frequency of engaging in maladaptive behaviors and school misconduct. A four-year follow-up study indicated that students in the Model Program continued to have higher GPAs than those in the control group (Tucker, Herman, Reid, Keefer, & Vogel, 1999), and unpublished data revealed that students in the Model Program had significantly lower numbers of school absences than those in the control group at the four-year follow-up (Tucker & Herman, 2002).

Although the program did produce significant effects, current research does not enable us to determine which component or components were responsible for those changes. Thus, it is not possible at this time to determine, for example, the extent to which the culturally sensitive aspects of the intervention (e.g., being based in an African American learning environment, linking academic achievement with an African American identity)—as opposed to some other component such as tutoring—is responsible for the effects that were obtained. Nevertheless, the Research-Based Model Partnership Education Program does provide one example of a culturally sensitive intervention that produces social and academic gains for students.

With respect to this type of program, the school counselor will be called on tofunction in a variety of creative and exciting ways. The most innovative and nontraditional of these is collaborating with neighborhood and other community-based groups to build and support this type of after-school initiative. Advocating for the program with teachers, administrators, and community organizations; collaborating with other professionals in the schools and with parents; coordinating referrals to the program; coordinating and/or providing training to tutors and parents; and even providing direct services (e.g., cognitive-behavioral groups) to students in the program are other relevant services that the school counselor might provide.

Interventions to Facilitate White Identity Development and Multicultural Competence

To our knowledge, facilitating ethnic identity development for White students has yet to be a subject of empirical research and remains primarily a topic that is discussed in the counselor-training literature (Ottavi, Pope-Davis, & Dings, 1994; Ponterotto & Casas, 1987; Pope-Davis & Ottavi, 1994); however, school counselors promoting White identity development could increase the strengths-enhancing capacity of the school environment for all students. Promoting this type of development involves White students adopting "attitudes, behaviors, and emotions that indicate acceptance and appreciation of diversity, greater interracial comfort, openness to racial concerns, an awareness of one's personal responsibility for racism, and an evolving nonracist White identity" (Parker, Moore, & Neimeyer, 1998, p. 302). Moreover, a study with counselor trainees demonstrated that an integrative, multicultural training program (a 15-week course) resulted in significant increases along three dimensions of White racial consciousness and in levels of interracial comfort for White trainees (Parker et al., 1998). Although we are not aware of similar research with children and adolescents, results from the Parker et al. study suggest the type of positive effects that might be obtained from facilitating White identity development in adolescent students.

Up to this point in this section, we have been discussing the value, in terms of student strengths and strengths-enhancing environments, of facilitating ethnic identity development in minority students of color, as well as in White students. Having a strong identification with members of one's own ethnic group is probably a necessary but not a sufficient personal strength either for ethnic minority or White students in our society. Implicit in our discussion is the notion of not only developing a strong identification with members of one's own culture but, at the same time, being able to function effectively with members of another culture.

LaFromboise, Coleman, and Gerton (1993) asserted the importance of bicultural competence for ethnic minority students. Bicultural competence presumes that an individual can alter his or her behavior to fit a particular social context. For example, Day-Vines et al. (2003) mention code switching, a practice in which African Americans alter their behavior patterns to conform to the current environment. Bicultural competence is the ability to gain competence within two cultures without losing one's cultural identity or having to choose one culture over the other. LaFromboise et al. (1993) view cultural competence within a multilevel continuum of social skill and personality development. The more levels in which students are competent, the fewer problems they will have functioning effectively within two cultures. Bicultural competence has important implications for the personal strengths that students need in a multicultural society, and for the ones that school counselors and other educators need to help them acquire. Based on their review of the literature, LaFromboise et al. (1993) proposed six bicultural strengths that ethnic minority[2] students need to develop: (a) knowledge of the beliefs and values of the minority and majority cultures; (b) positive, although not necessarily equal, attitudes toward both groups; (c) confidence that one can live effectively within the two groups without compromising one's sense of cultural identity (bicultural efficacy); (d) the ability to communicate effectively, both verbally and nonverbally, within the two cultures; (e) a range of culturally and situationally appropriate behaviors (role repertoire); and (f) a well-developed social support system (groundedness).

LaFromboise et al. (1993) summarized research about the value of bicultural competence for ethnic minority students. The research indicated that bicultural involvement/identification was related to self-esteem and well-being in Puerto Rican college students, to higher GPAs and more effective study habits in American Indian college students, to less rebellious behavior in Hispanic young men, to more positive educational outcomes and self-concepts for Korean American high-school students, and to higher self-esteem scores for Navajo elementary school students. Furthermore, it does not appear that bicultural adaptation entails a greater emotional cost than identification with a single cultural group (LaFromboise et al., 1993; Luthar & Burack, 2000). To date, there has not been much research about efforts to help students to acquire bicultural competence; however, the Bicultural Competence Skills Approach is one exception (Schinke et al., 1998).

The bicultural competence skills approach.   This approach, which is based on social-learning theory, consists of a group counseling intervention for substance abuse prevention with American Indian adolescents (Schinke et al., 1988). The groups were 10 sessions in length and led by two coleaders. Group members learned and practiced communication, coping, and discrimination skills. Communication skills involved biculturally relevant examples of verbal and nonverbal influences on substance abuse. The leaders modeled culturally relevant ways to turn down tobacco, alcohol, and drugs without offending American Indian and non-American Indian friends]. Coaching, feedback, and

---

[2]These bicultural strengths also seem applicable to White students who are functioning in an increasingly multicultural society.

praise from the leaders were used while students practiced the communication skills. Self-instruction and relaxation were coping skills used to avoid substance use situations and to deal with pressure to use the substances. With culturally meaningful examples, students were helped to discriminate high-risk occasions for substance use. They also learned and practiced ways to build networks with friends, family, and tribal members who could nurture and sustain responsible decisions about substance use. Homework assignments involved monitoring and supporting one another's preventive intervention attempts between sessions.

The average age for the students who participated in the evaluation of the program was 11.8 years. At post-test and a six-month follow-up, American Indian students who participated in the program improved significantly more than those who did not on measures of substance-use knowledge, attitudes, and interactive skills and on self-reported rates of tobacco, alcohol, and drug use. That is, they showed more knowledge about substance use and abuse, held less favorable attitudes about substance use in American Indian culture, and displayed more self-control, more alternative suggestions, and more assertiveness in a behavior test involving peer pressure to use substances. They also reported less use of smoke and smokeless tobacco, alcohol, marijuana, and inhalants.

But given changing demographics, more than bicultural competence may be needed to foster positive student development in the 21st century. The population in the United States has become more diverse than ever (Tang, 2001). The number of immigrants doubled from the 1960s to the 1990s, and the number of refugees also doubled from 1985 through the 1990s (Fix & Zimmermann, 1993). Moreover, the school-age immigrant population will increase to 9.1 million by 2010 and will account for more than half of the increase in the school-age population (Fix & Zimmermann, 1993). Furthermore, it is predicted that the rapid increase in U.S. minority population will reach its peak by 2050 (U.S. Bureau of the Census, 1998). As such, *all* students will need to develop not only bicultural but also multicultural competence in order to function effectively in a racially, ethnically, and culturally diverse society.

Multicultural competencies and proposed ways to achieve them. What are these multicultural strengths that students will need, and how does the school counselor facilitate and help other educators to foster these competencies in students? At this time, we are not aware of empirical data that have identified those strengths. As such, we must currently rely on expert opinion and informed speculation for examples of potentially relevant strengths. In that regard, our previous discussion about the importance of an achieved ethnic identity for both students of color and White students is clearly a relevant starting point.

In addition, Lonner and Hayes (2004) cited the recommendations of Kealey (1996). Kealey focused on selecting individuals for employment in other countries or in companies with many cultures. Kealey's profile of the model cross-cultural collaborator consisted of three parts: (a) adaptation skills (positive attitudes, flexibility, stress tolerance, patience, marital or family stability, emotional maturity, inner security), (b) cross-cultural skills (realism, tolerance, involvement in culture, political astuteness, cultural sensitivity), and (c) partnership skills (openness to others, professional commitment, perseverance, initiative, reliance building, self-confidence, problem solving). Many of the strengths that Kealey seeks in adults also appear relevant for students.

Matsumoto (2004), on the other hand, focused on emotion self-regulation, a strength that we discussed previously in this chapter.

> Whereas research had previously suggested that factors such as language proficiency, ethnocentrism, and knowledge of host and home cultures were the most important in predicting intercultural competence and adjustment . . ., the most recent research has indicated that skills such as emotion regulation, openness, flexibility, and critical thinking are in fact important skills that allow or do not allow such knowledge or proficiencies to be used in the development of intercultural competence. . . . Emotion regulation in particular has been shown to be the "gatekeeper" skill. . . . If individuals cannot regulate their emotional reactions in a constructive way that allows them to use their knowledge and skills, it is very difficult to develop intercultural competence. . . . Moreover, the available evidence appears to suggest that this role of emotional regulation is culturally invariant. (Matsumoto, 2004, p. 274)

The findings of Eidelson and Eidelson (2003) are also relevant to the development of multicultural competence. They studied conflicts between groups defined by factors such as ethnicity, nationality, and religion. In their review of relevant literatures (e.g., in psychology, political science, sociology, etc.), they identified five belief domains, or core beliefs of individuals and collective worldviews of groups, that may operate to trigger or constrain violence between those groups. The five beliefs are (a) *superiority*—the individual and the individual's group (the in-group) is better than other people in important ways in the sense of specialness, deservingness, and entitlement; (b) *injustice*—the out-group has mistreated the individual and his or her group, and there are significant and legitimate grievances against the out-group; (c) *vulnerability*—the individual and his or her group are perpetually vulnerable or in danger from the out-group; (d) *distrust*—the out-group is untrustworthy and harbors evil intentions toward the individual and the in-group; and (e) *helplessness*—the individual and the in-group are powerless and dependent on the out-group. In facilitating ethnic identity and multicultural competence, the school counselor needs to help students to identify, confront, and defuse these beliefs.

Finally, Sink (2002a) proposed that school counselors can play a valuable role in developing multicultural student-citizens through K–12 comprehensive guidance and counseling programs. By grade 12, these students would demonstrate a number of competencies:

- an understanding and appreciation for their own culture and the cultures of others
- critical thinking in the exploration of sociocultural and political ideas;
- an ability to reason about issues from local, national, and global perspectives
- an understanding of important American values (e.g., justice, tolerance, responsibility)
- an understanding of the basic rights of all human beings as embodied in the Bill of Rights
- the ability to express appropriately an opinion on important social and political issues while listening and respecting the views of others the ability to cooperate/collaborate with others in school and community settings
- how to resolve interpersonal conflicts peacefully (Sink, 2002a, p. 133).

Sink (2002a) indicated that a number of the student competencies in comprehensive guidance and counseling programs can be aligned with multicultural citizen development. Among these are effective communication, conflict resolution skills, and those that foster higher order thinking and reasoned discussion. Other competencies that address issues such as civic involvement, sociopolitical concerns, diversity, and character development would need to be added to these programs. Sink also recommended a variety of activities to facilitate the development of multicultural student-citizens. Among these were (a) collaborating with teachers to develop and deliver classroom guidance lessons that focus on controversial multicultural citizenship issues; (b) initiating the multicultural citizenship formation process starting with kindergarten or first grade; (c) incorporating sustained community service projects; and (d) eliciting parental and community involvement in developing a broad-based coalition of supporters of multicultural citizenship education.

As we have seen, there are a variety of interventions that school counselors can employ to promote the strengths in students that are associated with positive youth development. An equal, if not far more important, influence on development, however, is the characteristics of the environments in which students find themselves. Strengths-based school counselors need to be knowledgeable about the characteristics of environments that foster development and to be able to collaborate with other educational stakeholders to enhance those environments. We now turn to a consideration of the features of strengths-enhancing environments for personal and social student development.

STRENGTHS-ENHANCING
ENVIRONMENTS FOR POSITIVE
PERSONAL AND SOCIAL DEVELOPMENT

In Chapter 1, we considered the crucial role that social environments play in positive youth development. We also presented some of the research that has identified key environmental factors that nurture strengths development in youth (e.g., the external assets identified by Search Institute). In this chapter, we have discussed the work of Committee on Community-Level Programs for Youth with respect to personal and social assets. In addition to personal and social assets, the review by that Committee identified an empirically based, provisional list of environmental factors that promote the development of those assets (Eccles & Gootman, 2002; Larson, Eccles, & Gootman, 2004). Eight features of the person's interaction with the environment were identified—physical and psychological safety, clear and consistent structure and appropriate supervision, supportive relationships, opportunities to belong, positive social norms, support for efficacy and mattering, opportunities for skill building, and integration of family, school, and community efforts. These features are defined in Table 5–5.

These eight features bear a strong resemblance to the factors—caring and support, high expectations, opportunities for meaningful participation, prosocial bonding, clear and consistent boundaries, and life skills—that were independently identified by Henderson and Milstein (1996; see Chapter 1) as mitigating risk and building resiliency in the environment. In addition, a number of Search Institute's external asset categories (e.g., support, empowerment, boundaries and expectations) and specific external assets that also were discussed in Chapter 1 are consistent with those features. Furthermore, although the Search Institute publication, *Great Places to Learn* (Starkman, Scales, & Roberts, 1999), focuses on asset-building in schools rather than in community programs, its practical suggestions for teachers, counselors, and other educators address the environmental features identified by the Committee on Community-Level Programs for Youth.

INTERVENTIONS TO PROMOTE
STRENGTHS-ENHANCING ENVIRONMENTS
FOR PERSONAL AND SOCIAL DEVELOPMENT
IN ELEMENTARY AND MIDDLE SCHOOLS

A sense of community (e.g., belonging) has been shown to be related to a variety of positive educational and personal/social outcomes for students (Osterman, 2000), and over the years, educators have shown considerable interest in restructuring schools to increase sense of community (e.g., Noddings, 1992). But relatively little research has been generated about caring communities and their effects on students' personal, social, and academic development. Table 5–6

TABLE 5–5.
Features of Positive Developmental Settings

	Descriptors	Opposite Poles
Physical and Psychological Safety	Safe and health-promoting facilities; practice that increases safe peer group interaction and decreases unsafe or confrontational peer interactions.	Physical and health dangers; fear; feeling of insecurity, sexual and physical harassment; and verbal abuse.
Appropriate Structure	Limit setting; clear and consistent rules and expectations; firm-enough control; continuity and predictability; clear boundaries; and age-appropriate monitoring.	Chaotic; disorganized; laissez-faire; rigid; overcontrolled; and autocratic.
Supportive Relationships	Warmth; closeness; connectedness; good communication; caring; support; guidance; secure attachment; and responsiveness.	Cold; distant; overcontrolling; ambiguous support; untrustworthy; focused on winning; inattentive; unresponsive; and rejecting.
Opportunities to Belong	Opportunities for meaningful inclusion, regardless of one's gender, ethnicity, sexual orientation, or disabilities; social inclusion, social engagement and integration; opportunities for socio-cultural identity formation; and support for cultural and bicultural competence.	Exclusion; marginalization; and intergroup conflict.
Positive Social Norms	Rules of behavior; expectations; injunctions; ways of doing things; values and morals; and obligations for service.	Normlessness; anomic; laissez-faire practices; antisocial and amoral norms
Support for Efficacy and Mattering	Youth-based; empowerment practices that support autonomy; making a real difference in one's community; and being taken seriously. Practices that include enabling; responsibility granting; and meaningful challenge. Practices that focus on improvement rather than on relative current performance levels.	Unchallenging; overcontrolling; disempowering; and disabling. Practices that undermine motivation and desire to learn, such as excessive focus on current relative performance level rather than improvement.
Opportunities for Skill Building	Opportunities to learn physical, intellectual, psychological, emotional, and social skills; exposure to intentional learning experiences; opportunities to learn cultural literacies, media literacy, communication skills, and good habits of mind; preparation for adult employment; and opportunities to develop social and cultural capital.	Practice that promotes bad physical habits and habits of mind; and practice that undermines school and learning.
Integration of Family, School, and Community Efforts	Concordance; coordination' and synergy among family, school, and community.	Discordance; lack of communication; and conflict.

Reprinted with permission from *Community programs to promote youth development.* © (2002) by the National Academy of Sciences, Courtesy of the National Academy Press, Washington, D.C.

TABLE 5–6.
Selected Interventions to Promote Strengths-Enhancing Environments
for Personal and Social Development

Intervention	Type of Service/Function Performed by Counselor	Strength Promoted	Environment Addressed	School Level
Child Development Project	Advocating for the program, collaborating and teaming, coordinating, training	School connectedness	School Classroom	Elementary
Seattle Social Development Project	Advocating for the program, collaborating, coordinating, training, classroom guidance	School and family connectedness, social problem solving	School Classroom	Elementary
HiPlaces	Advocating for the program, collaborating	Academic School adjustment	School	Middle
School Transition Environment Project	Advocating for the program, collaborating, coordinating	Academic School Adjustment	School Classroom	High

presents selected interventions that were designed to promote strengths-enhancing environments for student personal and social development. Increasing connectedness (belonging) is one focus of several of these initiatives.

As we shall see, the school counselor's efforts in promoting these environments for students rely heavily on systemic-level functions (e.g., indirect services) and require assuming more of a leadership role for change within the school. Thus, the school counselor would be involved in advocating for these types of environments, in teaming and collaborating with other educators to foster them, and in consulting about and coordinating services within them.

The Child Development Project

The Child Development Project (CDP, 2004), which has been ongoing for over 20 years, is one research-based, elementary-school-restructuring initiative that focuses primarily on changing the school ecology to create schools that are caring communities of learners. Comprehensive in its approach, the CDP revamps teaching, learning, school organization, school climate, and teachers' work environments to promote the intellectual, social, and ethical development of students. The project is based in part on motivation theory (Deci & Ryan, 1985; Deci, Vallerand, Pelletier, & Ryan, 1991) that we discussed earlier (see Chapter 3) and strives to maximize students' feelings of autonomy, competence, and relatedness. It was initiated in three San Francisco area schools in 1982 (Solomon, Watson, Battistich, Schaps, & Delucchi, 1996) and is currently being implemented in more than 100 schools across the country (Posey et al. 1996). The project has been evaluated in a variety of locations, including Dade County, FL; White Plains, NY; Louisville, KY; and San Francisco, Cupertino, and Salinas, CA (CDP, 2004).

Three basic assumptions about children's motivation and four core principles guided the development of the CDP. The first assumption is that children will become more connected to school if they feel that it is a nurturing place and sensitive to their needs. Thus, the school will become a caring community for the student. Second, in order for the school to be a caring community, it must provide for the basic psychological needs of each student. These are (a) the need to belong and feel valued, (b) the need for autonomy and the freedom to do things on one's own initiative, and (c) the need for competence, which results from accomplishing goals and acquiring skills. Third, learning is an active process that is controlled by the learner not a passive process controlled by the teacher (Watson, Battistich, & Solomon, 1997). Coupled with these assumptions are four core principles on which the program is based: (a) build warm, stable, supportive relationships; (b) attend to the social and ethical dimensions of learning; (c) honor intrinsic motivation; and (d) teach in ways that support students' active construction of meaning (Watson et al., 1997). From these assumptions and core principles came five CDP program components. Three of the components—(a) collaborative learning, (b) developmental discipline, and (c) a literature-based reading and language arts program—focus primarily on the classroom environment. The fourth component is concerned with the school-wide environment, while the remaining component focuses on parent involvement.

Teachers use cooperative learning (see Chapter 3) to encourage students to develop prosocial skills within groups. Students participate in different groups throughout the year so that prosocial skills are developed with all classmates. Also, teachers are encouraged to allow student groups to work independently and problem solve on their own, although teacher intervention is emphasized for necessary guidance and instruction. Therefore, peer collaboration and adult guidance are both essential to fostering students' academic and prosocial development. Twenty-five group lessons used in the program are meant to be interesting to students, so that intrinsic motivation to learn can also be developed. The lessons employ a generic format that can be used in a variety of academic areas. In addition, 10 sample activities illustrate each format. Activities such as cooperative games or those that involve products in which all students contribute (e.g., class books or murals) help children interact while learning (Watson, Solomon, Battistich, Schaps, & Solomon, 1989). Also, the activities help avoid competition among groups, as there are no winners or losers among class groups. "Cooperative activities thus provide a kind of 'learning laboratory' for enhancing interpersonal understanding, developing a commitment to prosocial values and democratic processes, and acquiring important social skills, while also pursuing academic goals" (Battistich, Watson, Solomon, Schaps, & Solomon, 1991, p. 10).

Developmental discipline is the CDP component that is most explicitly directed toward developing and maintaining a caring classroom environment (Watson et al., 1997). The CDP emphasizes a child-centered approach that uses teaching and problem-solving, rather than rewards and punishments, to promote student competence, responsibility, and commitment to the community. Teachers are taught to use discipline as a way to develop prosocial values and self-control. It is expected that a sense of community in the classroom will create a shared commitment between students and teachers to the values and rules within the classroom. Specifically, teachers strive to establish positive and warm relationships with each student in the classroom. Students are involved in setting classroom rules and evaluating the classroom environment and effectiveness of rules throughout the year. Furthermore, teachers help students understand the reasons for the rules through the use of open discussion. Also, students are encouraged to work collaboratively to solve problems, especially in conflict resolution. Social skills and techniques for self-control are taught to students in order to prevent classroom misbehavior. Clear expectations are also given to avoid misbehavior. Rewards and punishment are not used with students in developmental discipline because punitive responses are viewed as likely to reduce self-esteem in students, deteriorate the positive student-teacher relationship, and induce fear or resentment toward the teacher by the student. If misbehavior does occur, teachers can address the problem by calling out the student's name, stating the relevant rule along with a demand for compliance, or asking the child to leave the class. If exclusion is required, it is important to involve the student in deciding how long the exclusionary time should last so that the student commits fully to the decision (Battistich et al., 1991).

The literature-based reading and language arts component focuses on integrating social and ethical content into the curriculum and helps students to develop greater empathy for others and understanding of themselves. While the other components of CDP specifically emphasize the use of prosocial values in the school and community settings, this component helps promote generalization of prosocial values to a broader range of settings. All stories are read out loud. Then, discussions about the moral dilemmas or conflicting values within the stories are conducted. Teachers are trained to ask open-ended questions that do not have "right" answers so that different opinions can be expressed by students. The discussions help children understand that there are many moral ways of behaving when presented with a difficult issue.

School-wide activities, the fourth CDP component, is a prime example of an area in which a school counselor's expertise, leadership, and coordination efforts could make a valuable contribution to restructuring the school environment to enhance positive youth development. In the CDP, school-wide activities are used to promote inclusion, non-competitiveness, and the values of a caring community (Watson et al. 1997). These activities provide extended opportunities for prosocial actions by students. Helping activities are planned using open discussion to obtain student input. Within school, buddy programs or tutoring programs that pair older students with younger students help develop a sense of responsibility and partnership in the school. School beautification projects promote a sense of inclusiveness for all students and create a sense of community. Also, individual chores or jobs can be used within the classroom setting so that students are responsible for some aspect of their classroom. Outside of school, students can participate in service activities to help community organizations (e.g., helping needy families during the holiday season or "trick or treating" for UNICEF). These activities can be done less frequently than those within school, but they are still important in creating personally rewarding experiences and exhibiting socially valued behavior. Once again, students are not offered rewards or prizes for participating in these activities. Instead, intrinsic motivation is encouraged as a reason to help others.

Parent involvement, another example of an area in which the school counselor's leadership and coordinating efforts could be extremely valuable, is the fifth CDP component. It includes both family participation activities that are coordinated within the curriculum, and membership on a teacher-parent coordinating team that plans activities to enhance the school-family bond. One example is *Homeside Activities*, which is a series of conversations and activities designed to explore the relationship between school and family (Watson et al., 1997). Parental involvement helps encourage warm and caring relationships between students and parents, and also provides a way for parents to talk to their children about school. Also, as students share their family history in class, classmates learn to appreciate different family cultures and traditions.

The Child Development Project of the Developmental Studies Center in Oakland, California has been the subject of extensive research over a 20-year period (e.g., Battistich et al., 1991; Solomon, Battistich, Watson, Schaps, & Lewis, 2000; Solomon, Watson, Battistich, Schaps, & Delucchi, 1996; Watson et al., 1989; Watson et al., 1997). The largest study involved an ethnically and socioeconomically diverse sample of over 14,000 students from 12 program and 12 matched comparison schools in six school districts across the country. After a three-year implementation period, positive student results were demonstrated in the five program schools in which the CDP was the most extensively implemented. Among the statistically significant differences favoring students in the high implementation schools as opposed to those in the corresponding comparison schools were the following:

- less use of alcohol and marijuana
- less weapons carrying and vehicle theft
- a greater sense of community and more liking for school

- stronger academic motivation and a higher sense of efficacy
- better conflict resolution skills, more concern for others, more frequent altruistic behavior
- stronger commitment to democratic values

The Developmental Studies Center (DSC) also reported follow-up data for students from three high-implementing CDP schools when the students were in middle school (Developmental Studies Center [DSC], 2004). Statistically significant differences favoring these students versus students in comparison schools included

- a greater sense of community and more liking for school
- greater trust in and respect for teachers and higher educational aspirations
- greater involvement in positive activities such as sports, clubs, and youth groups
- less misconduct at school and less delinquent behavior
- higher educational aspirations, grades in core academic subjects, and achievement test scores

As we have seen, the Child Development Project is a comprehensive elementary school restructuring initiative that has produced some impressive developmental gains with students in the personal/social as well as the academic area. It is clearly not an initiative that the school counselor can implement alone as it requires a whole-school team effort. It is the type of effective environmental restructuring, however, that the strengths-based counselor as a school leader can bring to the attention of teachers and administrators. Furthermore, the counselor can collaborate to build teams and coalitions of teachers, administrators, and parents that can advocate for developing and implementing CDP-type interventions. Providing training and helping to coordinate peer tutoring, buddy, and parent involvement are other important indirect or systems-level functions in which the school counselor can assume a key leadership role in environmental restructuring.

The Seattle Social Development Project

The Seattle Social Development Project (e.g., Hawkins et al., 1992; Hawkins, Catalano, Kosterman, Abbott, & Hill, 1999) is a comprehensive, longitudinal, prevention program in elementary schools that extends over a six-year period. It addresses multiple risk and protective factors, with a strong emphasis on maintaining strong school and family bonds, and is based on the social development strategy (Catalano & Hawkins, 1996; Wong et al. 1997) that we discussed in chapter one. The project began in 1981 with first graders in eight Seattle elementary schools and subsequently expanded to 18 elementary schools serving high-crime, high-poverty neighborhoods in Seattle. Since that time, students and parents have been contacted frequently to gather follow-up data, which are currently available for the participants through age 21.

Three intervention components—(a) teacher training, (b) child training, and (c) parent training—comprise the program. Teachers in grades one to six received five days of training annually on proactive classroom management, interactive teaching, and cooperative learning. Proactive classroom management involves training teachers to (a) maximize the time students are involved in learning, (b) minimize classroom disruptions, (c) give explicit instructions for student behavior, (d) recognize and reward compliance, and (e) keep minor discipline problems from interrupting learning. Interactive teaching includes (a) modeling skills to be learned, (b) teaching to explicit learning objectives, (c) breaking objectives into small steps, (d) constantly monitoring student comprehension, and (e) reteaching material when necessary. Cooperative learning, as we discussed earlier, involves small teams of students of different ability levels and backgrounds as learning partners, as well as providing recognition to teams for academic improvement of individual members.

The child training component includes social problem solving in the first grade using Shure's *I Can Problem Solve Program* that we reviewed earlier in this chapter. Students in grade 6 also receive four hours of training in recognizing and resisting social influences to engage in problem behaviors and generating positive alternatives for themselves and their peers to stay out of trouble. The school counselor could provide several key services with respect to this component of the program. These services could include providing or coordinating the ICPS training for teachers, as well as delivering the ICPS program directly to students through classroom guidance lessons or in conjunction with teachers.

The parent training component of the Seattle Social Development Project is voluntary. It is also another area in which the school counselor can make an important contribution either through coordinating this initiative or by providing services directly to parents. In the first and second grades, the parent training component consists of a seven-session curriculum, "Catch 'em Being Good," for child behavior management (e.g., using positive reinforcement and consequences). A four-session "How to Help Your Child Succeed in School" curriculum (e.g., seeking out teachers, creating a home learning environment, helping children to strengthen math and reading skills) is offered in second and third grades, while parents in grades five and six receive a five-session "Preparing for the Drug Free Years" curriculum (e.g., establishing a family policy on drug use and practicing refusal skills with children).

Evaluation of the Project used a nonrandomized control design with three conditions: (a) a full intervention group which received the intervention package from grade one to grade 5, (b) a later intervention group which received it in grades 5 and 6 only, and (c) a control group which received no special intervention (Hawkins, 2003; Hawkins et al., 1992, 1999). The final sample included 643 fifth-grade students assigned to the three conditions. A follow-up study was conducted six years after intervention at age 18, and then again at age 21. Ninety-three and ninety-four percent of the sample participated in the two follow-ups, respectively.

At the end of grade 6, significant differences were obtained primarily between the full intervention group and the control group students. Students who had received the full intervention demonstrated (a) more participation in class, (b) better social and schoolwork skills, (c) more commitment to school, (d) better behavior at school, (e) better achievement, and (f) less early onset of drug use and delinquency. At age 18, significantly fewer students in the full intervention group than the control group had (a) committed violent acts, (b) reported heavy alcohol use in past year, (c) engaged in sexual intercourse, (d) had multiple sex partners, or (e) had become pregnant or caused pregnancies. In addition, the full intervention students reported more commitment and attachment to school, better academic achievement, and less school misbehavior. At age 21, full intervention students were more likely to have graduated from high school and to have attended two or more years of college. They were also more likely to be employed, have more responsibility at work, and to be engaged in work or school. Moreover, they showed fewer problem behaviors as measured by selling drugs, symptoms of depression and social phobia, and unprotected sexual activity. Finally, the interventions resulted in particularly positive benefits for African American students, as fewer pregnancies were seen in African American females and increased condom use and fewer STDs were evident among African American males at age 21.

As was true for the Child Development Project, interventions in the Seattle Social Development Project provide the elementary-school counselor with opportunities to engage in a number of direct and system-level (indirect) service functions. Some of the most obvious of these are (a) classroom guidance, (b) parent workshops, (c) teacher training, (d) advocacy, (e) coordination, and (f) collaboration. Taken together, results from these two projects support the elementary school endorsing and participating in intensive, long-term promotion and prevention initiatives to improve the strengths-enhancing capacity of the elementary school environment. These initiatives have clearly been shown to be associated with long-term positive effects on student development in the personal-social domain, as well as in the academic and career domains.

The Project on High Performing Learning Communities (HiPlaces)

The Project on High Performing Learning Communities (HiPlaces; Felner, 2000; Felner et al., 1997) is an empirical study of the effects of different types of middle school environments on students' academic and personal/social development. The results of this study are important to middle school counselors and educators because they indicate the middle school environmental conditions that impede and enhance student development in the personal/social and academic areas. As such, they provide the middle school counselor with an empirical basis for advocating for these strengths-enhancing conditions.

In recent years, much of middle school reform initiatives have been driven by the recommendations of the Task Force on Education of Young Adolescents in the Carnegie Council's 1989 report, *Turning Points: Preparing American Youth for the 21st.* Among the recommendations (Carnegie Council, 1989) were the following:

- create small communities for learning (schools-within-schools, students and teachers grouped together as teams, and small group advisories)
- teach a core academic program that results in students who are literate, know how to think critically, lead a healthy life, behave ethically, and assume the responsibilities of citizenship in a pluralistic society
- ensure success for all students through eliminating tracking, and promoting cooperative learning, flexibility in arranging instructional time, and adequate resources (time, space, equipment, and materials) for teachers
- empower teachers and administrators to make decisions about the experiences of middle-grade students through creative control by teachers over the instructional program linked to greater responsibilities for student performance, governance committees, and autonomy to create environments tailored to enhance the intellectual and emotional development of all youth
- staff middle grade school with teachers who are experts at teaching young adolescents
- improve academic performance through fostering the health and fitness of young adolescents
- reengage families in education by giving them meaningful roles in school governance, communicating with them about student progress, and offering them opportunities to support the learning process
- connect schools with communities through service opportunities, collaborations to ensure students access to health and social services, and using community resources to enrich the instructional program and opportunities for constructive after-school activities.

The longitudinal effects of school restructuring in the Illinois Middle Grades Network (31 schools at the time of the study and 97 schools as of 1997) on students' academic achievement, socio-emotional development, and behavioral adjustment were the subjects of the HiPlaces study. The focus was on the effects of implementing the *Turning Points* structural recommendations for middle schools (e.g., team size, student/teacher ratio, amount of teacher common planning time). Data were reported for a three-year period, and the schools included in the study represented a range of geographic, demographic (urban, suburban, and rural), and size (from less than 200 to almost 2000) characteristics. The 31 schools were divided into three categories—(a) high implementation (9 schools), (b) partial implementation (12), and (c) low implementation (10)—based on the degree to which they had implemented *Turning Points* structural recommendations. High implementation schools, for example, had (a) teams with four to five common planning periods per week, (b) relatively small numbers of students (not more than 120) on the team, (c) relatively low teacher/student ratios (one teacher per 20–25 students), (d) advisories that occurred with relatively high frequency (e.g., four or five times per week), and (e) teacher/student ratios in advisories of approximately one to 22 or less. Although the three groups of schools differed in level of implementation of the recommendations, they were described as demographically comparable in terms of size, percentage of students eligible for free/reduced-priced lunch, and per-pupil expenditures.

Data were collected for sixth- and eighth-grade students and combined into a single sixth-eighth-grade index. Results on Illinois math, language arts, and reading achievement tests indicated that students in highly implemented schools achieved at much higher levels than those in non-implemented schools and substantially better than those in partially implemented schools. Teacher ratings of student behavioral problems (total of reported aggression, moodiness, shyness, and learning difficulties) revealed a lower level in highly implemented schools as compared to partially implemented schools and much lower than in non-implemented schools. In addition, students in more fully implemented schools reported better adjustment—less fearful of being victimized, less worried about something bad happening at school and about the future, and had higher levels of self-esteem—than those in partially implemented schools. Those in partially implemented schools, in turn, reported better adjustment than those in the least implemented schools.

Furthermore, the results indicated that, as schools moved up in their level of *Turning Points* recommendations over a one- and a two-year period, the increases in implementation were related to increases in achievement scores, student adjustment, and students' experiences of school climate. Felner et al. (1997) concluded that teams with more than 120 students, fewer than four common planning periods per week, and with student/teacher ratios beyond the middle 20s tend to show little impact on student well-being or on instructional practices. In addition, the study demonstrated a relationship between the level of implementation of the recommendations and the ability to prevent decline or enhance outcomes for at-risk students. Specifically, students in more traditionally structured middle schools showed declines in achievement and adjustment indicators. It was not until the schools had implemented a number of the recommendations that the declines were absent, and it took a high degree of implementation before enhancements in achievement and adjustment were obtained for at-risk students.

The HiPlaces research identified the types of structural components that are associated with strengths-enhancing school environments for middle school adolescents. Undoubtedly, these structural components increase the likelihood that student will experience a variety of the protective factors and assets that we have been discussing both in this chapter and in previous chapters. These factors include (a) caring relationships with adults, (b) high expectations, (c) opportunities for meaningful participation and mattering, (d) belonging, (e) prosocial bonding, (f) clear and consistent boundaries, and (g) opportunities for skill building. By providing information to teachers and administrators on the importance of these structural components—and by collaborating with educators, parents, and community members to advocate for these components—the middle school counselor can further the development of a strengths-enhancing environment in her or his school.

INTERVENTIONS TO PROMOTE STRENGTHS-ENHANCING ENVIRONMENTS FOR PERSONAL AND SOCIAL DEVELOPMENT IN HIGH SCHOOLS

In a previous chapter, we discussed the year-long School Transition Environment Project (STEP) conducted by Felner et al. (1993). As the reader may recall, STEP is a school restructuring project that was designed to prevent the deleterious effects that often result when students transition from the typically more personal and developmentally oriented middle school environment to the larger, and often less personal, high-school setting. STEP involves a variety of environmental modifications for ninth-grade students within the high school environment, including (a) smaller learning environments (STEP teams of 60–100) within the larger high school to increase belongingness; (b) classes in close proximity to each other in order to reduce the complexity of the environment and minimize social pressure from older students; (c) small homerooms with teachers serving as advisors; and (d) teachers identifying students who need additional assistance or other services. By the end of the project year, STEP participants exhibited higher self-concept scores, grades, and school attendance than control group students. A five-year follow-up also revealed a lower dropout rate, fewer absences, and a higher grade-point average for STEP participants indicating that long-term benefits were associated with this one-year school environmental restructuring project.

At this time, we are not aware of other high school restructuring efforts, which have empirically demonstrated that they enhance student development in the personal and social domains. To be sure, high-school reform has been a major issue in education for some time, but the focus has been almost exclusively on academic development and enhancing school and achievement test performance. One of the most common of these efforts is *High Schools That Work*, which began in 1987 and now has over 1,000 sites in 31 states (Southern Regional Education Board, 2004). The primary goal of the program is to increase the achievement of career-bound students by blending the content of traditional college preparatory studies with quality vocational and educational studies. The program changes the school environment by implementing 10 key practices: (a) high expectations; (b) challenging vocational studies; (c) increasing access to academic studies; (d) requiring four years of English, three of math, and three of science; (e) work-based learning; collaboration among academic and vocational teachers; (f) students actively engaged; (g) an individualized advising system; (h) extra help; and (i) using assessment and evaluation data to foster continuous improvement (Northwest Regional Educational Laboratory, 2004). The program has been extensively evaluated by its developers and has fairly consistently resulted in achievement test (mathematics, reading, and science) gains in the schools in which it was implemented, but these evaluations lacked a control group. Unfortunately, in a comparison study, the *HSTW* group was outperformed by the control group, prompting reviewers to assert that additional controlled research is needed to determine the effectiveness of *HSTW* (Borman et al., 2002).

As we have seen, there is a lack of definitive empirical evidence at the high-school level of environmental interventions that have clearly enhanced student development in the personal and social domains. As such, the school counselor who is concerned with fostering strengths-enhancing environments for high-school students must rely for guidelines on the more generic findings regarding strengths-enhancing environments that we discussed both in this chapter and previously. These recommendations include those by the Committee on Community-Level Programs for Youth contained in Table 5–5 as well as Henderson and Milstein's (1996) Resilience Wheel and Search Institute's external assets (e.g., Starkman et al., 1999), among others.

INTERVENTIONS TO PROMOTE STRENGTHS-ENHANCING ENVIRONMENTS FOR PERSONAL AND SOCIAL DEVELOPMENT OVER THE K–12 CONTINUUM

The challenges faced by counselors and other educators vary considerably from school to school. A number of schools are characterized by a large number of student discipline referrals and other student crises on a daily basis. In these instances, school counselors frequently report that they spend much of their time "putting out fires" and interacting with a relatively small percentage of the students and teachers in the school. Constantly having to function in this crisis mode with discipline and related referrals makes it difficult for them to implement a comprehensive school-guidance program. What does a Strengths-Based School Counseling framework have to offer counselors in this type of school environment?

An approach that is consistent with SBSC involves the school counselor conceptualizing the problem situation (e.g., frequent disciplinary incidents and crises) from a different vantage point. Rather than viewing the situation as one that involves intervening with an individual student (or teacher) or small groups of students, it may be more effective to view the situation and required interventions from a school or systems-level perspective. Thus, the cause of behavior doesn't reside solely within the student, but is the result of an interaction between the environment and the student. As such, that interaction becomes the target of intervention. Fix problem contexts, not problem behavior (Carr et al., 2002).

In this regard, school-wide Positive Behavior Support (PBS) is an evidenced-based approach for restructuring educational environments to improve school climate and positive behavior support for all students and to reduce school disciplinary incidents (Bohanon-Edmonson, Flannery, Eber, & Sugai, 2005; Center on Positive Behavioral Interventions and Supports, 2004; Sugai & Horner, 2002; U.S. Office of Special Education, www.pbis.org). Positive behavior includes skills that increase the likelihood of success and personal satisfaction in academic, work, social, recreational, community, and family settings; while support encompasses educational methods to teach, expand, and strengthen positive behavior, as well as system change methods to increase opportunities to display those positive behaviors (Carr et al., 2002). As such, skill building and environmental design are the change-producing interventions. School-wide Positive Behavior Support (PBS) involves collaboration among school counselors, administrators, teachers, special education specialists, school psychologists, parents, and school community councils, and focuses on violence prevention, social competencies, and bully-proofing the school. The purpose of school-wide PBS is to establish a climate in which appropriate behavior is the norm. The primary intervention strategy is to rearrange the environment to improve quality of life rather than to operate directly on reducing problem behavior per se (Carr et al., 2002). It includes teaching behavioral expectations and introducing, modeling, and reinforcing positive social behavior rather than waiting for misbehavior to occur before responding (e.g., and then punishing it). PBS involves implementing beliefs, practices, and interventions that support social competence and academic achievement, decision making, and student and staff behavior.

It's an interactive approach providing opportunities to correct and improve four key elements:

1. **Outcomes:** Academic and behavior targets endorsed and emphasized by students, families, and educators.

2. **Practices:** Evidence-based interventions and strategies.
3. **Data:** Information used to identify status, need for change, and effects of interventions.
4. **Systems:** Supports needed to enable the accurate and durable implementation of the PBS practices (Kay, 2005, pp. 20–21).

Kay (2005), a school counselor, reported on the effects of PBS. Kay described a middle school of 1,050 students in which there were 1,500 office referrals for discipline in a single year. Initially, discipline strategies were inconsistent, morale was low, and hallway behavior was out of control. In one year, discipline referrals were reduced by 60%, and students felt safer in the halls and the cafeteria. The reason for the change was the implementation of school-wide positive behavioral interventions and supports (Sugai & Horner, 2002; U.S. Office of Special Education, www.pbis.org).

PBS was led by a team consisting of the school counselor, assistant principal, teachers, and staff and parent representatives (Kay, 2005). A survey of student, faculty, and parent concerns resulted in the development of a set of school-wide expectations, specific hallway behaviors, and social skill instruction. The expectations were captured in a motto:

C—aring and Respectful Attitude

A—rrive on Time

T—ake responsibility

S—afety first.

Students learned the motto at the beginning of the year, followed by lessons taught about it by teachers throughout the year. School counselors made monthly classroom presentations about social skills relevant to the motto. Students were taught four simple rules for hallway behavior—(a) walk on the right, (b) no stopping at intersections, (c) pull to the side of the road to talk, and (d) safety first—and were reinforced with public recognition and small rewards for following those rules. In addition, teachers taught intelligent behavior (e.g., listening, accepting no, following directions, and asking for help) on a monthly basis and reinforced it daily.

PBS was implemented in three steps, each of which focused on three distinct groups of students. The first step focused on the vast majority of students (about 80%) and involved school-wide interventions. These interventions consisted of teaching behavioral expectations and modeling and reinforcing appropriate behaviors through public recognition and small rewards. Their purpose was to prevent new inappropriate behavior from occurring. At-risk students (approximately 15%) in the classroom for whom the school-wide interventions don't work all of the time were the focus of the second step. Interventions included "think time" (admitting misbehaving students into another class where they write descriptions of more appropriate behavior) and greater consistency in procedures from classroom to classroom. High-risk students (approximately 5%) for whom school-wide and classroom interventions were not effective were the focus of the third step in which individualized interventions were employed.

As Kay (2005) noted, the school counselor in PBS functions as a leader and systemic change agent working within the mission of the school. Moreover, PBS epitomizes a strengths-based approach as it "reflects a more general trend in the social sciences and education away from pathology-based models to a new positive model that stresses personal competence and environmental integrity" (Carr et al., 2002, p. 4).

The study by Kay (2005) is by no means the only one on the effects of PBS. School-wide PBS has been implemented in over 500 schools across the nation (Sugai & Horner, 2002), and research on its effectiveness was reviewed by Safran and Oswald (2003). PBS can be directed at four levels of support— (a) school-wide supports (e.g., a violence prevention program such as *Second Step* [Committee on Children, 1992a, 1992b, 1997]), (b) supports for nonclassroom or specific school settings (e.g., hallways, playgrounds, cafeterias, school entrances and exits), (c) classroom or group supports (e.g., a fourth-grade class or a basketball team), and (d) individual student supports for those with chronic problems requiring individualized interventions. The findings were positive across all types of PBS (Safran & Oswald, 2003). Thus, advocating, providing leadership for, and collaborating with others to institute school-wide PBS is one way in which the school counselor can function differently (e.g., not work in a direct-service mode with each individual crisis situation) and more effectively in a school that is characterized by a high number of disciplinary and crisis situations.

SUMMARY

In this chapter, we reviewed the empirically based personal and social strengths that are associated with positive student development. Next, we illustrated some evidence-based interventions that promote these strengths in the personal and social domains. Our discussion focused first on interventions for enhancing behavioral and emotional self-regulation. We then turned to importance of ethnic identity development both for students of color and for White students, and we reviewed interventions to foster that development. The strengths-based school counselor has a key role to play in helping students to acquire the skills that are needed to function effectively in an increasingly diverse, multicultural society.

We also discussed environmental factors that facilitate developing those strengths. We saw that many of those factors are the same as those which have been shown to be associated with positive student academic development.

Finally, we reviewed initiatives to restructure entire school environments in order to promote personal and social development. We found that these interventions often enhance development in the academic domain as well. Furthermore, some intensive, sustained school restructuring efforts, particularly during the elementary school years, have been shown to promote positive developmental changes that are sustained for a number of years after the intervention has ceased. As such, systemic-level interventions that improve the strengths-enhancing environment of the school need to be an essential component of the school counselor's efforts.

As is evident in this chapter, promoting student strengths and strengths-based environments for personal/social development is a complex endeavor. While "snap-shot, feel-good" interventions may be more manageable, they lack research support and neither impact nor empower students for meaningful change and development.

KEY POINTS

The Traditional Role of the School Counselor in Personal and Social Development

- The school counselor's traditional role typically involved a mental health focus with a small number of students.
- The primary focus was on problem reduction and resulted in the school counselor playing a supportive role to teachers and other educators.

The Contemporary Role of the School Counselor in Personal and Social Development

- As specified in the ASCA National Model, the contemporary role has a more developmental and preventative orientation toward personal and social development and results in the school counseling program being more central to the mission of schools.
- This model specifies standards as well as student competencies and indicators that students should be able to demonstrate as a result of participating in a comprehensive school counseling program.

The Strengths-Based School Counselor's Role in Personal and Social Development

- The strengths-based school counselor role's involves promoting evidence-based personal and social strengths and the environments that have been shown to foster them.
- Whenever possible, the counselor employs evidence-based interventions that support the development of those strengths and strengths-enhancing environments.

Personal and Social Strengths to Promote

- Research and theoretical advances from a variety of disciplines are increasingly converging on the specific strengths and strength areas that school counselors should promote.

- The Committee on Community-Level Programs for Youth of the National Research Council and Institute of Medicine compiled a research-based list of personal and social assets that promote the healthy development and well-being of adolescents and facilitate a successful transition from childhood through adolescence into adulthood. The four general categories of assets—(a) physical health, (b) cognitive development, (c) psychological and emotional development, and (d) social development—are relevant to ASCA's personal/social development domain, as well as the academic and career domains.

- Positive psychology researchers (Seligman and colleagues) have focused on developing a classification of character strengths and virtues that make the good life possible, buffer against misfortune and psychological disorders, and help build resilience. The 24 character strengths chosen satisfied a variety of criteria and are organized into six core moral virtues.

- Wellness/well-being literature has advanced a variety of strengths for both children and adults. Two examples are the multidimensional model of well-being in adults proposed by Ryff and Singer, and Cowen's five major strands that can enhance or pose threats to psychological wellness.

Strengths-Based Interventions to Promote Personal and Social Development

- Interventions that can increase students' ability to regulate behavior and emotions enhance social and personal development, and, in many instances, academic development. Many programs have been implemented that focus on these self-regulation skills. School counselors can coordinate these effective, evidence-based curricula to promote student strengths, as well as provide other services related to them.

- **The I Can Problem Solve Program (ICPS)** is a teacher-based, prevention-oriented classroom guidance program that teaches several cognitive problem-solving skills that are important to self-regulation and may be lacking in the thinking and actions of impulsive adolescents. The program has repeatedly demonstrated positive effects that result in increased generation of solutions to problems and increased thinking about the consequences of one's actions. The program is for students 4–12.

- **The Anger Coping Program** is a small group counseling intervention that targets the self-regulation skills of upper-elementary to early-middle-school students whose customary response to interpersonal problems is anger and depression. The purpose of the program is to (a) promote better perspective-taking skills, (b) increase awareness of the physiological signs of anger,(c) improve social problem-solving skills, and (d) increase the inventory of responses to problem situations. The program has been documented as an effective small group intervention.

- **Teaching Students to be Peacemakers** is a K–12 proactive, school-wide approach to violence prevention. Students learn conflict resolution and mediation skills and serve as peer mediators to their classmates. According to research, the program resulted in positive effects for general conflict resolution, reduced the amount of time that school staff spent on conflict resolution, improved the classroom climate, and was even linked to higher academic achievement.

- **The Penn Resilience or Penn Prevention Project (PPP)** is a small-group counseling program. It focuses on cognitive and social problem solving to help develop strengths that will provide a buffer against depression for all students and reduce the effects of depression for students already experiencing it. The cognitive component of the model incorporates Ellis' ABC model of dysfunction and Beck's cognitive therapy procedures, while the social problem-solving component incorporates assertiveness, negotiation, social-skills training, and the application of cognitive skills to the interpersonal domain. Research studies in four different countries over the past decade have shown the PPP to be effective.

- **The Life Skills Training (LST) Program** is an evidence-based, cognitive-behavioral, substance abuse prevention curriculum that has been the subject of research for more than 20 years. The LST curriculum teaches resistance skills within the larger context of acquiring basic life skills and enhancing personal and social competence. Knowledge and information, decision-making, self-directed behavior change, coping with anxiety, and social skills are the five main components of the curriculum. Results from the program research indicated that the LST program implemented in junior high can produce meaningful and durable reductions in tobacco, alcohol, and marijuana use.

- **The Teen Outreach Program (TOP)** is directed toward reducing rates of teenage pregnancy, school failure, and school suspension. The program attempts to provide students with a sense of empowerment by engaging teens in opportunities for meaningful participation and belonging in their community as well as opportunities that support efficacy and mattering. The year-long, high-school program has three components—(a) supervised community service, (b) classroom-based discussions of service experiences, and (c) classroom-based discussions and activities related to key social-developmental tasks of adolescence. Research results indicate that the program is effective even though the activities place very little emphasis on the topics of sexuality or school failure.

Enhancing Identity and Developing Multicultural Competence

- Context and environmental factors play an important role in all development processes and appear to be especially important for minority youth. For these youth, successful identity formation involves achieving a secure sense of racial, cultural, and/or ethnic identity in order to function in a healthy manner in the face of lower status, restricted opportunities, and the presence of stereotypes and racism. Research indicates that achieved ethnic identity for minority students is associated with positive attributes such as (a) high self-esteem, (b) a strong commitment to doing well in school, (c) a strong sense of purpose in life, self-efficacy, and (d) high academic achievement. Because schools are an important influence on racial identity development, school counselors have an important role to play in educating and training staff on identity development, creating an empowering climate for students to explore their ethnic heritage, and aiding all students in the identity development process.

Ethnic Identity Development Theories

- The school counselor needs to be knowledgeable about the specific issues that affect the identity developmental process of the particular ethnic groups with which she or he is involved. The counselor also needs to be aware of the developmental models and theories that have been proposed as well as the research on these models.
- The five-stage Minority Development model or Racial/Cultural Identity Model of Sue and Sue helps counselors understand culturally different clients' attitudes and behaviors. Each of the five stages of development is associated with a specific set of attitudes toward the self, others of the same minority, others of a different minority, and the dominant group. This model may be applied to White Identity development also.
- Another model by Phinney and Kohatsu involves a four-phase process rather than invariant stages. Each stage—(a) initial,(b) transition, (c) intermediate, and (d) final—is characterized by different feelings and thoughts. Also, it involves the resolution of three issues: (a) the individual's sense of belonging and commitment to his or her ethnic or racial group, (b) the individual's minority status in society and the associated effects of racism and discrimination, and (c) the individual's relationship to the dominant culture and to other ethnic groups.
- Helms developed a White racial-identity development model that occurs via a six-status process: (a) Contact,(b) Disintegration, (c) Reintegration, (d) Pseudo Independence, (e) Immersion/Emersion, and (f) Autonomy. Unlike ethnic identity development, White racial-identity formation is concerned with becoming aware of racism and privilege associated with being White and developing a non-racist White identity.

Interventions to Facilitate Ethnic Identity Development

- A variety of educational and counseling-related interventions have been proposed for facilitating ethnic identification due to its developmental importance. Unfortunately, little empirical research has been conducted on the effectiveness of most of the interventions; however, school counselors can advocate for and collaborate with teachers and administrators to implement recommended interventions.
- Cultural identity small groups, ethnic identity organizations in high schools, and community and school-based programs that include racial identification as an important component are all possible interventions that could be implemented. School counselors can encourage, mobilize support for, and facilitate the development of these interventions.
- **The Research-Based Model Partnership Education Program (Model Program)** is a culturally sensitive program that has generated data about its effectiveness. The program is a community-based, university-school-community partnership designed to empower low-income African American children for academic and social success. It is predicated on self-empowerment theory. Research studies found that the Model Program showed increases in adaptive skills and decreases in frequency of engaging in maladaptive behavior and school misconduct.
- Bicultural competence is the ability to gain competence within two cultures without losing one's cultural identity or having to choose one culture over the other. This competence has important implications for the personal strengths that students

need in a multicultural society and for the ones that school counselors should help them acquire. The six main bicultural strengths that ethnic minority students need to develop are (a) knowledge of the beliefs and values of the minority and majority cultures, (b) positive attitudes toward both groups, (c) confidence that one can live between the two groups without compromising one's sense of cultural identity, (d) the ability to communicate effectively within the two cultures, (e) a range of culturally and situationally appropriate behaviors, and (f) a well-developed social support system.

- **The Bicultural Competence Skills Approach** is one evidence-based, group-counseling intervention focused on preventing substance abuse with American Indian adolescents. The group sessions included culturally meaningful examples so students could identify with the situations. Research on the program indicates that participating students (a) showed more knowledge about substance use and abuse, (b) held less favorable attitudes about substance use in American Indian culture, (c) reported less use of substances, and (d) displayed more self-control, more alternative suggestions, and more assertiveness in a behavior test involving peer pressure to use substances.

- As the United States becomes more diverse, all students will need to develop not only bicultural but also multicultural competence in order to function effectively in a racially, ethnically, and culturally diverse society. Although empirical data have not identified the multicultural strengths that students will need at this time, school counselors can rely on expert opinion and informed speculation to implement appropriate interventions. Collaborating with teachers to (a) develop and deliver classroom guidance lessons, (b) create a school environment of cooperation and collaboration, (c) teach conflict resolution, and (d) elicit parental and community involvement in developing a broad-based coalition of supporters of multicultural citizenship education are just a few examples of ways that school counselors can help to develop these multicultural strengths in students.

Strengths-Enhancing Environments for Positive Personal and Social Development

- The Committee on Community-Level Programs for Youth identified an empirically based, provisional list of environmental factors that promote the development of personal and social assets. Eight features of the person's interaction with the environment were identified: (a) physical and psychological safety, (b) clear and consistent structure and appropriate supervision, (c) supportive relationships, (d) opportunities to belong, (e) positive social norms, (f) support for efficacy and mattering, (g) opportunities for skill building, and (h) integration of family, school, and community efforts.

Interventions to Promote Strengths-Enhancing Environments for Personal and Social Development in Elementary and Middle Schools

- A sense of community (e.g., belonging) has been shown to be related to a variety of positive educational and personal/social outcomes for students. Thus, educators have shown considerable interest in restructuring schools to increase the sense of community.

- **The Child Development Project (CDP)** is a research-based, elementary school restructuring initiative that focuses primarily on changing the school ecology to create schools that are caring communities of learners. CDP revamps teaching, learning, school organizations, school climate, and teachers' work environments to promote the intellectual, social, and ethical development of students; (a) collaborative learning, (b) developmental discipline, (c) a literature-based reading and language arts program, (d) parental involvement, and (e) schoolwide activities are the five components of the program. Research studies have indicated that the CDP produces impressive developmental gains with students in the personal/social and academic areas. School counselors can collaborate with school staff and community partners to advocate for and implement CDP-type interventions.

- **The Seattle Social Development Project** is a comprehensive, longitudinal prevention program in elementary schools that addresses multiple risk and protective factors; (a) teacher training, (b) child training, and (c) parent training are the three intervention components. Teachers learn about proactive classroom management, interactive teaching, and cooperative learning. Students learn social problem-solving skills. Parents learn strategies for incorporating school curriculum at home. Research studies indicate positive effects relating to academic development, social/personal development, and substance use prevention. School counselors can engage in a number of direct and indirect service functions within such a schoolwide program.

- **The Project on High Performing Learning Communities (HiPlaces)** is an empirical study of the effects of different types of middle-school environments on students' academic and personal/social development. In recent years, much of middle school reform initiatives have been driven by the recommendations of the Task Force on Education of Young Adolescents in the Carnegie Council's 1989 report, "Turning Points: Preparing American Youth for the 21st." The study focused on the effects of implementing recommendations from this report such as decreasing team size, increasing student/teacher ratios, and allowing teachers to have more flexibility in teaching students. Research studies indicated that as schools moved up in their level of implemented Turning Points recommendations, students increased achievement, levels of adjustment, and had more positive experiences within the school climate.

Interventions to Promote Strengths-Enhancing Environments for Personal and Social Development in High Schools

- **School Transition Environment Project (STEP)** is a year-long restructuring project that was designed to prevent the deleterious effects that often result when students move from middle school to high school. STEP involves a variety of environmental modifications for ninth-grade students such as (a) small learning environments, (b) classes in close proximity to each other, (c) small homerooms with teachers serving as advisors, and (d) teachers identifying students who need additional assistance or other services. STEP research results indicate that the program is associated with (a) a higher student self-concept, (b) higher academic achievement, (c) lower drop-out rates, and (d) increased school attendance.

- At this time, other high school restructuring efforts which have empirically demonstrated that they enhance student development in the personal and social domains are not readily available; however, efforts such as High Schools That Work are being developed and studied in the hopes that they will be successful in enhancing student development. As a result, the school counselor will need to rely on more general suggestions from areas such as resiliency research and the work The Committee on Community-Level Programs for Youth about characteristics of strengths-enhancing environments for high-school students.

Interventions to Promote Strengths-Enhancing Environments for Personal and Social Development over the K–12 Continuum

- **School-Wide Positive Behavior Support (PBS)** is an approach to improve school climate and behavior support for all students and to reduce student discipline referrals. It consists of skill building and environmental design and involves the school counselor in a variety of systems-level interventions, including advocacy, leadership, and collaboration.

6

Promoting Career Development

OUTLINE

The Traditional Role of the School Counselor in Career Development

The Contemporary Role of the School Counselor in Career Development

The Strengths-Based School Counselor's Role in Career Development

Career Strengths to Promote

Career Maturity/Adaptability (Elementary School example) • *Career Identity Development (Middle School example)* • *Career Self-Efficacy (High School example)*

Interventions to Promote Strengths for Career Development

Career Classes • *Computer-Career Development Programs*

Strengths-Enhancing Career Environments

Career Education • *Career Academies*

Visual Aids

2003 National Career Development Guidelines (Kobylarz et al., 2003) • *Six Primary Constructs that Promote Career Development Growth (Lapan, 2004)* • *Career-Maturity: A Basic Assessment (Super et al., 1992)* • *Education-Career Planning Framework for Middle School (Trusty et al., 2005)* • *Lesson Plan Titles and Course Content for Career Classes* • *Purposes of the Three Classes in the Career Horizons Program (O'Brien et al., 1999)* • *An Integrative Contextual Model of Career Development (Lapan, 2004)*

Summary

Key Points

Unlike with academic and personal/social development, school counselors' traditionally have approached career development from a more promotion and strengths-oriented perspective. Specifically for programming in K–12 education, rarely is remediation, crisis, or even developmental delay associated with approaches to enhancing career development as it is in academic or personal/social development. In fact, it is widely accepted that all students require career-development intervention and/or services. "Even students whose educational and personal-social development has been optimal, have needs relative to their continuing career development" (Niles, Trusty, & Mitchell, 2004, p. 109).

Although career-development programming typically targets all students, the lack of immediacy of career-development needs and the limited pressure for educators to demonstrate outcomes in this area diminish their priority in today's educational climate. Career-development outcomes are typically only recognized after high school and are associated with work and how adults negotiate and balance life roles. Instead, strengths-based school counselors need to promote skills and competencies throughout K–12 education that will enable all students to negotiate career development throughout their lifetime. Before we expand upon the career strengths and strengths-enhancing environments relevant for school counselors, we outline the shifting priorities and traditional and contemporary school-counselor role in career development.

THE TRADITIONAL ROLE OF THE SCHOOL COUNSELOR IN CAREER DEVELOPMENT

"The school counseling profession began as a vocational guidance movement that emerged from the Industrial Revolution at the beginning of the twentieth century" (Schmidt, 2003, p. 6). Before the school counselor role was even initiated, teachers served as vocational counselors in the schools in the early 1900s and provided vocational guidance as a supplementary part of the academic program. Often known as the founder of school counseling, Frank Parsons initiated vocational guidance by providing guidelines for choosing an occupation that were instrumental in changing the way school systems viewed the process of education (Schmidt). Parsons (1909) outlined three facets of the career-selection process that are still frequently addressed by school counselors today: (a) self understanding (e.g., personal interests, aptitudes, ability, limitations), (b) career knowledge (e.g., how to succeed, compensations, opportunities, advantages, and disadvantages), and (c) the ability to relate the two previous considerations to each other.

This early focus on career choice has endured. But throughout the first five decades of the 20th century (1910–1950), the emerging school counselor role expanded to include educational guidance (e.g., course selection) and meeting student personal or social needs. In fact, the American School Counselor Association (ASCA) was created in part because of the belief that the National Vocational Guidance Association (NVGA) was no longer representative of school counselors' needs as it was too narrowly focused on vocational guidance (Minkoff & Terres, 1985). During the first half of the 20th century, the school counselor role in career development (in reality career choice) relied on administering and interpreting standardized tests (e.g., interest inventories and aptitude tests) to advise students on vocational choices (Baker & Gerler, 2004). This process was referred to as the trait-and-factor approach and resulted in a directive style of counseling in which students were tested on who they were, what they were good at, and as a result, directed into particular career paths.

The National Defense Education Act of 1957 expanded the number of school counselors, with an underlying goal of getting school counselors to identify and encourage students who could be successful in math and science careers to prepare themselves for these careers. Although this movement renewed the focus on vocational choice, concurrent developments in school counseling expanded the school counselor role. "School counselor" emerged as a descriptor (as an alternative to vocational or guidance counselor) as the responsibilities of the position shifted toward a more diversified services orientation that included individual counseling and consultation about academic and personal and social needs. As a result, the school counselor's role in vocational guidance was no longer an exclusive responsibility, but one of many emerging services provided to students.

Models of career guidance underwent a significant transformation when several theorists proposed developmental models of career behavior (e.g., Ginzberg, Ginzberg, Axerlrad, & Herma, 1951). Ginzberg et al. (1951) suggested that factors such as early play, interests, values, and capacities influence career choice through a series of stages (fantasy, tentative, and realistic) that begin in childhood and extend through young adulthood. Donald Super (1957) also proposed a developmental perspective emphasizing career development as a lifelong process, rather than as an event occurring at a single point in time. Super's multidisciplinary theory shifted the focus of career interventions over time from career choice to career development. As a result, this shift directed school counselors to provide career-development services in a more sequential, progressive manner to students starting in elementary and middle school (rather than focusing exclusively on career choice in high school). For example, an understanding of self was not based solely on an aptitude or interest inventory taken in twelfth grade, but rather an examination of the culmination of experiences as students' moved through elementary, middle, and high school.

This developmental orientation to careers was pervasive in school counseling in the latter part of the 20th century. These theoretical advancements (i.e., Super) also coincided with emerging developmental models in school counseling (Dinkmeyer & Caldwell, 1970) and resulted in a shift from a solely testing or trait-and-factor orientation to career choice to an emphasis on career development as a process. As a result, school counselors now had theo-retical guides that recommended facilitating younger students' curiosity and exploring emerging interests and values as they relate to careers. School coun-selors also shifted their emphasis from career exploration as a one-time event to a process requiring skills for a lifetime. Along with these theoretical shifts in career development, school-counseling models and several career-oriented legislative initiatives emerged since the 1970s that reinforced a developmental approach to career counseling and a more programmatic approach (e.g., planned sequence of competencies to promote across K–12, shared responsi-bility with other educators) for contemporary school counselors.

THE CONTEMPORARY ROLE OF THE SCHOOL COUNSELOR IN CAREER DEVELOPMENT

Although early pioneers recommended comprehensive career-development programs, integration of career education into the school curriculum, and extension of career development into elementary school (Sink, 2005), these components of career-development programming are still forming today. The developmental and programmatic themes of career development are evident in Comprehensive Developmental Guidance Programs (CDGP) (Gysbers & Henderson, 2000) that emerged in the 1970s and still the primary school-counseling model cited today (see Chapter 1). In fact, one of the foundations of CDGP is the concept of life-career, a term that suggests a career is not a decision made at one point in time, but a series of decisions, experiences, and events that emerge over the course of one's life to influence the multiple roles, settings, and events in which we engage (Gysbers & Moore, 1975). The CDGP model also suggests that career-development services are provided as part of the school curriculum and that career guidance is a shared task between school counselors, teachers, parents, and others. Therefore, in CDGP, the school counselor's role in career development includes providing classroom guid-ance or providing leadership in schools to integrate career exploration into the planned curriculum for students (e.g., a career decisions elective class, inte-gration of career concepts into the academic curriculum). Although data on the effects of CDGP on career development are not yet abundant, the con-cepts have been influential in the school-counseling literature and seem com-patible with other contemporary influences.

A few key legislative contributions have also attempted to influence the school counselor's role in career development in a way similar to how NCLB influenced the counselor's role in academic development. For example, the National Occupational Information Coordinating Committee (NOICC, 1989) designed and field tested a set of competencies (e.g., self-knowledge, educa-tional and occupational exploration, and career planning) that seek to foster career education across the life span (and specifically for K–12 students). More recently, the School to Work Opportunities Act (STWOA) of 1994 called for career awareness and career-exploration interventions in school counseling programs no later than the seventh grade. These initiatives provided school counselors sequential guides, although not empirically validated, that are often congruent with career-development theory and serve to focus curricular and related career-programming interventions. They also were influential in providing funding and outside influence to school systems that focused attention on students' career development. As a result, a number of school-to-work programs and interventions (e.g., tech-prep programs, youth-apprenticeship programs) emerged due in part to legislative influence.

What Work Requires of Schools, a report issued by the Secretary's Commission on Achieving Necessary Skills (SCANS) (Academic Innovations, 2001) outlined a three-part foundation of skills that a student needs to be a successful employee. Of particular note, fundamental academic skills (e.g., reading, writing), thinking skills (e.g., decision making, problem solving) and personal qualities (e.g., sociability, self-management) were emphasized. What is most notable is the attention to basic academic and personal/social skills that are interrelated with career development. This report again reinforced (a) that the school counselor's role in career development was more comprehensive than merely facilitating; (b) that development in a broad sense needs to be a part of career development; and (c) that school counselors must work programmatically in collaboration with teachers, parents, and others.

Finally, just as with academic and personal/social development, ASCA outlines career-development standards to help school systems determine what students should know and be able to accomplish as the result of an effective school counseling program. The three ASCA National Standards for career development include:

> Standard A: Students are able to use self-awareness during their career search to help them make personal, informed career decisions.
>
> Standard B: Students should incorporate strategies to succeed in and be satisfied with their career.
>
> Standard C: Students should acquire an understanding of the interrelationship between their personal characteristics, education, and employment. (Campbell & Dahir, 1997, p. 24)

Although these standards are neither empirically derived nor articulated in a developmental framework and although the ASCA National Model does not offer specific interventions needed to facilitate these competencies, they do embody thematic strengths-oriented guides for school counselors. Further, the ASCA National Model (2003) encourages school counselors to develop specific competencies and indicators for these broad standards and conduct evaluation and research to determine effective interventions for accountability purposes.

Together, contemporary influences on the school counselor role in career development suggest a sequential (e.g., NOICC, STWOA), developmental (e.g., CDGP), integrated (CDGP, SCANS), and competency-based (e.g., NOICC, STWOA, ACSA) approach. Combined, they prompt school counselors to be intentional in providing a comprehensive career-development program to all students, rather than providing sporadic guidance interventions to selected students on career choice that leaves career development to chance. Unfortunately, no data exist that indicate the impact of legislative reforms on the school counselor role, and only minimal empirical data exist that demonstrate the impact of school-counseling models on the career development of students (e.g., Lapan, Gysbers, & Sun, 1997). Further, the legislative influences and ASCA guides are not necessarily empirically based, and they do not prescribe the interventions that promote the career-development competencies or strengths they outline. They also do not attend to the significant influence of the environment on student career development.

In addition to the absence of data about programmatic practice in career development, some evidence suggests that school counselors are not utilizing contemporary models. Although the more traditional school counselor role of matching people to careers (e.g., trait and factor) seems limited based on recent developments, Osborn and Baggerly (2004) found that school counselors still primarily utilize the classic (e.g., 1940s) trait-factor approach, and a fourth of their sample did not find current career theory applicable at all. In fact, they discovered that school counselors in Florida, especially elementary-school counselors, spent very little time with career counseling (Osborn & Baggerly). Although a focus on workforce development and job knowledge is needed, it has been overemphasized as compared to a career and human-development focus, "which emphasizes growth and development of the whole person for work and other life roles over the life span" (ACES/NCDA, 2000, p. 2).

Today the National Career Development Association (NCDA) defines career development as the total constellation of psychological, sociological, educational, physical, economic, and chance factors that combine to influence the nature and significance of work in the total life span of any given individual (NCDA, 2003; Sears, 1982). Careers are no longer primarily vertical in one company; rather the boundary-less career (Arthur, 1994) requires a continual emphasis on competency and exploration of self and the dynamic world of work (Meijers, 2002). Students need skills to enable them to access, evaluate, and utilize information effectively (e.g., how information can be received, how salient information is). Essentially, this changing career context suggests that the school counselor's role in career development must focus on enhancing students' strengths as lifelong learners, and applying these strengths to a dynamic, global workplace. An implication of these contemporary trends is the need to place less emphasis on providing occupational information and more on interventions and school environments that actively engage students in career planning, decision making, and models of transition and coping over one's life span.

THE STRENGTHS-BASED SCHOOL COUNSELOR'S ROLE IN CAREER DEVELOPMENT

Because theoretical guides for career development for K–12 students have focused on building competencies in a developmental sequence for the last half decade, the strengths orientation is already present to some degree in the career-development literature. "Career counselors have been particularly active in proposing taxonomies of human strengths as a means of operationally defining the domain and goals of developmental career counseling" (Savickas, 2004a, p. 230). In addition, the research we have covered in previous chapters on positive youth development offers several constructs appropriate for career development. For example, the 40 Developmental Assets (Search Institute) include planning and decision making, sense of purpose, and a positive view of personal future as core assets. The numerous youth-development programs described in Chapter 1 (Table 1–2) also seek to build on student strengths in structured activities that affect career development and potentially expand career possibilities.

Unlike the neglect of academic development (see Chapters 3 and 4) and the remedial focus on personal and social development in school counseling (see Chapter 5), the strengths-based school counselor can build on the existing developmental, competency-(strengths)-based, programmatic approaches to career development. Further, the school counselor can enhance current models with a focus on career development that is empirically based, with consideration of the environmental conditions in K–12 schools that support students' career development and knowledge of interventions that have been shown to influence career development strengths and strengths-enhancing environments.

CAREER STRENGTHS TO PROMOTE

As mentioned previously, theoretically based career-development competencies for K–12 students have been promulgated by a variety of sources. The NOICC guidelines (1989), the SCANS list of skills (Academic Innovations, 2001), and the ASCA National Standards for career development (Campbell & Dahir, 1997) provide a structure of recommended career competencies. More recently, the U.S. Department of Education Office of Vocational and Adult Education contracted with an outside agency in 2003 to update the NOICC guidelines based on the goals of No Child Left Behind (NCLB) and to create a Web resource for all stakeholders (America's Career Resource Network, 2007). The National Career Development Guidelines (NCDG) outline three domains (e.g., Personal Social Development, Educational Achievement and Lifelong Learning, and Career Management) and a series of goals and indicators (see Table 6–1) that can be utilized by school counselors as an organizational framework for career-development programming (see www.acrnet-

TABLE 6–1.
2003 National Career Development Guidelines

Personal Social Development Domain	
GOAL PS1	Develop understanding of yourself to build and maintain a positive self-concept.

PS1.K1	Identify your interests, likes, and dislikes.
PS1.A1	Demonstrate behavior and decisions that reflect your interests, likes, and dislikes.
PS1.R1	Assess how your interests and preferences are reflected in your career goals.
PS1.K2	Identify your abilities, strengths, skills, and talents.
PS1.A2	Demonstrate use of your abilities, strengths, skills, and talents.
PS1.R2	Assess the impact of your abilities, strengths, skills, and talents on your career development.
PS1.K3	Identify your positive personal characteristics (e.g., honesty, dependability, responsibility, integrity, and loyalty).
PS1.A3	Give examples of when you demonstrated positive personal characteristics (e.g., honesty, dependability, responsibility, integrity, and loyalty).
PS1.R3	Assess the impact of your positive personal characteristics (e.g., honesty, dependability, responsibility, integrity, and loyalty) on your career development.
PS1.K4	Identify your work values/needs.
PS1.A4	Demonstrate behavior and decisions that reflect your work values/needs.
PS1.R4	Assess how your work values/needs are reflected in your career goals.
PS1.K5	Describe aspects of your self-concept.
PS1.A5	Demonstrate a positive self-concept through your behaviors and attitudes.
PS1.R5	Analyze the positive and negative aspects of your self-concept.
PS1.K6	Identify behaviors and experiences that help to build and maintain a positive self-concept.
PS1.A6	Show how you have adopted behaviors and sought experiences that build and maintain a positive self-concept.
PS1.R6	Evaluate the affect of your behaviors and experiences on building and maintaining a positive self-concept.
PS1.K7	Recognize that situations, attitudes, and the behaviors of others affect your self-concept.
PS1.A7	Give personal examples of specific situations, attitudes, and behaviors of others that affected your self-concept.
PS1.R7	Evaluate the affect of situations, attitudes, and the behaviors of others on your self-concept.
PS1.K8	Recognize that your behaviors and attitudes affect the self-concept of others.
PS1.A8	Show how you have adopted behaviors and attitudes to positively affect the self-concept of others.
PS1.R8	Analyze how your behaviors and attitudes might affect the self-concept of others.

TABLE 6–1. (*Continued*)

Personal Social Development Domain

PS1.K9	Recognize that your self-concept can affect educational achievement (i.e., performance) and/or success at work.
PS1.A9	Show how aspects of your self-concept could positively or negatively affect educational achievement (i.e., performance) and/or success at work.
PS1.R9	Assess how your self-concept affects your educational achievement (performance) and/or success at work.
PS1.K10	Recognize that educational achievement (performance) and/or success at work can affect your self-concept.
PS1.A10	Give personal examples of how educational achievement (performance) and/or success at work affected your self-concept.
PS1.R10	Assess how your educational achievement (performance) and/or success at work affect your self-concept.
GOAL PS2	*Develop positive interpersonal skills including respect for diversity.*
PS2.K1	Identify effective communication skills.
PS2.A1	Demonstrate effective communication skills.
PS2.R1	Evaluate your use of effective communication skills.
PS2.K2	Recognize the benefits of interacting with others in a way that is honest, fair, helpful, and respectful.
PS2.A2	Demonstrate that you interact with others in a way that is honest, fair, helpful, and respectful.
PS2.R2	Assess the degree to which you interact with others in a way that is honest, fair, helpful, and respectful.
PS2.K3	Identify positive social skills (e.g., good manners and showing gratitude).
PS2.A3	Demonstrate the ability to use positive social skills (e.g., good manners and showing gratitude).
PS2.R3	Evaluate how your positive social skills (e.g., good manners and showing gratitude) contribute to effective interactions with others.
PS2.K4	Identify ways to get along well with others and work effectively with them in groups.
PS2.A4	Demonstrate the ability to get along well with others and work effectively with them in groups.
PS2.R4	Evaluate your ability to work effectively with others in groups.
PS2.K5	Describe conflict resolution skills.
PS2.A5	Demonstrate the ability to resolve conflicts and to negotiate acceptable solutions.
PS2.R5	Analyze the success of your conflict resolution skills.
PS2.K6	Recognize the difference between appropriate and inappropriate behavior in specific school, social, and work situations.
PS2.A6	Give examples of times when your behavior was appropriate and times when your behavior was inappropriate in specific school, social, and work situations.

(*continued*)

TABLE 6–1. (*Continued*)

Personal Social Development Domain

PS2.R6	Assess the consequences of appropriate or inappropriate behavior in specific school, social, and work situations.
PS2.K7	Identify sources of outside pressure that affect you.
PS2.A7	Demonstrate the ability to handle outside pressure on you.
PS2.R7	Analyze the impact of outside pressure on your behavior.
PS2.K8	Recognize that you should accept responsibility for your behavior.
PS2.A8	Demonstrate that you accept responsibility for your behavior.
PS2.R8	Assess the degree to which you accept personal responsibility for your behavior.
PS2.K9	Recognize that you should have knowledge about, respect for, be open to, and appreciate all kinds of human diversity.
PS2.A9	Demonstrate knowledge about, respect for, openness to, and appreciation for all kinds of human diversity.
PS2.R9	Assess how you show respect for all kinds of human diversity.
PS2.K10	Recognize that the ability to interact positively with diverse groups of people may contribute to learning and academic achievement.
PS2.A10	Show how the ability to interact positively with diverse groups of people may contribute to learning and academic achievement.
PS2.R10	Analyze the impact of your ability to interact positively with diverse groups of people on your learning and academic achievement.
PS2.K11	Recognize that the ability to interact positively with diverse groups of people is often essential to maintain employment.
PS2.A11	Explain how the ability to interact positively with diverse groups of people is often essential to maintain employment.
PS2.R11	Analyze the impact of your ability to interact positively with diverse groups of people on your employment.
GOAL PS3	*Integrate personal growth and change into your career development.*
PS3.K1	Recognize that you will experience growth and changes in mind and body throughout life that will impact on your career development.
PS3.A1	Give examples of how you have grown and changed (e.g., physically, emotionally, socially, and intellectually).
PS3.R1	Analyze the results of your growth and changes throughout life to determine areas of growth for the future.
PS3.K2	Identify good health habits (e.g., good nutrition and constructive ways to manage stress).
PS3.A2	Demonstrate how you have adopted good health habits.
PS3.R2	Assess the impact of your health habits on your career development.
PS3.K3	Recognize that your motivations and aspirations are likely to change with time and circumstances.
PS3.A3	Give examples of how your personal motivations and aspirations have changed with time and circumstances.

TABLE 6–1. (*Continued*)

Personal Social Development Domain

PS3.R3	Assess how changes in your motivations and aspirations over time have affected your career development.
PS3.K4	Recognize that external events often cause life changes.
PS3.A4	Give examples of external events that have caused life changes for you.
PS3.R4	Assess your strategies for managing life changes caused by external events.
PS3.K5	Identify situations (e.g., problems at school or work) in which you might need assistance from people or other resources.
PS3.A5	Demonstrate the ability to seek assistance (e.g., with problems at school or work) from appropriate resources including other people.
PS3.R5	Assess the effectiveness of your strategies for getting assistance (e.g., with problems at school or work) from appropriate resources including other people.
PS3.K6	Recognize the importance of adaptability and flexibility when initiating or responding to change.
PS3.A6	Demonstrate adaptability and flexibility when initiating or responding to change.
PS3.R6	Analyze how effectively you respond to change and/or initiate change.
GOAL PS4	*Balance personal, leisure, community, learner, family, and work roles.*
PS4.K1	Recognize that you have many life roles (e.g., personal, leisure, community, learner, family, and work roles).
PS4.A1	Give examples that demonstrate your life roles including personal, leisure, community, learner, family, and work roles.
PS4.R1	Assess the impact of your life roles on career goals.
PS4.K2	Recognize that you must balance life roles and that there are many ways to do it.
PS4.A2	Show how you are balancing your life roles.
PS4.R2	Analyze how specific life role changes would affect the attainment of your career goals.
PS4.K3	Describe the concept of lifestyle.
PS4.A3	Give examples of decisions, factors, and circumstances that affect your current lifestyle.
PS4.R3	Analyze how specific lifestyle changes would affect the attainment of your career goals.
PS4.K4	Recognize that your life roles and your lifestyle are connected.
PS4.A4	Show how your life roles and your lifestyle are connected.
PS4.R4	Assess how changes in your life roles would affect your lifestyle.
ED1.K1	Recognize the importance of educational achievement and performance to the attainment of personal and career goals.

(*continued*)

TABLE 6–1. (*Continued*)

GOAL ED1	Attain educational achievement and performance levels needed to reach your personal and career goals.
ED1.A1	Demonstrate educational achievement and performance levels needed to attain your personal and career goals.
ED1.R1	Evaluate how well you have attained educational achievement and performance levels needed to reach your personal and career goals.
ED1.K2	Identify strategies for improving educational achievement and performance.
ED1.A2	Demonstrate strategies you are using to improve educational achievement and performance.
ED1.R2	Analyze your educational achievement and performance strategies to create a plan for growth and improvement.
ED1.K3	Describe study skills and learning habits that promote educational achievement and performance.
ED1.A3	Demonstrate acquisition of study skills and learning habits that promote educational achievement and performance.
ED1.R3	Evaluate your study skills and learning habits to develop a plan for improving them.
ED1.K4	Identify your learning style.
ED1.A4	Show how you are using learning style information to improve educational achievement and performance.
ED1.R4	Analyze your learning style to develop behaviors to maximize educational achievement and performance.
ED1.K5	Describe the importance of having a plan to improve educational achievement and performance.
ED1.A5	Show that you have a plan to improve educational achievement and performance.
ED1.R5	Evaluate the results of your plan for improving educational achievement and performance.
ED1.K6	Describe how personal attitudes and behaviors can impact educational achievement and performance.
ED1.A6	Exhibit attitudes and behaviors that support educational achievement and performance.
ED1.R6	Assess how well your attitudes and behaviors promote educational achievement and performance.
ED1.K7	Recognize that your educational achievement and performance can lead to many workplace options.
ED1.A7	Show how your educational achievement and performance can expand your workplace options.
ED1.R7	Assess how well your educational achievement and performance will transfer to the workplace.
ED1.K8	Recognize that the ability to acquire and use information contributes to educational achievement and performance.

TABLE 6–1. (*Continued*)

Educational Achievement and Lifelong Learning Domain

ED1.A8	Show how the ability to acquire and use information has affected your educational achievement and performance.
ED1.R8	Assess your ability to acquire and use information in order to improve educational achievement and performance.
GOAL ED2	*Participate in ongoing, lifelong learning experiences to enhance your ability to function effectively in a diverse and changing economy.*

ED2.K1	Recognize that changes in the economy require you to acquire and update knowledge and skills throughout life.
ED2.A1	Show how lifelong learning is helping you function effectively in a diverse and changing economy.
ED2.R1	Judge whether or not you have the knowledge and skills necessary to function effectively in a diverse and changing economy.
ED2.K2	Recognize that viewing yourself as a learner affects your identity.
ED2.A2	Show how being a learner affects your identity.
ED2.R2	Analyze how specific learning experiences have affected your identity.
ED2.K3	Recognize the importance of being an independent learner and taking responsibility for your learning.
ED2.A3	Demonstrate that you are an independent learner.
ED2.R3	Assess how well you function as an independent learner.
ED2.K4	Describe the requirements for transition from one learning level to the next (e.g., middle school to high school, high school to postsecondary).
ED2.A4	Demonstrate the knowledge and skills necessary for transition from one learning level to the next (e.g., middle to high school, high school to postsecondary).
ED2.R4	Analyze how your knowledge and skills affect your transition from one learning level to the next (e.g., middle school to high school, high school to postsecondary).
ED2.K5	Identify types of ongoing learning experiences available to you (e.g., two- and four-year colleges, technical schools, apprenticeships, the military on-line courses, and on-the-job training).
ED2.A5	Show how you are preparing to participate in ongoing learning experiences (e.g., two- and four-year colleges, technical schools, apprenticeships, the military, on-line courses, and on-the-job training).
ED2.R5	Assess how participation in ongoing learning experiences (e.g., two- and four-year colleges, technical schools, apprenticeships, the military, on-line courses, and on-the-job training) affects your personal and career goals.
ED2.K6	Identify specific education/training programs (e.g., high school career paths and courses, college majors, and apprenticeship programs).
ED2.A6	Demonstrate participation in specific education/training programs (e.g., high school career paths and courses, college majors, and apprenticeship programs) that help you function effectively in a diverse and changing economy.

(*continued*)

TABLE 6–1. (*Continued*)

Educational Achievement and Lifelong Learning Domain

ED2.R6	Evaluate how participation in specific education/training programs (e.g., high school career paths and courses, college majors, and apprenticeship programs) affects your ability to function effectively in a diverse and changing economy.
ED2.K7	Describe informal learning experiences that contribute to lifelong learning.
ED2.A7	Demonstrate participation in informal learning experiences.
ED2.R7	Assess, throughout your life, how well you integrate both formal and informal learning experiences

Career Management Domain

GOAL CM1	*Create and manage a career plan that meets your career goals.*

CM1.K1	Recognize that career planning to attain your career goals is a life long process.
CM1.A1	Give examples of how you use career-planning strategies to attain your career goals.
CM1.R1	Assess how well your career planning strategies facilitate reaching your career goals.
CM1.K2	Describe how to develop a career plan (e.g., steps and content).
CM1.A2	Develop a career plan to meet your career goals.
CM1.R2	Analyze your career plan and make adjustments to reflect ongoing career management needs.
CM1.K3	Identify your short-term and long-term career goals (e.g., education, employment, and lifestyle goals).
CM1.A3	Demonstrate actions taken to attain your short-term and long-term career goals (e.g., education, employment, and lifestyle goals).
CM1.R3	Re-examine your career goals and adjust as needed.
CM1.K4	Identify skills and personal traits needed to manage your career (e.g., resiliency, self-efficacy, ability to identify trends and changes, and flexibility).
CM1.A4	Demonstrate career management skills and personal traits (e.g., resiliency, self-efficacy, ability to identify trends and changes, and flexibility).
CM1.R4	Evaluate your career management skills and personal traits (e.g., resiliency, self-efficacy, ability to identify trends and changes, and flexibility).
CM1.K5	Recognize that changes in you and the world of work can affect your career plans.
CM1.A5	Give examples of how changes in you and the world of work have caused you to adjust your career plans.
CM1.R5	Evaluate how well you integrate changes in you and the world of work into your career plans.

GOAL CM2	*Use a process of decision-making as one component of career development.*

CM2.K1	Describe your decision- making style (e.g., risk taker, cautious).
CM2.A1	Give examples of past decisions that demonstrate your decision-making style.
CM2.R1	Evaluate the effectiveness of your decision-making style.
CM2.K2	Identify the steps in one model of decision-making.
CM2.A2	Demonstrate the use of a decision-making model.

TABLE 6–1. (*Continued*)

Career Management Domain

CM2.R2	Assess what decision-making model(s) work best for you.
CM2.K3	Describe how information (e.g., about you, the economy, and education programs) can improve your decision-making.
CM2.A3	Demonstrate use of information (e.g., about you, the economy, and education programs) in making decisions.
CM2.R3	Assess how well you use information (e.g., about you, the economy, and education programs) to make decisions.
CM2.K4	Identify alternative options and potential consequences for a specific decision.
CM2.A4	Show how exploring options affected a decision you made.
CM2.R4	Assess how well you explore options when making decisions.
CM2.K5	Recognize that your personal priorities, culture, beliefs, and work values can affect your decision-making.
CM2.A5	Show how personal priorities, culture, beliefs, and work values are reflected in your decisions.
CM2.R5	Evaluate the affect of personal priorities, culture, beliefs, and work values in your decision-making.
CM2.K6	Describe how education, work, and family experiences might impact your decisions.
CM2.A6	Give specific examples of how your education, work, and family experiences have influenced your decisions.
CM2.R6	Assess the impact of your education, work, and family experiences on decisions.
CM2.K7	Describe how biases and stereotypes can limit decisions.
CM2.A7	Give specific examples of how biases and stereotypes affected your decisions.
CM2.R7	Analyze the ways you could manage biases and stereotypes when making decisions.
CM2.K8	Recognize that chance can play a role in decision-making.
CM2.A8	Give examples of times when chance played a role in your decision-making.
CM2.R8	Evaluate the impact of chance on past decisions.
CM2.K9	Recognize that decision-making often involves compromise.
CM2.A9	Give examples of compromises you might have to make in career decision-making.
CM2.R9	Analyze the effectiveness of your approach to making compromises.
GOAL CM3	*Use accurate, current, and unbiased career information during career planning and management.*
CM3.K1	Describe the importance of career information to your career planning.
CM3.A1	Show how career information has been important in your plans and how it can be used in future plans.
CM3.R1	Assess the impact of career information on your plans and refine plans so that they reflect accurate, current, and unbiased career information.
CM3.K2	Recognize that career information includes occupational, education and training, employment, and economic information and that there is a range of career information resources available.

(*continued*)

TABLE 6–1. (*Continued*)

Career Management Domain

CM3.A2	Demonstrate the ability to use different types of career information resources (i.e., occupational, educational, economic, and employment) to support career planning.
CM3.R2	Evaluate how well you integrate occupational, educational, economic, and employment information into the management of your career.
CM3.K3	Recognize that the quality of career information resource content varies (e.g., accuracy, bias, and how up-to-date and complete it is).
CM3.A3	Show how selected examples of career information are biased, out-of-date, incomplete, or inaccurate
CM3.R3	Judge the quality of the career information resources you plan to use in terms of accuracy, bias, and how up-to-date and complete it is.
CM3.K4	Identify several ways to classify occupations.
CM3.A4	Give examples of how occupational classification systems can be used in career planning.
CM3.R4	Assess which occupational classification system is most helpful to your career planning.
CM3.K5	Identify occupations that you might consider without regard to your gender, race, culture, or ability.
CM3.A5	Demonstrate openness to considering occupations that you might view as nontraditional (i.e., relative to your gender, race, culture, or ability).
CM3.R5	Assess your openness to considering non-traditional occupations in your career management.
CM3.K6	Identify the advantages and disadvantages of being employed in a non-traditional occupation.
CM3.A6	Make decisions for yourself about being employed in a non-traditional occupation.
CM3.R6	Assess the impact of your decisions about being employed in a non-traditional occupation.
GOAL CM4	*Master academic, occupational, and general employability skills in order to obtain, create, maintain, and/or advance your employment.*
CM4.K1	Describe academic, occupational, and general employability skills.
CM4.A1	Demonstrate the ability to use your academic, occupational, and general employability skills to obtain or create, maintain, and advance your employment.
CM4.R1	Assess your academic, occupational, and general employability skills and enhance them as needed for your employment.
CM4.K2	Identify job seeking skills such as the ability to: write a resume and cover letter, complete a job application, interview for a job, and find and pursue employment leads.
CM4.A2	Demonstrate the following job seeking skills: the ability to write a resume and cover letter, complete a job application, interview for a job, and find and pursue employment leads.
CM4.R2	Evaluate your ability to: write a resume and cover letter, complete a job application, interview for a job, and find and pursue employment leads.

TABLE 6–1. (*Continued*)

Career Management Domain

CM4.K3	Recognize that a variety of general employability skills and personal qualities (e.g., critical thinking, problem solving, resource, information, and technology management, interpersonal skills, honesty, and dependability) are important to success in school and employment.
CM4.A3	Demonstrate attainment of general employability skills and personal qualities needed to be successful in school and employment (e.g., critical thinking, problem solving, resource, information, and technology management, interpersonal skills, honesty, and dependability).
CM4.R3	Evaluate your general employability skills and personal qualities (e.g., critical thinking, problem solving, resource, information, and technology management, interpersonal skills, honesty, and dependability).
CM4.K4	Recognize that many skills are transferable from one occupation to another.
CM4.A4	Show how your skills are transferable from one occupation to another.
CM4.R4	Analyze the impact of your transferable skills on your career options.
CM4.K5	Recognize that your geographic mobility impacts on your employability.
CM4.A5	Make decisions for yourself regarding geographic mobility.
CM4.R5	Analyze the impact of your decisions about geographic mobility on your career goals.
CM4.K6	Identify the advantages and challenges of self-employment.
CM4.A6	Make decisions for yourself about self-employment.
CM4.R6	Assess the impact of your decision regarding self-employment on your career goals.
CM4.K7	Identify ways to be proactive in marketing yourself for a job.
CM4.A7	Demonstrate skills that show how you can market yourself in the workplace.
CM4.R7	Evaluate how well you have marketed yourself in the workplace.
GOAL CM5	*Integrate changing employment trends, societal needs, and economic conditions into your career plans.*
CM5.K1	Identify societal needs that affect your career plans.
CM5.A1	Show how you are prepared to respond to changing societal needs in your career management.
CM5.R1	Evaluate the results of your career management relative to changing societal needs.
CM5.K2	Identify economic conditions that affect your career plans.
CM5.A2	Show how you are prepared to respond to changing economic conditions in your career management.
CM5.R2	Evaluate the results of your career management relative to changing economic conditions.
CM5.K3	Identify employment trends that affect your career plans.
CM5.A3	Show how you are prepared to respond to changing employment trends in your career management.
CM5.R3	Evaluate the results of your career management relative to changes in employment trends.

America's Career Resource Network (2007). *The National Career Development Guidelines*. Retrieved September 1, 2006, from The World Wide Web: http://www.acrnetwork.org/ncdg/htm

work.org/ncdg for more information). The Web site also provides a crosswalk comparison to the previous NOICC guidelines, and to the ASCA National Standards, along with additional resources. These guidelines are more specific to the competencies students need to acquire for career development than the ASCA National Standards for career development, and further highlight the relationship between career development and academic and personal/social development. In addition to these guidelines, several states have put forth career-development guidelines (e.g., Missouri—http://www.dese.mo.gov/divcareered/guidance_placement_index.htm), and prominent career-development researchers (e.g., Niles & Trusty, 2004) have put forth lists of career-development tasks appropriate for K–12 students.

These various lists share commonalities (e.g., sequential outline of competencies) and provide a theoretical and conceptual structure for promoting career development. Even so, they neglect the significant interaction and impact of context (environment) on the career-development process. Perhaps more useful for strengths-based school counselors, Lapan (2004) presented six fundamental constructs that either promote or constrict career-development pathways (e.g., adaptive engagement of students in career development) within an integrative contextual model of career development. This model was based on a synthesis of decades of career-development research (empirically derived) and puts forth career-development strengths in a context that school counselors can seek to impact. Lapan's model is displayed in Fig. 6–1, and

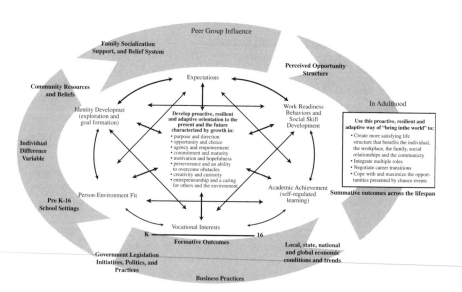

FIGURE 6–1.　An integrative contextual model of career development. Lapan, R. (2004). *Career development across the K–16 years: Bridging the present to satisfying and successful futures.* Alexandria, VA, ACA.

Table 6–2 lists these constructs and the theoretical or conceptual descriptions of each. These particular career-development constructs are not acquired in linear, chronological stages, but instead are interactive within social contexts as a fully integrative system that can enhance the career development of students at appropriate developmental levels. Simply, each one of the constructs influences the others (e.g., the level of exploration of self within identity development will impact career interests and expectations, and vice versa), and all of them are influenced by families, peers groups, business practices, and the varied contexts in which they develop. School counselors can utilize Lapan's model by considering how the six constructs or strengths can be integrated into a comprehensive, developmental school-counseling program.

As listed in Lapan's highlighted constructs, academic achievement (in particular self-regulated learning) and social-skill development are fundamental strengths that cut across developmental domains and relate to optimal career development. These are both discussed in previous chapters as strengths that enhance academic and personal/social development. The abilities to proactively engage self-regulated, lifelong learning strategies and demonstrate cultural and social competence are also necessities to thrive in economic and global work environments. Not only is academic achievement and postsecondary education a necessity for entry into the global economy, but students need to be able to plan, actively engage in learning, and process learning tasks (self-regulatory cycle) to be effective learners. Similarly, the elementary-school counselor running a social-skills group potentially impacts the ability of students to negotiate complex interpersonal situations with diverse people in the future workplace.

The remainder of this section will examine in more depth three empirically based constructs that have been prominent in the career-development literature. Specific to Lapan's (2004) model, career-identity development and career self-efficacy are outlined in depth. A third construct, career maturity or adaptability, is a broader, multidimensional construct that is the basis for many of the developmental, sequential guides for K–12 career. The three theoretical

TABLE 6–2.
Six Primary Constructs That Promote Career Development Growth

Construct	Theoretical or Conceptual Description
Positive Expectations	Self-efficacy, Attributions
Career Identity Development	Career exploration, Goal formation
Person-Environment Fit	Understanding of self, world of work, and best fit
Vocational Interests	Pursuit of one's intrinsic interests and preferences
Academic Achievement	Self-regulated, Lifelong learning
Social Skills	Use of everyday interactions to build social capacity
Workforce Readiness Behaviors	

constructs are presented as career-development strengths that school coun-selors can seek to promote for the optimal career development of students. We also present these strengths with practical examples within each level (ele-mentary, middle, high school), although each concept is relevant for all grade levels. We now turn to a discussion of career maturity/adaptability.

Career Maturity/Adaptability

Savickas (2004) noted that career development essentially is a "never ending process of transactional adaptation of career constructs that evolve in proba-bilistic ways" (p. 231). One multidimensional construct that captures the ex-tent to which a person is ready to cope with expected and unexpected de-mands in the vocational realm is career maturity (Savickas, 1984).

Super (1957) introduced the concept of vocational maturity or the age appropriateness of a person on the continuum of vocational development. Crites (1971) later refined the similar concept of career maturity as a readi-ness to make career decisions as they relate to age. Both terms evolved out of the initial Career Patterns Study of 1951 (Super), one of the first longitu-dinal (20-plus years) studies of career development. Crites (1971) model of career maturity has both a cognitive component (e.g., ability to make deci-sions) and an affective component (e.g., attitudes toward career decision making). In fact, Powell and Luzzo (1998) suggest career maturity is essen-tially a measure of readiness to make career decisions based on both knowl-edge and attitudes.

The Career Development Inventory (CDI) (Super & Thompson, 1979) and the Career Maturity Inventory (CMI) (Crites, 1976) emerged from these early studies and have been utilized extensively over the past few decades to further explore the concept of career maturity, which has become one of the most prevalent variables in research on career development (Powell & Luzzo, 1998). School counselors can use these instruments to assess the career maturity of students, or can use these data in the aggregate form to provide information for program planning or evaluation of career-development interventions. The CDI-S (a version designed for high school, grades 8–12) measures vocational maturity through eight scales including (a) career planning, (b) career explo-ration, (c) decision making, (d) world-of-work information, and (e) knowl-edge of preferred occupational group, (f) career-development attitudes, (g) career orientation, and (h) career-development knowledge and skills. The more recent CMI-R (designed for middle school through adult) includes an attitude scale (e.g., feelings toward making a career choice) and a competence scale (e.g., knowledge of occupations and decision making) that parallel Crites af-fective and cognitive components of career maturity (Crites, 1976). The revised CMI-R also includes a career-developer supplement (CDR) that helps a coun-selor engage discussion and teach a student or group of students about career decision making as they review items on the CMI-R (Crites & Savickas, 1996).

Although the CDI and CMI have been used extensively with high-school and college students, Super et al. (1992) outlined the theoretical components of career maturity, which included planfulness, exploration, information, decision making, and a reality orientation (see Table 6–3). For example, school counselors may use the career-maturity outline with individual or small groups as a checklist and/or informal assessment or they might use the major categories (e.g., planfulness, decision making) and specifics to audit career-development programs and interventions. With no specific measures available for elementary-school counselors as it relates to career maturity, Super's organizing framework can also be utilized in part as a guide for elementary- and middle-school counselors. Elementary-school counselors, for example, can do some informal as-

TABLE 6–3.
Career Maturity: A Basic Assessment

I. Planfulness
  a. Autonomy
  b. Time Perspective
    i. Reflect upon experience
    i. Anticipation of the future
    iii. Concepts of life stages
  c. Concepts of self
    i. Role of self-concepts
    ii. Self-esteem
    iii. Cognitive complexity

II. Exploration
  a. Querying: Self, situations, roles
  b. Resources: Awareness, use
  c. Participation in school, college, community

III. Information
  a. The world of education
  b. The world of work
    i. Career stages and tasks
    ii. Coping behaviors
    iii. Occupational structure
    iv. Typical occupations
    v. Access and entry
    vi. Rewards and drawbacks
    vii. Trends and changes
  c. The preferred occupational group
    i. Education and training needed
    ii. Entry requirements, routes

    iii. Duties, methods, materials, tools
    iv. Advancement, transfer, stability
    v. Conditions and rewards of work
    vi. Life style
    vii. Future prospects
  d. Life career roles
    i. Work, homemaking, leisure
    ii. Role relationships and effects
      1. Supplementary
      2. Complementary
      3. Conflicting
    iii. Multiple role realization

IV. Decision Making
  a. Principles
  b. Applications to people, situations
  c. Style: Rational, impulsive, intuitive, conforming

V. Reality orientation
  a. Self-knowledge
  b. Realism to outlets
  c. Consistency of preferences (exploratory and definitive)
  d. Crystallization of self-concepts, values, interest, and objectives
  e. Work experiences: Exploratory, instrumental, implementing, and stabilizing

sessment of the roles students utilize in fantasy play, the awareness of abilities and interests, future time perspective, and the role key figures play in students' conceptions of careers. Researchers (e.g., Schultheiss, Palma, & Manzi, 2005) are only beginning to propose initial instruments (e.g., Childhood Career Development Scale; Schultheiss & Stead, 2004) and more deeply examine elementary-age children in relation to career maturity and Super's developmental notions of career development. However, early indications confirm that assessing career maturity is a practical way to gain information about the rate and progress of career development of students, and suggestive of needs for intervention to enhance development (Crites, 1974; Herr, Cramer, & Niles, 2004).

For example, consider the elementary-school counselor for whom career development is rarely a top priority. The elementary-school counselor can focus on the career maturity of students by promoting self-awareness, curiosity, occupational fantasies, the exploration of interests and the environment, and help make the link between school and the world of work. Elementary-school counselors can provide multiple, positive career models and stimulate discovery and discussion of student strengths and how they may be useful in careers (Steen, Kachorek, & Petersen, 2003). Promoting career development in elementary school is less about making choices and more about avoiding premature closure of future options (Herr, Cramer, & Niles, 2004).

Career maturity is one of the most common constructs in career-development research, so debate about the concept is ongoing. While current definitions still focus on age [e.g., "denotes a readiness to engage in the developmental tasks appropriate to the age level at which one finds oneself" (Gysbers, Heppner, & Johnston, 2003, p. 24)], others (Patton & Creed, 2001; Watson & Van Aarde, 1986) have suggested that grade, due to grade-related career decisions and the influence of the educational system, is a more important indicator. Further, although the educational system imposes some career-development ho-mogeneity (e.g., all students being required to choose a course of study or track for high school in eighth grade), several researchers (Niles & Harris-Bowlsbey, 2005; Savickas, 1997) have proposed the term career adaptability instead of career maturity because of the heterogeneity of environmental obstacles and assets or affordances (Vondracek, Lerner, & Schulenburg, 1986) on the career development of children and adolescents. Vondracek and Reitzle (1998) suggest that a developmental-contextual perspective is needed for career maturity to account for demographic (e.g., ethnicity, socioeconomic status) and contextual factors. Career maturity/adaptability occurs within dynamic systems, and age and linear growth are not the only considerations (Vondracek & Reitzle). In particular, career maturity as it relates to the transition from school to work varies according to factors such as historical time, cultural and economic context, and the individuation of education (Vondracek & Reitzle). The theoretical debate is of lesser consequence for school counselors than the practical need to consider the contexts (e.g., parents, economic opportunity) around the student when considering career maturity. Although age or grade norms may exist, school counselors should also consider the potential impact of socioeconomic or cultural factors.

Whether school counselors use the term career maturity or career adaptability, most of the research on career maturity demonstrates an increasing progression of career-maturity scores of adolescents (Patton & Creed, 2001). Students with high levels of career maturity are more likely to obtain successful and satisfying careers due to more awareness, self-reliance, and commitment to the career decision-making process, and because they relate present behavior to future goals (Powell & Luzzo, 1998; Savickas, 1990). Career maturity has been positively associated with factors such as aptitude scores, interests, school subject preferences, realistic occupational aspirations and expectations, higher career decision-making self-efficacy, part-time employment experiences, and engagement in the educational planning process (Vondracek, Lerner, & Schulenberg, 1986; Westbrook, Sanford, & Donnelly, 1990). Although career maturity is not necessarily an end point to achieve, school counselors can utilize increases in career maturity or adaptation as a goal relative to a particular life stage. Another important strengths-based construct counselors seek to influence is a student's career identity development, a related, even embedded construct within career maturity.

Career-Identity Development

Scholars in a number of disciplines, such as adolescent psychology, have provided theoretical conceptions of identity development (e.g., Erikson, 1968; Marcia, 1966), and many suggest that people have multiple identities (e.g., gender, race) influenced by a variety of factors. Career identity relates to the part of one's perception of self that relates to work and working (What does work mean in and for my life?) (Meijers, 1998). Erickson (1968) suggested that attainment of an identity in the vocational domain is often the most challenging and overt aspect of the identity formation process (Blustein & Noumair, 1996). Although several definitions have been offered for earlier conceptions of vocational identity (Vondracek, 1992), Meijers (1998) defines it as "a structure or network of meanings in which the individual consciously links his own motivation, interests and competencies with acceptable career roles" (p. 200).

The career-identity construct is influenced by numerous career-development theories including Super's (1988) notions of self-concept in career development and Holland's (1985) notions of personal identity in having a clear picture of goals and talents. Most of these conceptualizations have centered on the often complex tasks of self-exploration and self-assessment as important to career-identity development (Blustein & Noumair, 1996). We will focus on the development and application of career identity for intervention purposes for the school counselor.

Career-identity development consists primarily of exploration of self- and goal formation and is an essential part of the resolution of identity crisis in late adolescence (Lapan, 2004). In particular, Flum and Blustein's (2000) work on establishing a self-constructed identity based on intrinsic goals provides a guide for helping students. Flum and Blustein identified three states of career identity (diffused, conferred, and self-constructed), similar to the identity taxonomy (diffused, foreclosed, moratorium, achieved) outlined by Marcia (1993]). A student who has not engaged in career exploration and is not committed to a particular occupation manifests a diffused career identity. The conferred (or foreclosed) career identity occurs when a student commits to a career (career-related goals, values, beliefs) prematurely due to explicit pressure or implicit influence from significant others, but has not engaged in exploration. These students may have pseudocrystallized choices, or career decisions dictated by parental figures rather than by an autonomous process of career exploration (Akos, Konold, & Niles, 2004). Marcia (1993), in articulating his ego-identity-status model, suggests that a high percentage of secondary students have a foreclosed identity (an identity determined by others rather then self). In these instances, school counselors should help students to explore options beyond those identified by influential figures (Santos & Coimbra, 2000). Santos and Coimbra and others (e.g., Meijers, 1998) suggest that career investment (commitment) derived through career exploration is an important component of an achieved career identity.

Essentially, Flum and Blustein advocate active exploration in creating a self-constructed identity (achieved career identity). "Just as the individual has to learn how to deal with forming his own identity, he also has to learn consciously to define that part of the world of work that fits in with his own identity" (Meijers, 1998, p. 194). In the self-constructed identity, the student's exploration and commitments are more intrinsic, based on exploration, rather than extrinsic or due to external expectations. While Flum and Blustein (2000) do not explicitly address Marcia's moratorium stage, it most closely aligns to the self-constructed identity in which intrinsic exploration is present without clear commitment. Based on the world of work today (e.g., changing workplace) and the career-development tasks confronting K–12 students (e.g., decision points), students ideally move between a career-identity moratorium and a self-constructed career identity seamlessly as they make career-related decisions (e.g., course selection, part-time work experiences) in K–12 school.

The process of developing a career identity is cyclical and multidimensional, and students move in and out of different identity statuses in career and a variety of other domains (e.g., politics, sexuality, ethnicity) based on significant life events. "What is crucial is the degree to which the individual's environment expects (or even forces) him to explore and make explicit choices" (Meijers, 1998, p. 198). The school counselor is in position to promote exploration by individual or systemic interventions throughout K–12 education. School counselors can help students in individual planning or counseling sessions to explore strengths and weaknesses as they relate to academic subjects or explore the student's conception of different roles, including student, peer, and sibling. Further, they might also advocate for programmatic attempts to engage students in exploration as with mentoring or job-shadowing programs with area businesses, job and career fairs, or information and Internet-based resources that enable students to explore careers and other interests. In fact, this type of purposeful exploration has particular salience in middle- or junior-high school.

By middle school or junior high, students begin to crystallize and specify occupational preferences (Super, Savickas, & Super, 1996), engaging in some choice and commitment as exploration of career identity continues. School counselors can utilize discovery and exploration of strengths when they align emerging career identities in educational planning. For example, the middle-school counselor can utilize career-development portfolios with students individually and in large groups in making choices for exploratory curriculum in middle school and for curricular tracks and vocational pathways in high school. Trusty, Niles, and Carney (2005) outline such an educational and career portfolio (see Table 6–4) that assures a level of exploration of self and career options to base plans for high school and beyond.

Exploration has been defined in a number of ways. Originally defined as an information-seeking behavior or a specific phase in the process of career decision making, researchers now define exploration as the major task in forming a career identity or even a life-span process that underlies career learning and development (Taveira & Moreno, 2003). Exploration itself has also been linked to a host of positive outcomes including expanding time perspective (the ability to plan ahead) (Savickas, 1990), decision making (Blustein, 1989), occupational satisfaction (Werbel, 2000), and self-efficacy in career decision making (O'Brien et al., 1999). Blustein (1989) suggested some exploration is self-determined, related to feelings of perceived competence, internal locus of control, and self-efficacy expectations. This is significant in that external incentives may be less useful to stimulate career-identity exploration. When some sense of imminence regarding career-development tasks is coupled with positive feelings of self (Taveira & Moreno, 2003), school counselors may need to provide the means and opportunity to explore.

It also seems evident that social and cultural factors influence both the content and process of exploratory activity for vocational purposes (Blustein & Flum, 1999). For example, Gottfredson's (1981) work on circumscription of career aspirations related to gender-identity-development theorizes the impact of individual variables on career-identity development. Her seminal work on female students limiting potential career futures based on gender highlights the salience of social roles and family and community expectations. The strengths-based school counselor may need to help students explore a full range of possible career futures, even investing time discussing options students initially dismiss (e.g., the cultural stereotype of nursing as a female occupation). Further, Crozier (1999) suggested viewing career behavior in the context of relationships and how the relational context for women has significance for career

TABLE 6–4.
Education-Career Planning Framework for Middle School

Data/Variable	Priority
STUDENT DATA	
• The student's self-knowledge	*
○ Strengths, personal resources, ability self-estimates	**
▪ Academic strengths	
▪ Non-academic strengths	
○ Obstacles, needs, ability self-estimates	**
▪ Academic obstacles	
▪ Non-academic obstacles	
○ Career interests	*
▪ Holland type	
▪ High-interest occupations	
○ Values	*
• The student's educational and occupational exploration	***
▪ Areas student explored	
▪ Areas student desire to explore	
• The student's current long-range career goals (or possible goals)	***
• Education, training, or certification steps required for the student to accomplish current long-range career goals	***
• The student's educational experiences	***
○ Courses completed, grades	***
○ Educational experiences outside school	***
• The student's educational plans	***
○ Courses planned	***
○ Plans for educational experiences outside school	***
○ Postsecondary education plans	***
• The student's extracurricular experiences	***
• The student's planned extracurricular experiences	***
• The student's leisure experiences	**
• The student's planned leisure experiences	**
PARENT DATA	
• Postsecondary educational level the parent expects the child to achieve	**
• School and career areas the parent discusses regularly with child	**
• Occupations for which child has expressed interest	**
• The child's strengths	**
• The child's obstacles	**
• Specific ways the parent can help with the child's education-career planning	***
TEACHER/COUNSELOR DATA	
• Perceptions of the student's actual achievement (performance in classes) as compared to his or her academic aptitude (potential, ability)	**
• The student's personal strengths	**
• The student's personal obstacles	**
• Particular resources in the student's environment (family, community, school, peers)	**
• Particular obstacles in the student's environment (family, community, school, peers)	**
• Postsecondary educational expectations for the student	**

* = important for education-career planning
** = highly informative for education-career planning
*** = essential for education-career planning

Trusty, J., Niles, S., & Carney, J. (2005). Education-career planning and middle school counselors. *Professional School Counseling, 9*(2), 136–143.

decision making and career choice. Meijers (1998) suggests that students must acquire genuine experience with work, have opportunity to use imagination as to how things might be in a future role, and have the ability to recognize and utilize emotion as an important contribution to career-identity development. According to Blustein and Noumair (1996):

> A careful examination of career development tasks throughout the life span suggests that implementing career choices and adjusting to the ever-increasing demands of one's work tasks necessitates ongoing interactions between an individual's self and identity and his or her social and cultural contexts. (p. 436)

Career Self-Efficacy

As students move into high school and further define diverse career identities, the educational system systematically engages students in somewhat homogenous career-development processes (e.g., class choices, club and extracurricular choices, part-time employment), and specific career-development behaviors (e.g., decision making) are required for crystallizing and implementing tentative career choices. Although career maturity and career identity are more multidimensional constructs, career self-efficacy is more specific to a student's "expectations or beliefs concerning one's ability to perform successfully a given behavior" (e.g., engage in career exploration, make a career-related decision) (Betz, 1994, p. 35). Career self-efficacy is an important part of social-cognitive-career theory (SCCT; Brown & Lent, 1996; Lent & Brown, 2002), which focuses on specific cognitive mediators and personal agency in learning experiences that guide career behavior.

Bandura's (1977) theory of self-efficacy was first applied to vocational behaviors by Betz and Hackett (1986). Career self-efficacy refers to "judgments of personal efficacy in relation to the wide range of behavior involved in career choice and adjustment" (Lent & Hackett, 1987, p. 349). Based on the social-learning theory, career self-efficacy theory (Lent, Brown, & Hackett, 1994) emphasizes how learning experiences and environmental factors influence individual belief systems in the career-development process. Simply, a student's view of her or his capability and the beliefs about probable outcomes influences career interests, goals, and behaviors.

To be efficacious within career development, internal (e.g., outcome expectations, perceived barriers) and external (e.g., opportunity and constraints) factors influence a student's sense of personal agency and therefore the formulation, pursuit, and attainment of career goals (Brown & Lent, 1996; McWhirter, Rasheeed, & Crothers, 2000). Self-efficacy beliefs are developed in experience through four sources: (a) performance accomplishments, (b) vicarious learning, (c) emotional arousal, and (d) verbal persuasion (Bandura, 1977).

Although most of the research to date on career self-efficacy has been on college students, especially as applied to women's career development (Herr, Cramer, & Niles (2004), high levels of career self-efficacy have been linked to low levels of career indecision, a greater range of perceived career options, and more persistence in academic pursuits (Betz & Hackett, 1983; Lent, Brown, & Larkin, 1986). Career self-efficacy or confidence in accomplishing career-development tasks also relates to a host of career-related factors including the range of occupations considered, interest development, choice, and performance (A. Hall, 2003). Betz (1992) suggested that consequences of perceived self-efficacy include choice versus avoidance, performance in the specific domain or task, and persistence in the face of obstacles or disconfirming experiences.

Lent, Brown, and Hackett (1994) also suggest that academic self-efficacy later translates into career self-efficacy. For example, female students with high self-efficacy in math may, in turn, have less anxiety related to math performance and choose to engage in traditionally male-dominated careers, such as engineering, which involve math. Taveira and Moreno (2003) suggest that it is important to increase individuals' feelings of self-efficacy in career exploration by providing verbal encouragement, demonstration of exploration processes, and support through the exploration process. Hackett (1995) suggests that attitudinal influences such as efficacy beliefs have not received as much attention as compared to objective skills development. Therefore, it is important to pair skill-building exercises (e.g., resume writing) with purposeful scaffolding of successful, confidence-building experiences.

Essentially, school counselors want to encourage students to become active participants in the career-development process by building successive experiences (vicarious, along with performance accomplishments) with career-development tasks throughout school. Counselors will need to assess (and help students self-assess) the influence of previous learning experiences and performance, the influence of context on the development of career interests, and how low perceptions of self-efficacy may limit career options, decision, or implementation (persistence in educational program or obstacles) (Betz, 1992). A helpful assessment tool may include the Career Decision-Making Self-Efficacy Scale (CDMSES) (Betz, Klein, & Taylor, 1996), which measures self-efficacy expectations relative to appraising self, gathering occupational information, selecting goals, making future plans, and solving problems. The CDMSES has been used primarily with college students (designed for high school use as well), but can be another tool for counselors to assess decision-making self-efficacy for students, or assess the impact of career-development interventions and programs. Most importantly, school counselors can provide mastery-oriented tasks (e.g., ungraded, but support efforts at building a resume and career portfolio) and successful performance accomplishments (e.g., mock interviews), role models or media illustrating successful models, and verbal encouragement.

INTERVENTIONS TO PROMOTE STRENGTHS FOR DEVELOPMENT

Several meta-analyses (a statistical analysis of a collection of studies) have examined the effects of career-development interventions, and career maturity, career self-efficacy, and career identity were common outcome measures in many of these studies. The reviews found overall positive effects for career interventions with high effect sizes (e.g., confidence that outcome differences found in the studies have substantial practical meaning) especially for junior-high-school students, individual counseling, and small-group interventions (most cost-effective) (Oliver & Spokane, 1988). These findings were supported by Whiston, Sexton, and Lasoff (1998) who found moderate effect sizes in a separate meta-analysis of more recent research. Those interventions targeting junior-high students and those that taught specific career "skills" were most effective. Individual career counseling, followed by group counseling and computer-assisted interventions had the most impact. In particular, it appears that just providing career information is not as effective as when another counseling component like individual planning is added (Whiston, Brecheisen, & Stephens, 2003).

Although meta-analyses provide a positive evaluation of career-development interventions overall, school counselors need data about the interventions that promote specific career-development strengths. The studies cited in the Whiston et al. (1998) review were conducted primarily with college students. Only one included elementary-school students and only two were conducted with junior-high-school students (11 on high school students) out of the 48 studies reviewed. Further, a review of outcome research in school counseling (Whiston & Sexton, 1998) documented nine individual career-planning interventions studies with positive results, although they were primarily descriptive studies lacking a control group. Some of these interventions are described here, along with more recent published intervention studies with positive empirical findings for our three profiled career-development strengths. We highlight two types of interventions, specific career classes that are often offered for middle- and high-school students and a diverse group of career programs.

Career Classes

A common intervention that seeks to boost career maturity for middle- and high-school students is various forms of career classes, an intervention that Whiston (2002a) found to be very effective in her meta-analyses. The formats of these courses vary greatly, but several outcome studies have found positive effects. For example, Savickas (1990) investigated the effectiveness of a *Career Decision-Making Course* that was created to help students more adequately make decisions relating to career choice. The course was based on

Crites's (1976) model for comprehensive career counseling that emphasizes how students choose the occupation they will pursue. The course focuses on developing decisional attitudes and competencies that help students manage career tasks and encourage behavioral responses that meet these tasks.

The course consists of 20 lessons, applicable from junior high through college. Table 6–5 presents the titles of each of the 20 lessons. In an empirical examination of outcomes, the course was field tested with 209 tenth-grade students. Six different teachers taught the course over the first six-week grading period for the same 40-minute period, five days a week. Compared to the control group, the treatment group demonstrated statistically and practically significant improvements in decision making and time, two important components of career maturity.

Although these classes were taught by regular classroom teachers who received preparation from the program developer, a similar decision-making curriculum delivered by a school counselor was evaluated by Kraus and Hughey (1999). The class consisted of 50-minute lessons, twice a week, for four weeks with high-school juniors. Specifically, the eight-session class focused on accurate self-appraisal, gathering occupational information, goal selection, making future plans, and problem solving (along with an introductory and review session). For example, in the problem-solving session, the school counselor initiated discussion of coping strategies and problem-solving models to a list of roadblocks and barriers to career goals brainstormed by students. For the entire class intervention, females in the treatment group had statistically significant higher scores on decision-making self-efficacy as compared with the control group The findings were not significant for males.

Another example of the effectiveness of a career class is in the McWhirter, Rasheed, and Crothers (2000) investigation of a required nine-week, 50-minute, career class for tenth-graders in a Midwest urban high school. The class included hands-on activities, lectures, small-group work and guest speakers. Details of the class content are also contained in Table 6–5. For each of the class topics, course assignments included active participation, including a live job interview near the end of the course. As compared to a control group, students in the career class had statistically significant higher scores on both the career decision-making self-efficacy scale (CDMSE; Betz & Luzzo, 1996) and the vocational skills self-efficacy scale both at posttest and at a six-week follow-up test. McWhirter, Rasheed, and Crothers (2000) note:

> Presumably, the career education class provided exposure to sources of self-efficacy expectations such as performance attainments (e.g., live interview), vicarious learning opportunities (e.g., guest speakers, small-group work), and social-persuasion experiences (e.g., feedback and encouragement). . . ." (p. 338)

While random assignment was not utilized in the study, the results show that school counselors and teachers can impact the career self-efficacy of students using a career-class intervention.

TABLE 6–5.
Lesson Plan Titles and Course Content for Career Classes

Savickas Course Content		McWhirter et al. Course Content
Attitudes and Concepts	Competencies and Tasks	Schedule of Content
Become involved now	Self-appraisal is crucial	Assessment of interests, abilities, and personality
Explore your future	Know yourself	Learning how to locate vocational information
Choose based on how things look to you	Appraise your activities	Learning how to develop and maintain a budget
Control your future	Know about jobs	Learning about standard employer expectations
Work: A problem or opportunity	Select goals	Exploring postsecondary career, educational, and training options
View work positively	Choose a job	Learning to identify educational requirements associated with specific occupations
Conceptualize career choice	Plan	Learning skills related to writing resumes, interviewing for jobs, finding and using career information, identifying sources of funding for postsecondary education, and calculating grade point averages
Clear up career-choice misconceptions	Look ahead	
Base your choice on yourself	Problem solve	
Use four aspects of self as choice basis	Course summary	

Other nonexperimental studies also suggest of the potential benefits of variations of career classes. For example, in a collaborative effort between school counselors and English instructors, Lapan, Gysbers, Hughey, and Arni (1993) highlighted an eight-week unit (13 class periods) in language arts class for eleventh-graders that demonstrated statistically significant improvements in vocational identity scores, increased understanding of the relationship of gender to careers, and positive grade improvements in language arts class. The first three days of the unit involved introductions and aptitude and interest surveys. The rest of the class time was devoted to interpreting the surveys, orienting students with the Guidance Resource Center (students spent four days using reference materials and computer career-information systems) and the vocational-technical area of the school, and providing information and training on job-seeking and job-keeping skills. Although the study did not include control groups, path analysis was used to provide some statistical control for confidence in the prepost design. Additionally, students self-reported that the unit was beneficial (90%), along with 80% of the girls reporting an understanding of how to enter careers that were traditionally male.

Although it is difficult to pinpoint the change mechanisms or the exact dosage needed to promote career-development strengths, it appears that middle- and high-school students can clearly benefit from a career exploration or career-development course. School counselors may teach this type of course as a regular elective or may consult and collaborate with an elective teacher to build students' career strengths in a specific course.

Computer-Career Development Programs

Computer programs are another form of intervention that have been shown to impact the career-development strengths highlighted previously. Studies of computer-career-development programs (e.g., DISCOVER, CHOICES) have also demonstrated increases in career maturity, career self-efficacy, and levels of career decidedness (Luzzo & Pierce, 1996; Pinder & Fitzgerald, 1984). The DISCOVER program (www.act.org/discover/), for example, is a multidimensional program that "incorporates Super's developmental stages, Teideman and O'Hara's decision-making model, the data-people-things classification of the DOT, the Holland categories, and the World-of-Work map" (Herr, Cramer, & Niles, 2004, p. 582). For example, the World-of-Work map is a circular graphic that organizes current job categories from the *Dictionary of Occupational Titles* by concepts (e.g., data, things, ideas, people) based on Holland's (1985) original occupational types. Students are able to use the map to see how their interests, abilities, and job values relate to career options. The current DISCOVER Web site markets both a middle-school and high-school version, and details the inventories, occupations, financial-aid opportunities, educational-planning material, along the support materials for schools or organizations utilizing the program.

In a study by Luzzo and Pierce, seventh- and eighth-grade students worked in pairs on the three modules (You and the World of Work, Exploring Occupations, Planning for High School) of DISCOVER (American College Testing [ACT], 1991) for one hour per week over a two-week period. A school counselor supervised and assisted students over the two-week period. The students using DISCOVER had statistically significant higher career maturity (attitude) scores on the CMI than the control group. Several other studies with college students (e.g., Garis & Bowlsbey, 1984) and adults (e.g., Sampson et al., 1993) have demonstrated an increase in career maturity by utilizing the DISCOVER program. Studies have also shown significant increases in career decision-making self-efficacy (Fukuyama, Probert, Neimeyer, Nevill, & Metzler, 1988) and vocational identity (Barnes & Herr, 1998) for college students.

O'Brien and her colleagues (O'Brien, Dukstein, Jackson, Tomlinson, & Kamatuka, 1999) developed the *Career Horizons Program* for middle-school students to enhance confidence in performing tasks related to investigating and selecting career choice for students at-risk for vocational underachievement. They specifically included means to enhance self-efficacy including multiple opportunities for performance accomplishment, vicarious learning through observation, verbal persuasion by staff, and expression of anxiety so emotional arousal could be used to facilitate learning. For example, in one of the class sessions, students focus on short- and long-term goals. In the session, students get feedback (e.g., verbal encouragement) from peers, parents, and staff about strengths and weaknesses that get translated into a vision of success for the future (O'Brien et al.). Further, other class sessions centered on vicarious and performance learning including students performing tie-dye to learn about chromatography from a chemist, and dissecting a pig heart to learn about the cardiovascular system from a biologist.

The intensive summer program (six hours a day for one week) for rising seventh-graders included career classes and exposure to college campus and team-building activities. The program consisted of three classes (Career Exploration, Career Self-Awareness, and Math and Science Careers) and a health and recreational component. A fuller description of the program is available in published research and through the first author (O'Brien et al., 1999). Table 6–6 lists the stated purposes of the three classes. Students also were invited to participate in a four- and nine-month follow-up activity (e.g., presentations by college admissions official, science museum visit). Although no control group was included in the evaluation, students who participated demonstrated statistically significant improvements in career planning and exploration efficacy, educational and vocational development efficacy, the number of careers they considered, and congruence between interests and career choice (O'Brien et al., 1999).

Also at the middle-school level, Killeen et al. (1999) examined the effectiveness of *The Real Game* (www.realgame.com). *The Real Game* simulates careers in a series of role-play scenarios in which students must navigate qualifications,

TABLE 6–6.
Purposes of the Three Classes in the Career Horizons Program

Career Exploration
    Broaden occupational perspectives
    Learn to explore and plan for careers
    Increase awareness of math/science career opportunities
    Understand how gender/ethnicity/SES relate to career choices

Career Self-Awareness
    Gain greater awareness and understanding of self
    Learn effective decision-making strategies
    Understand how drugs, alcohol, and pregnancy affect future career options
    Identify ways to improve personal study skills

Math and Science Careers
    Address under representation of White women and members of racial and ethnic
        minority groups in math and science related occupations
    Learn about careers related to math and science in hands-on activities

O'Brien, K., Dukstein, R., & Jackson, S. (1999). Broadening career horizons for students in at-risk environments. *Career Development Quarterly, 47*(3), 215–229.

transferable skills, salary, and leisure time. Students also can work to balance budgets and investigate gender-equality issues and the changing world of work. For example, for eight- to ten-year-old students (third- or fourth-graders), the unit, Play Real, centers on living and working in a community where students explore adult roles, job search, and work together as a community. The game requires 25–30 hours of curriculum time depending on topics and choices made (Killeen et al.). Teachers who administered the program reported a high rate of impact on student's learning (e.g., students more engaged in lessons, more frequent participation). Although these preliminary reports are positive, the National Center for Outcome Research in School Counseling (NCORSC) is currently conducting a more thorough evaluation of *The Real Game,* including an assessment of its impact on career self-efficacy.

Finally, *Kids and the Power of Work,* a national program aimed at exposing elementary-school children to the world of work, places volunteers in the classroom to teach students about workplace skills and careers (Grobe & Bailis, 1996), offers promising data. Survey data demonstrated that students who were involved with the program were more likely to realize how school activities relate to occupational experiences, understand the value of hard work, have a greater understanding of different jobs, and understand the importance of high-school and college educations. While empirical data is lacking, Grobe and Bailis suggested that the partnerships between business and schools (including a workplace visit) within a flexible curriculum seemed to be a critical element in engaging students.

STRENGTHS-ENHANCING
CAREER ENVIRONMENTS

As with academic and personal/social development, the strengths-based school counselor seeks to create or modify environments to facilitate career development for all students. Although much of the career-development research has examined the appropriate fit between career or work environments (person-environment fit) and interests, personality, and values, little research has specifically examined the impact of school environments on the career-development outcomes of K–12 students. Lapan's (2004) integrative contextual model (Fig. 6–1) highlights several environments (e.g., peer-group influences, family socialization, support, and belief systems, business practices) that impact students' career development. For example, "parents' practices, beliefs, and resources shape the expression of their children's career-related expectations, goals, and exploratory behaviors" (Lapan, 2004, p. 20). While multiple systems are both interactive and influential, this section will focus on the types of K–12 school environments (listed as pre-K–16 school settings in Lapan's model) as one of the systems school counselors can impact in order support the growth of career-development strengths.

Because development occurs in mutually interacting domains on many levels (e.g., developmental contextualism, Lapan's model), students need skills to adapt to school, work, and life transitions in general. Bronfenbrenner's (1979) ecological model of development suggests that social, cultural, and school environments influence career interests and education/career opportunities. Several career scholars (Gysbers & Henderson, 2000; Niles & Harris-Bowlsbey, 2005; Schmidt, 2003) have been explicit about the need for career-development programs to engage multiple stakeholders (e.g., administration, teachers, parents) and be an integral part of the school curriculum rather than an ancillary service. In fact, several preliminary studies demonstrate positive relationships between comprehensive developmental guidance models and students' career-development outcomes.

A fully implemented CDGP is not an intervention, rather an environment and systemic layer to the school itself. Studies have demonstrated students exposed to comprehensive developmental guidance models feel better prepared for the future, have more college and career information, believe their education was more relevant, show increases in scores on the Vocational Identity scale (Holland, Gottfredson, & Power, 1980), and exhibit greater awareness of the relationship between gender and careers (Lapan, Gysbers, & Petroski, 2001; Lapan, Gysbers, & Sun, 1997). While a CDGP may be conceptualized as an intervention, the comprehensive and programmatic nature of the model essentially influences several aspects of the school environment (e.g., curriculum, school mission, guidance priorities). Although we have highlighted some limitations of CDGPs in previous chapters, it appears that a well-implemented comprehensive, developmental school counseling program can be one important way the counselor can promote a strengths-enhancing environment as it relates to career development. Two school environments will be outlined in this section for the strengths-based school counselor: (a) career education (curricular) and (b) career academies (structural).

Career Education

Career education is the integration of career-related concepts into the traditional academic curriculum. Although similar to the career classes mentioned in the previous section, career-class interventions provide students information and skills *about* work (e.g., the career decision-making process) and are typically elective classes offered in secondary schools. In contrast, career education provides linkages between student's academic learning and its application *for* work (e.g., how fractions are utilized in various occupations). Various strategies have been part of the definition of career education (Isaacson & Brown, 2000), but the infusion of career-related concepts or work experiences into the core academic curriculum is broader than a simple intervention (such as a career class). With career education, *all* students are exposed to the treatment, and multiple school staff are engaged. Essentially the curricular environment is modified to foster student's career development and the connection between academic learning and the world of work.

Career education became popular in the 1970s as a federal priority, with a goal of ". . . preparing students to understand the linkages between educational opportunities and the subsequent implications of these in work choice and work adjustment" (Herr & Cramer, 1996, p. 34). In two meta-analyses of career education, Evans and Buck (1992) review of 67 studies reported a modest, but positive gain in academic achievement for students, whereas Baker and Taylor (1998) found a more robust positive effect for achievement and career development outcomes from a collection of 12 studies. Evans and Buck only examined academic achievement differences. In dissecting their results, Evans and Buck noted that the greatest increases were found in math and English classes among students with average ability and for situations in which career education was implemented in elementary school. They suggested that the larger impact for elementary school students may be due to the greater environmental consistency and uniformity as all students typically are in one classroom with one teacher. For average-ability students, Evans and Buck hypothesized that career education provides the additional motivation needed for students with potential to achieve. Finally, they also hypothesized that English and math are so basic to any occupation or life skill that these subjects can be easily integrated with work-related information.

Gillies, McMahon, and Carroll (1998) evaluated a career-education program in the upper-elementary school in Australia. They found that career-education programs have a positive effect on children's knowledge of where to find job information as well as on their interest in finding out more information about potential careers. Further, they found that the career-education program showed students the importance of school learning to future occupational success, even though the program did not explicitly target this skill.

School counselors can begin to influence the curricular environment of schools by collaborating with teachers to integrate career illustrations within core academic content. For example, school counselors can target core academic subjects like math and language arts and introduce exploration of a range of career applications. In working with persuasion within a language arts unit, school counselors can help teachers demonstrate content in careers like advertising, law, and/or retail sales. While many school counselors already do this type of collaboration, broad systematic inclusion of career content throughout the curriculum is reflective of a strengths-enhancing curricular environment.

Career Academies

Career academies emerged in the late 1970s and early 1980s in an effort to retain potential dropouts and prepare at-risk students for the labor force (Stern, Raby, & Dayton, 1992). There are about 1,500 academies across the nation (Underdue, 2000), although no one standard definition of career academies exists. Most academies include a smaller-learning-community format (e.g., school-within-a-school), college-prep curriculum with a career theme (e.g., health care, business), and partnerships with employers (Stern, Dayton, & Raby, 1988). Often these academies appear in low-income, urban areas and serve predominantly minority students whose grades and attendance are poor. The Manpower Development Research Corporation (MDRC;1993) described a career academy by three main criteria: (a) school-within-a-school organization, (b) courses that meet college entrance requirements (and technical courses) all related to an occupational theme and (c) employer partnerships for experiences related to the theme. Therefore, students in career academies learn about and experience occupational alternatives not only from counselors, but also from teachers, community and business collaborations, and employers themselves (e.g., externships).

A host of evaluations of career academies have demonstrated a lower dropout rate, better achievement and graduation rates, and more enrollments in postsecondary education as compared with randomly assigned high schools not utilizing an academy structure (Cannon & Reed, 1999; Kemple & Snipes, 2000; Steinberg, 1998). In the MDRC investigation, academy students reported more support from teachers and peers, more engagement in career-development activities, and work in jobs that connected to school as compared to the control-group students (Kemple, Poglinco, & Snipes, 1999). Further, in a four-year follow-up, students who participated in career academies earned higher hourly wages and worked more hours per week than students in traditional, control high schools (although no differences were found for educational attainment) (Kemple, 2004). The MDRC found that career academies, as compared to the control schools, provided more career guidance, technical classes, and school-supervised work experience during high school and had substantial positive impact for males and students at-risk for not finishing high school (Kemple, 2004).

Data are not yet available about which aspects of career academies are most salient to the academic and career development of students. Conchas and Clark (2002) emphasized smaller and more intimate school-within-a-school structures and teacher and student shared goals to maximize the benefits of career academies for urban and diverse youth. Even so, Catalano et al., (2003) suggest that the most successful career academies provided interpersonal supports (e.g., core group of teachers, team-like structure, and distinct physical space). Further, Kemple and Rock (1996) report real-world connections, integrated curriculum, rigor and inclusiveness, caring adults, and a professional learning community as contributing factors to success.

As with most environmental changes, school counselors most likely will not have the influence or ability to make large structural changes by themselves. Even so, school counselors can provide data and input to school administration and other school leaders (e.g., school boards) about the potential of career academies and the related mechanisms that appear to positively influence career development. They can also model and seek to advocate for many of the components of career academies (e.g., caring adults, professional learning communities) where more direct influence would be applicable.

SUMMARY

In this chapter, we reviewed the long tradition of the developmental and competence-based (although not empirically based) approach to career development. We also suggested that career development can not be disconnected from other areas of development as can be seen with many of the career strengths (e.g., self-regulated learning, social skills) (Niles, Trusty, & Mitchell, 2004). Similar to the progression of learning math, the sequential growth of career development through the K–12 years was presented in contemporary standards. "If the practice of career development is going to be a developmental process, the career guidance program must be continuous and cumulative" (Herr, Cramer, & Niles, 2004, p. 362). We also highlighted the significant changes occurring in the world of work, and how a focus on career-development strengths and strengths-enhancing environments is needed. Although we are unable to cover the broad theoretical (e.g., Holland) scope and range of environments (e.g., parents/families) relevant to career development, we highlighted three particular strengths and two environments worthy of school counselors' attention.

We described career maturity, career identity, and career self-efficacy, how they are associated with positive student outcomes, and conceptually how school counselors might seek to enhance these strengths in students. We also illustrated some evidence-based and promising interventions that promote these strengths. Even with limited empirical investigations of interventions that target K–12 students, the school counselor has a key role to play in helping students to build systematically the career-development skills to enable them to succeed in a dynamic, global economy. Finally, we also discussed environmental approaches that facilitate developing career strengths. We found that CDGP to an extent, and career education and career academies hold promise as strengths-enhancing environments.

KEY POINTS

The Traditional Role of the School Counselor in Career Development

- Before the school counselor role was even initiated, teachers served as vocational counselors in the schools in the early 1900s and provided vocational guidance as a supplementary part of the academic program.
- During the first half of the 20th century, the school counselor role in career development (in reality career choice) relied on administering and interpreting standardized tests (e.g., interest inventories and aptitude tests) to advise students about vocational choices (Baker & Gerler, 2004).
- Models of career guidance underwent a significant transformation when several theorists proposed developmental models of career behavior (e.g., Ginzberg, Ginzberg, Axelrad, & Herma, 1951). School counselors also shifted their emphasis from career exploration as a one-time event to a process requiring skills for a lifetime.

The Contemporary Role of the School Counselor in Career Development

- Therefore, in comprehensive developmental guidance programs (CDGP), the school counselor's role in career development includes providing classroom guidance or providing leadership in schools to integrate career exploration into the planned curriculum for students (e.g., a career-decisions elective class, integration of career concepts into the academic curriculum).
- Together, contemporary influences on the school counselor role in career development suggest a sequential (e.g., NOICC, STWOA), developmental (e.g., CDGP), integrated (CDGP, SCANS), and competency-based (e.g., NOICC, STWOA, ACSA) approach. Combined, they prompt school counselors to be intentional in providing a comprehensive career-development program to all students, rather than providing sporadic guidance interventions to selected students on career choice that leaves career development to chance.

- Essentially, this changing career context suggests that the school counselor's role in career development must focus on enhancing students' strengths as lifelong learners and that applying these strengths to a dynamic, global workplace will be required.

The Strengths-Based School Counselor's Role in Career Development

- Because theoretical guides for career development for K–12 students have focused on building competencies in a developmental sequence for the last half-decade, the strength orientation is already present to some degree in the career-development literature.
- Further, school counselors can enhance current models with a focus on career development that is empirically based, with consideration of the environmental conditions in K–12 schools which support students' career development and with knowledge of interventions that have been shown to influence career-development strengths and strengths-enhancing environments.

Career Strengths to Promote

- Career Maturity
  - One multidimensional construct that captures the extent to which a person is ready to cope with expected and unexpected demands in the vocational realm is career maturity (Savickas, 1984).
  - School counselors can use these instruments (CDI, CMI) to assess the career maturity of students, or can use these data in the aggregate form to provide information for program planning or evaluation of career-development interventions.
  - Students with high levels of career maturity are more likely to obtain successful and satisfying careers due to more awareness, self-reliance, and commitment to the career decision-making process, and because they relate present behavior to future goals (Powell & Luzzo, 1998; Savickas, 1990).
- Career Identity
  - Career identity relates to the part of one's perception of self that relates to work and working (What does work mean in and for my life?) (Meijers, 1998).
  - In the self-constructed identity, the student's exploration and commitments are more intrinsic, based on exploration, rather than extrinsic or due to external expectations.
  - Based on the world of work today (e.g., changing workplace) and the career-development tasks confronting K–12 students (e.g., decision points), students ideally move between a career-identity moratorium and a self-constructed career identity seamlessly as they make career-related decisions (e.g., course selection, part-time work experiences) in K–12 school.
  - School counselors can help students in individual planning or counseling sessions explore strengths and weaknesses as they relate to academic subjects or explore the student's conception of role as a student, peer, sibling, or any other role he or she may play. Further, students might also advocate for programmatic attempts to engage students in exploration as with mentoring or job-shadowing programs with area businesses, job and career fairs, or information and Internet-based resources that enable students to explore careers and other interests.

- Career Self-efficacy
  - Although career maturity and career identity are more multidimensional constructs, career self-efficacy is more specific to a student's "expectations or beliefs concerning one's ability to perform successfully a given behavior" (e.g., engage in career exploration, make a career-related decision) (Betz, 1994, p. 35).
  - Self-efficacy beliefs are developed in experience through four sources: (a) performance accomplishments, (b) vicarious learning, (c) emotional arousal, and (d) verbal persuasion (Bandura, 1977).
  - Essentially, school counselors want to encourage students to become active participants in the career-development process by building successive experiences (vicarious, along with performance accomplishments) with career-development tasks throughout school. Counselors will need to assess (and help students self-assess) the influence of previous learning experiences and performance, the influence of context on the development of career interests, and how low perceptions of self-efficacy may limit career options, decision, or implementation (persistence in educational program or obstacles) (Betz, 1992).

Interventions to Promote Strengths for Career Development

- Results of Meta-Analyses on Career Interventions
  - The reviews found overall positive effects for career interventions with high-effect sizes (e.g., confidence that outcome differences found in the studies have substantial practical meaning) especially for junior-high-school students, individual counseling, and small-group interventions (most cost-effective) interventions (Oliver & Spokane, 1988).
- Career Classes
  - Savickas (1990) investigated the effectiveness of a career decision-making course that was created to help students more adequately make decisions relating to career choice. The course was based on Crites's (1976) model for comprehensive career counseling, which emphasizes how students make the choice of which occupation they will pursue. The course focuses on developing decisional attitudes and competencies that help students to manage career tasks and encouraging behavioral responses that meet these tasks.
  - Kraus and Hughey (1999) eight-session class focused on accurate self-appraisal, gathering occupational information, goal selection, making future plans, and problem solving (along with an introductory and review session).
  - "Presumably, the career education class provided exposure to sources of self-efficacy expectations such as performance attainments (e.g., live interview), vicarious learning opportunities (e.g., guest speakers, small group work), and social persuasion experiences (e.g., feedback and encouragement). . ." (McWhirter, Rasheed, & Crothers, 2000, p. 338).
- Career Programs
  - Studies of computer career-development programs (e.g., DISCOVER, CHOICES) have also demonstrated increases in career maturity, career self-efficacy, and levels of career decidedness (Luzzo & Pierce, 1996; Pinder & Fitzgerald, 1984).
  - O'Brien and her colleagues (O'Brien, Dukstein, Jackson, Tomlinson, & Kamatuka, 1999) developed the Career Horizons Program for middle-school students to enhance confidence in performing tasks related to investigating and selecting

career choice for students at-risk for vocational underachievement. Although no control group was included in the evaluation, students who participated demonstrated statistically significant improvements in career planning and exploration efficacy, educational and vocational development efficacy, the number of careers they considered, and congruence between interests and career choice (O'Brien et al., 1999).

Strengths-Enhancing Career Environments

- Studies have demonstrated students exposed to comprehensive developmental guidance models feel better prepared for the future, have more college and career information, believe their education was more relevant, show increases in scores on the Vocational Identity scale (Holland, Gottfredson, & Power, 1980), and exhibit greater awareness of the relationship between gender and careers (Lapan, Gysbers, & Petroski, 2001; Lapan, Gysbers, & Sun, 1997).
- Career Education
  - Career education is the integration of career-related concepts into the traditional academic curriculum. In two meta-analyses of career education, Evans and Buck (1992) review of 67 studies reported a modest, but positive gain in academic achievement for students, whereas Baker and Taylor (1998) found a more robust positive effect for achievement and career-development outcomes from a collection of 12 studies.
- Career Academies
  - Most academies include a smaller-learning-community format (e.g., school-within-a-school), college-prep curriculum with a career theme (e.g., health care, business), and partnerships with employers (Stern, Dayton, & Raby, 1988).
  - A host of evaluations of career academies have demonstrated a lower drop-out rate, better achievement and graduation rates, and more enrollments in post-secondary education as compared with randomly assigned high schools not utilizing an academy structure (Cannon & Reed, 1999; Kemple & Snipes, 2000; Steinberg, 1998).
  - Data are not yet available about which aspects of career academies are most salient to the academic and career development of students. Even so, smaller and more intimate school-within-a-school structures and teacher- and student-shared goals; interpersonal supports (e.g., core group of teachers, team-like structure, and distinct physical space); and real-world connections, integrated curriculum, rigor and inclusiveness, caring adults, and a professional learning community have been cited as contributing factors to success.

7

Strengths-Based School Counseling in Perspective

OUTLINE

Twelve Key Questions about the Strengths-Based School Counseling Framework

TWELVE KEY QUESTIONS ABOUT
THE STRENGTHS-BASED SCHOOL
COUNSELING FRAMEWORK

We have advanced Strengths-Based School Counseling (SBSC) as a new framework to inform the practice of school counseling in the 21st century. But, as with any new perspective, questions arise about it such as how it fits with current theory and practice, what it offers that is better than what we already have, and why we should consider adopting it. We trust that we have provided the reader with the necessary answers to these questions in previous chapters, but we recognize that some questions may still remain. In this chapter, we attempt to answer some of the key questions about SBSC in an effort to put the importance and utility of this framework into perspective for school counselors. Specifically, we pose a dozen questions about SBSC, its relation to current theory and practice, and its potential contributions to school counseling and related disciplines.

1. What's development and why is it a central theme of this framework?

> Development generally refers to changes in patterns of overt and covert activity as people grow up or mature in their capacity to perform several culturally valued life functions. Individual development involves multiple changes as the person strives to master many life functions simultaneously. When such changes are judged as movement toward cultural ideals of maturity or healthiness, there is general agreement that the person made developmental changes. Developmental change is progressive and incremental, usually involving movement away from simple, dependent, self-centered activity patterns that are typical of younger members of a society and movement toward complex, independent, society-centered activity patterns that are typical of mature members of society. (Jepsen, 2004, p. 602)

In the National Model for School Counseling Programs (ASCA, 2003), development is conceptualized in terms of three domains: academic, personal/social, and career. Although we view development more holistically and contextually (e.g., that development in the three areas is interwoven and that change in one area impacts change in the other areas), we subscribe to ASCA's three-part view. Our emphasis is on promoting those developmental strengths which have been shown to be empirically linked either with positive functioning in adulthood or with positive youth development at a particular point in time.

School counselors function in educational settings, the mission of which in this country is to foster the development of individuals who can contribute to and function successfully in a democratic society. As a counseling professional working within an educational setting, the school counselor's role must be compatible with that developmental mission. Most recently, however, the overwhelming focus of that mission for teachers and administrators has been on the academic aspects of development (e.g., academic success for all students) almost to the exclusion of the other two developmental domains.

The school counselor has important contributions to make to that academic mission. However, the school counselor doesn't focus on test scores or on teaching academic content, but rather on factors that mediate academic performance. As a developmental specialist, the counselor recognizes that development in the personal/social and career domains positively impacts academic development and that academic development does not proceed effectively in the absence of personal/social and career development. Thus, the school counselor is both a counselor and an educator, but the core of what she or he is doing is intended to facilitate positive youth development. Unlike other educational professionals who focus primarily or exclusively on academic content mastery, the school counselor's focus is on holistic positive youth development. In that regard, the school counselor contributes a unique and complementary focus and set of skills that are both compatible with, and promote, the central mission of schools.

2. **We already have developmental approaches to counseling. Why is SBSC different from or better than the developmental approaches that we already have?**

Yes, a number of developmental approaches to counseling generally and/or school counseling in particular have been advanced over the years, including Dinkmeyer and Caldwell (1970), Gysbers and Henderson (1994, 2000), Ivey, Ivey, Myers, and Sweeney (2005), Myrick (1997), and Paisley and Hubbard (1994). These contributions have been important in a variety of ways and especially because they emphasize developmental issues as central considerations for counselors working with children. However, these approaches are also limited in a variety of ways. They tend to be predicated on earlier developmental theory (e.g., Piaget, 1950; Erickson, 1963; Kohlberg, 1969) and research which emphasize stage-invariant notions of development almost to the exclusion of environmental, cultural, and contextual influences. Some approaches focused almost exclusively on the counseling and therapy functions that a counselor provides and do not address the other functions (e.g., advocacy, consultation) that are essential to a school counselor's role. Finally, they fail to incorporate findings from contemporary developmental theory and research (e.g., resiliency, developmental assets) which have empirically identified operationally defined student strengths that are associated with positive youth development and environments that have clearly been shown to foster those strengths.

What SBSC offers that is an improvement over earlier developmental approaches is a framework that is built on contemporary developmental theory and research, and anchored to school counseling. SBSC identifies the empirically identified strengths that school counselors need to promote as well as the types of environments that have been shown to promote those strengths.

In addition, it recognizes the importance of cultural (e.g., ethnic identity) and other contextual factors (e.g., urban versus rural environments) that affect the acquisition and development of those strengths. Given the increasingly diverse student populations which characterize 21st century schools, counselors and other educators must address these factors if they are to facilitate positive youth development for all students.

3. **Advocacy. That's all I seem to hear about these days. I'm supposed to be an advocate for my client, an advocate for social and political change, an advocate for my profession, and so on and so forth. If I spend my time on all of the types of advocacy that counselors are supposed to be involved in, how will I have time for anything else?**

In recent years, the profession has recognized that just offering our traditional direct-counseling services to some clients, even to those client groups who have tended to be underserved by schools and mainstream society (e.g., minorities, immigrants, students with special educational needs), is often not sufficient to provide the necessary opportunities and resources that they need for positive youth development. As a result, school counselors have been urged to engage in a number of different types of advocacy initiatives in order to rectify historical imbalances and to provide needed resources and opportunities to client groups who have either been denied those opportunities or who have experienced greater difficulty in accessing them.

In SBSC, we support the importance of the different types of advocacy initiatives that have been proposed for school counselors. Advocating state and national policy that either promotes student development or removes barriers to development is clearly an important counseling function. Similarly, publicizing the accomplishments of school counselors and advocating support for our profession is essential to the survival and growth of school counseling.

However, for most school counselors and their stakeholders, we believe that greatest impact will accrue from emphasizing promotion-oriented, developmental client advocacy at the school-building level. Much of what has been written about advocacy is concerned with removing barriers to educational opportunities. Removing barriers to development is an important first step, but it does not automatically result in providing the resources and supports necessary for optimal development. For example, enabling more immigrant Hispanic students to access honors and advanced-placement classes in a school does not mean that these students have the necessary resources and supports to succeed in these classes that their more affluent, native-born, white peers often have. Promotion-oriented, developmental advocacy moves a step beyond barrier removal and emphasizes developing and sustaining the environmental contexts that foster the strengths associated with positive youth development. In this instance, it would involve not only removing the entrance barriers to these classes but also determining and providing the types of resources and supports needed in order to be successful in them. Client advocacy involves determining and advocating those client groups who currently are underserved or who have historically been underserved as a result of discrimination or other factors. In some instances, the composition of those groups is obvious. In other instances, disaggregating data such as representation in educational tracks, in special education, and in gifted and talented classes may reveal groups for whom advocacy efforts are needed. Finally, in SBSC we focus on advocacy at the school-building level. We believe that the building level is where most school counselors are likely to have their greatest influence and leverage and where their efforts will have the most immediate payoff for the stakeholders that they serve on a daily basis.

4. **I read somewhere that there are more than 200 theories of counseling and psychotherapy. Is SBSC another theory that I am going to have to learn?**

No. A theory is an attempt to organize and integrate knowledge in order to explain and/or predict events. In order to qualify as a theory, a conceptual formulation must include a variety of essential elements such as basic postulates and assumptions, key explanatory constructs, a set of relationships or rules that relate the constructs to each other, and a series of hypotheses about what the theory predicts to be true. These hypotheses are subject to empirical verification which, in turn, may result in the theory being revised. In counseling, a theory serves as a roadmap to help the practitioner to know what to do in order to help a client achieve desired goals.

Although we are strong supporters of theory- and data-driven practice in school counseling, SBSC is not a new theory. SBSC does not meet the criteria to qualify as a theory. It is simply a framework (a set of principles) to inform practice that was derived from a review of the literature on school counseling and related disciplines (e.g., education, social work, psychology). Six guiding principles comprise SBSC:

- Promoting Context-Based Development for All Students
- Promoting Individual Student Strengths
- Promoting Strengths-Enhancing Environments
- Emphasizing Strengths Promotion over Problem Reduction and Problem Prevention
- Emphasizing Evidence-Based Interventions and Practice
- Emphasizing Promotion-Oriented Developmental Advocacy at the School Level

SBSC draws upon knowledge and interventions from a variety of theories and conceptual frameworks (e.g., developmental contextualism, resiliency, developmental assets) that emphasize the development of evidence-based strengths in youth rather than the remediation and prevention of deficits. In that regard, the theories that underscore the work of the strengths-based school counselor may not be as familiar to many traditionally trained school counselors and counselor educators. However, we are confident that the rationale for SBSC discussed throughout this book together with the interventions that we have presented clearly demonstrate the utility of the framework for school counseling in the 21st century.

5. **My school system just decided to implement the ASCA National Model (ASCA, 2003). How can we turn around now and implement Strengths-Based School Counseling instead?**

The National Model represents a major step forward in the development and transformation of the school counseling profession. The National Model is comprehensive in scope and provides school counselors with important guidelines regarding the foundation of their school counseling programs as well as the management and delivery systems for those programs. In addition, it provides a much-needed focus on accountability.

It's not an either/or situation. You don't have to choose one or the other (e.g., National Model or Strengths-Based School Counseling). SBSC is not an alternative comprehensive school counseling program or an alternative to the National Model. It is a set of six guiding principles for implementing and focusing practice within a comprehensive school counseling program. The SBSC framework is compatible with, extends, and enhances the ASCA National Model in several ways.

One fundamental extension is that SBSC identifies the strengths (e.g., the student competencies) in the academic, personal/social, and career domains that are empirically linked to positive youth development as well as the strengths-enhancing environments associated with those strengths. It is these evidence-based strengths and strengths-enhancing environments that school counselors should promote. In addition, SBSC provides numerous examples of evidence-based interventions (e.g., the delivery system) that promote both the evidence-based student strengths and evidence-based strengths-enhancing environments which positively impact youth development in the academic, personal/social, and/or career domains. As such, SBSC reinforces and extends the accountability emphasis of the National Model. Finally, the six principles of SBSC provide the school counselor with flexible and applicable guidelines for focusing school counseling programs to meet local needs and incorporating future research findings.

6. **School counseling has been mostly ignored or marginalized by educational reform. How does Strengths-Based School Counseling respond to and fit with the educational reform movement?**

In its National Model, ASCA has been responsive to the major emphases of educational reform (e.g., No Child Left Behind). Specifically, comprehensive school counseling programs are to be aligned and made accountable with the central mission of schools (e.g., academic development and school success). With its emphases on empirically based positive youth development, evidence-based interventions, and evidence-based practice, SBSC is consistent with the alignment and accountability emphases of educational reform. In order to function effectively as educational leaders, school counselors must be knowledgeable about the effects of major educational reform efforts on academic achievement and other aspects of student development. In addition, they must know where to obtain updated information about these initiatives. Strengths-based school counselors have this knowledge (see Chapters 1 and 4).

7. **Evidence-based practice is costly. It requires money and other people. In order to do evidence-based practice, won't I have to stop doing something else?**

There is certainly some basis for this concern. Some of the evidence-based interventions are commercially produced and/or require a financial commitment to support needed professional development of counselors and other educators who will employ the interventions. Other aspects of evidence-based practice are costly with respect to a counselor's time. It's often quicker and easier to "do things yourself" rather than to collaborate with others. Similarly, collecting and analyzing data to demonstrate the effects of school counseling may also take time away from providing direct services. Moreover, evidence-based practice may necessitate that counselors devote time to acquiring and refining program-evaluation skills rather than to providing services to students, teachers, and parents.

But time and money are only part of the considerations in running a school counseling program. In this era of accountability, demonstrating effectiveness of services provided is frequently an overriding consideration as to whether a counseling position is funded or perhaps even whether school counseling will continue to be supported at all by taxpayers in the future. As you think about your school counseling program, consider what evidence base you have for the current services you provide to students, teachers, and parents. If your situation is like many others, you probably will find that you don't have much "hard" evidence for the effectiveness of those services. SBSC provides examples of a number of evidence-based interventions as well as suggestions for implementing evidence-based practice as a whole. Admittedly, it will take time and money to begin to integrate these ideas into practice, but, as you will see next, this type of focus can make a major difference even in very challenging school environments.

8. **I work in a school with a lot of tough kids and tough problems. Our school has an unbelievable number of discipline problems, and I'm always called upon to deal with one crisis or another. I don't have time for one more thing, let alone adding Strengths-Based School Counseling, with its promotion and prevention-oriented focus, to**

what I already do. How is adopting that framework going to help me deal with my students and all of their discipline problems and crises?

Continually dealing with student crises is time-consuming, difficult, and seemingly never-ending. On the one hand, it is an extremely important role for the school counselor as far as the students or teachers who are experiencing the crises are concerned. On the other hand, it typically results in the counselor expending a great deal of time and effort with a very small percentage of the school community. More importantly, it raises at least two unsettling questions for the school counselor: (1) how effective am I being with students (or teachers) with respect to their development if I am constantly dealing with their crises, and (2) how do the services that I am providing fit my profession's view (e.g., the ASCA National Model) of my role as a school counselor?

The history of school counseling and education is replete with examples of professionals being asked to assume more and more duties and responsibilities, often with fewer and fewer resources (e.g., the No Child Left Behind legislation). Moreover, it is rare that any duties or responsibilities are ever dropped from a professional's role. Similarly, in counselor education, faculty have been called upon to provide students more preparation, without recognizing that programs do not have ever-expanding resources and time (Pipes, Buckhalt, & Merrill, 1983).

With respect to these issues, SBSC is a dynamic rather than a static framework. That is, within its basic philosophy (e.g., the six guiding principles) of strengths promotion, etc., the specific type and amount of services provided by the school counselor will be impacted by local needs. In adopting SBSC, the counselor is not being asked to do more, but to do things differently. Central to SBSC is the principle of teaching students such skills as anger management, peacemaking, and problem solving (see Chapter 5) that help students both to avoid crisis situations as well as to manage them more effectively when they do occur. Of course, crises will inevitably occur. The strengths-based school counselor, however, does not function alone. He or she will have built the type of coordination and collaboration relationships that provide needed resources from the school and the community to assist with those crises and discipline problems. Thus, when crises do arise, both students and environmental supports should be better prepared and more available to address situational needs if a strengths-based framework has been implemented.

Yet another approach that is consistent with SBSC involves conceptualizing the problem situation (e.g., frequent disciplinary incidents and crises) and relevant interventions differently. Rather than viewing the situation as one that involves intervening with individual students or small groups of students, it may be more effective to view the situation and required interventions from a school- or system-level perspective. In this regard, the school counselor will find it helpful to refer to the systems approach for School-Wide Positive Behavior Support (Center on Positive Behavioral Interventions and Supports, 2004) discussed in Chapter 5.

9. So, if I am a strengths-based school counselor, do I just forget about reducing or eliminating disruptive and maladaptive behavior, attitudes, and emotions in my clients? In other words, you don't want me to help them deal with and resolve their problems?

Not at all. Helping students reduce or eliminate personal problems and other barriers to their development will always be an important function of school counselors. However, because students are problem-free does not mean that they now possess the skills and strengths necessary to meet the academic and other developmental challenges and opportunities that they will encounter in school and in life. Research has indicated that enhancing protective factors and reducing risk factors are *both* needed for positive youth development (e.g., Pollard et al., 1999).

In SBSC, we prioritize strengths enhancement over problem reduction and problem prevention, but we have not excluded problem reduction and problem prevention. We emphasize strengths enhancement for several reasons. First and foremost, school counselors, like other educators, are in the business of helping students to optimize development. Optimizing development involves helping students be academically successful, promoting their health and character, etc. Secondly, not only are these strengths important in their own right, but they have also been shown to buffer against the development of a variety of psychological problems among youth (Commission on Positive Youth Development, 2005). Thirdly, a deficit-reduction emphasis in school counseling tends to focus on what's wrong with students and can lead to labeling and blaming the victim, factors which limit the development of all students and especially those from groups who historically have been subjected to discrimination and restricted educational opportunities. In contrast, SBSC provides a more balanced perspective by emphasizing strengths but not overlooking deficits.

As a general rule, the strengths-based school counselor focuses first and foremost on increasing what students want to occur (e.g., strengths), and secondarily, if necessary, on decreasing what students doesn't want to occur (e.g., problems). As strengths increase, problems tend to decrease. On the other hand, if the focus is on reducing problems, it doesn't follow that strengths will invariably take their place.

10. I teach in a school counseling program that is accredited by the Council for Accreditation of Counseling and Related Educational Programs (CACREP). Is Strengths-Based School Counseling compatible with the CACREP standards, and are we going to have to modify our entire curriculum in order to prepare strengths-based counselors?

The SBSC principles are entirely compatible with the current CACREP Standards (CACREP, 2001). For example, the emphasis on promoting positive youth development exemplifies CACREP's Human Growth and Development standard (Section IIK 3d), strategies for facilitating optimum development across the lifespan. In fact, SBSC provides numerous examples of evidence-based strategies that facilitate such development. Similarly, the stress on evidence-based practice in SBSC is a good fit with the CACREP standards on assessment and research and program evaluation.

The SBSC principles also dovetail nicely with and even strengthen the CACREP School Counseling Program Standards. For example, the six principles (e.g., promoting context-based development for all students, individual student strengths, and strengths-enhancing environments; and emphasizing evidence-based practice, promotion over remediation, and promotion-oriented developmental advocacy) serve to (a) relate school counseling more closely to the academic services in schools (Foundations Standard), (b) provide the counselor with greater appreciation and knowledge of the influence of the school setting on youth development (Foundations), (c) integrate school counseling into the total school curriculum (Contextual Dimensions Standard), and (d) promote the use of counseling and guidance activities and programs by the total school community to enhance a positive school climate (Contextual Dimensions).

In order to incorporate this framework into school counselor education, infusion of the strengths-based principles, sequencing of courses, and some curriculum modification will be needed, but a revamping of the total curriculum does not seem to be necessary (see Chapter 8). Thus, school counselors will not necessarily need to receive more preparation. Rather, their preparation will need to have some different emphases than it currently has. For example, greater emphasis will need to be placed on counseling theories that emphasize strengths promotion, while less emphasis should be placed on theories that focus on deficit reduction. Leadership, indirect services, and environmental-change strategies will require greater attention along with the systemic and ecological theories from which those interventions are derived. Consequently, the coverage devoted to one-to-one counseling and other direct-service interventions may need to be adjusted vis-à-vis the coverage of systemic interventions and indirect services. Finally, evidence-based interventions both from school counseling and related fields as well as educational reform initiatives will need to receive greater attention than they currently do in most school counselor education programs.

11.   Is the strengths-based framework applicable by other professionals? Is it relevant to counselors in other settings?

The answer to both questions is definitely yes. At least five of the six principles are directly applicable by principals and other educational leaders who are concerned with operating accountable schools in which students are academically successful and develop the necessary career and personal/social skills that will enable them to contribute to and function successfully in a democratic society. Educational leaders have the professional responsibility to cultivate and maintain educational contexts (e.g., rules and procedures) and classroom environments that support achievement. When these efforts focus on student and staff strengths, the result is likely to be a more developmentally responsive environment for all students. The principle of promoting individual student strengths is a feature that supports the school's mission. As a result, SBSC is an endeavor which educational leaders are likely to support even though they are not directly involved in providing counseling themselves.

With the exception of the school-based principle (e.g., emphasize promotion-oriented developmental advocacy at the school-building level), SBSC is relevant to mental-health and agency counselors as well as to a variety of other mental-health professionals. For example, much of what occurs in mental-health counseling with children and families (e.g., solution-focused family counseling) involves attempting to build strengths in them and the systems of which they are a part, as opposed to remediating deficits which they manifest. Moreover, as we have discussed throughout the book, psychology is witnessing an emerging interest in positive and strengths-oriented, as opposed to pathology and deficit-reduction, models of intervention. We have seen that a similar orientation has previously appeared in social work as well (e.g., Saleebey, 1997).

12. **Does Strengths-Based School Counseling offer a practical framework that school counselors can implement and use successfully? Or is its strengths-based focus another passing fad that will be tried and discarded as unwieldy or ineffective?**

From a conceptual perspective, SBSC provides a flexible, data-driven approach that should be capable of being responsive to changes in education, society, etc. Because of the increasing diversity in school populations, cultures, and context, school counselors must remain flexible and responsive to client, community, and societal change. Even so, SBSC remains consistent in its conception of the school counselor's role and its focus on the six guiding principles. There is no reason to believe that principles such as strengths-promotion and accountability will be any less relevant to school counseling in the decades to come. Ultimately, however, only experience, the passage of time, and the accumulation of data will enable us to answer these questions. In the meantime, a number of challenges must be met if these questions are to receive a fair test. First, can school counselors move beyond traditional service models and adopt a promotion-focused orientation to service provision? Can they move beyond an ancillary, supportive role in schools and embrace a central leadership role for environmental change? Will school counselor educators provide future school counselors with the preparation necessary to function effectively from a strengths-based perspective? Finally, will school counselors, counselor educators, and other stakeholders be willing to collect the data necessary to evaluate the value of adopting a strengths-based framework?

8

School Counselor Preparation

OUTLINE

Historical Influences in School Counselor Education

Contemporary Influences in School-Counselor Preparation

Preparing the Strengths-Based School Counselor

Integration of Strengths-Based School Counseling in the CACREP Curriculum

The Strengths-Based School Counselor (Professional Identity) • *Promoting Human Development (Human Growth and Development)* • *Cultural Competence in Counseling and Schools (Social and Cultural Diversity)* • *Additional Core Infusion*

SBSC Intervention Sequence • *Clinical Course Integration and Supervision*

Visual Aids

Sample SBSC Program of Studies • *Sample Ecological Prevention Plan*

Summary

Key Points

In this chapter, we will discuss the type of changes in school counselor education that are needed in order to prepare strengths-based school counselors. The strengths-based school counseling (SBSC) framework requires distinctive practice from traditional and contemporary school counseling models. If practice is to be different, then school counselor preparation also needs to be adapted. Education and preparation impact both the capacity to implement the school counselor role and the ability to meet the demands of today's students and school communities. Before we discuss how to prepare strengths-based school counselors, we will first briefly consider some of the major historical and contemporary influences on school counselor education.

HISTORICAL INFLUENCES IN SCHOOL COUNSELOR EDUCATION

Although models for school counselor preparation date back to the 1920s (Aubrey, 1982), the creation of the American Personnel and Guidance Association (APGA) in 1952 and the passage of the National Defense Education Act (NDEA) in 1958 represent initial strides toward standardizing the preparation of school counselors (Baker, 2001b). The Act provided funds for school counseling essentially to enable schools to promote more students toward careers in math and science so that the country would be competitive in the space race. These events resulted in a dramatic increase in the number of school counselors and counselor-education programs. It also transformed much of school counselor preparation from teacher add-on programs and undergraduate preparation, to graduate-level preparation of school counselors. In the process, Rogerian client-centered counseling and the developmental-guidance model gained prominence in school counseling in the 1960s and 1970s and led many to advocate for a services (e.g., a focus on function) approach to school counseling (Baker, 2001a).

The Council for Accreditation of Counseling and Related Educational Programs (CACREP) provided formalized national accreditation standards for school counselor education programs starting in 1986. Accreditation standards provided one of the first attempts to standardize how students are trained to become school counselors. CACREP, as a part of the American Counseling Association (ACA), promulgated standards that emphasized counseling functions and an identity as a counselor. In 1990, the Association of Counselor Education and Supervision (ACES) sought to enhance school counselor education and preparation through a series of recommendations, such as the revision of national standards and uniformity of certification and licensure of school counselors nationally (ACES, 1990). Since the expansion of school counselor education in the 1950s, both a developmental focus and a concern for consistency and standardization of school counselor preparation have been thematic. Even so, contemporary school counselor preparation has not achieved consistency or a developmental focus, resulting in role ambiguity and confusion.

CONTEMPORARY INFLUENCES IN SCHOOL-COUNSELOR PREPARATION

Although Pate (1990) suggested that program accreditation is a topic of concern for counselor educators as it relates to professional identity, only one-third of school counselor preparation programs are accredited by CACREP (Hollis & Dodson, 2001; Schmidt, 1999). Examples of variability in school counselor preparation include the amount of influence of or responsiveness to national practice models of school counseling. Perusse, Goodnough, and Noel (2001) found that nearly one-third of school counselor educators did not incorporate the national standards for school counseling (Campbell & Dahir, 1997) into their curriculum. Those programs that did use the standards used them inconsistently. Additional variability in programs also appeared in faculty backgrounds (e.g., experience in schools) and field-experience requirements for students (both in hours required and expectations of duties in the field). In a more recent study, Akos and Scarborough (2004) similarly found that clinical assignments and pedagogical practices in clinical internship curricula in school counseling programs were highly variable.

This lack of consistency in school counselor preparation also extends to terminology. Although ASCA uses the term "professional school counselor" in recent models, the traditional term "guidance counselor" is often utilized in practice, and Sears and Granello (2002) suggested that counselor education has contributed to role confusion by often using the terms counseling and guidance inconsistently. Additionally, although ASCA uses the term professional school counselor, they also indicate that school counselors are "educators trained in school counseling" (O'Bryant, 1990). This assertion was based on a 1989 survey of ASCA leaders who were divided about the counselor versus educator identity (Hoyt, 1993). School counselor preparation as a whole has been characterized by this variation, which led Paisley and McMahon (2001) to highlight "ambiguous role definition" as one of the primary challenges for school counseling in the 21st century (p. 107). In fact, Bemak (2002) proposed that clarifying school counselor identity through a redefinition of implicit and explicit assumptions about the role is essential.

Since the mid-1990s, as calls for change and clarity in school counselor education have been increasing (Martin, 2002), the redefinition of the school counselor role and the preparation required for it continues. While school counselors traditionally were teachers, the erosion of previous teacher licensure and/or experience as a requirement by many states has opened the door to school counseling for many non-educators. Although the impact of this change has not been formally measured or researched, it may introduce a more pressing need to teach preservice school counselors to attend to and learn more about school culture and environmental impacts on the school counselor role (Peterson & Deuschle, 2006). Along with this change in school counselor licensure, national organizations have also impacted contemporary school counselor preparation.

The Transforming School Counseling Initiative (TSCI), set forth by the Education Trust (1999), sought to (a) assess the status of school counseling nationally, (b) develop plans for reforming graduate-level preparation programs, (c) partner with select institutions to implement the reforms, and (d) disseminate the reforms nationally. In their assessment of current school counseling programs, members of the TSCI found the school counselor "role/function is sometimes dictated by the district, the principal, the community in which they work, and/or their own personal preferences" (Martin, 2002, p. 150). Others have also suggested that special interests and other school personnel have dictated the school counselor's agenda (Walz & Bleuer, 1997).

The TSCI focused specifically on revising school counselor preparation in an effort to participate in national educational reform. This initiative asserts that school counselors need to be trained as leaders in their school and set academic achievement for all students, and especially minority students, as the top outcome priority (The Education Trust, 1999). The focus on academics is in response to glaring achievement gaps between white and minority students, and the importance of testing and "adequate yearly progress" as required by No Child Left Behind (NCLB) Act (Martin, 2002). Also, an academic focus is needed to advocate against disproportional placement of low-income and minority students in special-education and remedial curriculum (Martin, 2002). The TSCI offers a significant modification of current school counselor preparation models that focus primarily on traditional functions such as individual and group counseling. Leadership, advocacy, program development, and brokering services are all new school-counselor functions that the TSCI promotes.

Similar to the TSCI, another contemporary influence on school counselor preparation is the 2001 CACREP standards. This most recent revision of the CACREP standards require curricular experiences that emphasize newer school counselor functions like leadership and advocacy, and topics such as systemic theories, opportunities and barriers, and competencies that promote student success. For example, CACREP now requires experiences in "strategies of leadership designed to enhance the learning environment of schools" and the "relationship of the school counseling program to the academic and student services program in the school" (p. 92). Other curricular revisions include "identification of student academic, career, and personal/social competencies and the implementation of processes and activities to assist students in achieving these competencies" (p. 93). The CACREP standards are scheduled to be revised again in 2008 and most likely will continue to influence the evolution of school counselor preparation.

Finally, the recent ASCA National Model (2003), which incorporates the popular and widespread Comprehensive Developmental Guidance Program model (Gysbers & Henderson, 2000), reflects another potential contemporary influence on school counselor preparation. Data are not yet available on the impact of the National Model on school counselor preparation. Even so, being the first model to emerge from the national professional association and with responsiveness to the accountability trend for educational reform, it seems likely to impact the preparation of school counselors. These contemporary influences (change in the teaching experience requirement, TSCI, CACREP Standards, ASCA National Model) help shape SBSC in the intentional teaching about and increased use of indirect or systemic services and focus on accountability. At the same time, they also add to the complexity of the school counselor identity issue, increase demands on school counselor preparation, and yet again raise the question of the precise school counselor role.

PREPARING THE STRENGTHS-BASED SCHOOL COUNSELOR

Although education and school counselor reform continue, to date standards and revisions of school counselor preparation are still based primarily on function or services (e.g., to deliver individual counseling, group counseling, classroom guidance, advocacy) rather than on a vision of a role. Our informal review of many school counseling programs suggests that classes are often offered around one of the functions that school counselors are expected to perform (e.g., group counseling, consultation, individual counseling). This traditional focus on functions or services (process) contributes to the unresolved debate about the role of the school counselor.

Ideally, counselor functions or actions should be conceptualized around an overarching role (foundation) and the outcomes that these functions are designed to produce. Although school counselors in practice provide education, guidance, individual and group counseling, and advocacy, all of these functions are essentially centered on student development. In SBSC, the role of the school counselor is focused on developmental promotion (e.g., the six principles outlined in Chapter 1). The specific functions are the means by which the role is implemented (outlined in Chapter 2) and employed differently depending on student developmental needs and the specific school context.

Even though a developmental framework may be the key in distinguishing counseling from other social occupations, developmental theory has not been the focus of many school counseling programs (Ivey & Goncalves, as cited in Granello & Hazler, 1998). In general, some contemporary school counseling role statements (e.g., TSCI) have neither been focused on development nor informed by contemporary developmental research. Criticism has also been raised about a shift toward a role solely focused on academic achievement. For example, authors have noted that personal and social development should not be underemphasized in response to pressure to raise test scores (Whiston, 2002b), school counselors should not be held accountable for test scores (Sink, 2002), and riding the wave of educational reform may not be useful (Borders, 2002).

Green and Keys (2001) suggested that outmoded counselor education or outright neglect of developmental principles may be partially responsible for role ambiguity. In fact, ACES (1990) specifically targeted curricular weaknesses in "developmentally based intervention strategies" in school counselor programs in its recommendations. Although school counselors must be responsive to reform efforts such as NCLB and be cognizant that academic *development* is an essential focus, the school counselor's role should center on promoting positive youth development and be based on contemporary developmental research. This position is exemplified in Chapter 4, which outlines research important to promoting academic *development*. Additionally, because the areas of academic, career, and personal/social development interact and are mutually influential, a more inclusive focus on positive youth development is most appropriate. Without this core focus, school counselors negate the unique, complementary, and necessary contribution they can provide to students, parents, educators, and schools themselves. This chapter will illustrate how the core principles of SBSC can be operationalized in school-counselor preparation.

INTEGRATION OF STRENGTHS-BASED SCHOOL COUNSELING IN THE CACREP CURRICULUM

Change in school counselor education historically has been about "adding-on" new content or skills to an already extensive curriculum. What is needed instead is a clear articulation of vision (Martin, 2002). Rather than continuing to add to the curriculum, implementing the SBSC framework prioritizes and enhances aspects of CACREP requirements for school counselor preparation. Although CACREP standards lack a significant evidence base that demonstrates the necessity and utility of these standards, we utilize CACREP standards for school counselor preparation as a framework in this chapter because they are most visible in the counseling profession and have been created by a collection of scholars. As such, they represent a collective view of ideal counselor preparation. The following shows how a CACREP-type school counseling program might incorporate SBSC.

Prerequisite courses that establish a common organizational framework should center on the principles of SBSC. Three CACREP core areas in particular provide the opportunity to cover the SBSC principles of context-based development (human growth and development, social and cultural diversity), orientation to strengths and strengths-enhancing environments (professional identity), and evidence-based practice (professional identity). These CACREP core areas (professional identity, human growth and development, and social and cultural diversity) are often represented in individual and distinct courses in school counselor education programs. Preparing strengths-based school counselors not only requires a comprehensive focus on these singular courses, but also an infusion of content from these three SBSC areas throughout the curriculum and in clinical experiences. Creating a theoretically strong professional identity based on culturally relevant and evidence-based developmental promotion is critical for clarity in the school counselor's role.

Not only is infusion of key principles programmatically important, but sequencing and focusing other courses for preservice school counselors is also critical (Hayes & Paisley, 2002). As Hayes, Dagley, and Horne (1996) suggested, graduate-student mastery and skill development require active engagement that promotes a developmental path to learning. As illustrated in Fig. 8–1, research and assessment course work is a necessary complement or precursor to academic and career development course work to ensure students'

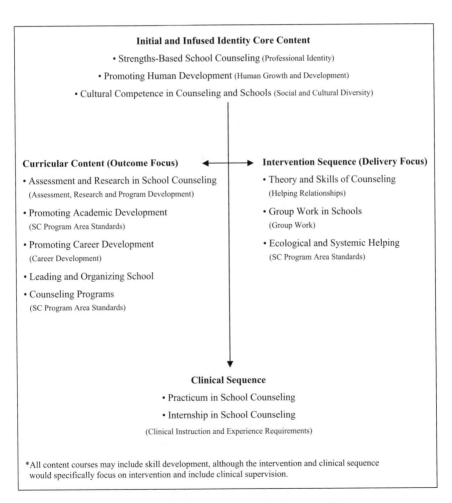

Initial and Infused Identity Core Content

• Strengths-Based School Counseling (Professional Identity)

• Promoting Human Development (Human Growth and Development)

• Cultural Competence in Counseling and Schools (Social and Cultural Diversity)

Curricular Content (Outcome Focus)

• Assessment and Research in School Counseling
(Assessment, Research and Program Development)

• Promoting Academic Development
(SC Program Area Standards)

• Promoting Career Development
(Career Development)

• Leading and Organizing School

• Counseling Programs
(SC Program Area Standards)

Intervention Sequence (Delivery Focus)

• Theory and Skills of Counseling
(Helping Relationships)

• Group Work in Schools
(Group Work)

• Ecological and Systemic Helping
(SC Program Area Standards)

Clinical Sequence

• Practicum in School Counseling

• Internship in School Counseling

(Clinical Instruction and Experience Requirements)

*All content courses may include skill development, although the intervention and clinical sequence would specifically focus on intervention and include clinical supervision.

FIGURE 8–1.   Sample SBSC Program of Studies (2001 CACREP requirements in parentheses).

abilities as consumers of evidence-based practice. In the assessment course for example, students need to learn about the assessment matrix (e.g., strengths/ risks X individuals/systems) and the associated assessment instruments used by school counselors; while in the research course, they need to learn about the importance of data collection and the type of data to collect (e.g., outcomes) in order to evaluate the services they provide. This sequence enables them to do program evaluation and research on the strength-based interventions they use in their clinical (e.g., practicum and internship) work (accountability). The academic and career-development course work also focus on promoting strengths, strengths-enhancing environments, and the outcomes that school counselors are trying to produce at the school level, rather than focusing on the types of services (e.g., individual counseling, classroom guidance) that they deliver.

Although Fig. 8–1 illustrates a sample SBSC program, this type of sequencing has relevance for institutions with students in multiple counseling tracks as well. While career development has been a traditional core area in all counseling tracks, academic development is more reflective of school counselor program area standards in CACREP and aligns school counselor preparation with educational reform and the academic mission of schools. Even so, all counseling students can benefit from a purposeful sequence in which a research/ program evaluation base is established prior to engaging in practice in other core areas (such as marriage, family and couples counseling, addictions counseling) because that sequence emphasizes the importance of evidence-based practice and accountability in counseling generally.

For school counseling students, the core courses then can culminate in a course focused on organizing and leading school counseling services. This course can explore the SBSC framework as applied to comprehensive school counseling models (e.g., the ASCA National Model) and serve as a culmination of content-based courses in the curriculum. For example, students in the course can apply strengths-based and context-based developmental theories to the foundation component of the ASCA National Model in order to construct a comprehensive program based on SBSC.

Similar to the way core courses are sequenced, intervention-based classes can be sequenced to emphasize promoting individual strengths (through direct service) and evidence-based practice (e.g., collecting pre-post data for the services provided) as a precursor to promoting strengths-enhancing environments (indirect service) with associated data collection. This sequence is sensitive to the professional development of counselors and builds competence in more traditional functions (e.g., individual and group counseling) that seek to build client strengths before expanding to more complex system-wide efforts (e.g., advocacy, leadership) that target strengths-enhancing environments. This may be of particular importance today as many preservice school counselors may have limited to no experience in the school context. For example, a strengths-based theory and skills of individual counseling course (helping relationships) should precede group work. This intervention-centered sequence would then culminate with ecological or systemic helping, a course that represents some of the CACREP core (e.g., consultation) but is also based on a variety of standards in the CACREP school program area. For example, coordination, collaboration, referral, and team-building efforts that promote program objectives and facilitate successful student development and achievement of all students are relevant means to promote strengths-enhancing environments within CACREP requirements for school counselors. This type of intentional prioritizing and sequencing of core and intervention-based courses throughout the curriculum provides a developmental learning progression for knowledge and skills as they relate to SBSC principles.

Another important aspect is how SBSC principles can be integrated into core courses, and how these courses can be focused for school counselors. The next section of this chapter explores examples of how infusion can be achieved.

The Strengths-Based School Counselor (Professional Identity)

As mentioned previously, several scholars have written that professional identity may be one of the most crucial, and yet debated aspects of school counselor preparation. Paisley and Borders (1995) called school counseling an "evolving specialty" and as a result of societal trends, school counselors "find themselves too frequently in a reacting role" (p. 153). School counselors often find themselves in an "unrealistic position of trying to be all things to all people" (Paisley & McMahon, 2001, p. 107). Instead, Paisley and McMahon indicated "it is crucial that school counselors focus their role within the school" (p. 110). Others have also advocated for more clarity and vision in the school counselor role (House & Hayes, 2002) in both purpose and mission (Herr, 2001).

In courses that address professional identity (e.g., Introduction to Counseling), counseling students are able to track the history and evolution of the core theme of development in counseling. For example, Sweeney (2001) noted the historical roots in both a development and wellness orientation in professional identity. Through an examination of professional organizations (APGA to AACD to ACA), licensure and credentials, and counselor's relationships with other professionals, the evolution of the school counselor role is put in context.

In addition to reading about counseling's foundation in development, an important way to encourage a focus on developmental promotion is to stimulate new graduate students to think deeply about and articulate why they chose counseling as a profession. School counseling students typically share stories about an influential school counselor in their own lives, how they feel passionate about helping others, or perhaps that they want to help students beyond traditional instruction in the classroom. Faculty can facilitate discussion related to this assignment around specifically what *strengths or competence* their own school counselor helped promote within them and what *outcomes* they want to see in students. Noting the competence one felt or observed in others centers students on a role in promoting strengths. A similar discussion can originate about the types of *strength-enhancing environments* students feel passionate about cultivating in schools, as well as the specific classrooms and other school settings that enhanced their own development. This is particularly relevant with students without prior working experience in K–12 schools. While this type of guided discussion may be common in introductory courses, often the discussion is problem-focused (e.g., how a problem was resolved) rather than centered on the principles of SBSC (e.g., developmental promotion, strengths, strengths-enhancing environments, evidence-based practices).

Another useful assignment is to engage students in conceptions (e.g., research papers, presentations) of the "role of the school counselor." Faculty can introduce and explain the six core principles of SBSC and discuss how they define and shape the school counselor role and how the school counseling preparation program itself seeks to prepare students to implement the school counselor role. For example, school counselor educators can (a) emphasize evidence-based practice by including reviews of school counseling outcome research (e.g., Whiston & Sexton, 1998), (b) reference various outcome research centers emerging in school counseling (e.g., UMass, ASCA, University of San Diego), and (c) comment on evidence-based practices that emerge from school psychology, educational psychology, social work, and a variety of fields. Faculty can also introduce current developments (e.g., NCLB) and initiatives (see comprehensive school reform in Chapter 4) in educational reform and specifically share how school counselor developmental advocacy at the building level should focus on promoting strengths and strengths-enhancing environments. This type of introduction to the role of the school counselor is essential and further emphasized through instruction and learning about context-based development.

Promoting Human Development (Human Growth and Development)

As highlighted throughout the book, this particular CACREP core curricular area is the most salient for SBSC. Most school counseling programs are built on traditional foundations such as developmental guidance (Myrick, 1997). Most existing developmental school counseling models emphasize stage theories for the various realms of development (e.g., cognitive, physical, social, moral) or developmental tasks to be accomplished at appropriate times. Research on stage theories and developmental tasks has certainly provided a foundation for and shaped school counselor preparation (Paisley, 2001), but most applied research in development has then focused on developmental delays, problems, and risks. This seems particularly true for other counseling program tracks (e.g., community counseling, mental-health counseling) and has specifically influenced school counselor preparation to emphasize a risk and remediation orientation to development.

The "leading developmental theories that might provide a foundation for counseling practice are at best incomplete" (Lapan, 2001, p. 293). School counseling needs to evolve beyond a reliance on traditional developmental themes, as the traditional themes are not sufficient to address many complex factors of development (Green & Keys, 2001). Paisley (2001, p. 275) proposed that "school counseling programs have as their purpose promotion of development . . . to serve as developmental specialists . . . and incorporate the best-known information from developmental principles as a method for promoting success." Further, Whiston (2002b, p. 152) observed that "theoretical and empirical advancements in childhood and adolescent development are occurring, but this information needs to be more consistently applied to school counseling programs."

Rather than reiterate the research presented in the first six chapters of the book (e.g., the types of evidence-based, developmental strengths and strength-enhancing environments that should complement traditional stage-development theories in human growth and development course work), it is important to note that this newer developmental content aligns with CACREP requirements and is relevant for all programs. For example, CACREP requires instruction in "strategies that facilitating optimum development over the life-span" as part of the human growth-and-development core. These more contemporary theories of human development (e.g., developmental contextualism) take into account the systems and cultural factors that constitute major developmental influences.

Cultural Competence in Counseling and Schools (Social and Cultural Diversity)

Although human development encompasses much of the context-based development principles of SBSC, social and cultural diversity (defined broadly) related course work enables preservice school counselors to learn and reflect on important aspects of context and how they impact strengths and strengths-enhancing environments. Also, demographic trends in schools, the limited diversity in the school counseling profession (e.g., gender and race), and emerging research on multicultural competencies make this area a priority. Increasing preservice school counselors' awareness of their own cultural and contextual influences, knowledge of other cultures and contexts, and counseling skills that are culturally relevant enables school counselors to be more effective in today's diverse schools. In terms of school counselor development, cultural competency is actually framed as a strength orientation. Lee's (2001) concept of a "student development facilitator" (p. 259) includes a school counselor who is culturally sensitive, promotes positive self-identity, and facilitates school staff professional development in cultural relations.

CACREP standards are often interpreted to give race and ethnicity primary attention in social and cultural diversity curriculum. Attention to race and ethnic identity development is absent in most comprehensive developmental school counseling programs (Sink & MacDonald, 1998). School counselors need to learn techniques that promote concepts such as racial or cultural-identity development (Akos & Ellis, in press; Day-Vines, Patton, & Baytops, 2003) and programs that seek to build strengths for diverse students (see Chapter 5).

Context-based development also includes the types of peer groups and classroom and school environments that contribute to or detract from cultivating students strengths. As part of the social and cultural diversity core, CACREP requires instruction about factors such as disabilities, sexual orientation, socioeconomic status, as well as characteristics of families and communities. Not only will preservice school counselors need to learn about the risks for and laws (e.g., sexual harassment) that protect sexual-minority students, but they also need to learn about techniques to facilitate positive sexual identities and school climates that are supportive of differences. Bemak (2002) forecasted that teachers and schools will look to school counselors in regard to how the school culture is affected by cultural differences, race relations, and learning styles. School counselors in particular must "collaboratively determine what optimal development is in cultural context" (Granello, 2002, p. 1).

Although these notions of promoting school counselors' own awareness, knowledge, and skills may be typical of pedagogy in school counseling, strengths-based school counselors will also need to learn specific strategies and be aware of research on effective programs that promote the cultural competence of K–12 students and school environments that capitalize on cultural strengths and diversity. While evidence-based programs are not abundant in the literature, Chapter 5 outlines relevant concepts, and ongoing monitoring of emerging research should provide important information. Again, Lee (2001) noted the necessity for school counselors to play a large role in building culturally responsive schools.

For example, preservice school counselors can be taught to examine data about the importance of minority enrollment in advanced curriculum (e.g., TSCI reforms). Research about tracking has shown that low-ability tracks are essentially "social spaces" that are often dominated by low-income and minority students (Gamoran, 1992). School counselors will have to help teachers create classroom environments (social spaces) in advanced academic classes that are more welcoming and supportive of diverse enrollment, and perhaps promote teaching practices like differentiation that seek to support heterogeneous ability grouping. Students can examine data from local school districts or their own internship site on factors such as criteria for advanced placement, support services for students, and what classroom conditions seem to contribute to student success. While this school-based developmental advocacy would not be sufficient alone to close the achievement gap, this strengths-based approach is an important proactive step and does not stigmatize minority students with respect to achievement. This important aspect of context-based development, coupled with broader human growth and development theories and research and a professional identity formed around SBSC, builds the foundation for the rest of the core, intervention, and clinical courses.

Additional Core Infusion

Just as the content of these three traditional courses requires revision, SBSC impacts the rest of the curriculum. For example, in research and assessment, students can develop risk *and asset* profiles of both students *and school environments* (classroom, grade, or whole school) to determine the optimal place and focus (or places and foci) of interventions. In this way, students are balancing risk reduction and prevention-based interventions, with the strengths-based focus of SBSC, as well as considering the costs/benefits of intervening with individuals and small groups versus classes and systems. The assessment and research curriculum also connects well to the accountability focus in the ASCA National Model. Students can start with assessment and research on intervention with individual clients or small groups and progress to whole-program evaluation in the leading and organizing school counseling program course. This culminating course can then again examine the evidence base for the program activities, which include evaluation of the need for and effectiveness of school-based developmental advocacy. Much of the content of this book was dedicated to the research and concepts relevant to courses such as Promoting Academic Development (Chapters 3 and 4), and Promoting Career Development (Chapter 6). While extensive conceptual and research based information is presented, these are but a sample of the dynamic and expanding research base on relevant strengths, environments, and interventions.

SBSC Intervention Sequence

As important as the core curriculum, courses that focus on delivery and intervention should flow from the foundation established in prerequisite courses. Previous chapters have outlined the need to exercise initiative, leadership, and advocacy, and Chapter 2 examined the types of functions in which strengths-based school counselors engage. Preparing preservice school counselors to engage and help students in individual counseling remains a core skill for school counselors. Traditional microskills and Rogerian conditions that enhance the ability of school counselors to form relationships with students, teachers, and parents continue to be an important contribution. Placing a priority on strength-focused approaches to counseling (e.g., Solution-Focused Brief Counseling) will be important. These strengths-oriented approaches have not yet accumulated the amount of empirical evidence that problem-based approaches have, but emerging research in positive psychology and trends in clinical work hold promise. As this evidence emerges, counselor educators might also consider the use of treatment manuals and evidence-based practices as a supplement for neophyte counselors. Whiston and Coker (2000) note that counselor education needs to integrate more information on empirically validated treatments into both our curriculums and our professional identity. Unfortunately, the positive psychology movement is only just starting to develop an empirical catalogue of strengths and strengths-enhancing environments that might serve as a seminal resource (much like the problem-focused Diagnostic and Statistical Manual).

As with individual counseling, instruction in group work should include how to promote student development and strengths-enhancing environments through task groups, such as IEP meetings and other working groups in the school. School counselors can approach IEP meetings, teacher-team meetings, and school committees from a solution-focused perspective with the goal of promoting student assets and the environments that support positive youth development. Centering parents and teachers on a positive goal is a more inviting process to parents who may have had negative experience in the school and also allows them to contribute in constructing strategies for success.

Instruction on group work can also focus on positive development through strengths-building psychoeducational groups that increase tolerance and peaceful resolution of conflicts (Johnson & Johnson, 2001), using evidence-based programs such as those described in *Safe and Sound* (CASEL, 2003), or other positive youth-development programs mentioned previously. These topics can also be incorporated into classroom guidance in which developmental promotion can be connected to the curriculum. Moreover, counseling groups can be reframed for developmental promotion (e.g., family-change versus divorce groups). Thus, the content of a family-change group can focus on the benefits of new family structures and how to form new relationships within a blended family as a source of support rather than on focusing on the conflict resulting from the divorce. While these yet lack an evidence base, they align with the orientation of SBSC.

The course, Ecological and Systemic Helping, can focus on promoting evidence-based, strengths-enhancing environments through functions and programs that are supportive of youth development. This course in particular is rather novel to the traditional counselor preparation curriculum in that it should challenge and expand on ways school counselors think about change and intervention. For example, school counselors and counselor educators are much less likely to be familiar with existing theoretical perspectives that can effectively guide intervention at the systems and ecological level as compared with those that guide intervention in individual and group counseling. Further, as noted previously, many school counseling students may enter programs with limited or no knowledge of school culture of how the school system functions. Yet, a sound conceptual/theoretical framework may be even more instrumental to the school counselor in facilitating change and strengths-enhancing environments at these levels. While a complete discussion of this topic is beyond the scope of this chapter, a systems-ecological perspective (Fine, 1992), multisystemic intervention plans (Henggeler, Schoenwald, Borduin, Rowland, & Cunningham, 1998), and systems psychology in the schools (Plas, 1986) provide three examples of conceptual guides for environmental level-interventions. These conceptual frameworks will be extremely helpful to the counselor educator in preparing school counselors to be skillful change agents.

A systemic-ecological perspective views student behavior as purposeful adaptation of the individual to the interactive relationships in his or her environment. In order to understand an individual's behavior from a systems perspective, one focuses on the context in which the behavior occurs and the reciprocal influences between the student and all of the persons who are connected with the situation (Fine, 1992). This focus, which emphasizes recurring circular or reciprocal processes or patterns within the context in which the student is embedded, is in marked contrast to the focus that has traditionally been emphasized in school counseling. The traditional focus emphasizes the student's individual psychological development and a simple linear (e.g., uni-directional) cause-effect or stimulus-response view of student behavior and development. In the traditional focus, the locus of problem behavior is primarily viewed as residing within the student or, at most, as resulting from simple reinforcement of maladaptive behavior by the student's environment (e.g., the student who is having difficulty learning to read is acting out to get attention). In contrast, from a system perspective, "disturbed or problem behavior of a child is considered to be a symptom of a dysfunctional system, including the fit of the setting(s) to the child" (Fine, 1992, p. 15). Moreover, unlike the traditional focus in helping *students* change, school counselors must also examine how relationships, boundaries, patterns of interaction, dysfunctional sequences, and the functionality of the *systems* around children might be altered. The emphasis is on creating a better fit between the student and the learning environment (e.g., the student who is having difficulty learning to read may learn faster and behave more appropriately with a different teacher, in a different classroom-learning environment, and with a different instructional approach). As such, ". . . the environment must be given attention equal to that shown to the individual. . . ." (Fine, 1992, p. 8).

Thus, systemic and ecological models of intervention challenge the school counselor's traditional linear thinking of causality. School counselors must instead assess systems as units of study and units of intervention, and how these nested systems (e.g., student within peer group within classroom within school) interact and change during intervention (Plas, 1986). In effect, the cause of a behavior is less important than the search for rules that govern interaction within the system. Keys and Lockhart (1999) asserted that multisystemic interventions require school counselors to view student behavior change as interactive and circular within peer groups, classrooms, and schools. Even though a school counselor might find utility in working individually with a student on homework completion, intervention with the teachers (e.g., type of homework assigned), family (e.g., setting aside appropriate space and monitoring homework), and homework policy (e.g., amount or type of homework assigned) also may be required for meaningful and sustained change. Plas (1986) draws on systemic family therapy to suggest that intervention should seek to effect nodal points, or the places where the optimal number of functions within a system converge. This type of thinking about the utility and importance of systemic intervention or indirect service may be in contrast with the ASCA National Model (80% direct-service recommendation) and most traditional thinking about intervention (individual counseling skills).

Urie Bronfenbrenner (1979) in his classic book, *The Ecology of Human Development: Experiments in Nature and Design*, outlined four systems (microsystem, mesosystem, exosystem, and macrosystem) that describe how individual relationships in peer groups, classrooms, and families interact with one another within a large system like the school itself or the cultural norms associated with the school. The microsystem refers to interactions in systems such as the classroom, the family, and the school in which the student is directly involved. In contrast, the mesosystem involves interrelationships among the student's various microsystems. The exosystem refers to the transportation system, government agencies and other societal institutions and structures, while the macrosystem is the general cultural system of which all of these other systems are parts. Because interactions between and among these systems impact students and, in turn, are impacted by them, school counselors need to think of change in terms of multisystemic intervention in order to cultivate strengths-enhancing environments. However, the locus of most of these systemic interventions is likely to be the micro- and mesosystems (Fine, 1992), and this locus is entirely compatible with SBSC.

Figure 8–2 presents an example of school-based prevention plans for dating or relationship violence based on the Bronfrenbrenner model that a school counselor might consider (Chronister, McWhirter, & Kerewsky, 2004). These authors use a case example of Smith Middle School to illustrate ecological practices that are based in research and focus on person-environment interactions and the use of strengths. For example, school counselor actions at the microsystem level focus on increasing student awareness and competencies (e.g., assertiveness, conflict resolution) to empower them to build healthy relationships and make positive changes in their school environments (McWhirter et al., 2004). "Interventions at the mesosystemic level may include increasing students' identification of people and communities that are sources of support as well as increasing their use of these available resources" (Chronister, McWhirter, & Kerewsky, 2004, p. 326). This type of multi-level systemic intervention, utilized here to promote healthy relationships, is an important extension of traditional school-counselor action.

Ecological Level	Examples of Best Prevention Practice With Smith Middle School
Macrosystem	• Identify and address influence of adolescents' community, culture gender roles, media, peers, and societal messages about sex and dating • Facilitate counselor awareness of how adolescent development and urban culture may influence effectiveness of traditional therapy approaches
Exosystem	• Identify ecological influence of educational and school policies on curriculum, availability of counselors, and campus safety • Identify relationship violence resources for adolescents and their families • Facilitate counselor, school, and students working together for social change regarding relationship violence, public policy, and the provision and allocation of resources to youth
Mesosystem	• Identify and facilitate students' connections with community resources • Include family, teachers, school officials, and community members in prevention program • Identify and consider mesosystemic relationships and influences
Microsystem	• Facilitate students' awareness and understanding of healthy and unhealthy relationships • Facilitate students' abilities to identify emotional, mental, physical, and spiritual dating violence • Facilitate students' awareness and identification of ecological factors, across all system levels, impacting their individual and social development • Facilitate counselor critical consciousness, self-reflection, and power analysis, across all ecological system levels
Individual	• Facilitate students' awareness of their strengths, skills, and power to make changes within their relationships • Facilitate students' identification and examination of their own academic, personal, and interpersonal goals

FIGURE 8–2. Sample Ecological Prevention Plan. Reprinted from Chronister, K., McWhirter, B., & Kerewsky, S. (2004). Counseling and ecological practice. In R. Conyne & E. Cook (Eds), *Ecological counseling: An innovative approach to conceptualizing person-environment interaction.* Alexandria, VA: American Counseling Association, p. 324. © American Counseling Association. Reprinted with permission. No further reproduction without written permission from the American Counseling Association.

A starting point for faculty can be a focus on resiliency and developmental assets as a basis for helping counseling students learn how to restructure school environments to promote positive youth development. For example, in promoting preservice school counselor knowledge and skills to "facilitate educational transitions" (CACREP, 2001, p. 93), curriculum can be designed to help students explore interventions such as STEP (Felner et al., 1993) that demonstrate methods of shaping the structure of the student-teacher relationships in the high-school ecology to promote more success in the transition to high school (see Chapter 4). STEP undoubtedly capitalizes on a variety of resiliency factors and developmental assets such as providing caring and support, prosocial bonding, opportunities for meaningful participation, high expectations, and clear boundaries.

In general, Fine (1992) outlined structural (e.g., drawing clearer boundaries, breaking dysfunctional alliances) and strategic (e.g., reframing behavior, specific strategies) approaches as two alternatives that school counselors can use to influence the ecology of a school. For example, developing, promoting, and even co-coordinating developmentally appropriate extracurricular activities (see Chapter 2) is a structural approach (Fine, 1992) that fosters more opportunities for meaningful relationships and engagement in school. Coordinating programs such as peer mediation and peer mentoring are prime examples of strategic intervention (Fine, 1992) that seek to utilize peers in supportive and more functional ways. Counselor preparation in consultation, collaboration, and coordination should also focus on building a school climate that promotes prosocial bonding, high expectations, and meaningful opportunities for students to participate in their schools and community (Henderson & Milstein, 1996).

In summary, the intervention preparation sequence that we are suggesting helps to build school counseling students' competencies developmentally. That is, the sequence progresses from individual to group to more systemic or ecological interventions, capitalizes on school counselors access to and leverage with systems (e.g., peers, classrooms, school culture), and, in the process, provides students with a broader intervention perspective than is currently developed in most school counseling programs.

Clinical Course Integration and Supervision

The school counselor role is implemented by preservice school counselors in clinical practice in practicum and internship. A year-long, intensive internship experience (either full- or part-time) may be most appropriate for the strengths and strengths-enhancing environment building that school counselors will do. Influencing and restructuring environments require intimate familiarity with the school ecology and the related processes and politics associated with schools. For example, getting approval, buy-in, and funding for particular programs (e.g., peer mediation) requires school counselors to utilize relationships of influence and present evidence-based proposals that show the importance of programs for the overall school mission. "Counselor training programs providing early and frequent practice along with theory were considered by practitioners to be the best models for preparation for working in the schools" (Martin, 2002, p. 150). Although concerns about teachers' inability or unwillingness to give up full-time employment shifted CACREP guidelines from requiring full-time internships (Pate, 1990; Smaby & D'Andrea, 1995), it seems debatable whether students can learn to negotiate the political system or ecology of the school, or "perform, under supervision, a variety of counseling activities that a professional counselor is expected to perform" (CACREP, 2001, p. 67) in after school, summer, or snapshot experiences.

In a year-long, intensive field experience in the school, counseling interns can start by building competence in counseling (individual and group), completing developmental risk and asset profiles in case conceptualization, practice and refine counseling skills, create and deliver classroom-guidance curriculum (e.g., Second Step), and utilize racial-identity development or family-change groups to build experience through supervised practice. Requirements for indirect service then can be assigned in the second half of the year and might include designing multisystemic intervention plans, efforts to restructure parts of the school environment (e.g., positive-behavior support programs), or identifying opportunities to advocate for a student (or group of students) and to form an advocacy plan for one of these opportunities. In the process, interns can be instructed about appropriate ways to plan and deliver an advocacy intervention and can implement it under close supervision by site and faculty supervisors.

Dollarhide and Miller (2006) described supervision as a rite of passage, "the means by which . . . trainees explore their new professional identities in preparation for induction into their profession" (pp. 242–243). Traditional school counseling supervision generally has been labeled as inadequate (few trained supervisors, supervision from non-counselors) (Dollarhide & Miller), and most practicing school counselors that serve as supervisors for preservice school counselors have been trained under traditional models of counselor preparation. It is therefore incumbent upon counselor education faculty to prepare and mentor school-based supervisors in SBSC principles. Several authors in a recent special issue of *Counselor Education and Supervision* explored supervision of the systemic aspects of school counselor work (Wood & Rayle, 2006) and supervision of students without teaching experience (Peterson & Deuschle, 2006). Both examine elements of school counselor supervision that begin to align with systemic or environmental components of SBSC. Counselor-education faculty will also have to provide supervision on the systemic aspects of school counseling, as well as provide insight and direction in strengths-based and evidence-based practices.

SUMMARY

Sequencing and infusing the SBSC principles is relevant for all counseling program areas, although it may be more challenging to implement these reforms in school-counseling preparation programs taught in departments with multiple-counselor preparation tracks. Most often, school counselor preparation programs offer a "generic counseling" orientation (Martin, 2002), a limitation of school counselor preparation as viewed by the Educational Trust and TSCI reforms. Further, Perusse, Goodnough, and Noel (2001) found that few courses in school counseling programs are designed specifically for school counseling students. When multiple tracks (e.g., community counselors, marriage, family, and couples counseling) are represented in institutions, setting or population specific courses can replace or mirror school counseling specific courses (e.g., strengths-based community counseling, leading and organizing college counseling programs). Also, within courses that include students from multiple tracks, school counseling students can focus on the school context through differentiated instruction (e.g., individualized or group assignments, early field experiences, or by contextualizing learning).

For example, a group work course can include more extensive content and projects related to task groups in the school setting for preservice school counselors (Akos, Goodnough, & Milsom, 2004). While concepts such as group stages and group dynamics will be applicable for all counselors, it is important for school counselors to consider unique aspects such as leading IEP meetings, working with children and adolescents, screening and recruiting students for group work, and scheduling to minimize student's absence from academic classes. Finally, a school counseling focus might also be enhanced by teaching specific school counseling courses in a public school-based facility, thereby providing early induction to the school as a learning environment (House, Martin, & Ward, 2002). Preservice school counselors without prior experience in the school may especially benefit from informal and experiential learning in the public-school setting. This type of specificity and application of general counseling knowledge would be useful for students entering community agencies, higher education, or other settings where practice is highly context dependant. Obviously, patience and persistence is necessary for any change in higher education and institutional context and resources will dictate the appropriate means and pace for implementation of the SBSC framework.

SBSC expands and enhances developmental counseling models of school counselor preparation (e.g., Dinkmeyer & Caldwell, 1970; Myrick, 1997; Gysbers & Henderson, 2000; Wittmer, 2000). To be sure, all of these earlier developmental approaches share the common assumption that attention to overall student development is what is distinctive about school counseling as compared to other educational specialties. They view the school counselor's role as that of an applied developmental specialist. What is distinctive about the SBSC framework is its application of advocacy for developmental promotion of strengths and strengths-enhancing environments that is grounded in evidence-based practice and focused at the school level.

Just as new models continue to be developed to guide the practice of school counseling, school counselor educators must also seek to renew preparation methods and improve their models. In 1952, Hobbs suggested the need to invent some new terminology due to the confusion with guidance, and, in 1993, Hoyt expressed similar concern that counseling was not the proper word for guidance. As we have repeated in this book, role articulation is much more than semantics. The SBSC framework seeks to teach and prepare students for a professional role in school counseling that is substantive, stable, yet adaptable and one that complements the roles of other educators in order to facilitate positive youth development for all students.

KEY POINTS

Historical Influences in School Counselor Education
- NDEA (1958) helped expand school counseling greatly, while initial CACREP standards (1986) and ACES (1990) sought consistency and uniformity in school counselor preparation
- School counselor preparation has not achieved consistency or a developmental focus, resulting in role ambiguity and confusion

Contemporary Influences in School Counselor Preparation
- Variability is still common in school counselor preparation today (e.g., use of national standards, field requirements, terminology, guidance)
- The Transforming School Counseling Initiative(TSCI) focused school counselors on educational reform, specifically with preparing school counselors to impact academic achievement and eliminate achievement gaps
- 2001 CACREP standards and the ASCA National Model both point to systemic services and increase the demands on school counselor preparation

Preparing the Strengths-Based School Counselor
- Most school counselor preparation reforms still focus on function, rather than role
- In Strengths-Based School Counseling (SBSC), the role of the school counselor is focused on developmental promotion

Integration of Strenghs-Based School Counseling the CACREP Curriculum
- Rather than being an add-on, SBSC prioritizes and sequences the curriculum
- Focus is on context-based development, orientation to strengths and strengths-enhancing environments, and evidence-based practice
- Core and intervention courses are sequenced on individual strengths and interventions first, and move to environments and system-level interventions
- *The Strengths-Based School Counselor (Professional Identity)*
  - Outline the developmental roots of the profession and focus students on strengths, environments, and outcomes

- *Promoting Human Development (Human Growth and Development)*
  - Provide contemporary developmental theories and research (e.g., resiliency, developmental assets, positive psychology)
- *Cultural Competence in Counseling and Schools (Social and Cultural Diversity)*
  - Increase both the cultural competence of your preservice school counselor and his or her ability to promote cultural competence of K–12 students and school environments
  - Inclusion of racial identity theories and research and culturally appropriate, evidence-based interventions as these emerge
- *Additional Core Infusion*
  - In research and assessment courses, provide students both at-risk and asset-based focus including an accountability focus that aligns with the ASCA National Model and education reform
- *SBSC Intervention Sequence*
  - Continue, but perhaps with less emphasis, individual-based interventions such as Solution-Focused Brief Counseling and evidence-based practices
  - Provide group-work instruction on task groups from a strength-building perspective
  - Create ecological and systemic helping course work that teaches both theory (e.g., systems-ecological perspective, systems psychology, ecological development) and practice (e.g., multisystemic intervention)
- *Clinical Course Integration and Supervision*
  - Consider year-long internship experiences that enable sequential and developmental practice (e.g., from individual focused intervention to systemic or environmental plans) and that enhance student's understanding of the school ecology
  - Counselor-education faculty will also have to provide supervision on the systemic aspects of school counseling, as well as provide insight and direction in strengths-based and evidence-based practices
- *Summary*
  - SBSC can be applicable to multiple tracks (e.g., community counseling) through similar focus and sequencing and by differentiating instruction
  - SBSC expands and enhances traditional, developmental-counseling models and provides a substantial, stable, and clear role for school counselors

References

Academic Innovations. (2001). *Secretary's commission on achieving necessary skills (SCANS): Final report available.* Retrieved August 30, 2003, from www.academicinnovations.com/report

Adelman, H. S., & Taylor, L. (2001). *Framing new directions for school counselors, psychologists, and social workers.* Los Angeles: Center for Mental Health in Schools.

Adelman, H. S., & Taylor, L. (2002). School counselors and school reform: New directions. *Professional School Counseling, 5,* 235–238.

Akin-Little, K. A., Little, S. G., & Delligatti, N. (2004). A preventative model of school consultation: Incorporating perspectives from positive psychology. *Psychology in the Schools, 4,* 155–162.

Akos, P. (2002). The developmental needs of students in transition from elementary to middle school. *Professional School Counseling, 5,* 339–345.

Akos, P., & Ellis, C. (in press). Racial identity development in middle school: School counselor individual and systemic intervention. *Journal of Counseling and Development.*

Akos, P., & Galassi, J. P. (2004a). Gender and race as factors in psychosocial adjustment to middle and high school. *Journal of Educational Research, 98,* 102–108.

Akos, P., & Galassi, J. P. (2004b). Middle and high school transitions as viewed by students, parents, and teachers. *Professional School Counseling, 7,* 212–221.

Akos, P., Goodnough, G., & Milsom, A. (2004). Preparing school counselors for group work. *The Journal for Specialists in Group Work, 29*(1), 137–146.

Akos, P., Konold, T., & Niles, S. (2004). A career readiness typology and typal membership in middle school. *Career Development Quarterly, 53*(1), 53–66.

Akos, P., Queen, J., & Lineberry, C. (2005). *Promoting a successful transition to middle school.* Larchmont, NY: Eye on Education.

Akos, P., & Scarborough, J. (2004). An examination of the clinical preparation of school counselors. *Counselor Education and Supervision, 44*(4), 96–107.

Allen, J. P., Kuperminc, G. P., Philliber, S., & Herre, K. (1994). Programmatic prevention of adolescent problem behaviors: The role of autonomy, relatedness, and volunteer service in the Teen Outreach Program. *American Journal of Community Psychology, 22,* 617–638.

Allen, J. P., Philliber, S., Herrling, S., & Kuperminc, G. P. (1997). Preventing teen pregnancy and academic failure: Experimental evaluation of a developmentally based approach. *Child Development, 68,* 729–742.

Allen, J. P., Philliber, S., & Hoggson, N. (1990). School-based prevention of teenage pregnancy and school dropout: Process evaluation of the national replication of the Teen Outreach Program. *American Journal of Community Psychology, 18,* 505–524.

Alspaugh, J. W. (1998). Achievement loss associated with the transition to middle school and high school. *The Journal of Educational Research, 92,* 20–25.

Ames, C. (1992). Classrooms: Goals, structures, and student motivation. *Journal of Educational Psychology, 84*, 261–271.

American Career Resource Network. (2007). The National Career Development Guidelines. Retrieved September 1, 2006, from the World Wide Web: http://www.acrnetwork.org/ncdg.htm

American Counseling Association (ACA). (1995). *Code of ethics and standards of practice.* Alexandria, VA: Author.

American School Counselor Association. (1998). *Ethical standards for school counselors.* Alexandria, VA: Author.

American School Counselor Association. (2003). *The ASCA national model: A framework for school counseling programs.* Alexandria, VA: Author.

Amrein, A. L., & Berliner, D. C. (2002, March 28). High-stakes testing, uncertainty, and student learning. *Education Policy Analysis Archives, 10*(18). Retrieved September 16, 2002, from http://epaa.asu.edu/epaa/v10n18/

Andrews, G. R., & Debus, R. L. (1978). Persistence and the causal perception of failure: Modifying cognitive attributions. *Journal of Educational Psychology, 70*, 154–166.

Anderman, E. M., & Maehr, M. L. (1994). Motivation and schooling in the middle grades. *Review of Educational Research, 64*, 287–309.

Arce, C. A. (1981). A reconsideration of Chicano culture and identity. *Daedalus, 110*, 177–192.

Arreaga-Mayer, C., Terry, B. J., & Greenwood, C. R. (1998). Classwide peer tutoring. In K. Topping & S. Ehly (Eds.), *Peer-assisted learning* (pp. 105–119). Mahwah, NJ: Lawrence Erlbaum Associates.

Arredondo, P., & Lewis, J. (2001). Counselor roles for the 21st century. In D. C. Locke, J. E. Myers, & E. L. Herr (Eds.), *The handbook of counseling* (pp. 257–267). Thousand Oaks, CA: Sage Publications.

Arthur, M. (1994). The boundaryless career: A new perspective for organisational inquiry. *Journal of Organisational Behavior, 15*, 295–306.

Association of Counselor Education and Supervision (ACES). (1990). Standards and procedures for school counselor training and certification. *Counselor Education & Supervision, 29*, 213.

Astramovich, R. L., & Coker, J. K. (in press). Program evaluation: The Accountability Bridge Model for counselors. *Journal of Counseling & Development.*

Atkinson, D. R., Morten, G., & Sue, D. W. (1998). *Counseling American minorities: A cross cultural perpective* (5th ed.). Dubuque, IA: William C. Brown Publishers.

Aubrey, R. (1982). A house divided: Guidance and counseling in 20th century America. *The Personnel and Guidance Journal, 61*, 198–204.

Bailey, D. F., & Paisley, P. O. (2004). Developing and nurturing excellence in African American male adolescents. *Journal of Counseling & Development, 82*, 10–17.

Baker, S. B. (2001a). Reflections on forty years in the school counseling profession: Is the glass half full or half empty? *Professional School Counseling, 5*, 75–83.

Baker, S. B. (2001b). *School counseling for the twenty-first century.* Upper Saddle River, NJ: Prentice Hall.

Baker, S., & Gerler, E. (2004). *School counseling for the twenty-first century.* Upper Saddle River, NJ: Merrill.

Baker, S. B., Swisher, J. D., Nadenichek, P. E., & Popowicz, C. L. (1984). Measured effects of primary prevention strategies. *The Personnel and Guidance Journal, 62*, 487–498.

Baker, S., & Taylor, J. (1998). Effects of career education interventions: A meta-analysis. *The Career Development Quarterly, 46*, 376–385.

Bandura, A. (1977). Self-efficacy: Toward a unifying theory of behavioral change. *Psychological Review, 84*, 191–215.

Bandura, A. (1986). *Social foundations of thought and action.* Englewood Cliffs, NJ: Prentice Hall.

Bandura, A. (1997). *Self-efficacy: The exercise of control.* New York: Freeman.

Bangert-Drowns, R. L., Kulik, J. A., & Kulik, C. C. (1983). Effects of coaching programs on achievement test scores. *Review of Educational Research, 53*, 571–585.

Banks, J. A. (1981). The stages of ethnicity: Implications for curriculum reform. In J. A. Banks (Ed.), *Multi-ethnic education: Theory and practice* (pp. 129–139). Boston: Allyn and Bacon.

Banks, V. (1999). A solution focused approach to adolescent group work. *A.N.Z.J. Family Therapy, 20*, 78–82.

Barnes, J., & Herr, E. (1998). The effects of interventions on career progress. *Journal of Career Development, 24*, 179–193.

Barron, K. E., & Harackiewicz, J. M. (2001). Achievement goals and optimal motivation: Testing multiple goal models. *Journal of Personality and Social Psychology, 80*, 706–722.

Battistich, V., Watson, M., Solomon, D., Schaps, E., & Solomon, J. (1991). The Child Development Project: A comprehensive program for the development of prosocial character. In W. M. Kurtines & J. L. Gewirtz (Eds.), *Handbook of moral behavior and development: Vol. 3. Application* (pp. 1–34). Hillsdale, NJ: Lawrence Erlbaum Associates.

Beck, A. T. (1976). *Cognitive therapy and the emotional disorders.* New York: Guilford Press.

Bemak, F. (2000). Transforming the role of the counselor to provide leadership in educational reform through collaboration. *Professional School Counseling, 3*, 323–331.

Bemak, F. (2002). Paradigms for future school counseling programs. In C. Johnson & S. Johnson (Eds.), *Changing school counselor preparation: A critical need* (pp. 185–208). Alexandria, VA: ASCA.

Bemak, F., Chung, R. C., & Siroskey-Sabdo, L. A. (2005). Empowerment groups for academic success: An innovative approach to prevent high school failure for at-risk, urban African American girls. *Professional School Counseling, 8*, 377–389.

Benard, B. (1991). *Fostering resiliency in kids: Protective factors in the family, school, and community.* Portland, OR: Western Regional Center for Drug-Free Schools and Communities.

Benard, B. (1999). Mentoring: New study shows the power of relationship to make a difference. In N. Henderson, B. Benard, & N. Sharp-Light (Eds.), *Resiliency in action: Practical ideas for overcoming risks and building strengths in youth, families, & communities* (pp. 93–99). Gorham, ME: Resiliency in Action, Inc.

Benson, P. L. (1997). *All kids are our kids: What communities must do to raise caring and responsible children and adolescents.* San Francisco, CA: Jossey-Bass Publishers.

Benson, P. L., Galbraith, J., & Espeland, P. (1998). *What kids need to succeed: Proven, practical ways to raise good kids.* Minneapolis, MN: Free Spirit Publishing Inc.

Benson, P. L., Scales, P. C., & Mannes, M. (2003). Developmental strengths and their sources: Implications for the study and practice of community building. In R. M. Lerner, F. Jacobs, & D. Wertlieb (Eds.), *Handbook of applied developmental science: Vol. 1. Applying developmental science for youth and families: Historical and theoretical foundations* (pp. 369–406). Thousand Oaks, CA: Sage Publications, Inc.

Bergan, J. R., & Kratochwill, T. R. (1990). *Behavioral consultation and therapy.* New York: Plenum.

Betz, N. (1992). Counseling uses of career self-efficacy theory. *The Career Development Quarterly, 41*, 22–26.

Betz, N. (1994). Basic issues and concepts in career counseling for women. In W. Walsh & S. Osipow (Eds.), *Career counseling for women* (pp. 1–42). Hillsdale, NJ: Erlbaum.

Betz, N., & Hackett, G. (1983). The relationship of mathematics self-efficacy expectations to the selection of science-based college majors. *Journal of Vocational Behavior, 23,* 329–345.

Betz, N., & Hackett, G. (1986). Applications of self-efficacy theory to understanding career choice behavior. *Journal of Social & Clinical Psychology, 4*(3), 279–289.

Betz, N., Klein, K., & Taylor, K. (1996). Evaluation of a short form of the Career Decision-Making Self-Efficacy scale. *Journal of Career Assessment, 4,* 47–57.

Betz, N., & Luzzo, D. (1996). Career assessment and the Career Decision-Making Self-Efficacy Scale. *Journal of Career Assessment, 4*(4), 413–428.

Bloom, V. S. (1984). The 2 sigma problem: The search for methods of group instruction as effective as one-to-one tutoring. *Educational Researcher, 13,* 4–16.

Blustein, D. (1989). The role of goal instability and career self-efficacy in the career exploration process. *Journal of Vocational Behavior, 35,* 194–293.

Blustein, D., & Flum, H. (1999). A self-determination perspective of interests and exploration in career development. In M. Savickas & A. Spokane (Eds.), *Vocational interests: Meaning measurement, and counseling use* (pp. 345–368). Palo Alto, CA, US: Davies-Black Publishing.

Blustein, D., & Noumair, D. (1996). Self and identity in career development: Implications for theory and practice. *Journal of Counseling & Development, 74*(5), 433–441.

Bodiford, C. A., Eisenstadt, T. H., Johnson, J. H., & Bradlyn, A. S. (1988). Comparison of learned helpless cognitions and behavior in children with high and low scores on the Children's Depression Inventory. *Journal of Clinical Child Psychology, 17,* 152–158.

Bohanon-Edmonson, K., Flannery, B., Eber, L., & Sugai, G. (Eds.) (2005). *Positive behavior support in high schools: Monograph from the 2004 Illinois forum of positive behavioral interventions and supports.* Retrieved August 4, 2006, from http://www.pbis.org/files/PBSMonographComplete.pdf

Bolman, L. G., & Deal, T. E. (1997).*Reframing organizations: Artistry, choice, and leadership* (2nd ed.). San Francisco: Jossey-Bass.

Borders, L. D. (2002). School counseling in the 21st century: Personal and professional reflections. *Professional School Counseling, 5,* 180–185.

Borders, L. D., & Drury, S. M. (1992). Comprehensive school counseling programs: A review for policymakers and practitioners. *Journal of Counseling & Development, 70,* 487–498.

Borman, G. C., Hewes, G. M., Overman, L. T., & Brown, S. (2002). *Comprehensive school reform and student achievement: A meta-analysis.* Retrieved December 15, 2004, from http://www.csos.jhu.edu/CRESPAR/techReports/Report59.pdf

Bornstein, M. H., Davidson, L., Keyes, C. L. M., & Moore, K. A. (2003). *Well-being: Positive development across the life course.* Mahwah, NJ: Lawrence Erlbaum Associates.

Botvin, G. J. (1983). *Life skills training: Teacher's manual.* New York: Smithfield Press.

Botvin, G. J. (2000). Preventing drug abuse in schools: Social and competence enhancement approaches targeting individual-level etiologic factors. *Addictive Behaviors, 25,* 437–446.

Botvin, G. J., Baker, E., Dusenbury, L., Botvin, E. M., & Diaz, T. (1995). Long-term follow-up results of a randomized drug abuse prevention trial in a white middle-class population. *Journal of the American Medical Association, 273,* 1106–1112.

Botvin, G. J., Baker, E., Filazzola, A. D., & Botvin, E. M. (1990). A cognitive behavioral approach to substance abuse prevention: One-year follow-up. *Addictive Behaviors, 15,* 47–63.

Botvin, G. J., Baker, E., Renick, N., Filazzola, A. D., & Botvin, E. M. (1984). A cognitive-behavioral approach to substance abuse prevention. *Addictive Behaviors, 9*, 137–147.

Botvin, G. J., & Tortu, S. (1988). Preventing adolescent substance abuse through life skills training. In R. H. Price, E. L. Cowen, R. P. Lorion, & J. Ramos-McKay (Eds.), *14 ounces of prevention: A casebook for practitioners* (pp. 98–110). Washington, DC: The American Psychological Association.

Bowen, G. L., & Richman, J. M. (2001). *School success profile*. Chapel Hill: Jordan Institute for Families, School of Social Work, The University of North Carolina.

Bowen, G. L., Woolley, M. E., Richman, J. M., & Bowen, N. K. (2001). Brief intervention in schools: The school success profile. *Brief treatment and crisis intervention, 1*, 43–54.

Bowers, J. L., & Hatch, P. A. (2002). *The national model for school counseling programs: Draft*. Alexandria, VA: American School Counselor Association.

Bowers, J., Hatch, T., & Schwallie-Giddis, P. (2001, September/October). The brain storm. *ASCA School Counselor*, 17–18.

Bradley, L., & Lewis, J. (2000). Introduction. In J. Lewis & L. Borders (Eds.), *Advocacy in counseling: Counselors, clients & community* (pp. 3–4). Greensboro, NC: ERIC Clearinghouse on Counseling and Student Services.

Brigman, G., & Campbell, C. (2003). Helping students improve academic achievement and school success behavior. *Professional School Counseling, 7*, 91–98.

Brigman, G., & Goodman, B. E. (2001). Academic and social support: Student success skills. In G. Brigman & B. E. Goodman, *Group counseling for school counselors: A practical guide* (pp. 106–131). Portland, MA: J. Weston Walch.

Brody, G. H., Stoneman, Z., & Flor, D. L. (1996). Parent religiosity, family processes, and youth competence in rural two-parent African American families. *Developmental Psychology, 32*, 696–706.

Bronfenbrenner, U. (1979). *The ecology of human development*. Cambridge, MA: Harvard University Press.

Brown, D., Galassi, J. P., & Akos, P. (2004). School counselors' perceptions of the impact of high-stakes testing. *Professional School Counseling, 8*, 31–39.

Brown, S., & Lent, R. (1996). A social cognitive framework for career choice counseling. *The Career Development Quarterly, 44*, 354–366.

Buckley, M., Storino, M., & Saarni, C. (2003). Promoting emotional competence in children and adolescents: Implication for school psychologists. *School Psychology Quarterly, 18*, 177–191.

Burnham, J. J., & Jackson, J. J. (2000). School counselor roles: Discrepancies between actual practice and existing models. *Professional School Counseling, 4*, 41–49.

Campbell, C., & Brigman, G. (2005). Closing the achievement gap: A structured approach to group counseling. *Association for Specialists in Group Work, 30*(1), 67–82.

Campbell, C. A., & Dahir, C. A. (1997). *Sharing the vision: The national standards for school counseling programs*. Alexandria, VA: American School Counselor Association.

Cannon, D., & Reed, B. (1999). Career academies: Teaming with a focus. *Contemporary Education, 70*, 48–51.

Cardemil, E. V., Reivich, K. J., & Seligman, M. E. P. (2002). The prevention of depressive symptoms in low-income minority middle school students. *Prevention and Treatment, 5*, Article 8. Retrieved January 18, 2004, from http//journals.apa.org/prevention/volume5/pre0050008a.html

Carnegie Council on Adolescent Development Task Force on the Education of Young Adolescents. (1989). *Turning points: Preparing American youth for the 21st century: The report of the Task Force on Education of Young Adolescents*. Washington, DC: Author.

Carns, A. W., & Carns, M. R. (1991). Teaching study skills, cognitive strategies, and metacognitive skills through self-diagnosed learning styles. *The School Counselor, 38,* 341–346.

Carr, E. G., Dunlap, G., Horner, R. H., Koegel, R. L., Turnbull, A. P., Sailor, W., et al. (2002). Positive behavior support: Evolution of an applied science. *Journal of Positive Behavior Interventions, 4,* 4–16, 20.

Catalano, R. F., Berglund, M. L., Ryan, A. M., Lonczak, H. S., & Hawkins, J. D. (2002). Positive youth development in the United States: Research findings on evaluations of positive youth development programs. *Prevention & Treatment, 5,* Article 15. Retrieved February 3, 2003, from http://journals.apa.org/prevention/volume5/pre0050015a.html

Catalano, R. F., & Hawkins, J. D. (1996). The social development model: A theory of antisocial behavior. In J. D. Hawkins (Ed.), *Delinquency and crime: Current theories* (pp. 149–197). New York: Cambridge University Press.

Center on Positive Behavioral Interventions and Supports. (2004). *School-wide Positive Behavior Support: Implementers' blueprint and self-assessment.* Eugene: University of Oregon, Office of Special Education Programs.

Chapin, M., & Dyck, D. L. (1976). Persistence in children's reading behavior as a function of N length and attribution retraining. *Journal of Abnormal Psychology, 85,* 511–515.

Chávez, A. F., & Guido-DiBrito, F. (1999). Racial and ethnic identity and development. *New directions for adult and continuing education, 84,* 39–47.

Chavous, T. M., Bernat, D. H., Schmeelk-Cone, K., Caldwell, C. H., Kohn-Wood, L., & Zimmerman, M. A. (2003). Racial identity and academic attainment among African American adolescents. *Child Development, 74,* 1076–1090.

Child Development Project. (2004). *SAMHSA model programs: Effective substance abuse and mental health programs for every community.* Retrived December 3, 2004, from http://modelprograms.samhsa.gov/template_cf.cfm?page=model&pkProgramID=3&section=background

Christophersen, E. R., & Mortweet, S. L. (2001). *Empirically supported strategies for managing childhood problems.* Washington, DC: American Psychological Association.

Christenson, S. L., & Anderson, A. R. (2002). Commentary: The centrality of the learning context for students' academic enabler skills. *School Psychology Review, 31,* 378–393.

Christenson, S. L., & Peterson, C. J. (1998). *Family, school, and community influences on children's learning: A literature review.* Minneapolis: All Parents are Teachers Project, University of Minnesota Extension Service.

Christenson, S. L., & Sheridan, S. M. (2001). *Schools and families: Creating essential connections for learning.* New York: Guilford Press.

Chronister, K., McWhirter, B., & Kerewsky, S. (2004). Counseling and ecological practice. In R. Conyne & E. Cook (Eds.), *Ecological counseling: An innovative approach to conceptualizing person-environment interaction.* Alexandria, VA: American Counseling Association.

Chung, H., Elias, M., & Schneider, K. (1998). Patterns of individual adjustment changes during middle school transition. *Journal of School Psychology, 36,* 83–101.

Cimbricz, S. (2002, January 9). State-mandated testing and teachers' beliefs and practice. *Education Policy Analysis Archives, 10*(2). Retrieved September 16, 2002 from, http://epaa.asu.edu/epaa/v10n2

Clifton, D. (2003). Foreword. In S. J. Lopez & C. R. Snyder (Eds.), *Positive psychological assessment: A handbook of models and measures* (pp. xiii). Washington, DC: American Psychological Association.

Collaborative for Academic, Social, and Emotional Learning (CASEL). (2003). *Safe and sound: An educational leader's guide to evidence-based social and emotional learning (SEL) programs.* Chicago: University of Illinois.

Commission on Positive Youth Development. (2005). The positive perspective on youth development. In D. L. Evans, E. B. Foa, R. E. Gur, H. Hendin, C. P. O'Brien, M. E. P. Seligman, et al. (Eds.), *Treating and preventing adolescent mental health disorders: What we know and what we don't know. A research agenda for improving the mental health of our youth* (pp. 498–527). New York: Oxford University Press, Inc.

Committee for Children. (1992a). *Second step: A violence prevention curriculum; Grades 1–3.* Seattle, WA: Author.

Committee for Children. (1992b). *Second step: A violence prevention curriculum; Grades 4–5.* Seattle, WA: Author.

Committee for Children. (1997). *Second step: A violence prevention curriculum; Middle school/junior high.* Seattle, WA: Author.

Conchas, G., & Clark, P. (2002). Career academies and urban minority schooling: Forging optimism despite limited opportunity. *Journal for Education for Students Placed at Risk, 7,* 287–311.

Cook, J. B., & Kaffenberger, C. J. (2003). Solution shop: A solution-focused counseling and study skills programs for middle school. *Professional School Counseling, 7,* 116–123.

Cooper, H. (1989). *Homework.* White Plains, NY: Longman.

Cooper, H. (2001). *The battle over homework: Common ground for administrators, teachers and parents* (2nd. ed.). Thousand Oaks, CA: Corwin Press, Inc.

Cooper, H., Lindsay, J. J., & Nye, B. (2000). Homework in the home: How student, family, and parenting-style differences relate to the homework process. *Contemporary Educational Psychology, 25,* 464–487.

Cooper, H., Lindsay, J. J., Nye, B., & Greathouse, S. (1998). Relationships among attitudes about homework, amount of homework assigned and completed, and student achievement. *Journal of Educational Psychology, 90,* 70–83.

Cooper, H., & Nye, B. (1994). Homework for students with learning disabilities: The implications of research for policy and practice. *Journal of Learning Disabilities, 27,* 470–479.

Cooper, H., Valentine, J. D., Nye, B., & Lindsay, J. J. (1999). Relationships between five after-school activities and academic achievement. *Journal of Educational Psychology, 91,* 369–378.

Cornell, D. G., & Loper, A. B. (1998). Assessment of violence and other high-risk behaviors with a school survey. *School Psychology Review, 27,* 317–330.

Cosden, M., Morrison, G., Albanese, A. L., & Macias, S. (2001). When homework is not home work: After-school programs for homework assistance. *Educational Psychologist, 36,* 211–221.

Council for Accreditation of Counseling and Related Educational Programs (CACREP). (2001). *CACREP Accreditation Manual.* Alexandria, VA: American Counseling Association.

Cowen, E. L. (1994). The enhancement of psychological wellness: Challenges and opportunities. *American Journal of Community Psychology, 22,* 149–179.

Cowger, C. (1997). Assessing client strengths: Assessment for client empowerment. In D. Saleebey (Ed.), *The strengths perspective in social work practice* (2nd ed., pp. 59–73). White Plains, NY: Longman.

Craighead, L. W., Craighead, W. E., Kazdin, A. E., & Mahoney, M. J. (1994). *Cognitive and behavioral interventions: An empirical approach to mental health problems.* Boston: Allyn and Bacon.

Crites, J. (1971). Acquiescence response style and the Vocational Development Inventory. *Journal of Vocational Behavior, 2,* 189–200.

Crites, J. (1974). A reappraisal of vocational appraisal. *Vocational Guidance Quarterly, 22*, 272–279.

Crites, J. (1976). A comprehensive model of career development in early childhood. *Journal of Vocational Behavior, 9*, 105–116.

Crites, J., & Savickas, M. (1996). Revision of the career maturity inventory. *Journal of Career Assessment, 4*(2), 131–138.

Crockett, L., Peterson, A., Graber, J., Schulenberg, J., & Ebata, A. (1989). School transitions and adjustment during early adolescence. *Journal of Early Adolescence, 9*, 181–210.

Cross, W. E., Jr. (1971). The Negro-to-black conversion experience. *Black World, 29*(9), 13–27.

Cross, W. E., Jr.(1991). *Shades of black: Diversity in African American identity.* Philadelphia: Temple University Press.

Crozier, S. (1999). Women's career development in a "relational context." *International Journal for the Advancement of Counselling, 21*, 231–247.

Dahir, C. A. (2001). The national standards for school counseling programs: Development and implementation. *Professional School Counseling, 4*, 320–327.

Dahir, C. A., & Stone, C. B. (2003). Accountability: A M.E.A.S.U.R.E. of the impact school counselors have on student achievement. *Professional School Counseling, 6*, 214–225.

Dahlsgaard, K., Peterson, C., & Seligman, M. (2001). *Values In Action Inventory of Strengths for Youth (VIA-Y).* Retrieved December 7, 2004 from http://www.authentichappiness.org/perl/Children.pl

DAP. (2004). *Developmental Assets Profile.* Retrieved December 7, 2004 from http://www.search-institute.org/surveys/dap.html

Day-Vines, N. L., Patton, J. M., & Baytops, J. L. (2003). Counseling African American adolescents: The impact of race, culture, and middle class status. *Professional School Counseling, 7*, 40–51.

Deci, E. L., & Ryan, R. (1985). *Intrinsic motivation and self-determination in human behavior.* New York: Plenum Press.

Deci, E. L., Vallerand, R. J., Pelletier, L. G., & Ryan, R. M. (1991). Motivation and education: The self-determination perspective. *Educational Psychologist, 26*, 325–346.

deShazer, S. (1985). *Keys to solution in brief therapy.* New York: Norton.

Developmental Studies Center. (2004). *Summary of evaluation findings on the Child Development Project.* Retrieved December 7, 2004, from http://www.devstu.org/cdp/pdfs/cdp_eval_summary.pdf

Dimmitt, C. (2003). Transforming school counseling practice through collaboration and the use of data: A study of academic failure in high school. *Professional School Counseling, 6*, 340–349.

Dinkmeyer, D., & Caldwell, E. (1970). *Developmental counseling and guidance: A comprehensive school approach.* New York: McGraw-Hill.

DiPerna, J. C., & Elliott, S. N. (1999). Development and validation of the academic competence evaluation scales. *Journal of Psychoeducational Assessment, 17*, 207–225.

DiPerna, J. C., & Elliott, S. N. (2002). Promoting academic enablers to improve student achievement: An introduction to the mini-series. *School Psychology Review, 31*, 293–297.

DiPerna, J. C., Volpe, R. J., & Elliott, S. N. (2002). A model of academic enablers and elementary reading/language arts achievement. *School Psychology Review, 31*, 298–312.

Dodge, K. A., & Frame, C. L. (1982). Social cognitive biases and deficits in aggressive boys. *Child Development, 53*, 620–635.

Dollarhide, C. T. (2003). School counselors as program leaders: Applying leadership contexts to school counseling. *Professional School Counseling, 6*, 304–308.

Dollarhide, C., & Miller, G. (2006). Supervision for preparation and practice of school counselors: Pathways to excellence. *Counselor Education & Supervision, 45*, 242–252.

Dollarhide, C. T., & Saginak, K. A. (2003). *School counseling in the secondary school: A comprehensive process and programs.* Boston: Allyn and Bacon.

Dougherty, E. H., & Dougherty, A. (1977). The daily report card: A simplified and flexible package for classroom behavior management. *Psychology in the Schools, 14*, 191–195.

Dunn, R., Deckinger, E. L., Withers, P., & Katzenstein, H. (1990). Should college students be taught how to do homework? The effects of stydying marketing trough individual perceptual strengths. *Illinois School Research and Development, 26*, 96–113.

Dunn, R., & Dunn, K. (1992). *Teaching elementary students through their individual learning styles: Practical approaches for grades 3–6.* Boston: Allyn & Bacon.

Dunn, R., & Dunn, K. (1993). *Teaching secondary students through their individual learning styles: Practical approaches for grades 7–12.* Boston: Allyn & Bacon.

Durlak, J. A., Fuhrman, T., & Lampman, C. (1991). Effectivenss of cognitive-behavior therapy for maladapting children: A meta-analysis. *Psychological Bulletin, 110*, 204–214.

Dweck, C. S. (1975). The role of expectations and attributions in the alleviation of learned helplessness. *Journal of Personality and Social Psychology, 31*, 674–685.

Dweck, C. S., & Leggett, E. L. (1988). A social-cognitive approach to motivation and personality. *Psychological Review, 95*, 256–273.

Eccles, J., & Gootman, J. A. (Eds.). (2002). *Community programs to promote youth development.* Washington, DC: National Academy Press. Retrieved September 17, 2004, from http://www.nap.edu/books/0309072751/html/

Eccles, J., & Templeton, J. (2002). Extracurricular and other after-school activities for youth. *Review of Research in Education, 26*, 113–180.

Eccles, J. S., Midgley, C., Wigfield, A., Buchanan, M., Reuman, D., Flanagan, C., et al. (1993). Development during adolescence: The impact of stage-environment fit on young adolescents' experiences in schools and in families. *American Psychologist, 48*, 90–101.

Eccles, J. S., Wigfield, A., Midgley, C., Reuman, D., Mac Iver, D., & Feldlaufer, J. (1993). Negative effects of traditional middle schools on students' motivation. *The Elementary School Journal, 93*, 553–574.

Eccles, J. S., Wigfield, A., & Schiefele, U. (1998). Motivation to succeed. In W. Damon (Series Ed.) & N. Eisenberg (Vol. Ed.), *Handbook of child psychology: Vol 3. Social, emotional and personality development* (5th ed., pp. 1017–1095). New York: Wiley.

Eder, K. C., & Whiston, S. C. (2006). Does psychotherapy help some students? An overview of psychotherapy outcome research. *Professional School Counseling, 9*, 337–343.

Edwards, S. L., Bell, L., & Hunter-Geboy, C. (1996). *Changing scenes: A curriculum of the Teen Outreach Program.* Houston: Cornerstone Consulting Group.

The Education Trust. (1999). *Transforming school counseling.* Retrieved January 18, 2002, from http://www.edtrust.org/main/school_counseling.asp

Eidelson, R. J., & Eidelson, J. I. (2003). Dangerous ideas: Five beliefs that propel groups toward conflict. *American Psychologist, 58*, 182–192.

Ellis, A. (1962). *Reason and emotion in psychotherapy.* New York: Lyle Stuart.

Epstein, J. L., Salinas, K. C., & Jackson, V. E. (1995). *Manual for teachers and prototype activities: Teachers Involve Parents in Schoolwork (TIPS) language arts, science/health, and math interactive homework in the middle grades.* Baltimore, MD: Johns Hopkins University, Center on School, Family, and Community Partnerships.

Epstein, J. L., & Van Voorhis, F. L. (2001). More than minutes: Teachers' roles in designing homework. *Educational Psychologist, 38,* 181–193.

Epstein, M. H., & Sharma, J. (1998). *Behavioral and Emotional Rating Scale: A strength-based approach to assessment.* Austin, TX: PRO-ED.

Erford, B. T., House, R., & Martin, P. (2003). Transforming the school counseling profession. In B. T. Erford (Ed.), *Transforming the school counseling profession* (pp. 1–20). Upper Saddle River, NJ: Merrill Prentice Hall.

Eriksen, K. (1997). *Making an impact: A handbook on counselor advocacy.* Washington, DC: Accelerated Development.

Erikson, E. H. (1963). *Childhood and society.* New York: W. W. Norton.

Erikson, E. H. (1968). *Identity: Youth and crisis.* New York: W. W. Norton.

Eschenauer, R., & Chen-Hayes, S. F. (2005). The Transformative Individual School Counseling model: An accountability model for urban school counselors. *Professional School Counseling, 8,* 244–248.

Evans, J., & Buck, H. (1992). The effects of career education interventions on academic achievement: A meta-analysis. *The Journal of Counseling and Development, 71,* 63–71.

Fairchild, T. N., & Seeley, T. J. (1995). Accountability strategies for school counselors: A baker's dozen. *The School Counselor, 42,* 377–392.

Fantuzzo, J., & Ginsburg-Block, M. (1998). Reciprocal peer tutoring: Developing and testing effective peer collaborations for elementary school students. In K. Topping & S. Ehly (Eds.), *Peer-assisted learning* (pp. 121–144). Mahwah, NJ: Lawrence Erlbaum Associates.

Fava, G. A., & Ruini, C. (2003). Development and characteristics of a well-being enhancing psychotherapeutic strategy: Well-being therapy. *Journal of Behavior Therapy and Experimental Psychiatry, 34,* 45–63.

Feldman, A. F., & Matjasko, J. L. (2005). The role of school-based extracurricular activities in adolescent development: A comprehensive review and future directions. *Review of Educational Research, 75,* 159–210.

Felner, R. D. (2000). Educational reform as ecologically-based prevention and promotion: The Project on High Performance Learning Communities. In D. Cicchetti, J. Rappaport, I. Sandler, & R. P. Weissberg (Eds.), *The promotion of wellness in children and adolescents* (pp. 271–307). Washington, DC: CWLA Press.

Felner, R. D., Brand, S., Adan, A., Mulhall, P., Flowers, N., Sartain, B., et al. (1993). Restructuring the ecology of the school as an approach to prevention during school transitions: Longitudinal follow-ups and extensions of the School Transition Environment Project (STEP). *Prevention in Human Services, 10,* 103–136.

Felner, R. D., Jackson, A. W., Kasak, D., Mulhall, P., Brand, S., & Flowers, N. (1997). The impact of school reform for the middle years: Longitudinal study of a network engaged in *Turning Points*-based comprehensive school transformation. *Phi Delta Kappan, 78,* 528–550.

Fine, M. (1992). A systems-ecological perspective on home-school intervention. In M. Fine & C. Carlson (Eds.), *The Handbook of Family-School Intervention* (pp. 1–17). Needham Heights, MA: Allyn and Bacon.

Finn, J. D. (1993). *Social engagement and students at risk.* Washington, DC: National Center for Educational Statistics, U.S. Department of Education.

Fish, M. C., & Mendola, L. R. (1986). The effect of self-instruction training on homework completion in an elementary special education class. *School Psychology Review, 15,* 268–276.

Fix, M., & Zimmermann, W. (1993). *Educating immigrant children: Chapter 1 in the changing city.* Washington, DC: Urban Institute Press.

Flum H., & Blustein, D. (2000). Reinvigorating the study of vocational exploration: A framework for research. *Journal of Vocational Behavior, 56,* 380–404.

Fonagy, P., Target, M., Cottrell, D., Phillips, J., & Kurtz, Z. (2002). *What works for whom? A critical review of treatments for children and adolescents.* New York: The Guilford Press.

Foot, H., & Howe, C. (1998). The psychoeducational basis of peer-assisted learning. In K. Topping & S. Ehly (Eds.), *Peer-assisted learning* (pp. 27–43). Mahwah, NJ: Lawrence Erlbaum Associates.

Fordham, S., & Ogbu, J. (1986). Black students' school success. Coping with the burden of "acting white." *The Urban Review, 18*(3), 31–58.

Foster, L. H., Watson, T. S., Meeks, C., & Young, J. S. (2002). Single-subject research design for school counselors: Becoming an applied researcher. *Professional School Counseling, 6,* 146–154.

Fowler, J. W., & Peterson, P. L. (1981). Increasing reading persistence and altering attributional style of learned helpless children. *Journal of Educational Psychology, 73,* 251–260.

Frederickson, B. L. (2000). Cultivating positive emotions to optimize health and well-being. *Prevention and Treatment, 3,* Article 0001a. Retrieved February 6, 2002, from http://journals.apa.org/prevention/volume3/pre0030001a.html

Fredrickson, B. L. (2001). The role of positive emotions in positive psychology. *American Psychologist, 56,* 218–226.

Frederickson, B. L. (2002). Positive emotions. In C. R. Snyder & S. J. Lopez (Eds.), *Handbook of positive psychology* (pp. 120–134). New York: Oxford University Press.

Friend, M., & Cook, L. (2003). *Interactions: Collaboration skills for school professionals* (4th ed.). Boston: Allyn & Bacon.

Freiberg, H. J. (1998). Measuring school climate: Let me count the ways. *Educational Leadership, 56,* 22–26.

Freiberg, H. J. (1999). *School climate: Measuring, improving and sustaining healthy learning environments.* London: Falmer Press.

Fukuyama, M., Probert, B., Neimeyer, G., Nevill, D., & Metzler, A. (1988). Effects of DISCOVER on career self-efficacy and decision making of undergraduates. *Career Development Quarterly, 37,* 56–62.

Galassi, J. P., & Akos, P. (2004). Developmental advocacy: 21st century school counseling. *Journal of Counseling & Development, 82,* 146–157.

Galassi, J. P., & Gersh, T. L. (1991). Single-case research in counseling. In C. E. Watkins & L. J. Schneider (Eds.), *Research in counseling* (pp. 119–161). Hillsdale, NJ: Lawrence Erlbaum Associates.

Galloway, J., & Sheridan, S. M. (1994). Impementing scientific practices through case studies: Examples using home-school interventions and consultation. *Journal of School Psychology, 32,* 385–413.

Gamoran, A. (1992). The variable effects of high school tracking. *American Sociological Review, 57,* 812–828.

Gamoran, A., & Berends, M. (1987). The effects of stratification in secondary schools: Synthesis of survey and ethnographic research. *Review of Educational Research, 57,* 415–435.

Garmezy, N., Masten, A. S., & Tellegen, A. (1984). Studies of stress-resistant children: A building block for developmental psychopathology. *Child Development, 55,* 97–111.

Garrett, J. T., & Walking Stick Garrett, M. (1994). The paths of good medicine: Understanding and counseling Native American Indians. *Journal of Multicultural Counseling and Development, 22,* 134–144.

Garis, J., & Bowlsbey, J. (1984). *DISCOVER and the counselor: Their effect upon college student planning and progress* (ACT Research Report No. 85). Iowa City, IA: ACT Publications.

Gay, G. (1985). Implications of selected models of ethnic identity development for educators. *The Journal of Negro Education, 54*, 43–55.

Gelso, C. J., & Woodhouse, S. (2003). Toward a positive psychotherapy: Focus on human strength. In W. B. Walsh (Ed.), *Counseling psychology and optimal human functioning* (pp. 171–197). Mahwah, NJ: Lawrence Erlbaum Associates.

Gerler, E. R. (1985). Elementary school counseling research and the classroom learning environment. *Elementary School Guidance & Counseling, 20*, 39–48.

Gerler, E. R., Jr. (1992). What we know about school counseling: A reaction to Borders and Drury. *Journal of Counseling & Development, 70*, 499–501.

Gettinger, M., & Seibert, J. K. (2002). Contribution of study skills to academic competence. *School Psychology Review, 31*, 350–365.

Gholson, R. (1985). Student achievement and cocurricular activity participation. *NASSP Bulletin, 69*, 17–20.

Gillham, J. E., & Reivich, K. J. (1999). Prevention of depressive symptoms in schoolchildren: A research update. *Psychological Science, 10*, 461–462.

Gillham, J. E., Reivich, K. J., Jaycox, L. H., & Seligman, M. E. P. (1995). Prevention of depressive symptoms in schoolchildren: Two-year follow-up. *Psychological Science, 6*, 343–351.

Gillies, R., McMahon, M., & Carroll, J. (1998). Evaluating a career education intervention in the upper elementary school. *Journal of Career Development, 24*, 267–287.

Gilligan, C. (1982). *In a different voice: Psychological theory and women's development.* Cambridge, MA: Harvard University Press.

Gilman, R., Meyers, J., & Perez, L. (2004). Structured extracurricular activities among adolescents: Findings and implications for school psychologists. *Psychology in the Schools, 41*, 31–41.

Ginzberg, E., Ginzburg, S., Axelrad, S., & Herma, J. (1951). *Occupational choice: An approach to a general theory.* New York: Columbia University Press.

Good, C., Aronson, J., & Inzlicht, M. (2003). Improving adolescents' standardized test performance: An intervention to reduce the effects of stereotype threat. *Applied Developmental Psychology, 24*, 645–662.

Gottfredson, L. (1981). Circumscription and compromise: A developmental theory of occupational aspirations. *Journal of Counseling Psychology, 28*, 545–579.

Granello, D. H., & Hazler, R. J. (1998). A developmental rationale for curriculum order and teaching styles in counselor education programs. *Counselor Education and Supervision, 38*, 89–105.

Granello, P. (2002, November). *Wellness . . .* Presentation at the Association of Counselor Education and Supervision, Park City, UT.

Green, A., & Keys, S. (2001). Expanding the developmental school counseling paradigm: Meeting the needs of the 21st century student. *Professional School Counseling, 5*, 84–95.

Greenberg, M. T., Domitrovich, C., & Bumbarger, B. (2001). The prevention of mental disorders in school-aged children: Current state of the field. *Prevention and Treatment, 4*, Article 1. Retrieved September 27, 2004, from http://journals.apa.org/prevention/volume4/pre0040001a.html

Greenberg, M. T., Weissberg, R. P., O'Brien, M. U., Zins, J. E., Fredericks, L., Resnik, H., et al. (2003). Enhancing school-based prevention and youth development through coordinated social, emotional, and academic learning. *American Psychologist, 58*, 466–474.

Greenwood, C. R., Carta, J. J., Kamps, D., & Hall, E. V. (1988). The use of classwide peer tutoring strategies in classroom management and instruction. *School Psychology Review, 17*, 258–275.

Greenwood, C. R., Horton, B. T., & Utley, C. A. (2002). Academic engagement: Current perspectives on research and practice. *School Psychology Review, 31*, 326–349.

Gresham, F. M., & Elliott, S. N. (1990). *Social Skills Rating System manual*. Circle Pines, MN: American Guidance Services.

Grobe, T., & Bailis, L. (1996). *Final report of a two year evaluation of the Kids and the Power of Work (KAPOW) program*. Waltham, MA: Brandeis University, American Youth Policy Forum, Center for Human Resources.

Grolnick, W. S., & Ryan, R. M. (1989). Parent styles associated with children's self-regulation and competence in school. *Journal of Educational Psychology, 81*, 143–154.

Gysbers, N. C. (2001). School guidance and counseling in the 21st century: Remember the past into the future. *Professional School Counseling, 5*, 96–105.

Gysbers, N. C., & Henderson, P. (1994). *Developing and managing your school guidance program* (2nd ed.) . Alexandria, VA: American Counseling Association.

Gysbers, N. C., & Henderson, P. (2000). *Developing and managing your school guidance program* (3rd ed.). Alexandria, VA: American Counseling Association.

Gysbers, N. C., & Henderson, P. (2001). Comprehensive guidance and counseling programs: A rich history and a bright future. *Professional School Counseling, 4*, 246–256.

Gysbers, N. C., & Henderson, P. (2006). *Developing and managing your school guidance counseling program* (4th ed.). Alexandria, VA: American Counseling Association.

Gysbers, N., Heppner, M., & Johnston, J. (2003). *Career counseling: Process, issues, and techniques* (2nd ed). New York: Allyn & Bacon.

Gysbers, N., & Moore, E. (1975). Beyond career development—life career development. *Personnel and Guidance Journal, 53*, 647–652.

Hackett, G. (1995). Self-efficacy in career choice and development. In A. Bandura (Ed.), *Self-efficacy in changing societies* (pp. 232–258). New York: Cambridge University Press.

Hadley, H. R. (1988). Improving reading scores through a self-esteem intervention program. *Elementary School Guidance & counseling, 22*, 248–252.

Hall, A. (2003). Expanding academic and career self-efficacy: A family systems framework. *Journal of Counseling and Development, 81*(1), 33–40.

Hall, K. R. (2003). Strength in numbers. *ASCA School Counselor, 44*(1), 28–32.

Hardiman, R. (1982). White identity development: A process oriented model for describing the racial consciousness of white Americans. *Dissertation Abstracts International, 43*, 104A. (UMI No. 82-10330).

Harrington, R., Fudge, H., Rutter, M., Pickles, & Hill. (1990). Adult outcomes of childhood and adolescent depression. *Archives of General Psychiatry, 47*, 465–473.

Harris, A. H. S., & Thoresen, C. E. (2003). Strength-based health psychology: Counseling for total human health. In W. B. Walsh (Ed.), *Counseling psychology and optimal human functioning* (pp. 199–227). Mahwah, NJ: Lawrence Erlbaum Associates.

Hart, P. J., & Jacobi, M. (1992). *From gatekeeper to advocate: Transforming the role of the school counselor*. New York: College Entrance Examination Board.

Harter, S. (1981). A new self-report scale of intrinsic versus extrinsic orientation in the classroom: Motivational and informational components. *Developmental Psychology, 17,* 300–312.

Harter, S., & Jackson, B. J. (1992). Trait vs. nontrait conceptualizatons of intrinsic/extrinsic motivational orientation. *Motivation and Emotion, 16,* 209–230.

Harvey, S., & Goudvis, A. (2000). *Strategies that work: Teaching comprehension to enhance understanding.* York, ME: Stenhouse.

Havighurst, R. J. (1972). *Human development and education.* New York: David McKay.

Hawkins, J. D. (2003). *Long term effects of the SOAR program: The Seattle social development project.* Retrieved October 12, 2004 from http://depts.washington.edu/sdrg/SOAR_LongTermEffects_SPR/index.html.

Hawkins, J. D., Catalano, R. F., & Associates. (1992). *Communities that care: Action for drug abuse prevention.* San Francisco: Jossey-Bass.

Hawkins, J. D., Catalano, R. F., & Miller, J. Y. (1992). Risk and protective factors for alcohol and other drug problems in adolescence and early adulthood: Implications for substance abuse prevention. *Psychological Bulletin, 112,* 64–105.

Hawkins, J. D., Catalano, R. G., Morrison, D., O'Donnell, J., Abbott, R., & Day, L. (1992). The Seattle social development project: Effects of the first four years on protective factors and problem behaviors. In J. McCord & R. Tremblay (Eds.), *Preventing antisocial behavior: Interventions from birth through adolescence* (pp. 139–161). New York: Guilford Press.

Hawkins, J. D., Catalano, R. F., Kosterman, R., Abbott, R., & Hill, K. (1999). Preventing adolescent health-risk behaviors by strengthening protection during childhood. *Archives of Pediatric and Adolescent Medicine, 153,* 226–234.

Hayes, R., Dagley, R., & Horne, A. (1996). Restructuring school counselor education: Work in progress. *Journal of Counseling & Development, 74,* 378–384.

Hayes, R. L., Nelson, J., Tabin, M., Pearson, G., & Worthy, C. (2002). Using school-wide data to advocate for student success. *Professional School Counseling, 6,* 86–94.

Hayes, R., & Paisley, P. (2002). Transforming school counselor preparation programs. *Theory into Practice, 41,* 169–176.

Helms, J. E. (1984). Toward a theoretical explanation of the effects of race on counseling: A black and white model. *The Counseling Psychologist, 12,* 163–165.

Helms, J. E. (1990). *Black and white racial identity: Theory, research, and practice.* New York: Greenwood Press.

Helms, J. E. (1994a). The conceptualization of racial identity and other racial constructs. In E. J. Trickett, R. J. Watts, & D. Birman (Eds.), *Human diversity: Perspective on people in context* (pp. 185–211). San Francisco: Jossey-Bass.

Helms, J. E. (1994b). Racial identity in the school environment. In P. Pedersen & J. C. Carey (Eds.), *Multicultural counseling in schools: A practical handbook.* Boston: Allyn & Bacon.

Helms, J. E. (2003). Racial identity and racial socialization as aspects of adolescents' identity development. In R. M. Lerner, F. Jacobs, & D. Wertlieb (Eds.), *Handbook of applied developmental science: Vol. 1. Applying developmental science for youth and families: Historical and theoretical foundations* (pp. 143–163). Thousand Oaks, CA: Sage.

Henderson, N., & Milstein, M. (1996). *Resiliency in schools: Making it happen for students and educators.* Thousand Oaks, CA: Corwin Press.

Heppner, P. P. (1988). *The problem-solving inventory.* Palo Alto, CA: Consulting Psychologist Press.

Heppner, P. P., Manley, C. M., Perez, R. M., & Dixon, W. A. (1994). *An adolescent version of the problem-solving inventory: Initial reliability and validity estimates.* Unpublished manuscript.

Henggeler, S., Schoenwald, S., Borduin, C., Rowland, M., & Cunningham, P. (1998). Empirical, conceptual, and philosophical bases of MST. In S. Henggeler, S., Schoenwald, C. Borduin, M. Rowland, & P. Cunningham (Eds.), *Multisystemic treatment of antisocial behavior in children and adolescents* (pp. 3–20). New York: Guilford Press.

Herr, E. L. (2001). The impact of national policies, economics, and school reform on comprehensive guidance programs. *Professional School Counseling, 4,* 236–245.

Herr, E. L. (2002). School reform and perspectives on the role of school counselors: A century of proposals for change. *Professional School Counseling, 5,* 220–234.

Herr, E. L. (2003). Historical roots and future issues. In B. T. Erford (Ed.), *Transforming the school counseling profession* (pp. 21–38). Upper Saddle River, NJ: Merrill Prentice Hall.

Herr, E., & Cramer, S. (1996). *Career guidance and counseling through the life span* (5th ed.). New York: HarperCollins.

Herr, E., Cramer, S., & Niles, S. (2004). *Career guidance and counseling through the life span* (6th ed.). New York: HarperCollins.

Hidi, S., & Harackiewicz, J. M. (2000). Motivating the academically unmotivated: A critical issue for the 21st century. *Review of Educational Research, 70,* 151–179.

Hobbs, N. (1952). Guidance: Is it snark or boojum? *Clearing House, 26*(9), 525.

Holcomb-McCoy, C. C. (1997, June-July). *Who am I? The ethnic identity development of adolescents.* Paper presented at the annual meeting of the American School Counselor Association, Nashville, TN.

Holland, J. (1985). *Making vocational choices: A theory of vocational personalities and work environments* (2nd ed.). Englewood Cliffs, NJ: Prentice Hall.

Holland, J., Gottfredson, D., & Power, P. (1980). Some diagnostic scales for research in decision making and personality: Identity, information, and barriers. *Journal of Personality and Social Psychology, 39,* 1191–1200.

Hollis, J., & Dodson, T. (2001). *Counselor preparation 1999–2001.* New York: Accelerated Development.

Holloway, J. (2002). Extracurricular activities and student motivation. *Educational Leadership, 60,* 80–81.

Holmes, M., & Croll, P. (1989). Time spent on homework and academic achievement. *Educational Research, 31,* 36–45.

Hong, E., & Lee, K. (1999, April). *Chinese parents' awareness of their children's homework style, achievement, and attitude.* Paper presented at the American Educational Research Association, Montreal, Quebec, Canada

Hong, E., & Milgram, R. M. (2000). *Homework: Motivation and learning preference.* Westport, CT: Bergin & Garvey.

Hong, E., & Milgram, R. M. (2001). *The homework motivation and preference questionnaire.* NV: University of Nevada Las Vegas.

Hong, E., Milgram, R. M., & Perkins, P. G. (1995). Homework style and homework behavior of Korean and American children. *Journal of Research and Development in Education, 28,* 197–207.

Hong, E., Topham, J., Wozniak, E., Carter, S., & Topham, A. (2000, April). *Parent and student attitudes toward homework intervention and their effects on homework achievement and attitude.* Paper presented at the meeting of the American Educational Research Association, New Orleans, LA.

Hoover, J. P. (2002). A dozen ways to raise students' test performance. *Principal, 81*(3), 17–18.

Hoover-Dempsey, K. V., Battiato, A. C., Walker, J. M. T., Reed, R. P., DeJong, J. M., & Jones, K. P. (2001). Parental involvement in homework. *Educational Psychologist, 36*, 195–209.

House, R. M., & Hayes, R. L. (2002). School counselors: Becoming key players in school reform. *Professional School Counseling, 5*, 249–256.

House, R. M., & Martin, P. J. (1998). Advocating for better futures for all students: A new vision for school counselors. *Education, 119*, 284–291.

House, R., Martin, P., & Ward, C. (2002). Changing school counselor preparation: A critical need. In C. Johnson & S. Johnson (Eds.), *Changing school counselor preparation: A critical need* (pp. 185–208). Alexandria, VA: ASCA.

Hoyt, K. (1993). Guidance is not a dirty word. *The School Counselor, 40*(4), 267–274.

Hughes, J. (1993). Behavior therapy. In T. R. Kratochwill, & R. J. Morris (Eds.), *Handbook of psychotherapy with children and adolescents* (pp. 185–220). Boston: Allyn and Bacon.

Isaacs, M. L. (2003). Data-driven decision making: The engine of accountability. *Professional School Counseling, 6*, 288–295.

Isaacson, L., & Brown, D. (2000). *Career information, career counseling, and career development.* Boston: Allyn and Bacon.

Ivey, A. E., Ivey, M. B., Myers, J. E., & Sweeney, T. J. (2005). *Developmental counseling and therapy: Promoting wellness over the lifespan.* Boston: Lahaska Press.

Jagers, R. J., & Mock, L. O. (1993). Culture and social outcomes among inner city African American children: An Afrographic exploration. Emotional development of African American children. [Special issue] *Journal of Black Psychology, 19*, 391–405.

Jaycox, L. H., Reivich, K. J., Gillham, J., & Seligman, M. E. P. (1994). Prevention of depressive symptoms in school children. *Behaviour Research and Therapy, 32*, 801–816.

Jepsen, D. A. (2004). Developmental counseling. In C. Spielberger (Ed.), *Encyclopedia of applied psychology* (pp. 601–606). San Diego, CA: Elsevier.

Johnson, D. W., & Johnson, R. T. (1995). *Teaching students to be peacemakers.* Edina, MN: Interaction Book Company.

Johnson, D. W., & Johnson, R. T. (2001, April). *Teaching students to be peacemakers: A meta-analysis.* Paper presented at the annual meeting of the American Educational Research Association, Seattle, WA.

Johnson, R. T., & Johnson, D. W. (1994). An overview of cooperative learning. In J. S. Thousand, R. A Villa, & A. I. Nevin (Eds.), *Creativity and collaborative learning: A practical guide to empowering students and teachers* (pp. 31–58). Baltimore, MD: Paul H. Brookes.

Joiner, T. E., Jr., Pettit, J. W., Perez, M., Burns, A. B., Gencoz, T., Gencoz, F., et al. (2001). Can positive emotion influence problem-solving attitudes among suicidal adults? *Professional Psychology: Research and Practice, 32*, 507–512.

Jurich, S., & Estes, S. (2000). *Raising academic achievement: A study of 20 successful programs.* Washington, DC: American Youth Policy Forum.

Kahn, B. B. (2000). A model of solution-focused consultation for school counselors. *Professional School Counseling, 3*, 248–254.

Katz, J. H. (1989). The challenge of diversity. [Monograph No.11, 1–17] In C. Woolbright (Ed.). *College Unions at Work,*. Bloomington, Indiana: Association of College Unions International.

Kay, D. (2005). A team approach to positive behaviors. *ASCA School Counselor, 42*(5), 17–21.

Kazdin, A. E., & Weisz, J. R. (Eds.), (2003). *Evidenced-based psychotherapies for children and adolescents*. New York: The Guilford Press.

Kealey, D. J. (1996). The challenge of international personnel selection. In D. Landis & R. S. Bhagat (Eds.), *Handbook of intercultural training* (2nd ed., pp. 81–105). Thousand Oaks, CA: Sage.

Keith, T. Z. (1982). Time spent on homework and high school grades: A large-sample path analysis. *Journal of Educational Psychology, 74*, 248–253.

Keith, T. Z. (2002). Commentary: Academic enablers and school learning. *School Psychology Review, 31*, 394–402.

Kemple, J. (2004). *Career academies: Impacts on labor market outcomes and educational attainment*. New York: MDRC.

Kemple, J., Poglinco, S., & Snipes, J. (1999). *Career academies: Building career awareness and work-based learning activities through employer partnerships*. New York: MDRC.

Kemple, J., & Rock, J. (1996). *Career academies: Early implementation lessons from a 10-site evaluation*. New York: MDRC.

Kemple, J., & Snipes, J. (2000). *Career academies: Impacts on students' engagement and performance in high school*. New York: MDRC.

Keys, S. G., Bemak, F., & Lockhart, E. J. (1998). Transforming school counseling to serve the mental health needs of at-risk youth. *Journal of Counseling & Development, 76*, 381–388.

Keys, S. G., & Green, A. (2005). Enhancing developmental school counseling programs through collaboration. In C. A. Sink (Ed.), *Contemporary school counseling: Theory, research, and practice* (pp. 361–389). Boston: Lahaska Press.

Keys, S. G., & Lockhart, E. J. (1999). The school counselor's role in facilitating multisystemic change. *Professional School Counseling, 3*, 101–107.

Keys, S. G., Green, A., Lockhart, E., & Luongo, P. F. (2003). Consultation and collaboration. In B.T. Erford (Ed.), *Transforming the school counseling profession* (pp. 171–190). Upper Saddle River, NJ: Merrill Prentice Hall.

Killeen, J., Edwards, A., Barnes, A., & Watts, A. (1999). *Evaluating the UK national pilot of The Real Game: Technical report on the quantitative analysis of learning outcomes*. NICEC Project Report. Cambridge, England: Careers Research and Advisory Centre.

Kim, J. (1981). The process of Asian American identity development: A study of Japanese-American women's perceptions of their struggle to achieve personal identities as Americans of Asian ancestry. *Dissertation Abstracts International, 42* (155), 1A. (UMI No. 81-18180).

Kiselica, M. S., & Robinson, M. (2001). Bringing advocacy counseling to life: The history, issues, and human dramas of social justice work in counseling. *Journal of Counseling & Development, 79*, 387–397.

Kohlberg, L. (1969). Stage and sequence: The cognitive developmental approach to socialization. In D. Goslin (Ed.), *Handbook of socialization theory and research* (pp. 347–480). Chicago: Rand-McNally.

Kratochwill, T. R., & Bergan, J. R. (1990). *Behavioral consultation in applied settings: An individual guide*. New York: Plenum

Kraus, L., & Hughey, K. (1999). The impact of an intervention on career decision-making self-efficacy and career indecision. *Professional School Counseling, 2*, 384–390.

Krumboltz, J. D. (1974). An accountability model for counselors. *Personnel and Guidance Journal, 52*, 639–646.

LaFountain, R., Garner, N., & Boldosser, S. (1995). Solution-focused counseling groups for children and adolescents. *Journal of Systemic Therapies, 14*, 39–51.

LaFountain, R., Garner, N., & Eliason, G. T. (1996). Solution-focused counseling groups: A key for school counselors. *The School Counselor, 43*, 256–267.

LaFromboise, T., Coleman, H. L. K., & Gerton, J. (1993). Psychological impact of biculturalism: Evidence and theory. *Psychological Bulletin, 114*, 395–412.

Lapan, R. T. (2001). Results-based comprehensive guidance and counseling programs: A framework for planning and evaluation. *Professional School Counseling, 4*, 289–299.

Lapan, R. T. (2004). *Career development across the K–16 years: Bridging the present to satisfying and successful futures.* Alexandria, VA: American Counseling Association.

Lapan, R. T., Gysbers, N., Hughey, K., & Arni, T. J. (1993). Evaluating a guidance and language arts unit for high school juniors. *Journal of Counseling & Development, 71*, 444–451.

Lapan, R. T., Gysbers, N. C., & Petroski, G. F. (2001). Helping seventh graders be safe and successful: A statewide study of the impact of comprehensive guidance and counseling programs. *Journal of Counseling & Development, 79*, 320–330.

Lapan, R. T., Gysbers, N. C., & Sun, Y. (1997). The impact of more fully implemented guidance programs on the school experiences of high school students: A statewide evaluation study. *Journal of Counseling & Development, 75*, 292–302.

Lapan, R. T., Kardash, C., & Turner, S. (2002). Empowering students to become self-regulated learners. *Professional School Counseling, 5*, 257–265.

Larson, R. W. Eccles, J., & Gootman, J. A. (2004). Features of positive developmental settings. *The Prevention Researcher, 11*(2), 8–13.

Larson, R. W. (2000). Toward a psychology of positive youth development. *American Psychologist, 55*, 170–183.

Larson, R. W., & Verma, S. (1999). How children and adolescents spend time across the world: Work, play, and developmental opportunities. *Psychological Bulletin, 125*, 701–736.

Lauer, P. A., Akiba, M., Wilkerson, S. B., Apthorp, H. S., Snow, D., & Martin-Glenn, M. L. (2006). Out-of-school-time programs: A meta-analysis of effects for at-risk students. *Review of Educational Research, 76*, 275–313.

Lee, C. C. (1992). *Empowering young black males.* Ann Arbor, MI: ERIC/CASS Publications.

Lee, C. C. (2001). Culturally responsive school counselors and programs: Addressing the needs of all students. *Professional School Counseling, 4*, 257–261.

Lee, C. C., & Walz, G. R. (Eds.). (1998). *Social action: A mandate for counselors.* Alexandria, VA: American Counseling Association.

Lee, F. Y. (1991). *The relationship of ethnic identity to social support, self-esteem, psychological distress, and help-seeking behavior among Asian American college students.* Unpublished doctoral dissertation, University of Illinois, Urbana-Champaign.

Lee, R. S. (1993). Effects of classroom guidance on student achievement. *Elementary School Guidance & Counseling, 27*, 163–171.

Lenehan, M. C., Dunn, R., Inghan, J., Signer, B., & Murray, J. B. (1994). Effects of learning-style intervention on college students' achievement, anxiety, anger, and curiosity. *Journal of College Student Development, 35*, 461–464.

Lennon, T., Blackwell, P., Bridgeforth, C., & Cole, P. (Eds.). (1996). *Pathways: School guidance and counseling in Equity 2000.* New York: College Entrance Examination Board.

Lerner, R. M. (1984). *On the nature of human plasticity.* New York: Cambridge University.

Lerner, R. M. (1986). *Concepts and theories of human development* (2nd ed.). New York: Random House.

Lerner, R. M. (1995). *America's youth in crisis: Challenges and options for programs and policies.* Thousand Oaks, CA: Sage.

Lerner, R. M., Walsh, M. E., & Howard, K. A. (1998). Developmental-contextual considerations: Person-context relations as the bases for risk and resiliency in child and adolescent development. In T. Ollendick (Ed.), *Comprehensive clinical psychology: Vol. 5. Children and adolescents: Clinical formulation and treatment* (pp. 1–24). New York: Elsevier Science Publishers.

Lent, R., & Brown, S. (2002). Social cognitive career theory and adult career development. In S. Niles (Ed.), *Adult career development: Concepts, issues and practices* (3rd ed., pp. 76–97). Columbus, OH: National Career Development Association.

Lent, R., Brown, S., & Hackett, G. (1994). Toward a unifying social cognitive theory of career and academic interest, choice, and performance. *Journal of Vocational Behavior, 45,* 79–122.

Lent, R., Brown, S., & Larkin, K. (1986). Self-efficacy in the prediction of academic performance and perceived career options. *Journal of Counseling Psychology, 33,* 165–169.

Lent, S., & Hackett, G. (1987). Career self-efficacy: Empirical status and future directions. *Journal of Vocational Behavior, 30,* 347–382.

Lewinsohn, P. M., Hops, H., Roberts, R., & Seeley, J. (1996). Adolescent suicidal ideation and attempts: Prevalence, risk factors, and clinical implications. *Clinical Psychology: Science and Practice, 3,* 25–46.

Lewis, J., & Bradley, L. (Eds.). (2000). *Advocacy in counseling: Counselors, clients & community.* Greensboro, NC: ERIC Clearinghouse on Counseling and Student Services.

Lewis, J. A., Cheek, J. R., & Hendricks, C. B. (2001). Advocacy in supervision. In L. J. Bradley & N. Ladany (Eds.), *Counselor supervision: Principles, process, and practice* (3rd ed., pp. 330–341). Philadelphia, PA: Brunner-Routledge.

Linnenbrink, E. A., & Pintrich, P. R. (2002). Motivation as an enabler for academic success. *School Psychology Review, 32,* 313–327.

Lipsey, M. W., & Wilson, D. B. (1993). The efficacy of psychological, educational, and behavioral treatment: Confirmation from meta-analysis. *American Psychologist, 48,* 1181–1209

Littrell, J. M., Malia, J. A., & Vanderwood, M. (1995). Single-session brief counseling in a high school. *Journal of Counseling & Development, 73,* 451–458.

Lochman, J. E. (1992). Cognitive-behavioral intervention with aggressive boys: Three-year follow-up and preventive effects. *Journal of Consulting and Clinical Psychology, 60,* 426–432.

Lochman, J. E., Burch, P. R., Curry, J. F., & Lampron, L. B. (1984). Treatment and generalization effects of cognitive-behavioral and goal-setting interventions with aggressive boys. *Journal of Consulting and Clinical Psychology, 52,* 915–916.

Lochman, J. E., Curry, J. F., Dane, H., & Ellis, M. (2001). The anger coping program: An empirically-supported treatment for aggressive children. . In S. I. Pfeiffer & L. A Reddy (Eds.), *Innovative mental health interventions for children: Programs that work* (pp. 63–73). New York: The Haworth Press, Inc.

Lochman, J. E., & Lampron, L. B. (1988). Cognitive behavioral interventions for aggressive boys: Seven months follow-up effects. *Journal of Child and Adolescent Psychotherapy, 5,* 15–23.

Lochman, J. E., Lampron, L. B., Gemmer, T. C., & Harris, S. R. (1987). Anger coping intervention with aggressive children: A guide to implementation in school settings. In P. A. Keller & S. R. Heyman (Eds.), *Innovations in clinical practice: A source book* (Vol. 6, pp. 339–356). Sarasota, FL: Professional Resource Exchange.

Lochman, J. E., Nelson, W. M., & Sims, J. P. (1981). A cognitive behavioral program for use with aggressive children. *Journal of Clinical Child Psychology, 10,* 146–148.

Lochman, J. E., & Wells, K. C. (1996). A social-cognitive intervention with aggressive children: Prevention effects and contextual implementation issues. In R. D. Peters & R. J. McMahon (Eds.), *Prevention and early intervention: Childhood disorders, substance use, and delinquency* (pp. 111–143). Newbury Park, CA: Sage.

Lochman, J. E., & Wells, K. C. (2002). *The Duke coping power program (Adapted version for use with the Durham public schools)*. Unpublished manuscript.

Lonner, W. J., & Hayes, S. A. (2004). Understanding the cognitive and social aspects of intercultural competence. In R. J. Sternberg & E. L. Grigorenko (Eds.), *Culture and competence: Contexts of life success* (pp. 89–109). Washington, DC: American Psychological Association.

Lopez, S. J., Floyd, R. K., Ulven, J. C., & Snyder, C. R. (2000). Hope therapy: Helping clients build a house of help. In C. R. Snyder (Ed.), *Handbook of hope: Theory, measures, & applications* (pp. 123–150). San Diego, CA: Academic Press.

Lopez, S. J., Snyder, C. R., & Rasmussen, H. N. (2003). Striking a vital balance: Developing a complementary focus on human weakness and strength through positive psychological assessment. In S. J. Lopez & C. R. Snyder (Eds.), *Positive psychological assessment: A handbook of models and measures* (pp. 3–20). Washington, DC: American Psychological Association.

Luthar, S. S., & Burack, J. A. (2000). Adolescent wellness: In the eye of the beholder? In D. Cicchetti, J. Rappaport, I. Sandler, & R. P. Weissberg (Eds.), *The promotion of wellness in children and adolescents* (pp. 29–57). Washington, DC: CWLA Press.

Luzzo, D., & Pierce, G. (1996). Effects of DISCOVER on the career maturity of middle school students. *The Career Development Quarterly, 45,* 170–172.

MacDonald, G., & Sink, C. A. (1999). A qualitative developmental analysis of comprehensive guidance programmes in schools in the United States. *British Journal of Guidance and Counselling, 27,* 415–430.

Maheady, L. (1998). Advantages and disadvantages of peer-assisted learning strategies. In K. Topping & S. Ehly (Eds.), *Peer-assisted learning* (pp. 45–64). Mahwah, NJ: Lawrence Erlbaum Associates.

Mahoney, J. (2000). School extracurricular activity participation as a moderator in the development of antisocial patterns. *Child Development, 71,* 502–516.

Mahoney, J., Cairns, B., & Farmer, T. (2003). Promoting interpersonal competence and educational success through extracurricular participation. *Journal of Educational Psychology, 95,* 409–418.

Mahoney, J., & Cairns, R. (1997). Do extracurricular activities protect against early school dropout? *Developmental Psychology, 33,* 241–253.

Marcia, J. (1966). Development and validation of ego-identity status. *Journal of Personality and Social Psychology, 3,* 551–558.

Marcia, J. (1993). The ego identity status approach to ego identity. In J. Marcia, A. Waterman, D. Matteson, S. Archer, & J. Orlofsky (Eds.), *Ego identity: A handbook for psychosocial research.* New York: Springer-Verlag.

Marcia, J., Waterman, A., Matteson, D., Archer, S., & Orlofsky, J. (1994). *Ego identity: A handbook of psychosocial research.* New York: Springer-Verlag.

Martens, B. K. (1993). A behavioral approach to consultation. In J. E. Zins, T. R. Kratochwill, & S. N. Elliott (Eds.), *Handbook of consultation services for children: Applications in educational and clinical settings* (pp. 65–86). San Francisco: Jossey-Bass.

Martin, P. (2002). Transforming school counseling: A national perspective. *Theory Into Practice, 41,* 148–154.

Masten, A. S. (2001). Ordinary magic: Resilience processes in development. *American Psychologist, 56,* 227–238.

Masten, A. S., & Coatsworth, J. D. (1998). The development of competence in favorable and unfavorable environments: Lessons from successful children. *American Psychologist, 53,* 205–220.

Masten, A. S., & Reed, M. J. (2002). Resilience in development. In C. R. Snyder & S. J. Lopez (Eds.), *Handbook of positive psychology* (pp. 74–88). New York: Oxford University Press.

Matsumoto, D. (2004). Reflections on culture and competence. In R. J. Sternberg & E. L. Grigorenko (Eds.), *Culture and competence: Contexts of life success* (pp. 273–282). Washington, DC: American Psychological Association.

McCall-Perez, Z. (2000). The counselor as advocate for English language learners: An action research approach. *Professional School Counseling, 4,* 13–22.

McDougall, D., & Smith, D. (2006). Recent innovations in small-N designs for research and practice in professional school counseling. *Professional School Counseling, 9,* 392–400.

McGannon, W., Carey, J., & Dimmitt, C. (2005). *The current status of school counseling outcome research* [Research Monograph, No. 2]. Retrieved July 7, 2005, from University of Massachusetts Amherst, Center for School Counseling Outcome Research Web site: http://www.umass.edu/schoolcounseling/PDFs/OutcomeStudy Monograph.pdf

McWhirter, E., Rasheed, S., & Crothers, M. (2000). The effects of high school career education on social-cognitive variables. *Journal of Counseling Psychology, 47,* 330–341.

McWhirter, J. J., McWhirter, B. T., McWhirter, E. H., & McWhirter, R. J. (2004). *At-risk youth: A comprehensive response* (3rd ed.). Pacific Grove, CA: Brooks/Cole.

Meijers, F. (2002). *Career policy for the contemporary world: Dictat or stimulant?* Cambridge, UK: The Career-Learning Network.

Meijers, F. (1998). The development of career identity. *International Journal for the Advancement of Counselling, 20,* 191–207.

Metcalf, L. (1995). *Counseling toward solutions: A practical solution-focused program for working with students, teachers, and parents.* Englewood Cliffs, NJ: Center for Applied Research in Education.

Metropolitan Life Survey of the American Teacher. (1994). *Violence in America's public schools: The family perspective.* New York: Louis Harris.

Midgley, C. (1993). Motivation and middle level schools. In M. L. Maehr & P. R. Pintrich (Eds.), *Advances in motivation and achievement: Motivation and adolescence* (Vol. 8, pp. 271–274). Greenwich, CT: JAI Press.

Minkoff, H., & Terres, C. (1985). ASCA perspectives: Past, present, and future. *Journal of Counseling and Development, 63,* 424–427.

Mitchell, M. (1993). Situational interest: Its multifaceted structure in the secondary school mathematics classroom. *Journal of Educational Psychology, 85,* 424–436.

Mizelle, N. B., & Irvin, J. L. (2000). Transition from middle school to high school. *Middle School Journal, 31,* 57–61.

Moore, K. A., & Keyes, C. L. M. (2003). A brief history of the study of well-being in children and adults. In M. H. Bornstein, L. Davidson, C. L. M. Keyes, & K. A. Moore (Eds.), *Well-being: Positive development across the life course* (pp. 1–11). Mahwah, NJ: Lawrence Erlbaum Associates.

Murphy, J. J. (1997). *Solution-focused counseling in middle and high schools.* Alexandria, VA: American Counseling Association.

Murphy, J. J., & Duncan, B. L. (1997). *Brief interventions for school problems: Collaborating for practical solutions.* New York: The Guilford Press.

Myers, J. E., Sweeney, T. J., & White, V. E. (2002). Advocacy for counseling and counselors: A professional imperative. *Journal of Counseling & Development, 80,* 394–402.

Myers, J. E., Sweeney, T. J., & Witmer, J. M. (2000). The wheel of wellness counseling for wellness: A holistic model for treatment planning. *Journal of Counseling & Development, 78,* 251–266.

Myers, J. E., Sweeney, T. J., & Witmer, J. M. (2001). Organization of behavior: Promotion of wellness. In D. C. Locke, J. E. Myers, & E. L. Herr (Eds.), *The handbook of counseling* (pp. 641–652). Thousand Oaks, CA: Sage Publications.

Myrick, R. D. (1997). *Developmental guidance and counseling: A practical approach* (3rd ed.). Minneapolis, MN: Educational Media Corporation.

Myrick, R. D. (2003). Accountability: Counselors count. *Professional School Counseling, 6,* 174–184.

National Center for Education Statistics. (1997). Principals/school disciplinarian survey on school violence. *Fast response survey, system, 63.* Washington, DC: U.S. Government Printing Press.

National Commission on Excellence in Education. (1983). *A nation at risk.* Washington, DC: Author.

National Education Association. (2006). *Closing achievement gaps: An association guide.* Retrieved July 13, 2006, from http://www.achievementgaps.org/articleDetail_content.php?recid=18363

Nicholls, J. (1984). Achievement motivation: Conceptions of ability, subjective experience, task choice, and performance. *Psychological Review, 91,* 328–346.

Niles, S., Trusty, J., & Mitchell, N. (2004). Fostering positive career development in children and adolescents. In R. Perusse and G. Goodnough (Eds.), *Leadership, advocacy, and direct service strategies for professional school counselors* (pp. 102–124). Wadsworth Publishing, NY.

Niles, S., & Harris-Bowlsbey, J. (2007). *Career development interventions in the 21st century,* (2nd ed.) NY: Prentice Hall.

No Child Left Behind. (2002). *It's a new era in education.* Retrieved May 12, 2003, from http://www.nochildleftbehind.gov/index.html

Noddings, N. (1992). *The challenge to care in schools: An alternative approach to education.* New York: Teachers College Press.

Nolen-Hoeksema, S., Girgus, J. S., & Seligman, M. E. P. (1986). Learned helplessness in children: A longitudinal style of depression, achievement, and explanatory style. *Journal of Personality and Social Psychology, 51,* 435–442.

Northwest Regional Educational Laboratory. (2004). *The catalog of school reform models.* Retrieved December 15, 2004, from http://www.nwrel.org/scpd/catalog/modellist.asp

O'Brien, K. M. (2003). Measuring career self-efficacy: Promoting confidence and happiness at work. In S. J. Lopez & C. R. Snyder (Eds.), *Positive psychological assessment: A handbook of models and measures* (pp. 109–126). Washington, DC: American Psychological Association.

O'Brien, K. M., Dukstein, R., Jackson, S., Tomlinson, M., & Kamatuka, N. (1999). Broadening career horizons for students in at-risk environments. *Career Development Quarterly, 47,* 215–229.

O'Bryant, B. (1990). The year of the school counselor cometh. *The ASCA Counselor, 27*(4), 4.

Ogbu, J. (1987). Opportunity structure, cultural boundaries, and literacy. In J. Langer (Ed.), *Language, literacy, and culture: Issues of society and schooling* (pp. 149–177). Norwood, NJ: Ablex.

Oliver, L., & Spokane, A. (1988). Career-intervention outcome: What contributes to client gain? *Journal of Counseling Psychology, 35,* 447–462.

Olympia, D. E., Jenson, W. R., & Hepworth-Neville, M. (1996). *Sanity savers for parents: Tips for tackling homework.* Longmont, CO: Sopris West.

Olympia, D. E., Sheridan, S. M., Jenson, W. R., & Andrews, D. (1994). Using student-managed interventions to increase homework completion and accuracy. *Journal of Applied Behavior Analysis, 27,* 85–89.

Ormrod, J. E. (1999). *Human learning* (3rd. ed.). Upper Saddle River, NJ: Prentice Hall.

One Hundred Third Congress of the United States of America. (1994). School-to-Work Opportunities Act of 1994 Public Law 103-239. Retrieved August 30, 2003, from http://www.fessler.com/SBE/act.htm

Osborn, D., & Baggerly, J. (2004). School counselors' perceptions of career counseling and career testing: Preferences, priorities, and predictions. *Journal of Counseling and Development, 31,* 45–59.

Osterman, K. F. (2000). Students' need for belonging in the school community. *Review of Educational Research, 70,* 323–367.

Ottavi, T. M., Pope-Davis, D. B., & Dings, J. G. (1994). Relationship between white racial identity attitudes and self-reported multi-cultural counseling competencies. *Journal of Counseling Psychology, 41,* 149–154.

Paisley, P. O. (2001). Maintaining and enhancing the developmental focus in school counseling programs. *Professional School Counseling, 4,* 271–277.

Paisley, P. O., & Borders, L. D. (1995). School counseling: An evolving specialty. *Journal of Counseling & Development, 74,* 150–153.

Paisley, P. O., & Hayes, R. L. (2003). School counseling in the academic domain: Transformations in preparation and practice. *Professional School Counseling, 63,* 198–204.

Paisley, P. O., & Hubbard, G. T. (1994). *Developmental school counseling programs: From theory to practice.* Alexandria, VA: American Counseling Association.

Paisley, P. O., & McMahon, H. (2001). School counseling for the 21st century: Challenges and opportunities. *Professional School Counseling, 5,* 106–115.

Paisley, P. O., & Peace, S. D. (1995). Developmental principles: A framework for school counseling programs. *Elementary School Guidance & Counseling, 30,* 85–93.

Parham, T. (1989). Cycles of psychological Nigrescence. *The Counseling Psychologist, 17,* 187–226.

Parker, W. M., Moore, M. A., & Neimeyer, G. J. (1998). Altering white racial identity and interracial comfort through multicultural training. *Journal of Counseling & Development, 76,* 302–310.

Parsons, F. (1909). *Choosing a vocation.* Boston: Houghton-Mifflin.

Pate, R. (1990). The potential effect of accreditation standards on the type of students who will enter counselor education programs. *Counselor Education and Supervision, 29,* 179–187.

Patton, W., & Creed, P. (2001). Developmental issues in career maturity and career decision status. *Career Development Quarterly, 49,* 336–351.

Pedersen, P. B. (2003). Multicultural training in schools as an expansion of the counselor's role. In P. B. Pedersen & J. C. Carey (Eds.), *Multicultural counseling in schools* (2nd ed., pp. 190–210). Boston: Allyn and Bacon.

Perusse, R., Goodnough, G., & Noel, C. (2001). A national survey of school counselor preparation programs: Screening methods, faculty experiences, curricular content, and fieldwork requirements. *Counselor Education and Supervision, 40,* 252–262.

Peseschkian, N., & Tritt, K. (1998). Positive psychotherapy: Effectiveness study and quality assurance. *The European Journal of Psychotherapy, Counseling & Health, 1,* 93–104.

Peterson, C., & Seligman, M. E. P. (2004). *Character strengths and virtues: A handbook and classification.* New York: American Psychological Association and Oxford University Press, Inc.

Peterson, J., & Deuschle, C. (2006). A model for supervising school counseling students without teaching experience. *Counselor Education & Supervision, 45,* 267–281.

Phillips, P. L., Sears, S., Snow, B. M., & Jackson, C. M. (2005). The professional school counselor as a leader. In T. Davis (Ed.), *Exploring school counseling: Professional practices and perspectives* (pp. 215–234). Boston: Lahaska Press.

Phinney, J. S. (1990). Ethnic identity in adolescents and adults: Review of research. *Psychological Bulletin, 108,* 499–514.

Phinney, J. S. (1996). Understanding ethnic diversity: The role of ethnic identity. *American Behavioral Scientist, 40,* 143–152.

Phinney, J. S., & Kohatsu, J. S. (1997). Ethnic and racial identity development and mental health. In J. S. Schulenberg, J. L. Maggs, & K. Hurrelmann (Eds.), *Health risks and developmental transitions during adolescence* (pp. 420–443). Cambridge, United Kingdom: Cambridge University Press.

Piaget, J. (1950). *The psychology of intelligence.* New York: Harcourt, Brace, & Company.

Pinder, F., & Fitzgerald, P. (1984). The effectiveness of a computerized guidance system in promoting career decision making. *Journal of Vocational Behavior, 24,* 123-131.

Pintrich, P. R. (2000). The role of goal orientation in self-regulated learning. In M. Boekaerts, P. R. Pintrich, & M. Zeidner (Eds.), *Handbook of self-regulation* (pp. 451–502). San Diego, CA: Academic Press.

Pintrich, P. R., & Schunk, D. (2002). *Motivation in education: Theory, research, and applications* (2nd ed.). Upper Saddle River, NJ: Prentice Hall.

Pipes, R. B., Buckhalt, J. A., & Merrill, H. D. (1983). Counselor education and the psychology of more. *Counselor Education and Supervsion, 22,* 282–286.

Pittman, K. J., & Fleming, W. E. (1991). *A new vision: Promoting youth development.* Testimony by Karen J. Pittman before the House Select Committee on Children, Youth and Families. Washington, DC: Center for Youth Development and Policy Research.

Pittman, K. J., Irby, M., Tolman, J., Yohalem, N., & Ferber, T. (2001). *Preventing problems, promoting development, encouraging engagement: Competing priorities or inseparable goals?* Takoma Park, MD: The Forum for Youth Investment.

Plas, J. (1986). *Systems psychology in the schools.* New York: Pergamon Press.

Pollard, E. L., & Rosenberg, M. L. (2003). The strengths-based approach to child well-being: Let's begin with the end in mind. In M. H. Bornstein, L. Davidson, C. L. M. Keyes, & K. A. Moore (Eds.), *Well-being: Positive development across the life course* (pp. 13–21). Mahwah, NJ: Lawrence Erlbaum Associates.

Pollard, J. A., Hawkins, J. D., & Arthur, M. W. (1999). Risk and protection: Are both necessary to understand diverse behavioral outcomes in adolescence? *Social Work Research, 23,* 145–158.

Ponterotto, J. G. (1988). Racial consciousness development among white counselors' trainees: A stage model. *Journal of Multicultural Counseling and Development, 16,* 146–156.

Ponterotto, J. G., & Casas, J. M. (1987). In search of multicultural competence within counselor education programs. *Journal of Counseling and Development, 65*, 430–434.

Pope-Davis, D. B., & Ottavi, T. M. (1994). Examining the association between self-reported multicultural counseling competencies and demographic variables among counselors. *Journal of Counseling and Development, 74*, 651–654.

Porter, G., Epp, L., & Bryant, S. (2000). Collaboration among school mental health professionals: A necessity, not a luxury. *Professional School Counseling, 3*, 315–322.

Posey, R., Wong, S. C., Catalano, R. F., Hawkins, J. D., Dusenbury, L., & Chappell, P. J. (1996). *Communities that care prevention strategies: A research guide to what works.* Seattle, WA: Developmental Research and Programs, Inc.

Powell, D., & Luzzo, D. (1998). Evaluating factors associated with the career maturity of high school students. *Career Development Quarterly, 47*, 145–158.

Prout, H. T., & DeMartino, R. A. (1986). A meta-analysis of school-based studies of psychotherapy. *Journal of School Psychology, 24*, 285–292.

Quiggle, N. L., Garber, J., Panak, W. F., & Dodge, K. A. (1992). Social information processing in aggressive and depressed children. *Child Development, 63*, 1305–1320.

Rawsthorne, L. J., & Elliot, A. J. (1999). Achievement goals and intrinsic motivation: A meta-analytic review. *Personality and Social Psychology Review, 3*, 326–344.

Rayle, A. D., & Myers, J. E. (2004). Counseling adolescents toward wellness: The roles of ethnic identity, acculturation, and mattering. *Professional School Counseling, 8*, 81–90.

Riley, R., & Cantu, N. (2000). *The use of tests as part of high-stakes decision-making for students: A resource guide for educators and policy makers.* Washington, DC: U.S. Department of Education, Office of Civil Rights.

Ripley, V., Erford, B. T., Dahir, C., & Eschbach, L. (2003). Planning and implementing a 21st-century comprehensive developmental school counseling program. In B. T. Erford (Ed.), *Transforming the school counseling profession* (pp. 63–119). Upper Saddle River, NJ: Merrill Prentice Hall.

Roberts, M. C., Brown, K. J., Johnson, R. J., & Reinke, J. (2002). Positive psychology for children: Development, prevention, and promotion. In C. R. Snyder & S. J. Lopez (Eds.), *Handbook of positive psychology* (pp. 663–675). New York: Oxford University Press.

Rotheram-Borus, M. J. (1990). Adolescents' reference-group choices, self-esteem, and adjustment. *Journal of Personality and Social Psychology, 59*, 1075–1081.

Rowell, L. L., & Hong, E. (2002). The role of school counselors in homework intervention. *Professional School Counseling, 5*, 285–291.

Ruiz, A. S. (1990). Ethnic identity: Crisis and resolution. *Journal of Multicultural Counseling and Development, 18*, 29–40.

Rutter, M. (1985). Resilience in the face of adversity: Protective factors and resistance to psychiatric disorder. *British Journal of Psychiatry, 147*, 598–611.

Ryan, R. M., Stiller, J., & Lynch, J. H. (1994). Representations of relationships to teachers, parents, and friends as predictors of academic motivation and self-esteem. *Journal of Early Adolescence, 14*, 226–249.

Ryan, R. R., & Deci, E. L. (2000). Self-determination theory and the facilitation of intrinsic motivation, social development, and well-being. *American Psychologist, 55*, 68–78.

Ryff, C. D. (1985). Adult personality development and the motivation for personal growth. In D. Kleiber & M. Maehr (Eds.), *Advances in motivation and achievement: Motivation and adulthood* (Vol. 4, pp. 55–92). Greenwich, CT: JAI Press.

Ryff, C. D., & Singer, B. (2003). Ironies of the human condition: Well-being and health on the way to mortality. In L. G. Aspinwall & U. M. Staudinger (Eds.), A psychology of human strengths: Fundamental questions and future directions for a positive psychology (pp. 271–287). Washington, DC: American Psychological Association.

Sabnani, H. B., Ponterotto, J. G., Borodovsky, L. G. (1991). White racial identity development and cross-cultural counselor training. The Counselor Psychologist, 19, 76–102.

Safran, S. P., & Oswald, K. (2003). Positive behavior supports: Can school reshape disciplinary practices? Exceptional Children, 69, 361–373.

Saleebey, D. (1997). The strengths approach to practice. In D. Saleebey (Ed.), The strengths perspective in social work practice (2nd ed., pp. 49–57). White Plains, NY: Longman Publishers.

Sampson, J., Reardon, R., Lez, J., Ryan-Jones, R., Peterson, G., & Levy, R. (1993). The impact of DISCOVER for Adult Learners and SIGI PLUS on the career decision making of adults. (ERIC Document Reproduction Service No. ED 363 824)

Samson, G. E. (1985). Effects of training in test-taking skills on achievement test performance: A quantitative synthesis. Journal of Educational Research, 78, 261–265.

Sanders, M. G. (1998). The effects of school, family, and community support on the academic achievement of African American adolescents. Urban Education, 33, 385–409.

Sansone, C., & Smith, J. L. (2000). Interest and self-regulation: The relation between having to and wanting to. In C. Sansone & J. M. Harackiewicz (Eds.), Intrinsic and extrinsic motivation: The search for optimal motivation and performance (pp. 341–372). San Diego, CA: Academic Press.

Santos, P., & Coimbra, J. (2000). Psychological separation and dimensions of career indecision in secondary school students. Journal of Vocational Behavior, 56, 346–362.

Savickas, M. (2004). Toward a taxonomy of human strengths: Career counseling's contribution to positive psychology. In W. Walsh (Ed.), Counseling psychology and optimal human functioning (pp. 229–249). Mahwah, NJ: Lawrence Erlbaum Associates.

Savickas, M. (1997). Career adaptability: An integrative construct for life-span, life-space theory. The Career Development Quarterly, 45(3), 247–259.

Savickas, M. (1990). The career decision-making course: Description and field test. Career Development Quarterly, 38, 275–285.

Savickas, M. (1984). Career maturity: The construct and its measurement. Vocational Guidance Quarterly, 32, 222–231.

Scales, P. C. (2005). Developmental assets and the middle school counselor. Professional School Counseling, 9, 104–111.

Schinke, S. P., Botvin, G. J., Trimble, J. E., Orlandi, M. A., Gilchrist, L. D., & Locklear, V. S. (1988). Preventing substance abuse among American-Indian adolescents: A bicultural competence skills approach. Journal of Counseling Psychology, 35, 87–90.

Schmidt, J. (1999). Two decades of CACREP and what do we know? Counselor Education and Supervision, 39, 34–46.

Schmidt, J. (2003). Counseling in schools: Essential services and comprehensive programs. Boston: Allyn and Bacon.

Schultheiss, D., Palma, T., & Manzi, A. (2005). Career development in middle childhood: A qualitative inquiry. The Career Development Quarterly, 53, 246–262.

Schultheiss, D., & Stead, G. (2004). Childhood career development scale: Scale construct and psychometric properties. Journal of Career Assessment, 12, 113–134.

Schunk, D. H. (1983). Ability versus effort attributional feedback: Differential effects on self-efficacy and achievement. Journal of Educational Psychology, 75, 848–856.

Scruggs, T. E., White, K. R., & Bennion, K. (1986). Teaching test-taking skills to elementary grade students: A meta-analysis. *The Elementary School Journal, 87,* 69–82.

Sears, S. (1982). A definition of career guidance terms: A national vocational guidance association perspective. *Vocational Guidance Quarterly, 31,* 137–143.

Sears, S., & Granello, D. (2002). School counseling now and in the future: A reaction. *Professional School Counseling, 5,* 164–171.

Seligman, M. E. P. (2002). Positive psychology, positive prevention, and positive therapy. In C. R. Snyder & S. J. Lopez (Eds.), *Handbook of positive psychology* (pp. 3–9). New York: Oxford University Press.

Seligman, M. E. P., & Csikszentmihalyi, M. (2000). Positive psychology: An introduction. *American Psychologist, 55,* 5–14.

Seligman, M. E. P., & Peterson, C. (Eds.). (2003). Positive clinical psychology. In L. G. Aspinwall & U. M. Staudinger (Eds.), *A psychology of human strengths: Fundamental questions and future directions for a positive psychology* (pp. 305–317). Washington, DC: American Psychological Association.

Seligman, M. E. P., Schulman, P., DeRubeis, R., & Hollon, S. (1999). The prevention of depression and anxiety. *Prevention and Treatment, 2,* Article 8. Retrieved January 18, 2004 from http//journals.apa.org/prevention/volume2/pre0020008a.html

Sexton, T. L. (2001). Evidence-based counseling intervention programs. In D. C. Locke, J. E. Myers, & E. L. Herr (Eds.), *The handbook of counseling* (pp. 499–512). Thousand Oaks, CA: Sage.

Sexton, T. L., Whiston, S. C., Bleuer, J. C., & Walz, G. R. (1997). *Integrating outcome research into counseling practice and research.* Alexandria, VA: American Counseling Association.

Shadish, W. R., Cook, T. D., & Campell, D. T. (2002). *Experimental and quasi-experimental design for generalized causal inference.* Boston: Houghton Mifflin.

Shatté, A., & Reivich, K. (1997–2003). *Penn Resiliency Project: A depression-prevention and life-skills program for children and adolescents.* Unpublished manuscript.

Shatté, A. J., Seligman, M. E. P., Gillham, J. E., & Reivich, K. (2003). The role of positive psychology in child, adolescent, and family development. In R. M. Lerner, F. Jacobs, & D. Wertlieb (Eds.), *Handbook of applied developmental science: Vol. 1. Applying developmental science for youth and families: Historical and theoretical foundations* (pp. 207–226). Thousand Oaks, CA: Sage.

Shechtman, Z. (2002). Child group psychotherapy in the school at the threshold of a new millennium. *Journal of Counseling & Development, 80,* 293–299.

Shechtman, Z., Gilat, Il., Fos, L., & Flasher, A. (1996). Brief group therapy with low-achieving elementary school children. *Journal of Counseling Psychology, 43,* 376–382.

Sheldon, K. M., & King, L. (2001). Why positive psychology is necessary. *American Psychologist, 56,* 216–217.

Sheley, J. F., McGee, Z. T., & Wright, J. D. (1992). Gun-related violence in and around inner-city schools. *American Journal of Diseases of Children, 46,* 677–682.

Sheridan, S. M. (1997). Conceptual and empirical bases of conjoint behavioral consultation. *School Psychology Quarterly, 12,* 119–133.

Sheridan, S. M., Eagle, J. W., Cowan, R. J., & Mickelson, W. (2001). The effects of conjoint behavioral consultation: Results of a 4-year investigation. *Journal of School Psychology, 39,* 361–385.

Sheridan, S. M., Kratochwill, T. R., & Elliott, S. N. (1990). Behavioral consultation with parents and teachers: Delivering treatment for socially withdrawn children at home and school. *School Psychology Review, 19,* 33–52.

Shure, M. B. (1993). *Interpersonal problem solving and prevention: A five-year longitudinal study—kindergarten through grade 4. Final report #MH-40801*, Washington, DC: National Institute of Mental Health.

Shure, M. B. (1996). I can problem solve (ICPS): An interpersonal cognitive problem solving program for children. In M. C. Roberts (Ed.), *Model programs in child and family mental health* (pp. 47–62). Mahwah, NJ: Lawrence Erlbaum Associates.

Shure, M. B. (2000). I can problem solve: An interpersonal cognitive problem-solving program (2nd Ed.). Champaign, IL: Research Press.

Shure, M. B. (2001). I can problem solve (ICPS): An interpersonal cognitive problem-solving program for children. In S. I. Pfeiffer & L. A Reddy (Eds.), *Innovative mental health interventions for children: Programs that work* (pp. 3–14). New York: The Haworth Press.

Shure, M. B., & Spivack, G. (1972). Means-ends thinking, adjustment and social class among elementary school-aged children. *Journal of Consulting and Clinical Psychology, 38*, 348–353.

Simmons, R., & Blyth, D. (1987). *Moving into adolescence: The impact of pubertal change and school context*. Hawthorne, NY: Aldine de Gruyter.

Sims, S. J., & Sims, R. R. (1995). Learning and learning styles: A review and look to the future. In R. R. Sims & S. J. Sims (Eds.), *The importance of learning styles: Understanding the implication for learning, course design, and education* (pp. 193–210). Westport, CT: Greenwood Press.

Sink, C. A. (2002a). Comprehensive guidance and counseling programs in the development of multicultural students-citizens. *Professional School Counseling, 6*, 130–137.

Sink, C. A. (2002b). In search of the professions' finest hour: A critique of four views of 21st century school counseling. *Professional School Counseling, 5*, 156–163.

Sink, C. (2005). Fostering academic development and learning: Implications and recommendations for middle school counselors. *Professional School Counseling, 9*, 128–135.

Sink, C. A., & MacDonald, G. (1998). The status of comprehensive guidance and counseling in the United States. *Professional School Counseling, 2*, 88–94.

Sink, C. A., & Stroh, H. R. (2003). Raising achievement test scores of early elementary school students through comprehensive school counseling programs. *Professional School Counseling, 6*, 350–364.

Sklare, G. B. (1997). *Brief counseling that works: A solution-focused approach for school counselors*. Thousand Oaks, CA: Corwin Press.

Slavin, R. E. (1983). *Cooperative learning*. New York: Longman.

Slavin, R. (1985). An introduction to cooperative learning research. In R. Slavin, S. Sharan, S. Kaga, R. Hertz-Lazarowitz, C. Webb, & R. Schmuck (Eds.), *Learning to cooperate: Cooperating to learn* (pp. 1–15). New York: Plenum Press.

Slavin, R. E. (1990). *Cooperative learning: Theory, research, and practice*. Upper Saddle River, NJ: Prentice Hall.

Smaby, M., & D'Andrea, L. (1995). 1994 CACREP standards: Will we make the grade? *Journal of Counseling and Development, 74*, 105–109

Smith, E., Walker, K., Fields, L., Brookins, C., & Seay, R. (1999). Ethnic identity and its relationship to self-esteem, perceived efficacy and prosocial attitudes in early adolescence. *Journal of Adolescence, 22*, 867–880.

Smith, E. J. (2006). The strength-based counseling model. *The Counseling Psychologist, 34*, 13–79.

Smith, S. H. (2000). *Schoolwide test preparation: One elementary school's instructional approach that dramatically raised standardized test scores*. Arlington, VA: Educational Research Service.

Snyder, C. R., & Taylor, J. D. (2000). Hope as a common factor across psychotherapy approaches: A lesson from the Dodo's verdict. In C. R. Snyder (Ed.), *Handbook of hope: Theory, measures, & applications* (pp. 89–108). San Diego, CA: Academic Press.

Snyder, C. R., Feldman, D. B., Shorey, H. S., & Rand, K. L. (2002). Hopeful choices: A school counselor's guide to hope theory. *Professional School Counseling, 5*, 298–307.

Snyder, C. R., Lopez, S. J., Edwards, L. M., Teramoto Pedrotti, J., Prosser, E. C., LaRue Walton, S., et al. (2003). Measuring and labeling the positive and the negative. In S. J. Lopez & C. R. Snyder (Eds.), *Positive psychological assessment: A handbook of models and measures* (pp. 21–39). Washington, DC: American Psychological Association.

Sodowsky, G. R., Kwan, K. K., & Pannu, R. (1995). Ethnic identity of Asians in the United States. In J. G. Ponterotto, J. M. Casas, L. A. Suzuki, & C. M. Alexander (Eds.), *Handbook of multicultural counseling* (pp. 123–154). Thousand Oaks, CA: Sage.

Solomon, D., Battistich, V., Watson, M., Schaps, E., & Lewis, C. (2000). A six-district study of educational change: Direct and mediated effects of the Child Development Project. *Social Psychology of Education, 4*, 3–51.

Solomon, D., Watson, M., Battistich, V., Schaps, E., & Delucchi, K. (1996). Creating classrooms that students experience as communities. *American Journal of Community Psychology, 24*, 719–748.

Southern Regional Education Board (2004). *High schools that work*. Retrieved December 15, 2004 from http://www.sreb.org/programs/hstw/hstwindex.asp

Spivack, G., & Levine, M. (1963). Self-regulation in acting-out and normal adolescents. Report #M-4531. Washington, DC: National Institute of Mental Health.

St. Clair, K. L. (1989). Middle school counseling research: A resource for school counselors. *Elementary School Guidance and Counseling, 23*, 219–226.

Starkman, N., Scales, P. C., & Roberts, C. (1999). *Great places to learn: How asset-building schools help students succeed*. Minneapolis, MN: Search Institute.

Steen, T., Kachorek, L., & Peterson, C. (2003). Character strengths among youth. *Journal of Youth and Adolescence, 32*(1), 5–17.

Steinberg, A. (1998). *Real learning, real work: School-to-school and high school reform*. New York: Routledge.

Stern, D., Dayton, C., & Raby, M. (1988). *Career academies and high school reform*. CA: Career Academy Support Network, University of California at Berkeley.

Stern, D., Raby, M., & Dayton, C. (1992). *Career academies: Partnerships for reconstructing American high schools*. San Francisco: Jossey-Bass.

Stevahn, L., Johnson, D. W., Johnson, R. T., Green, K., & Laginski, A. M. (1997). Effects on high school students of conflict resolution training integrated into English literature. *Journal of Social Psychology, 137*, 302–315.

Stevahn, L., Oberle, K., Johnson, D. W., & Johnson, R. T. (2001, April). *Effects of role reversal training and use of integrative negotiation for classroom management on conflict resolution in kindergarten*. Paper presented at the annual meeting of the American Educational Research Association, Seattle, WA.

Stone, C. B., & Clark, M. A. (2001). School counselors and principals: Partners in support of academic achievement. *NASSP Bulletin, 85*(624), 46–52.

Stone, C. B., & Dahir, C. A. (2004). *School counselor accountability: A MEASURE of student success*. Upper Saddle River, NJ: Pearson Education.

Strayhorn, J. M. (1988). *The competent child: An approach to psychotherapy and preventive mental health.* New York: The Guilford Press.

Strukoff, P. M., McLaughlin, T. F., & Bialozor, R. C. (1987). The effects of a daily report card system in increasing homework completion and accuracy in a special education setting. *Techniques, 3,* 19–26.

Sue, D. W., & Sue, D. (2003). *Counseling the culturally diverse: Theory and practice* (4th ed.). New York: John Wiley & Sons.

Sugai, G., & Horner, R. (2002). The evolution of discipline practices: School-wide positive behavior supports. *Child & Family Behavior Therapy, 24,* 23–50.

Super, D. (1957). *The psychology of careers.* New York: Harper.

Super, D. (1988). Vocational adjustment: Implementing a self-concept. *Career Development Quarterly, 36*(4), 351–357.

Super, D. E., Thompson, A. (1979). A six-scale, two-factor measure of adolescent career or vocational maturity. *Vocational Guidance Quarterly, 28*(1), 6–15.

Super, D., Savickas, M., & Super, C. (1996). The life-span, life-space approach to careers. In D. Brown & L. Brooks (Eds.), *Career choice and development,* (3rd ed., pp. 122–178). San Francisco: Jossey-Bass.

Super, D., Osborne, W., Walsh, D., Brown, S., & Niles, S. (1992). Developmental career assessment and counseling: The C-DAC model. *Journal of Counseling and Development, 71,* 74–80.

Sweeney, T. (2001). Counseling: Historical origins and philosophical roots. In D. Locke, J. Myers, & E. Herr (Eds.), *The Handbook of Counseling* (pp. 3–26), London: Sage.

Szapocznik, J., Santisteban, D., Kurtines, W. M., Hervis, O. E., & Spencer, F. (1982). Life enhancements counseling: A psychosocial model of services for Cuban elders. In E. E. Jones & S. J. Korchin (Eds.), *Minority mental health* (pp. 296–329). New York: Praeger.

Tang, M. (2001). Counseling immigrant children in school settings: What school counselors should do. In D. S. Sandhu (Ed.). *Elementary school counseling in the new millennium* (pp. 209–222). Alexandria, VA: American Counseling Association.

Taveira, M., & Moreno, M. (2003). Guidance theory and practice: The status of career exploration. *British Journal of Guidance and Counselling, 31,* 189–207.

Taylor, K., & Betz, N. (1983). Applications of self-efficacy theory to the understanding and treatment of career indecision. *Journal of Vocational Behavior, 22,* 63–81.

Taylor, L., & Adelman, H. S. (2000). Connecting schools, families, and communities. *Professional School Counseling, 3,* 298–307.

Teresa, J. S. (1991). *Increasing self-efficacy for careers in young adults from migrant farmworker backgrounds.* Unpublished doctoral dissertations, Washington State University, Pullman.

Terjesen, M. D., Jacofsky, M., Froh, J., & DiGiuseppe, R. (2004). Integrating positive psychology into schools: Implications for practice. *Psychology in the Schools, 4,* 163–172.

Thomas, C. W. (1970). Different strokes for different folks. *Psychology Today, 4,* 48–53, 78–80.

Thompson, C. L., & O'Quinn, S. D. III. (2001). *Eliminating the black-white achievement gap: A summary of research.* Chapel Hill, NC: The North Carolina Education Research Council.

Tierney, J. P., Grossman, J. B., & Resch, N. L. (1995). *Making a difference: An impact study of Big Brothers/Big Sisters.* Philadelphia, PA: Public/Private Ventures.

Topping, K. (2001). *Peer assisted learning: A practical guide for teachers.* Cambridge, MA: Brookline Books.

Topping, K., & Ehly, S. (1998). Introduction to peer-assisted learning. In K. Topping & S. Ehly (Eds.), *Peer-assisted learning* (pp. 27–43). Mahwah, NJ: Lawrence Erlbaum Associates.

Townsend, B. L., & Patton, J. M. (1995). *Three "warring souls" of African American high school students*. (ERIC Document Reproduction Service No. ED400250).

Trammel, D. L., Schloss, P. J., & Alper, S. (1995). Using self-recording, evaluation, and graphing to increase completion of homework assignments. In W. D. Bursuck (Ed.)., *Homework: Issues and practices for students with learning disabilities* (pp. 169–180). Austin, TX: PRO-ED.

Trickett, E. J., & Moos, R. H. (1995). *Classroom environment scale manual* (3rd ed.). Palo Alto, CA: Consulting Psychologist Press.

Trusty, J., Niles, S., & Carney, J. (2005). Education-career planning and middle school counselors. *Professional School Counseling, 9*, 136–143.

Tucker, C. M., Chennault, S. A., Brady, B. A., Fraser, K. P., Gaskin, V. T., Dunn, C., et al. (1995). A parent, community, public schools, and university involved partnership education program to examine and boost academic achievement and adaptive functioning skills of African-American students. *Journal of Research and Development in Education, 28*, 174–185.

Tucker, C. M., & Herman, K. C. (2002). Using culturally sensitive theories and research to meet the academic needs of low-income African American children. *American Psychologist, 57*, 762–773.

Tucker, C. M., Herman, K. C., Reid, A., Keefer, N., & Vogel, D. (1999). The Research-Based Model Partnership Education Program: A four-year outcome study. *Journal of Research and Development in Education, 32*, 32–37.

Underdue, T. (2000). It's academic. *Techniques: Connecting Education and Careers, 75*, 16–19.

U.S. Bureau of the Census. (1998). *Growth of U.S. population by race and ethnicity*. Washington, DC: U.S. Government Printing Office.

U.S. Department of Education. (1997). *Individuals with Disabilities Education Act Ammendments of 1997*. Retrieved September 5, 2002, from http://www.ed.gov/offices/OSERS/Policy/IDEA/

U.S. Department of Education. (2001a). *No Child Left Behind Act of 2001 (H.R.1)*. Washington, DC: U.S. Department of Education.

U.S. Department of Education, Institute of Education Sciences, National Center for Educational Statistics. (2001b). *Percent of high school dropouts (status dropouts) among persons 16 to 24 years old, by income level, and distribution of dropouts by labor force status and educational attainment: October 1970 to October 2001*. Retrieved September 9, 2003, from http://www.nces.ed.gov/pubs2003/digest02/tables/dt109.asp

U.S. Department of Education, Institute of Education Sciences, National Center for Educational Statistics. (2001c). *Percent of high school dropouts (status dropouts) among persons 16 to 24 years old, by sex and race/ethnicity: April 1960 to October 2001*. Retrieved September 9, 2003, from http://www.nces.ed.gov/pubs2003/digest02/tables/dt108.asp

U.S. Department of Education. (2002). *Comprehensive school reform program*. Retrieved December 16, 2004, from http://www.ed.gov/print/programs/compreform/2pager.html

Vondracek, F. (1992). The construct of identity and its use in career theory and research. *Career Development Quarterly, 41*, 130–144.

Vondracek, F., Lerner, R., & Schulenburg, J. (1986). *Career development: A life-span development approach*. Hillsdale, NJ: Lawrence Erlbaum Associates.

Vondracek, F., & Reitzle, M. (1998). The viability of career maturity theory: A developmental-contextual perspective. *Career Development Quarterly, 47*, 6–15.

Wagner, W. G. (1996). Optimal development in adolescence: What is it and how can it be encouraged? *The Counseling Psychologist, 24*, 360–399.

Walberg, H. J. (1986). Synthesis of research on teaching. In M. C. Wittrock (Ed.), *Handbook of research on teaching* (3rd ed., pp. 214–229). New York: Macmillan.

Walsh, M. E., Galassi, J. P., Murphy, J. A., & Park-Taylor, J. A. (2002). A conceptual framework for counseling psychologists in schools. *The Counseling Psychologist, 30*, 682–704.

Walsh, M. E., Howard, K. A., & Buckley, M. (1999). School counselors in school-community partnerships: Opportunities and challenges. *Professional School Counseling, 2*, 349–356.

Walz, G., & Bleuer, J. (1997). *Emerging priorities and emphases in school counseling, guidance, and student services.* (ERIC Reproduction Service No. ED425413).

Wampold, B. E. (2001). *The great psychotherapy debate: Models, methods, and findings.* Mahwah, NJ: Lawrence Erlbaum Associates.

Wang, M. C., Haertel, G. D., & Walberg, H. J. (1997). Learning influences. In H. J. Walberg & G. D. Haertel (Eds.), *Psychology and educational practice* (pp. 199–211). Berkeley, CA: McCutchan.

Ware, W. B., & Galassi, J. P. (2006). Using correlational and prediction data to enhance student achievement in K–12 schools: A practical application for school counselors. *Professional School Counseling, 9*, 344–366.

Washington, E. D., Crosby, T., Hernandez, M., Vernon-Jones, R., Medley, R., Nishamura, B., et al. (2003). Cultural identity groups and cultural maps: Meaning making in groups. In P. B. Pedersen & J. C. Carey (Eds.). *Multicultural counseling in schools* (2nd ed., pp. 26–43). Boston: Allyn and Bacon.

Watson, M., Battistich, V., & Solomon, D. (1997). Enhancing students' social and ethical development in schools: An intervention program and its effects. *International Journal of Educational Research, 27*, 571–586.

Watson, M., Solomon, D., Battistich, V., Schaps, E., & Solomon, J. (1989). The Child Development Project: Combining traditional and developmental approaches to values education. In L. P. Nucci (Ed.), *Moral development and character education: A dialogue* (pp. 51–92). Berkeley, CA: McCutchan Publishing Corporation.

Watson, M., & Van Aarde, J. (1986). Attitudinal career maturity of South African colored high school pupils. *Journal of Vocational Behavior, 29*, 7–16.

Webb, L. D., Brigman, G. A., & Campbell, C. (2005). Linking school counselors and student success: A replication of the student success skills approach targeting the academic and social competence of students. *Professional School Counseling, 8*, 407–413.

Weiner, B. (1986). *An attributional theory of motivation and emotion.* New York: Springer-Verlag.

Weiner, R. K., Sheridan, S. M., & Jenson, W. R. (1998). The effects of conjoint behavioral consultation and a structured homework program on math completion and accuracy in junior high students. *School Psychology Quarterly, 13*, 281–309.

Weinstein, C. E., & Mayer, R. F. (1985). The teaching of learning strategies. In M.C. Wittrock (Ed.), *Handbook of research on teaching* (3rd ed., pp. 315–329). New York: Macmillan.

Weissberg, R. P., Caplan, M., & Harwood, R. L. (1991). Promoting competent young people in competence-enhancing environments: A systems-based perspective on primary prevention. *Journal of Consulting and Clinical Psychology, 59*, 830–841.

Weller, L. D., & Weller, S. J. (1998). Raising test scores through the continuous improvement model. *Clearing House, 71*, 159.

Wentzel, K. R., & Watkins, D. E. (2002). Peer relationships and collaborative learning as context for academic enablers. *School Psychology Review, 31*, 366–377.

Werbel, J. (2000). Relationships among career exploration, job search intensity, and job effectiveness in graduating college students. *Journal of Vocational Behavior, 57*, 379–394.

Werner, E., & Smith, R. (1992). *Overcoming the odds: High risk children from birth to adulthood.* New York: Cornell University Press.

Westbrook, B., Sanford, E., & Donnelly, M. (1990). The relationship between career maturity test scores and appropriateness of career choices: A replication. *Journal of Vocational Behavior, 36*, 20–32.

Wheeler, P. T., & Loesch, L. (1981). Program evaluation and counseling: Yesterday, today, and tomorrow. *Personnel and Guidance Journal, 51*, 573–578.

Whiston, S. (2002a). Applications of the principles: Career counseling and interventions. *The Counseling Psychologist, 30*, 218–237.

Whiston, S. C. (2002b). Response to the past, present, and future of school counseling: Raising some issues. *Professional School Counseling, 5*, 148–155.

Whiston, S. C. (2003). Outcomes research on school counseling services. In B. T. Erford (Ed.), *Transforming the school counseling profession* (pp. 435–447). Upper Saddle River, NJ: Merrill Prentice Hall.

Whiston, S. C., Brecheisen, B., & Stephens, J. (2003). Does treatment modality affect career counseling effect? *Journal of Vocational Behavior, 62*, 390–410.

Whiston, S. C., & Coker, K. (2000). Reconstructing clinical training: Implications from research. *Counselor Education and Supervision, 39*(4), 228–53.

Whiston, S. C., & Sexton, T. L. (1998). A review of counseling outcome research: Implications for practice. *Journal of Counseling & Development, 76*, 412–426.

Whiston, S. C., Sexton, T., & Lasoff, D. (1998). Career-intervention outcome: A replication and extension of Oliver and Spokane. *Journal of Counseling Psychology, 45*, 150–165.

White, R. W. (1959). Motivation reconsidered: The concept of competence. *Psychological Review, 66*, 297–333.

Widaman, K. F., & Kagan, S. (1987). Cooperativeness and achievement: Interaction of student cooperativeness with cooperative versus competitive classroom organization. *Journal of School Psychology, 25*, 355–365.

Wigfield, A., Eccles, J. S., Mac Iver, D., Reuman, D., & Midgley, C. (1991). Transitions during early adolescence: Changes in children's domain specific self-perceptions and general self-esteem across the transition to junior high school. *Developmental Psychology, 27*, 552–566.

Wilson, N. S. (1986). Effects of a classroom guidance unit on sixth graders' examination performance. *The Journal of Humanistic Education and Development, 25*, 70–79.

Wittmer, J. (2000). *Managing your school counseling program: K–12 developmental strategies* (2nd ed.). Minneapolis, MN: Educational Media Corp.

Wolin, S., & Wolin, S. (1993). *The resilient self: How survivors of troubled families rise above adversity.* New York: Villard.

Wong, S. C., Burgoyne, K., Catalano, R. F., Chappell, P. J., & Hawkins, J. D. (1997). *Communities that care team handbook.* Seattle, WA: Developmental Research and Programs, Inc.

Wood, C., & Rayle, A. (2006). A model of school counseling supervision: The goals, functions, roles, and systems model. *Counselor Education & Supervision, 45*, 253–266.

Wright, B. A., & Lopez, S. J. (2002). Widening the diagnostic focus: A case for including human strengths and environmental resources. In C. R. Snyder & S. J. Lopez (Eds.). *Handbook of positive* psychology (pp. 26–44). New York: Oxford University Press.

W. T. Grant Consortium on the School-Based promotion of Social Competence. (1992). Drug and alcohol prevention curricula. In J. D. Hawkins, R. F. Catalano & Associates (Eds.), *Communities that care* (pp. 129–148). San Francisco: Jossey-Bass.

Zaff, J., Moore, K., Papillo, A., & Williams, S. (2003). Implications of extracurricular activity participation during adolescence on positive outcomes. *Journal of Adolescent Research, 18*, 599–630.

Zaff, J. F., Smith, D. C., Rogers, M. F., Leavitt, C. H., Halle, T. G., & Bornstein, M. H. (2003). Holistic well-being and the developing child. In M. H. Bornsetin, L. Davidson, C. L. M. Keyes, & K. A. Moore (Eds.), *Well-being: Positive development across the life course.* (pp. 23–32). Mahwah, NJ: Lawrence Erlbaum Associates.

Zimmerman, B. J. (2000). Attaining self-regulation a social cognitive perspective. In M. Boekaerts, P. R. Pintrich, & M. Zeidner (Eds.), *Handbook of self-regulation* (pp. 13–37). San Diego, CA: Academic Press.

Zimmerman, B. J. (2001). Theories of self-regulated learning and academic achievement: An overview and analysis. In B. J. Zimmerman & D. H. Schunk (Eds.), *Self-regulated learning and academic achievement: Theoretical perspectives* (2nd ed., pp. 1–37). Mahwah, NJ: Lawrence Erlbaum Associates.

Zimmerman, B. J., & Kitsantas, A. (1999). Acquiring writing revision skill: Shifting from process to outcome self-regulatory goals. *Journal of Educational Psychology, 91*, 1–10.

Zimmerman, B. J., & Martinez-Pons, M. (1986). Development of a structured interview for assessing students' use of self-regulated learning strategies. *American Educational Research Journal, 23*, 614–628.

Zimmerman, B. J., & Martinez-Pons, M. (1988). Construct validation of a strategy model of student self-regulated learning. *Journal of Educational Psychology, 80*, 284–290.

Zins, J. E., & Wagner, D. I. (1997). Educating children and youth for psychological competence. In R. J. Illback, C. T. Cobb, & H. M. Joseph, Jr. (Eds.), *Integrated services for children and families: Opportunities for psychological practice* (pp. 137–156). Washington, DC: American Psychological Association.

Author Index

Subject Index